Historical Turns

Historical Turns

Weimar Cinema and the Crisis of Historicism

NICHOLAS BAER

University of California Press

University of California Press
Oakland, California

© 2024 by Nicholas Baer

Library of Congress Cataloging-in-Publication Data

Names: Baer, Nicholas, 1985- author.
Title: Historical turns : Weimar cinema and the crisis of historicism / Nicholas Baer.
Description: Oakland, California : University of California Press, [2024] | Includes bibliographical references and index.
Identifiers: LCCN 2023051393 (print) | LCCN 2023051394 (ebook) | ISBN 9780520398818 (cloth) | ISBN 9780520398825 (paperback) | ISBN 9780520398832 (ebook)
Subjects: LCSH: Motion pictures—Germany—20th century—History and criticism. | Silent films—Germany—History and criticism.
Classification: LCC PN1993.5.G3 B28 2024 (print) | LCC PN1993.5.G3 (ebook) | DDC 791.0943087—dc23/eng/20240229
LC record available at https://lccn.loc.gov/2023051393
LC ebook record available at https://lccn.loc.gov/2023051394

33 32 31 30 29 28 27 26 25 24
10 9 8 7 6 5 4 3 2 1

In loving memory of Alfred and Eva Baer

Contents

Acknowledgments — IX

INTRODUCTION — 1

1. HISTORICAL TURNS — 10
2. THINGS AS THEY COULD HAVE HAPPENED: SIEGFRIED KRACAUER AND THE HISTORICAL FILM — 29
3. RELATIVIST PERSPECTIVISM: *THE CABINET OF DR. CALIGARI* — 57
4. METAPHYSICS OF DEATH: *DESTINY* — 84
5. THE NONSIMULTANEITY OF THE SIMULTANEOUS: *RHYTHM 21* — 104
6. NATURAL HISTORY: *THE HOLY MOUNTAIN* — 128

EPILOGUE. THE WEIMAR ANALOGY: *METROPOLIS* AND THE GLOBAL PRESENT — 147

Notes — 167
Bibliography — 215
Index — 247

Acknowledgments

Like Stephen Dedalus in James Joyce's *Ulysses* (1922), I found myself trying to awake from the nightmare of history over the course of this project. For my work on cinema and the crisis of historicism in the Weimar Republic has coincided with a metastasizing set of political, economic, and environmental crises in the global present. Writing this book often felt like Pomodoro-ing amid ongoing catastrophe. While my temporal distance from interwar Germany never dissolved in what Frank Ankersmit calls a "sublime historical experience"—a direct, immediate encounter with the past; a sudden revelation through an "opening in the contextualist clouds"—the contemporary juncture at least afforded some glimmers of insight into another highly fraught, turbulent period.

As Siegfried Kracauer remarks in his final work, *History: The Last Things before the Last* (1969), one of the great difficulties for the historian is tracing lines of influence over time. Ascertainable evidence is scant and elusive. An offhand comment might have exerted an indelible impact: "One word . . . , long since forgotten, may have changed the mind of the man to whom it was once spoken." The promiscuous path of ideas has undoubtedly posed a challenge for me in reconstructing the German debates over historicism from a full century ago. No less daunting, however, is the task of acknowledging those who shaped and informed my own research, which has spanned many years, locations, and institutions.

I owe my first debt of gratitude to the three scholars who advised the dissertation from which this book emerged. It has been the privilege of a lifetime to work with Tony Kaes, counting him as a *Doktorvater*, coeditor, interlocutor, and now neighbor and friend. He provided the conditions of possibility for this undertaking and remains tirelessly dedicated and generous beyond measure. Martin Jay offered an indispensable map for my own expeditions into the field of modern intellectual history. His brilliance is matched only by his unwavering graciousness and self-deprecating charm. Linda Williams treated me as a peer from day one, giving rigorously incisive and refreshingly blunt feedback.

During my years of graduate coursework at the University of California, Berkeley, my thinking on historicism and the philosophy of history was further animated and enriched by seminars with Deena Aranoff, Judith Butler, John Efron, Deniz Göktürk, Anne Nesbet, Hans Sluga, and Kristen Whissel. It was exhilarating to participate in such seminars and in broader university life with many people who remain friends and colleagues to this day: Mason Allred, Yael Almog, Kurt Beals, Jennifer Blaylock, Erik Born, Angela Botelho, Alex Bush, Paul Dobryden, Patrick Ellis, Robin Ellis, Shaina Hammerman, Sebastian Haselbeck, Lisa Jacobson, Ramsey McGlazer, Annika Orich, Renée Pastel, Eli Rosenblatt, Sasha Rossman, Althea Wasow, Damon Young, and Nepomuk Zettl.

I had the fortune to research and write my dissertation in Berlin. Gertrud Koch welcomed me into her orbit at the Freie Universität Berlin, where I profited from her doctoral colloquium along with her "Geschichtsbilder" seminar and lecture series, suffused with stunning insights and dry humor. Karin Krauthausen, Ethel Matala de Mazza, and Burkhardt Wolf included me in invigorating and generative discussions at the Humboldt-Universität zu Berlin.

This book benefited from the detailed input of three readers at a workshop held over Zoom amid the COVID-19 pandemic. Johannes von Moltke is a role model and consummate colleague, extending extraordinary guidance and consideration to junior scholars. Patrice Petro has imparted her deep knowledge of the history of our discipline, lending me a sharper sense of past and present battles—and the interventions that still need to be staged. Katharina Loew has shared her expertise on film technology and aesthetics with delightful irreverence and an astounding lack of pretension. I hope they all find traces of their valuable comments in the pages that follow.

My work would not have been possible without several archives, libraries, museums, and academic institutions. I conducted research at the Bundesarchiv-Filmarchiv, Deutsche Kinemathek, Filmarchiv Austria, Österreichisches Filmmuseum, and Staatsbibliothek zu Berlin, with friendly assistance from Christian Dewald, Cordula Döhrer, Oliver Hanley, Regina Hoffmann, and Michael Skowronski. The research was enabled by fellowships from the Leo Baeck Institute/German Academic Scholarship Foundation (Studienstiftung), German Academic Exchange Service

(DAAD), Alfried Krupp Institute for Advanced Study in Greifswald, and UC Berkeley's Graduate Division and Institute of European Studies. Additional funding has come from the Fritz Thyssen Foundation, Phi Beta Kappa, the University of Groningen's Institute for the Study of Culture, Utrecht University's Institute for Cultural Inquiry, and UC Berkeley's Division of Arts & Humanities and Office of the Vice Chancellor for Research. A stipend from the Institute for Critical Social Inquiry at the New School allowed me to participate in Nancy Fraser's fabulous "Critique of Capitalism" summer seminar. (Shoutout to the #CrisisGirls!)

Many colleagues invited me to share my work in progress at conferences, symposia, and film festivals, where they raised vital questions: Nora Alter, Ofer Ashkenazi, Nathaniel Brennan, Daniel Fairfax, Jennifer Fay, Jane Gaines, Rasmus Greiner, Mathias Grote, Malte Hagener, Boaz Hagin, Vinzenz Hediger, Josef Jünger, Antonia Lant, Leila Mukhida, Kartik Nair, Winfried Pauleit, Patrice Petro, Dana Polan, Ying Qian, John David Rhodes, Caroline Rothauge, Martin Ruehl, Joachim Schätz, Christian Suhm, Takuya Tsunoda, Kerry Wallach, Andrew Webber, Daniel Wildmann, Marie-Noëlle Yazdanpanah, Raz Yosef, Samuel Zeitlin, and Yvonne Zimmermann. On such occasions, I had stimulating and enjoyable exchanges with numerous scholars: Tim Bergfelder, Oliver Botar, James Leo Cahill, Erica Carter, Steve Choe, Michael Cowan, the late Thomas Elsaesser, Paul Flaig, Mila Ganeva, Carl Gelderloos, Christina Gerhardt, Michael B. Gillespie, Pablo Gonçalo, Barbara Hales, Sara Hall, Britta Hartmann, Noah Isenberg, Jan-Christopher Horak, Lutz Koepnick, Ervin Malakaj, Barbara Mennel, Matthew Noble-Olson, Francesco Pitassio, Eszter Polonyi, Eric Rentschler, Philip Rosen, Lucia Ruprecht, Tanvi Solanki, Chris Tedjasukmana, Cynthia Walk, Michael Weinman, and Valerie Weinstein.

Shorter and earlier versions of chapters 3, 4, and 6 appeared as "Historical Turns: On *Caligari*, Kracauer, and New Film History," in *Film and History: Producing and Experiencing History in Moving Images and Sound*, ed. Delia González de Reufels, Rasmus Greiner, and Winfried Pauleit (Berlin: Bertz + Fischer, 2015), 153–64; "Post-Perspectival Aesthetics in 'The Cabinet of Dr. Caligari,'" in *The New Berlin, 1912–1932*, ed. Inga Rossi-Schrimpf (Tielt, Belgium: Lannoo Publishers, 2018), 93–99; "Relativist Perspectivism: *Caligari* and the Crisis of Historicism," in *How Film Histories Were Made: Materials, Methods, Discourses*, ed. Malte Hagener and Yvonne Zimmermann (Amsterdam: Amsterdam University Press, 2024), 85–118; "Metaphysics of Finitude: *Der müde Tod* and the Crisis of Historicism," in *A Companion to Fritz Lang*, ed. Joe McElhaney (Malden, MA, and Oxford: Wiley-Blackwell, 2015), 141–60; and "Natural History:

Rethinking the *Bergfilm*," in *"Doch ist das Wirkliche auch vergessen, so ist es darum nicht getilgt": Beiträge zum Werk Siegfried Kracauers*, ed. Jörn Ahrens, Paul Fleming, Susanne Martin, and Ulrike Vedder (Wiesbaden: Springer, 2017), 279–305. Thank you to the publishers for permission to reprint these texts in expanded and revised form.

Wissenschaft is an often-precarious vocation, as Max Weber knew. At an especially troubled and worrisome moment for higher education, I have been lucky to find phenomenal colleagues and committed mentors at multiple institutions: Casey Haskins, Morris Kaplan, Anne Kern, Michelle Stewart, Jennifer Uleman, and Agustín Zarzosa at the State University of New York at Purchase; Julian Hanich, Sara Strandvad, and Annie van den Oever at the University of Groningen; and Jochen Hung, Frank Kessler, and Nanna Verhoeff at Utrecht University. Deb Neibel fostered a wonderful intellectual environment for the Society of Fellows at the University of Chicago; I was particularly grateful for workshops with Tom Gunning and Benjamin Morgan, who offered astute suggestions on individual chapters, as well as the "Time After Time" writing group with Meghanne Barker, Nadine Chan, Natacha Nsabimana, and Adam Spanos. The final stages of this project overlapped with a return to Berkeley, where Lilla Balint, Jeroen Dewulf, Nikolaus Euba, Karen Feldman, Deniz Göktürk, Niklaus Largier, and Chenxi Tang have warmly welcomed me into the Department of German.

Over the peripatetic past years, my friends have been a source of constancy. Maggie Hennefeld has been a daily purveyor of prodigious advice, effusive support, and good cheer; Doron Galili is unassumingly brilliant, hilariously eccentric, and exceedingly loyal; Kristina Köhler has relayed crucial insights and precious references; Philipp Stiasny is tremendously fun and endlessly generous with his encyclopedic knowledge; Kartik Nair has supplied discerning wisdom at decisive moments; and Samuel England always slides into my DMs with high-quality content. I cherish the friendship of Priyanka Basu, Simon Böckle, Eugenie Brinkema, Iggy Cortez, Pardis Dabashi, Emily Dreyfus, Tobias Faßhauer, Susanne Fontaine, Lilian Gergely, Sarah Goodrum, Ron Gregg, Paul Haacke, Laura Horak, Katerina Korola, Astrid Korporaal, Mikki Kressbach, Henryk Paciorek, Jennifer Peterson, Sergio Rigoletto, Kathryn Roberts, Jordan Schonig, Aurore Spiers, Kyle Stevens, Jaap Verheul, Federico Windhausen, and Ling Zhang.

At the University of California Press, Raina Polivka championed this project and kept it on track with unabated enthusiasm, and Sam Warren helped bring it to publication. Jeff Anderson shepherded the book through various stages of production, and Kevin Barrett Kane designed the elegant cover, inspired by Joost Schmidt's 1923 Bauhaus exhibition poster. I am grateful to Carl Walesa for meticulously copyediting the manuscript, Linus Mao for final proofreading, Chris van der Vegt for assembling and formatting the bibliography, and Celia Braves for crafting the index. All translations are mine unless otherwise noted.

Lastly, I thank my late grandparents, Alfred and Eva, who were firsthand witnesses to the crisis-ridden Weimar era and nurtured my budding interest in German culture and thought, despite bearing the scars of dispossession and exile; and my parents, Alan and Maria, who have provided loving support and unflagging encouragement, even as I became the wrong kind of doctor. An academic career in the humanities involves struggles and setbacks, protracted uncertainty and profound distances. My partner, Matt, has shown boundless devotion in the face of these challenges and has been an ideal companion with whom to navigate, protest, and endure the multiplying crises of our own time. Amid the long nightmare of history, I am glad to be sleeping in his arms.

Introduction

> I realized in a flash the many existing parallels between history and the photographic media, historical reality and camera-reality.
>
> SIEGFRIED KRACAUER

> Kracauer must think we read books on the movies to get our knowledge of history and philosophy.
>
> PAULINE KAEL

This book reassesses Weimar cinema in light of the "crisis of historicism" widely diagnosed by German philosophers in the early twentieth century. I argue that films of the Weimar Republic lent vivid expression to the crisis of historical thinking, revealing the capacity of the medium to engage with fundamental questions of the philosophy of history. Reconstructing the extensive debates over historicism that unfolded during the initial decades of moving-image culture, I propose a more reflexive mode of historiography, exploring how the medium itself meditates on problems of historicism. Not least, I suggest an approach to studying cinema in conjunction with enduring historical-philosophical concerns.

In drawing attention to the philosophical critiques of historicism that gained an acute urgency and popular currency during the Weimar period, this book participates in critical reflection on the import and legacy of the "historical turn" in Cinema and Media Studies. Emerging in the mid-1970s, New Film History was animated by several impulses: a reaction against the monolithic assumptions of apparatus theory; the archival preservation and restoration of early cinema and the concomitant challenge to traditional conceptions of film history; an interest in the genealogy of nonnarrative, documentary, and avant-garde cinemas; the counterhistories associated with feminism, postcolonialism, and further political liberation movements; and, finally, a Marxist view of historical change that deemphasized individual inventors and pioneers in favor of uneven technological, socioeconomic, and institutional developments. These disparate strands wove together as television and analog video posed increasing threats to cinema's status as the dominant *dispositif* and cultural form. The history of cinema could no longer be studied in isolation from a broader system and multimedia environment, and the hermeneutic analysis of filmic texts gave way to forensic and contextualist approaches.[1]

New Film History has remade our understanding of cinema, correcting the inadequacies of prior accounts and opening areas of inquiry that have remained enormously generative. Yet the past years have seen stirrings of discontent with the methodological commitments that informed the discipline's historical turn. For, in seeking to establish the study of cinema as an academic pursuit, revisionist film historians appealed to nineteenth-century practices and ideals of primary-source research, rigorous documentation, and precise, factual representation. Where New Film History aspired to what Thomas Elsaesser glossed as "scientific or empirical standards of exactitude and knowledge," more recent scholarship has confronted absences and irreducible ambiguities in the archive, embracing approaches or artifacts often deemed speculative, unstable, dubious, or otherwise illegitimate.[2] Questioning the objectivist and recuperative investments of New Film History, scholars such as Mark Lynn Anderson, Jane Gaines, Katherine Groo, Priya Jaikumar, and Samantha N. Sheppard have engaged with theories of history and the archive by Michel Foucault, Jacques Derrida, Joan Wallach Scott, Saidiya Hartman, and others.[3]

This book contributes to contemporary efforts to provide a more robust philosophical foundation for film and media historiography. Drawing film history into the history of ideas—especially ideas of history—I analyze five pioneering works of German silent cinema: Robert Wiene's *The Cabinet of Dr. Caligari* (*Das Cabinet des Dr. Caligari*, 1920), Fritz Lang's *Destiny* (*Der müde Tod*, 1921), Hans Richter's *Rhythm 21* (*Rhythmus 21*, 1923–25), Arnold Fanck's *The Holy Mountain* (*Der heilige Berg*, 1926), and Lang's *Metropolis* (1927). With their experiments in cinematic form and style (e.g., intricate narrative structures, Expressionist mise-en-scène, abstract animation), these highly innovative and influential films gave expression to the early-twentieth-century crisis of historical thinking, demonstrating the ability of the medium to carry out complex thought on ontological, epistemological, and historiographical questions of the philosophy of history. Placing Weimar films in conversation with concurrent debates over historicism, I create intellectual commerce between cinema and the philosophy of history, and indeed show that this commerce has taken place since the advent of moving-image culture.

In this way, *Historical Turns* not only proposes a more reflexive and philosophically grounded mode of historiography, but also historicizes and expands the field of film philosophy. The status of theory in Cinema and Media Studies has been contested over the past decades on account of the discipline's historical turn as well as the "post-theory" debate launched by David Bordwell and Noël Carroll, who polemicized against the grand frameworks of semiology, Lacanian psychoanalysis, and Althusserian Marxism that had shaped apparatus theory of the 1970s. Where Bordwell and Carroll have embraced "middle-level research" and "piecemeal theorizing" modeled on cognitivist science, D. N. Rodowick has sought to defend the unique character of humanistic inquiry by offering a "philosophy of the humanities"—one that entails a shift from film theory to film philosophy, which he traces back to writings by Stanley Cavell and Gilles Deleuze that place cinema in the service of ontological and ethical examination.[4] Among the key problems with Rodowick's move to film philosophy, as commentators have observed, is that it forgoes the explicitly political concerns of 1970s film theory, including the emancipatory project of feminism and the Marxist tradition of ideology critique.[5]

Historical Turns further challenges Rodowick's programmatic work on film philosophy, particularly insofar as it has jettisoned questions of history. Much as Theodor W. Adorno critiqued Martin Heidegger for his turn to existential ontology amid the crisis of historicism (as subsequent chapters of this book discuss), I take issue with Rodowick's focus on ontological and ethical questions during our own period of pervasive crisis rhetoric across the humanities. Where Rodowick has restricted his purview to the writings of Cavell and Deleuze from the 1970s forward, I significantly broaden the parameters of film philosophy by probing the nexus of film, history, and philosophy in the early twentieth century. Drawing sustained attention to the rich tradition of historical-philosophical debate in Germany, I position Weimar films as philosophical texts that engaged with the crisis of historicism, exploring the medium's potential to complicate and reconfigure concepts of time and historicity—concepts that have assumed a central position in Cinema and Media Studies through books such as Philip Rosen's *Change Mummified* (2001), Mary Ann Doane's *The Emergence of Cinematic Time* (2002), and Laura Mulvey's *Death 24x a Second* (2006).[6]

In pursuing the interconnections between film, history, and philosophy, *Historical Turns* opens an enormous cross-disciplinary and intermedial archive of historiographical, philosophical, artistic, literary, and other works. My main guide in this endeavor is Siegfried Kracauer, a journalist, critic, sociologist, and foundational film scholar whose career was bookended by questions of the philosophy of history. In a letter to Leo Löwenthal from March 1, 1922, Kracauer expressed interest in Heidegger's "The Concept of Time in the Science of History" ("Der Zeitbegriff in der Geschichtswissenschaft," 1916) and mentioned his own plans to begin a "metaphysics of history with a discussion of concepts of time."[7] While this project did not take expansive form during the Weimar period, the subject of history would move to the fore in the final years of Kracauer's life. In his correspondence with Löwenthal from the early 1960s, Kracauer again conveyed his strong desire to write about historical methodology and content, noting the affinities between film theory and the philosophy of history: "This essay on history, I suddenly realized, is the direct continuation of my *Theory of Film* [1960]: the historian has traits of the photographer, and historical reality resembles camera-reality."[8]

The unfinished and posthumously published essay in question, *History: The Last Things before the Last* (1969), returned to Kracauer's abiding historical-philosophical concerns and further pursued the analogy between modern historiography and technological media. Kracauer may thus be placed within a trajectory of thinkers (e.g., Franklin H. Giddings, Walter Benjamin, Marc Bloch, Arthur Danto, A.R. Louch, Michel de Certeau, Hayden White, Frank Ankersmit) who have drawn comparisons with film in addressing issues of historical method and narration, suggesting the interrelation between the popular media and historical imagination of any epoch.[9] In the following chapters, I revisit and sometimes revise Kracauer's seminal contributions to the study of film and history, from his criticism of the 1920s up to his fragmentary final work. Where *History* has often been overshadowed by Kracauer's earlier writings, my book moves it into the spotlight, reconstructing the extensive network of ideas and debates from which it emerged. Moreover, in illuminating the manifold links between cinema and the philosophy of history, *Historical Turns* serves as a corrective to the logocentrism of existing accounts of the crisis of historicism, which have commonly neglected the sphere of audiovisual culture.

Weimar cinema has been a privileged site for considering issues of film historiography and hermeneutics since Kracauer's *From Caligari to Hitler* (1947). Where scholars have long contested Kracauer's claim that the films of "pre-Hitler Germany" reveal protofascist psychological dispositions—Anton Kaes, for instance, has reversed Kracauer's teleology, arguing that the films retrospectively registered the "shell shock" of World War I—this book redirects focus to the Weimar period's own vital and prevalent historical-philosophical debates.[10] I explore various aspects of the crisis of historicism by tracking across a full spectrum of film styles, modes, and genres: from the Expressionism of *Caligari* to the metaphysical allegory of *Destiny*, from the geometrical abstraction of Richter's "absolute film" to the natural history of Fanck's mountain film, and concluding with the summative pastiche of *Metropolis*. In analyzing these works on a formal and aesthetic level for their modernist experiments in nonlinear time, this book remains committed to the practice of interpretative close reading. The five films under examination serve as tutor texts that help elucidate debates about time and history that permeated all realms of Weimar culture and remain relevant to the present day.

Chapter 1, "Historical Turns," defines and situates the book's central terms—historicism, the crisis of historicism, and the historical turn in Cinema and Media Studies—and lays out its interventions in key fields of study: film and media historiography, film and critical theory, philosophy of history, history and film, film philosophy, and Weimar cinema. As mentioned above, scholarship within the field of intellectual history has largely neglected the intersections between the crisis of historical thinking and the advent of moving-image culture; conversely, New Film History has seldom engaged with critical reflections on the theory and practice of history, often appealing to the very model of historical scholarship that came under intense scrutiny at the time of cinema's emergence. Challenging the oversights of prior accounts, I emphasize the concurrence of the early-twentieth-century debates over historicism and the increasing recognition of film's capacity as a medium of philosophical thought. In this way, I also historicize contemporary interest in film philosophy, unearthing a vast archive of writings that long predates the work of Cavell and Deleuze. Subsequent chapters then develop and substantiate the book's argument, exploring facets of the crisis of historicism through the prism of disparate philosophers and films. Across the book's chapters, I intend not only to offer novel interpretations of familiar, much-discussed films, but also to map out the historiographical implications of the technological medium, generating a loose typology of thinking about time and history through the moving image.

While cinema was quickly recognized for its ability to capture the phenomena of the contemporary world—Thomas Edison heralded his Kinetoscope as "a new way of recording history"—the invention also immediately gave rise to an enduring genre of films that restage and reenact the past.[11] My second chapter, "Things As They Could Have Happened," examines the genre of the historical film through the lens of Kracauer's voluminous, often-untranslated writings across nearly half a century. Moving from Kracauer's first film reviews in the Weimar Republic up to his final books in American exile, I demonstrate how his emerging critique of the genre developed into an aesthetics and theory of film as well as a general philosophy of history. In my analysis, the historical film was problematic for Kracauer, given the genre's attempts to resurrect an irretrievably bygone past. Where a founder of modern historical science, Leopold von Ranke, aspired to show "how it essentially was [*wie es eigentlich gewesen*]," the historical film can only render "things as they *could* have happened."[12]

Kracauer thus rethought the long-standing Aristotelian distinction between history and poetry, curiously locating the *poetics* of film in the medium's documentary function as a *historian* of present-day life.

Robert Wiene's classic of Expressionist cinema, *The Cabinet of Dr. Caligari*, has often served as a linchpin of arguments about the Weimar Republic. Repositioning *Caligari* as a deliberation on the period's own debates on time and history, my third chapter, "Relativist Perspectivism," studies the film at the nexus of two interlocking sets of developments: the popularization of Albert Einstein's theory of relativity and widespread recognition of the relativist implications of historicist thought; and the rejection of perspectival conventions in the visual arts and the emergence of perspectivism in philosophy. Eliciting comparisons to Einstein's theory upon its release, Wiene's film challenges basic historicist tenets, conveying a radical skepticism regarding the possibility of detached, disinterested observation. With its enigmatic narrative and distorted, postperspectival set design, *Caligari* dismisses Ranke's ideal of faithfully and impartially reconstructing the past. Instead, the film follows Friedrich Nietzsche's early writings in suggesting a perspectivist sense of historical reality as the interplay of finite interpretations. *Caligari's* legacy thus consists not only in its modernist aesthetics, but also in its engagement with fundamental historical-philosophical questions.

Appearing one year after *Caligari*, Fritz Lang's *Destiny* similarly explores the potential of film, in the director's own words, "to photograph *thoughts*, that is, render them visually."[13] My fourth chapter, "Metaphysics of Death," approaches *Destiny* as a film-philosophical meditation on being and time after "the end of metaphysics" (Heidegger). I argue that *Destiny* is concerned with the status of death in a period of shattered faith in the meaning and coherence of history. Where the German historicist tradition treated historical entities (e.g., epochs, peoples, states) as irreducibly individual and unique—"every epoch is immediate to God [*unmittelbar zu Gott*]," in Ranke's well-known phrase—Lang's episode film conveys a visual poetics of parallelism and analogy, emphasizing transhistorical affinities and commonalities rather than distinct inner principles.[14] Recognizing the collapse of historicism into relativism in the aftermath of a world war and global pandemic, the film contributed to Weimar philosophical debates by indicating that the very inescapability of death remains an abiding and universal truth. Lang's film thus participated in the theorization of finitude that characterized Weimar intellectual and cultural life, offering what might be deemed a postmetaphysical metaphysics.

"History is what is happening today," declared Hans Richter in a 1926 issue of his avant-garde journal *G: Zeitschrift für elementare Gestaltung* (*G:*

Journal for Elementary Construction).[15] Calling for a mode of historiography that serves present-day artistic practice, Richter's manifesto is at odds with his later writings that retrospectively chronicle the Dada movement, early documentary and experimental film, and the cinematic avant-garde in Germany. In Chapter 5, "The Nonsimultaneity of the Simultaneous," I examine questions of time and history in Richter's abstract films and theoretical writings of the Weimar era—works, in my analysis, that seek to negate the past and establish a temporality of pure presence. Analyzing *Rhythm 21* as a response to the crisis of historicism, I argue that Richter paradoxically relied on aesthetic and intellectual traditions in the very act of rejecting the past, articulating an antihistoricist presentism caught in a performative contradiction. Moreover, engaging with texts by interwar thinkers on the concept of nonsimultaneity (*Ungleichzeitigkeit*), I problematize Richter's manifesto and suggest a reflexive approach to the "historical avant-garde"—one that historicizes it in relation to contemporaneous debates on the philosophy of history.

The genre of the mountain film (*Bergfilm*) is often characterized as a conservative retreat from the contingencies of sociopolitical history into a timeless, mythical nature. My sixth chapter, "Natural History," argues that the genre participated in interwar debates on historicism by rethinking the very dualism of nature and history. Where Heidegger rendered the two terms identical, essentializing historicity as the basic ontological structure of *Dasein*, Adorno sought to overcome the reified antithesis of nature and history through a dialectical concept of natural history (*Naturgeschichte*). In my analysis, Arnold Fanck's *The Holy Mountain* marks an instantiation of Adorno's dialectics, tracing the interaction of nonidentical, ultimately irreconcilable human characters and geophysical forces. While the film appeals to what I call a cinematic jargon of authenticity, it also reveals seemingly fixed, lawful forces to be transient and finite. In this way, I show that early-twentieth-century Germany was already the site of nascent recognition of the mutability and potential destructibility of the Alpine landscape. Weimar films thereby prefigure contemporary efforts to reconsider the relationship between nature and history against the backdrop of global warming and climate catastrophe.

A culmination of silent-film aesthetics, *Metropolis* brought together heterogeneous elements of Weimar cinema. My epilogue, "The Weimar Analogy," demonstrates that despite Weimar culture's "hunger for wholeness" (Peter Gay), there was no return from fragmentation to cohesive unity, and from relativist skepticism to transcendental values and timeless, universal truths. While symptomatizing what Ernst Troeltsch identified as a widespread longing for "synthesis, system, worldview, structure, and position," *Metropolis* betrayed the promiscuous set of forms assumed by a younger generation's revolt against its liberal bourgeois inheritance.[16] I place *Metropolis* in conversation with two recent works of global cinema: *Sorry to Bother You* (Boots Riley, 2018) and *Parasite* (Bong Joon-ho, 2019). While these two films follow *Metropolis* in their use of vertically organized cityscapes to visualize class stratification, they extend and challenge the legacy of Lang's film in allegorizing racial capitalism and environmental injustice. Finally, I contribute to ongoing scholarly discussions over the potential for drawing analogies between the Weimar Republic and our own moment of political, economic, and environmental crises, identifying vital questions that still emerge from the interwar debates over historicism.

Given my concern with a crisis of historicism, it may seem paradoxical that my book itself focuses on a particular cultural-linguistic context. As the following chapter elaborates, Germany was the site of a specific tradition of historiography and historical thinking that entered a state of acute, widely diagnosed crisis in the early twentieth century. This crisis gave rise to significant historical-philosophical debates that not only extended across academic disciplines, but also—as I argue—found more popular expression in the vibrant intellectual and film culture of the 1920s, when cinema gained increasing recognition as a novel medium of thought. Yet instead of presenting Weimar as a bounded, uniform epoch with a distinct zeitgeist, I trace longer-term inheritances and uneven, nonsynchronous developments, foregrounding German intellectuals' own critiques of periodizing topoi that lend undue consistency, homogeneity, and unified coherence to the historical process. And rather than treating Weimar Germany as irreducibly unique or "immediate to God," I draw numerous connections to other contexts and also reflect on the ability of cross-temporal analogies to bring into relief the contours of the global present, helping us to write what Hans Richter invoked as a history of "what is happening today."

To the extent that this book examines an earlier revolt against historicism even as it remains committed to aspects of the tradition at the levels of method and prose (e.g., contextualization, chronological succession, continuous or linear narration), it gestures to the basic antinomy of historical time identified by Kracauer, enacting what he ultimately proposed as "the 'side-by-side' principle."[17] In offering a historical account of antihistoricism, the book also signals an unavoidable irony, as flagged more recently by Frank Ankersmit: "Historicism quietly awaits us at the end of the route we had chosen in our attempt to escape from it."[18] If we are unable to evade a historicist mode of thinking, we can nonetheless develop a more reflexive and philosophically grounded approach, exploring how the medium of film itself reflects on problems of historicism and engaging with broader historical-philosophical debates of the past. For, as I hope to demonstrate, we may yet learn from the interwar critiques of historicism in our own period of metastasizing crises. It is the wager of this book that Weimar philosophy and film provide new ways of thinking about the decisive issues of our own crisis-ridden time.

1. Historical Turns

The age of historicism is over.

CARL HEINRICH BECKER

Historicism is and will be our fate, whether we like it or not.

FRANK ANKERSMIT

Conceived in Kantian terms as a "critique of historical reason," Wilhelm Dilthey's *Introduction to the Human Sciences* (*Einleitung in die Geisteswissenschaften*, 1883) recognized the limits of the historical consciousness that arose in the nineteenth century.[1] As part of the Romantic reaction to the French Revolution, German historicism had challenged the natural-law theory of the Enlightenment and prompted a "historical turn" across disciplines—from history and theology to economics, law, and politics. Emancipating these fields from an abstract, metaphysical system of thought, the German Historical School adopted an empirical mode of observation, studying the concrete particularities of human history and society with reference to their contexts of development. Dilthey emphasized, however, that the school never established a firm philosophical grounding in epistemology and psychology. Rather than grasping historical reality by analyzing "the facts of consciousness given in inner experience," it followed Leopold von Ranke's methodological ideal of self-extinguishment (*Selbstauslöschung*).[2] Thus, as Charles R. Bambach notes, "although Dilthey still respected the Historical School for helping to break down metaphysical notions of *Wissenschaft*, ultimately he believed that the 'historical turn' of nineteenth-century German scholarship lacked a genuinely scientific foundation."[3]

As outlined in the introduction, this book contributes to efforts to provide a more solid philosophical foundation for Cinema and Media Studies following the discipline's own "historical turn." Emerging in the mid-1970s, New Film History served as a corrective to the universalisms of apparatus theory and the guiding assumptions of previous generations of historiography (e.g., cinema's evolutionary development, unique essence, or narrative vocation), compromised by insufficient access to film prints and archival materials.[4] Where revisionist scholarship of the past decades has radically expanded and complicated understandings of film history, it has seldom engaged sustainedly with debates on the philosophy of history and on the legacy and status of the historicist tradition.[5] In Jane Gaines's words, "While the leading historical works in new film history have been what is often termed *theoretically informed*, there have been too few attempts to foreground, let alone critique, the methods and assumptions that film and cinema historiography picked up along with the professional historian's method."[6] This book rethinks the tenets of film and media historiography by examining works of German silent cinema in relation to the philosophical critiques of historicism of the late nineteenth and early twentieth centuries. I argue that New Film History has often made recourse to the very model of historical scholarship that Dilthey and other thinkers called into question.

Of course, an analogy between the historical turn in nineteenth-century German scholarship and that of film studies is an imperfect one. Employed by Jay Leyda in 1974, the phrase "New Film History" recalled the New History championed in the early twentieth century by James Harvey Robinson, who had distinguished it from traditional narratives of preeminent political figures and events as well as more scientific efforts to establish the objective truth of the past.[7] Promoting an understanding and improvement of contemporary conditions, Robinson and fellow Progressive historians such as Charles A. Beard broadened the purview and methods of the historical sciences and foregrounded economic and social forces. Programmatic works of New Film History, including Robert C. Allen and Douglas Gomery's *Film History: Theory and Practice* (1985), followed the New History in conceiving the history of cinema not as a tale of individual inventors and pioneers, but rather as an open system shaped by artistic, technological, economic, and sociocultural factors. In their introductory theoretical discussion, Allen and Gomery quoted Beard's "That Noble Dream" (1935) and posited critical realism as an alternative to the "empiricism" of Carl Hempel and the "conventionalism" of Saussurean structural linguistics.[8]

Emerging alongside the *nouvelle histoire* of the Annales School's third generation and the New Historicism in literary studies, New Film History was one of many concurrent movements that pronounced their difference from antiquated historical scholarship. Yet New Film History was itself curiously old-fashioned, for it sought legitimacy as a field of academic study through an implicit appeal to the German Historical School's central methods and ideals, from primary archival research and philological source criticism to scientific exactitude and objective, detached neutrality.[9] Compounding this sense of untimeliness was a lack of historical reflexivity about the rapid media-technological transformations of the mid to late twentieth century—

transformations that facilitated a more rigorously empirical mode of investigation but also challenged the very autonomy, specificity, and stability of cinema as an object of inquiry, threatening it with obsolescence. In a 1986 review essay on works of New Film History, Thomas Elsaesser presciently noted that "none of these books . . . pays attention to the new technologies as they affect not only the cinema but how we come to view its history. The New History, depending on the one hand on archivists and restorers and on the other on video and television, may well be the phoenix that rises from the ashes of the cinema we once knew."[10]

In his later work, Elsaesser responded to the historiographical challenge of digital technologies by recasting New Film History as a form of "media archaeology."[11] Drawing from Michel Foucault, media archaeology extends and radicalizes many facets of New Film History, most notably an emphasis on heterogeneity, rupture, and discontinuity rather than singular origins, linear causality, and teleological progression; an exploration of media practices beyond narrative entertainment and theatrical exhibition; and, finally, a shift from the interpretive analysis of individual works to a material consideration of institutions, industries, and networks.[12] At the same time, media archaeology diverges from New Film History in provincializing cinema within media history and also in depriviliging realistic historical representation (Ranke's "how it essentially was") in favor of alternate, even counterfactual trajectories (Elsaesser's "what might have been and could still be, along with what has been, has been forgotten, or is poised to return").[13] While the present book likewise deviates from a Rankean approach, it issues a more immanent critique of the historical turn in Cinema and Media Studies, highlighting the tension between the tacit historicism of New Film History and the "crisis of historicism" that unfolded alongside the emergence of cinema.

HISTORICISM AND ITS CRISIS

Modeled after the German noun *Historismus*, historicism (sometimes rendered as *historism*) bears varying, often-contradictory meanings in cultural and intellectual history. The *Oxford English Dictionary* defines the term as a stylistic epoch in art and architecture, a deterministic theory of historical processes (à la Karl Popper's *The Poverty of Historicism* [1957]), and a belief in the importance of historicity, the past, and the contextual understanding of sociocultural phenomena and values.[14] The present book, by contrast, uses the word to denote a specific movement of historiography and historical thinking that flourished in nineteenth-century Germany and revolutionized modern thought. The classic account of this movement is Friedrich Meinecke's *Historism: The Rise of a New Historical Outlook* (*Die Entstehung des Historismus*, 1936), which identified the essence of historicism as "the substitution of a process of *individualising* observation for a *generalising* view of human forces in history."[15] Emerging in the latter half of the eighteenth century and culminating in the writings of Justus Möser, Johann Gottfried Herder, Johann Wolfgang von Goethe, and Ranke, historicism displaced an atemporal conception of human nature and reason with a new emphasis on the development and irreducible uniqueness of historical entities such as epochs, peoples, and states.

Meinecke's *Historism* has been a touchstone for subsequent studies of the German historical outlook. In *The German Conception of History* (1968), Georg G. Iggers complicated Meinecke's quasi-Hegelian narrative of historicism as a "general Western movement" that attained its full development in Germany, and he also criticized the author for bracketing the movement's political connotations and broader social contexts.[16] Tracing German historicism back to Wilhelm von Humboldt and Ranke, Iggers emphasized that it arose from a nationalist response to the French Revolution and Napoleonic Wars and maintained an optimistic faith in the harmony of state power, ethics, and freedom. More recently, Frederick C. Beiser's *The German Historicist Tradition* (2011) faults Meinecke for ignoring or misinterpreting major figures and for employing a facile, misleading conceptual scheme.[17] Examining a lineage of thinkers from Johann Martin Chladenius to Max Weber, Beiser redefines historicism in terms of a nominalist emphasis on the omnipresence of change and on the principles of individuality and holism. Moreover, identifying the aim of historicism as the justification of the scientific status of history, Beiser dismisses the objective existence of the crisis of historicism, attributing the intellectual movement's demise to its success in legitimating history as an academic discipline.

This monograph diverges from Beiser in approaching the crisis of historicism as a major, widely diagnosed phenomenon that remains relevant to the present day. Although the advent of this crisis is commonly dated back to the late nineteenth century, the German phrase "*die Krisis des Historismus*" itself was coined by Ernst Troeltsch in a 1922 essay of that title. Invoking the general revolt against science that Weber had addressed in "Science as a Vocation" ("Wissenschaft als Beruf," 1919), Troeltsch nonetheless argued that the crisis of historical science arose primarily from within the movement of historicism, which he defined as "the historicization of our entire knowledge and perception of the spiritual-intellectual [*geistigen*] world as it came in the course of the nineteenth century. We see here everything in the flow of becoming, in endless and ever-new individualization, in the determination by the past and in the direction of an unrecognized future. State, law, morality, religion, and art are dissolved into the flow of historical becoming and are comprehensible to us everywhere only as part of historical developments."[18]

In associating historicism with the dissolution of all eternal truths into a continuous, ever-changing flux, Troeltsch's essay recalled Friedrich Nietzsche's "On the Uses and Disadvantages of History for Life" ("Vom Nutzen und Nachteil der Historie für das Leben," 1874), which had also deployed Heraclitean metaphors to describe nineteenth-century historiography as the erosion of all foundations "into a continual evolving that flows ceaselessly away."[19] Yet where Nietzsche had challenged foundational values of European culture, Troeltsch sought an ethically oriented "cultural synthesis [*Kultursynthese*]" of inherited values—an idea he advanced in his final, unfinished work, *Historicism and Its Problems* (*Der Historismus und seine Probleme*, 1922).[20]

Published in a disorienting postwar period that saw a heightened interest in the philosophy of history (as signaled by the massive currency of Oswald Spengler's two-volume *The Decline of the West* [*Der Untergang des Abendlandes*, 1918 and 1922]), Troeltsch's work served as the primary basis for the Weimar debate over historicism, including interventions by Meinecke, Karl Mannheim, and Otto Hintze.[21] Taken together, these writings identified ontological, epistemological, and historiographical reasons for the crisis of historical thinking: a shattered faith in the logic, meaning, and directionality of the historical process; skepticism regarding the possibility of securing objective knowledge of a dynamic historical world, especially given the subjective and spatiotemporally determined perspective of all cognition; and, finally, acknowledgment of the aesthetic dimensions of historical contemplation and writing. No less vital were concerns about the antinomy between historical science and contemporary life, or between specialized research and general problems, as well as about the apparent lack of certain values, firm standards of judgment, and absolute, universally valid truths.[22] If, in Ranke's well-known formulation, "every epoch is immediate to God," then the Nietzschean death of God threatened to collapse historicism into sheer relativism.[23]

Though the acute sense of crisis largely subsided by the end of the 1920s, German-speaking commentators continued to reassess the legacy of historicism in subsequent decades.[24] In *The Crisis of Historicism* (*Die Krisis des Historismus*, 1932), Karl Heussi argued that the crisis had partly disintegrated and partly reshaped the dominant model of historiography from circa

1900, with two notable transformations: where, at the beginning of the century, the objects of historical cognition were seen as permanently fixed, now they seemed to shift in relation to the mobile position of the observer, such that the past became "something living, constantly changing and growing, ... an inexhaustible stimulus for ever-new historical interpretations."[25] Previously restricted to a positivist realm of verifiable facts, historical science had also been supplemented and enriched in recent years through more speculative philosophical thinking. In a 1942 essay, "On the Crisis of Historicism" ("Von der Krisis des Historismus"), Meinecke objected to Heussi's definition of historicism, deeming his opposition between turn-of-the-century and postwar historical thinking "fundamentally nonexistent."[26] Meinecke further noted that the crisis of historicism appeared resolved after the Nazi attempt to create a new form of society and state along with fixed guidelines for historical thinking and understanding.[27]

KRACAUER'S AND BENJAMIN'S CRITIQUES

The crisis of historicism figured into German film and critical theory in its formative stages, particularly via the work of Siegfried Kracauer and Walter Benjamin. Having written philosophical and sociological studies during and after the Great War (most notably *Sociology as a Science* [*Soziologie als Wissenschaft*, 1922]), Kracauer commented on intellectual developments for the *Frankfurter Zeitung* throughout the Weimar era, publishing essays, tributes, book reviews, and lecture and conference reports.[28] Within this vast corpus of texts, Kracauer's most sustained intervention into the historicism debate was the 1923 article "The Crisis of Science" ("Die Wissenschaftskrisis"). Discussing Troeltsch's *Historicism and Its Problems* alongside Weber's *Collected Essays on Epistemology* (*Gesammelte Aufsätze zur Wissenschaftslehre*, 1922), Kracauer noted that empirical disciplines such as history and sociology confronted a dilemma as they made claims to general validity: either they retained their objectivity, yielding a "senseless *accumulation of material* [*Stoffanhäufung*]," or they employed value-laden criteria at the cost of an "unavoidable *relativism.*"[29] In Kracauer's analysis, both Troeltsch and Weber had sought in vain to address the antinomies between relativism and absolute meaning, historical science and religious faith—antinomies that could be reconciled only through a transformation of the entire spiritual-intellectual situation.

Kracauer's essay "Photography" ("Die Photographie," 1927) adopted a more immanent, Marxist mode of critique, suggesting that an "*accumulation of material*" is not the byproduct of value-free objectivity, but rather the ideological veil of a bourgeois society that conceals mortality: "What the photographs by their accumulation [*Häufung*] attempt to banish is the recollection of death."[30] Integrating historicism into a theorization of visual culture, he wrote:

> The principle of Goethe philology is that of *historicist* thinking, which became established at around the same time as modern photographic technology. Its advocates—Dilthey, for instance—believe that they can explain any phenomenon purely from its genesis; that is, they believe in any case that they can grasp historical reality by reconstructing the series of events in their temporal succession without any gaps. Photography presents a spatial continuum; historicism seeks to provide the temporal continuum. According to historicism, the complete mirroring of an intratemporal sequence simultaneously contains the meaning of all that occurred within that time. . . . Historicism is concerned with the photography of time. The equivalent of its temporal photography would be a giant film depicting the temporally interconnected events from all sides.[31]

Referencing the philological research published in the *Jahrbuch der Goethe-Gesellschaft,* Kracauer noted the contemporaneous rise of historicism and photography in the nineteenth century along with their common drive toward comprehensive coverage. Where historicist scholarship constructs an unbroken continuum of chronological events, the photographic images that proliferate in illustrated magazines aim at a complete reproduction of the world—in both cases, however, reifying the prevailing social order and hindering an understanding of the true history, relationality, and meaning of phenomena. Film unites the two axes of time and space, with the potential for epic, multiperspectival representation. In a dialectical turn, however, the essay's final section argued that the medium also bears the more radical possibility of reassembling the "*general inventory*" of spatiotemporal elements through montage.[32]

Divided into eight chapters (like the eight sections of "Photography"), Kracauer's final, posthumously published book, *History: The Last Things before the Last* (1969), returned to the concerns of his 1927 essay, further pursuing the analogy between historiography and photographic media, or "historical reality" and "camera-reality."[33] (In the book's introduction, he wrote, "Lately I came across my piece on 'Photography' and was completely amazed at noticing that I had compared historism with photography already in this article of the 'twenties.")[34] Extending key concepts from his *Theory of Film* (1960), Kracauer addressed questions of historical methodology such as genre, scale, subject matter, and the balance between "realistic" and "formative" tendencies.³⁵ Moreover, acknowledging the challenges that historicism had posed for modern philosophy, Kracauer took up pivotal issues of the late-nineteenth- and early-twentieth-century crisis of historical thought: the constitution and structure of the historical universe; the position of historiography vis-à-vis literature, philosophy, theology, and the natural sciences; the influence of the historian's subjectivity and contemporary environment on their rendering of the past; and, finally, the disjuncture between the relativity of historical knowledge and the quest for significant, generally valid truths.

A key interlocutor on historical-philosophical questions was Kracauer's late friend and fellow German-Jewish émigré, Walter Benjamin. In "Eduard Fuchs, Collector and Historian" ("Eduard Fuchs, der Sammler und der Historiker," 1937) and "On the Concept of History" ("Über den Begriff der Geschichte," 1940), Benjamin had drawn a comparison between historical materialism and historicism, associating the latter with an eternal, contemplative image of the past along with the additive procedure and epic narrative principle of universal history.³⁶ Written under desperate circumstances, Benjamin's 1940 essay—his last known text—argued that historicism empathized with history's victors, whose seizures of power were normalized in the name of progress. Recalling Kracauer's description of the "accumulation [*Häufung*]" of all photographs in a vast inventory of crumbling natural elements, Benjamin's essay presented an allegorical vision of progress as a ruinous storm that drives the backward-facing angel of history into the future: "Where a chain of events appears before *us*, *he* sees one single catastrophe, which relentlessly piles [*häuft*] wreckage upon wreckage and hurls it at his feet."³⁷ Yet while Kracauer looked to cinematic montage to "stir up the elements of nature," Benjamin sought more violently to "blast open the continuum of history," shattering the causal nexus established by historicism.³⁸

Benjamin's thetic essay nonetheless suggested its own points of conjunction between the critique of historicism and moving-image media. Dismissing Rankean efforts to ascertain "how it essentially was," Benjamin argued that the "true image of the past" is one that "flashes up [*aufblitzt*]" and "flits by [*huscht vorbei*]," evanescently available to the historical subject in a moment of danger.³⁹ While the metaphoric language recalled passages in Sigmund Freud's "A Note upon the 'Mystic Writing-Pad'" ("Notiz über den 'Wunderblock,'" 1925) and Benjamin's own texts on astrology, dialectical images, and the mimetic faculty, it also evoked the lightning speed and irretrievable ephemerality of cinematic images.⁴⁰ (In later writings, Theodor W. Adorno would similarly characterize film and television in terms of "images that flash up and slip away [*aufblitzenden und entgleitenden Bilder*].")⁴¹

Benjamin's allusion to film became explicit later in the essay, as he contended that the French Revolution had accelerated the historical process, inaugurating a novel temporal order: "The Great Revolution introduced a new calendar. The initial day of a calendar acts as a historical time lapse."[42] For Benjamin as for Kracauer, then, cinema suggested critical alternatives to the temporal regime of historicism, especially through modernist techniques such as montage and time-lapse photography.

HISTORICISM AND CONTEMPORARY DIGITAL CULTURE

Beyond film and critical theory of the interwar period, the critique of historicism has remained integral to cultural criticism and the philosophy of history over the past half century. A cursory, incomplete sketch of major interventions would include Roland Barthes's and Hayden White's accounts of historiography as a form of narrative prose discourse or emplotment, Foucault's archaeological and genealogical methods, and Reinhart Koselleck's practice of conceptual history.[43] Likewise influential have been theoretical concepts such as trauma, memory, and the limits of representation; the singular "event" that disrupts coherent narratives and exceeds meaningful contextual explanation; and "sublime historical experience" (Frank Ankersmit) or "presence" (Eelco Runia) as instances of an overwhelming sensation of the past.[44] Nineteenth-century historicism has also been a central target of feminist and postcolonial critique: Bonnie G. Smith argued that the emergence of professional historical writing was predicated on a feminized, nonscientific amateurism devoted to "superficial" subjects, while Dipesh Chakrabarty contended that historicism buttressed European colonialism, deeming non-Western societies asynchronous in their political development.[45] Most recently, Chakrabarty has shifted attention to the Anthropocene, addressing the challenges it poses to the historicist division between human and natural history, and the historical and natural sciences.[46]

In the present discussion, however, I wish to focus on how the digital turn has extended and reoriented scholarly debates over historicism. It is by now a commonplace to acknowledge that digital technologies of preservation, storage, and dissemination have powerfully reshaped historical consciousness and means of knowledge production, transforming the material bases of the sort of Goethe philology that Kracauer mocked in 1927 (and encouraging us to reenvision his "general inventory" of elements as a data center or digital archive of ever-accumulating files). While Andreas Fickers has called for the revitalization of Ranke's critical-historical method in the service of "a new digital historicism," other commentators have expressed concern about a lapse into scientistic positivism, as evidenced by the often-naive, unreflective integration of empirical and quantitative research techniques into the humanities.[47] Among the most outspoken of these detractors is Tom Eyers, who polemicizes against computational approaches to literary macroanalysis such as "distant reading" and "algorithmic criticism," condemning their disregard for "the lessons of the critiques of historicism that characterized the best of critical theory in the twentieth century."[48]

Debates on the digital humanities unfold at a moment of mounting skepticism of historicism as a methodology and broader order of time. Literary scholars are increasingly challenging the New Historicism's privileging of the work's unique cultural context above other concerns (e.g., aesthetics, form, cross-temporal resonance, present-day relevance) along with its promotion of narrow specialization within historical periods. If, in Rita Felski's gloss, "restiveness with historicism is beginning to make itself felt across the spectrum of literary studies," this disciplinary trend notably coincides with more general claims about a cessation of the historicist experience of time.[49] François Hartog contends that presentism has emerged as the "regime of historicity" since 1989, as the short-termism of financial capitalism has become both omnipresent and omnipotent. Where Koselleck famously characterized the modern era (*Neuzeit*) in terms of an ever-widening separation between the "space of experience" and "horizon of expectation," Hartog now senses "a permanent, elusive, and almost immobile present."[50] Elaborating on Hartog's work, Enzo Traverso argues that the collapse of communism paralyzed the utopian imagination that had animated the revolutionary movements of the prior two centuries. For Traverso, recent decades have witnessed a transition from utopia to memory, or from a "principle of hope" (Ernst Bloch) to a "principle of responsibility" (Hans Jonas).[51]

Perhaps most vocal on the shift away from historicism, however, is Hans Ulrich Gumbrecht. In *Our Broad Present* (*Unsere breite Gegenwart*, 2011), Gumbrecht argues that the historicist chronotope that developed in the early nineteenth century has been succeeded by another temporal regime: "the 'imperceptibly short' present of the historicist construction of time . . . has now been replaced by an ever broadening present of simultaneities. In today's electronic present, there is neither anything 'from the past' that we need to leave behind nor anything 'from the future' that could not be made present by simulated anticipation."[52] Invoking Charles Baudelaire's "The Painter of Modern Life" ("Le Peintre de la vie moderne," 1863), Gumbrecht posits that historicism understood the present as a brief moment of transition between a bygone past and an open future. In his analysis, however, this configuration of time is now obsolete: the past has become unrelinquishable, and the future is no longer a spectrum of possibilities (Koselleck's "horizon of expectation"), but rather menacingly foreclosed on account of global warming, nuclear weapons, and other existential threats. As Gumbrecht indicates, digital technologies contribute to the posthistoricist expansion of the present, since they render all traces of the past readily accessible and can also simulate elements of an anticipated future.

Illuminating as it is, Gumbrecht's book nonetheless overlooks compelling signs that the historicist construction of time persists in the twenty-first-century media environment. Where Kracauer envisaged the equivalent of historicism's temporal photography as "a giant film depicting the temporally interconnected events from all sides" (and later cited Fernand Léger's idea for a "monster film that would have to record the life of a man and a woman throughout twenty-four consecutive hours"), we might think today of the television channels, websites, and mobile apps that evoke an imaginary of total coverage and the complete, multiperspectival representation of human reality via constant news alerts and a continuous, 24/7 interface.[53] Notable in this regard is Facebook, which maps one's life events onto ceaselessly flowing timelines while offering unprompted "memories" that seek to extend, reduplicate, or even outsource the operations of individual subjectivity (recalling Kracauer's Bergsonian-cum-Proustian opposition between the spatiotemporal continuum of photographic representation and the fragmentary, irreducibly personal nature of human memory).[54] Contra Gumbrecht, then, I argue that historicism remains both a powerful chronotope and an essential target of critique, especially as Facebook and other platforms come under heightened political scrutiny. Not least, I suggest that contemporary digital culture affords vital new perspectives on the long-standing relation between historicism and technological media.

THE RELATIONSHIP BETWEEN HISTORY AND FILM

Memorably theorized in Kracauer's writings and Barthes's *Camera Lucida* (*La chambre claire*, 1980), the nexus of history and photographic media has endured as a rich site of inquiry in recent decades.[55] In *Romanticism and the Rise of History* (1995), Stephen Bann studied representations of the past across various media in early-nineteenth-century Europe—from the novels of Sir Walter Scott to the paintings and lithographs of Richard Parkes Bonington, and from museums such as Alexandre du Sommerard's Musée de Cluny to the panoramas, dioramas, and photographs of Louis Daguerre.[56] Rearticulating Bann's art-historical research in media-archaeological terms, Wolfgang Ernst draws a parallel between Ranke's self-effacing quest to show "*wie es eigentlich gewesen*" and the impartiality of nascent optical technologies: "Ranke's ambition to let archival documents speak for themselves and his determination to use nothing but original sources found their visual equivalent in the media-epistemological fiction of an unmediated record of the reality of the past.... Daguerre achieved in the visual representation of photography exactly what was attempted in textual historiography of the period."[57] While professional historians sought to recover the objective truth of the past through primary sources, the daguerreotype process thus promised a direct photochemical inscription of the real.

Though the first commercial public exhibitions of film did not occur until 1895, the new medium emerged from a regime of historicity and art that had arguably existed for an entire century. As Jacques Rancière contends in "The Historicity of Cinema" ("L'historicité du cinéma," 1998), film marked the realization of a utopian program that dates as far back as Friedrich Schiller's "On the Aesthetic Education of Man" ("Über die ästhetische Erziehung des Menschen," 1795).[58] Where scholars have traditionally linked history and film by rendering one the object of the other (i.e., the history of film, film as a document or dramatic re-creation of history), Rancière conceives the two terms together within the broader framework of a Romantic movement that regarded all subjects as equal and sought to overcome the traditional divides between life and art, thought and feeling, and the intelligible and the sensible. For Rancière, film dissolves these oppositions through its dual constitution by the mechanical eye of the camera and an artistic subjectivity that frames and assembles the recorded footage. Developing ideas from Rancière's essay, Antoine de Baecque's *Camera Historica* (*L'Histoire-caméra*, 2008) defines "cinematographic forms of history" as instances in which history irrupts into the particular mise-en-scène developed by filmmakers to lend form to their visions of past or present.[59]

De Baecque follows an extended lineage of commentators who have examined the relationship between history and film, or between written and audiovisual renderings of the past. Emerging concurrently with New Film History, the field of History and Film was initiated by journals such as *Film & History* (1971–); books like Marc Ferro's *Cinema and History* (*Cinéma et histoire*, 1977) and Pierre Sorlin's *The Film in History* (1980); and the 1988 forum in the *American Historical Review* in which Hayden White introduced the term *historiophoty* to denote "the representation of history and our thought about it in visual images and filmic discourse."[60] Proceeding from White's claim that historical films are no more constructed or shaped than works of academic historiography, Robert Rosenstone's *Visions of the Past* (1995) and *History on Film/Film on History* (2006) argued that film is a legitimate form of historical discourse that should be evaluated not according to scholarly standards of factual accuracy and argumentation, but with regard to the medium's own practices and possibilities.[61] Where Rosenstone studied dramatic features, documentaries, and experimental films, Steve Anderson, Alison Landsberg, and others have opened the discussion to include television, video games, and digital media, addressing cultural memory and modes of spectatorial engagement.[62]

Work within the field of History and Film has often focused on the genre of the historical film, characterized by the rebuilding of historical worlds and their reenactment with real and/or fictional figures. While historians like Natalie Zemon Davis have approached the genre with an eye to its "truth status" and its potential as a "thought experiment about the past," film scholars have considered how the genre's "'surge and splendor'" (Vivian Sobchack) stimulates a viscerally embodied, sensory-affective experience and also prompts historical reflection, contributing to understandings of the past along with conceptions of nation and culture.[63] In *Film Nation* (1997) and *The Hollywood Historical Film* (2008), Robert Burgoyne analyzed American historical films that articulate a counternarrative of national history and identity, and he set forth a taxonomy of the historical film with five distinct subtypes (the war film, epic, biopic, topical film, and metahistorical film).[64] Philip Rosen, Eleftheria Thanouli, and others have further theorized the historical film and its aesthetic problematics, emphasizing its ambiguous position between history and poetics, document and fiction, and past affairs and present concerns.[65] In the next chapter, I explore these issues through the lens of Kracauer's largely unknown writings on the genre, beginning with his film reviews and essays from the Weimar period.

Weimar Germany was the site of extensive discourse about the historical film genre along with cinema's potential role in historical research and instruction. Within the immense archive of texts from the era, we find, for example, a spirited exchange from 1921 in the daily film periodical *Der Kinematograph* on the relative merits of film as a vivid means of reimagining the past or as a faithful record of contemporary life that effortlessly captures "how it essentially was" for future generations; a chapter of Oskar Kalbus's book *The German Educational Film in Science and the Classroom* (*Der deutsche Lehrfilm in der Wissenschaft und im Unterricht*, 1922) on the moving image as a livelier and more emotionally immersive form of historical instruction than the spoken word; and, finally, a 1928 essay in the monthly journal for history teachers *Vergangenheit und Gegenwart* heralding cinema as a pedagogical tool that could reawaken the younger generation's interest in historical study amid the crisis of historicism.[66] As

Mason Allred has argued, such writings should be understood in the context of progressive education (*Reformpädagogik*) and especially the institutional initiatives of the Weimar period, including the Bildstelle im Zentralinstitut für Erziehung und Unterricht (est. 1919), the Deutsche Bildwoche (est. 1920), and the Deutscher Ikonographischer Ausschuss (est. 1930).[67]

FILM AND THE PHILOSOPHY OF HISTORY

Alongside the proliferation of writings and institutional initiatives, the early years of the Weimar Republic witnessed what Lotte H. Eisner would later describe as a "flood of historical films"—among them Ernst Lubitsch's historical spectacles (e.g., *Madame DuBarry* [1919], *Sumurun* [1920], *Anna Boleyn* [1920], *The Loves of Pharaoh* [*Das Weib des Pharao*, 1922]) as well as the cycle of "Prussian films" beginning with the four-part *Fridericus Rex* (Arzén von Cserépy, 1922–23).[68] While the following chapter addresses such historical films via Kracauer's writings, my book as a whole does not restrict its attention to this single genre. Given that Weimar cinema was "a tremendously diverse popular cinema that developed a variety of genre forms," as Christian Rogowski has emphasized, I adopt a much broader scope, tracking the question of history across films that helped inaugurate the genres of horror, fantasy, the avant-garde, the mountain film, and science fiction.[69] Through analyses of five influential works—*The Cabinet of Dr. Caligari* (1920), *Destiny* (1921), *Rhythm 21* (1923–25), *The Holy Mountain* (1926), and *Metropolis* (1927)—I argue that Weimar cinema lent vivid expression to the critique of historicism, engaging with ontological, epistemological, and historiographical questions of the philosophy of history. In developing this argument, I not only challenge the historicist tenets of New Film History, but also expand the field of film philosophy, probing the nexus between cinema and historical-philosophical inquiry.

A key passage on the relationship between film and the philosophy of history is found in Gilles Deleuze's *Cinéma 1* (1983). Defending the strength and coherence of Hollywood's conceptions of history, Deleuze relates the formal and stylistic features of American silent epics to the modes of historiographical engagement delineated by Nietzsche in "On the Uses and Disadvantages of History for Life":

> It is easy to make fun of Hollywood's historical conceptions. It seems to us, on the contrary, that they bring together the most serious aspects of history as seen by the nineteenth century. Nietzsche distinguished three

of these aspects, "monumental history," "antiquarian history," and "critical," or rather ethical, history. The monumental aspect concerns the physical and human encompasser, the natural and architectural milieu. Babylon and its defeat, in Griffith, the Hebrews, the desert and the sea which opens; . . . According to Nietzsche's analysis, such an aspect of history favours the analogies or parallels between one civilisation and another: the great moments of humanity, however distant they are, are supposed to communicate via the peaks, and form a "collection of effects in themselves" which can be more easily compared and act all the more strongly on the mind of the modern spectator.[70]

Invoking D.W. Griffith's *Intolerance* (1916) and Cecil B. DeMille's *The Ten Commandments* (1923), Deleuze overlooks the transnational circulation of the analogical or parallelist narrative form during the silent era, from Luigi Maggi's *Satan* (*Satana*, 1912) to works by Joe May (*Veritas vincit*, 1919), Friedrich Wilhelm Murnau (*Satan* [*Satanas*, 1920]), Carl Theodor Dreyer (*Leaves from Satan's Book* [*Blade af Satans bog*, 1920]), Michael Kertész (*Sodom and Gomorrah* [*Sodom und Gomorrha*, 1922]), and Alexander Korda (*Samson and Delilah* [*Samson und Delila*, 1922]).[71] At the same time, in viewing transhistorical films such as *Intolerance* through a Nietzschean lens (and, later in the passage, with reference to Sergei Eisenstein's theory of dialectical montage), Deleuze neglects the various American traditions of historical discourse from which Griffith drew—traditions that Miriam Hansen would elucidate in *Babel and Babylon* (1991).[72]

With his two *Cinema* books, Deleuze joined Stanley Cavell in inaugurating the field of film philosophy, as developed over the past two decades by Daniel Frampton, Paisley Livingston, Stephen Mulhall, John Mullarkey, Patricia Pisters, Robert Sinnerbrink, and Thomas Wartenberg, among many others.[73] While this burgeoning and somewhat amorphous field includes continental, analytic, cognitivist, and neuroscientific schools, it has been broadly shaped by a number of terms and methodological distinctions. For example, Sinnerbrink characterizes "film-philosophy" as a romanticist exploration of cinema's potential as a unique mode of thinking, delineating it from a rationalist "philosophy of film" that offers conceptual analysis and explanation of cinematic experience.[74] And Livingston juxtaposes a "bold thesis"—namely, that films make independent and innovative contributions to philosophy through exclusively cinematic means—with a "modest thesis," according to which films illustrate or express preexisting philosophical ideas through devices that are not medium specific.[75] Linked to these distinctions are issues such as the nature and interrelation of film and philosophy, or art and knowledge, as well as the value of nominalist arguments about particular films, directors, and genres versus more general or a priori claims about cinema's inherent philosophical capacities or concerns.

One of the most significant recent interventions into film philosophy is D. N. Rodowick's *Philosophy's Artful Conversation* (2015). The third in a trilogy of books rethinking the study of cinema following the digital turn and the "post-theory" debate, Rodowick's monograph positions philosophy at the dual bookends of the history of film theory: "It is a delicious irony that at the beginning of the last century, Hugo Münsterberg, arguably the first film theorist, was in fact a philosopher who grasped completely that the medium of moving images asks both ontological and ethical questions of us. And so it is most fitting that as film bows from the stage of history, it leaves us with our thoughts and returns us to philosophy. After a one-hundred-year history, what becomes of theory? Philosophy. Films still entertain and move us, but they also move us to thought."[76]

For Rodowick, the return from film theory to philosophy is one from epistemological inquiry to ontological and ethical investigation, and from the explanation of the nature, logics, and effects of film to the use of moving images to examine and clarify philosophy's own concepts. Among the problems with Rodowick's account is its bracketing of philosophy from the histories of cinema and film theory.[77] Restricting his purview to the writings of Cavell and Deleuze from the 1970s forward, Rodowick elides the wealth of philosophical engagement with film over the full course of the twentieth century, including a wide range of thinkers (both canonized and lesser known) from myriad cultural-linguistic contexts and intellectual genealogies. Moreover, in characterizing philosophy as "inward directed" or "self-referring"—"a (film) philosophy is not necessarily a part of film studies; rather, it belongs to philosophy alone"—Rodowick dismisses the potential for a more dynamic, mutually illuminating exchange between the two disciplines.[78]

Where Rodowick views Münsterberg's *The Photoplay* (1916) as the historical pivot from philosophy to film theory, I instead examine the first decades of the twentieth century as the initial moment of a sustained conversation between film and philosophy, particularly in the German-speaking world. Though sometimes tacit or indirect, this exchange can often be explicitly documented, as with screenwriters and directors who cited their intellectual influences, film and cultural critics who drew connections in their articles, and philosophers who discussed their experience of individual screenings or looked to cinema more generally as a novel medium of thought. (Already in 1911, for instance, one commentator asked in the weekly journal *Die Zukunft*, "Couldn't the cinematograph even be placed in the service of the highest theoretical knowledge of nature, or in the service of philosophy?")[79] A study of early-twentieth-century German culture thus reveals a diverse array of imagined and actualized possibilities at the junction of film and philosophy—possibilities that exceed or complicate established distinctions between "film-philosophy" and the "philosophy of film," and the "bold thesis" and "modest thesis." Not least, the following chapters demonstrate that a bidirectional interaction between film and philosophy has occurred since the silent era of cinema.

THE HISTORIOGRAPHY OF WEIMAR CINEMA

The study of German silent cinema has been formatively shaped by two midcentury books by Jewish émigrés who had worked as film critics and journalists during the Weimar Republic: Kracauer's *From Caligari to Hitler* (1947) and Eisner's *The Haunted Screen* (*L'écran démoniaque*, 1952). While Kracauer offered a psychosocial analysis, arguing that films from the pre-Hitler era revealed "deep psychological dispositions predominant in Germany from 1918 to 1933," Eisner drew attention to Weimar cinema's stylistic inheritances from Expressionist art along with Max Reinhardt's theatrical productions.[80] Despite their varied emphases and methodological premises, both authors posited a relationship between Weimar cinema's distinct textual features (e.g., recurring themes, motifs, aesthetic and narrative devices) and the German collective mind or soul, as impacted by social, political, and economic developments. Establishing interwar Germany as a privileged site for considering major issues of film historiography, the two books have sparked fierce debates and criticisms. Where *The Haunted Screen* is often faulted for its indiscriminate use of the term *Expressionism*, *From Caligari to Hitler* has been condemned, inter alia, for its teleological backshadowing, homogenization and selective treatment of Weimar cinema, and reductionist analyses of individual films.[81]

For Kracauer and Eisner, Weimar cinema appeared hopelessly overdetermined, whether by its prefiguration of Nazism or by the proliferation of fantastic or supernatural elements from past aesthetic movements. Revisiting both books following the historical turn in film studies, Thomas Elsaesser sought to restore a hermeneutical openness to pre-Nazi cinema:

> The lesson of the New film history in so many areas has been to de-idealise film history, by recalling its socio-economic base, by reminding one of the materialist conditions at once enabling and constraining the existence of films. In the case of the German cinema, this anti-idealist tendency has also had the effect of "normalising" this

cinema: to relieve the films, along with the idealist expectation of cinema giving us "art," also of their "demonic" and "haunted" burden, mitigating the horrified stare at a cinema apparently so much in the grip of a symptomology, so much fevering towards the political apocalypse, as it did appear to hindsight accounts.[82]

Whereas Kracauer and Eisner had employed the method of *Geistesgeschichte*, studying the development of German silent cinema with reference to a national mentality or worldview (*Weltanschauung*), New Film History shifted from an *idealist* to a *materialist* approach. Rather than viewing films primarily as sociopsychological symptoms or as masterful achievements in artistic technique, film historians now foregrounded the basic conditioning factors of commerce and industry. One of the central questions of Elsaesser's book is why so many films of the Weimar era thematize issues of narrative authority or control, often including framing tales, flashbacks, nested stories, and *mise en abyme* structures. With a tacit nod to Jürgen Habermas, Elsaesser attributes these reflexive formal features to a "double 'legitimation crisis'" vis-à-vis the established arts and the threat of Hollywood hegemony, as the Weimar film community struggled for cultural recognition at home and financial success internationally.[83]

In a more recent book, Anton Kaes powerfully challenges Kracauer's "prefascistic" interpretation of Weimar cinema, characterizing this corpus instead as a "posttraumatic" or "shell shock cinema."[84] For Kaes, German films of the 1920s were haunted by the experience of the Great War and its devastating outcome, reenacting and working through the repressed memory of military combat and defeat. In their efforts to visualize the psychological wounds of World War I, classic works by Robert Wiene, Friedrich Wilhelm Murnau, and Fritz Lang developed innovative narrative and aesthetic strategies to express extreme mental states, thereby contributing to a modernist language of film that would later inspire film noir, horror, and science-fiction cinema. While forcefully positioning his argument in opposition to the overarching thesis of *From Caligari to Hitler*, Kaes preserves Kracauer's conception of films as psychological sensors that can lend insight into the unconscious preoccupations of a national collective. And although Kaes reverses the teleology of Kracauer's narrative, he maintains his predecessor's approach to cinema as a key medium for explicating sociopolitical developments. In so doing, Kaes's book runs the risk of overdetermining the First World War over other salient phenomena that came to bear on the cinema and audiovisual culture of the Weimar Republic.

Where Elsaesser and Kaes account for Weimar cinema's innovations with reference to a "double 'legitimation crisis'" and the aftershocks of war, respectively, I place German films of the 1920s in conversation with the philosophical critique of historicism that gained an acute urgency and widespread currency in the postwar period. In problematizing the acts of vision and narration through distinctive formal and stylistic features (e.g., nonlinear storytelling, distorted mise-en-scène, geometrical abstraction), many Weimar films engage with fundamental questions of the philosophy of history, such as the structure and directionality of the historical process, the possibility of objective cognition, and the validity of any chronicle of the past. While such metahistorical issues were extensively debated in the immediate postwar period, the decisiveness of World War I should not be overstated. As both primary and secondary sources attest, the Great War intensified rather than precipitated the crisis of historicism; Charles R. Bambach, for instance, posits the experience of war "less as a cause of crisis-consciousness than as a force of acceleration."[85] The Weimar-era critiques of historicism were prefigured by late-nineteenth-century writings of thinkers including Nietzsche, Jacob Burckhardt, and Dilthey, who had already recognized the internal problems of the German historicist tradition.

To the extent that film scholars have long disputed the proper analytical lens for German silent cinema—whether psychosocial or stylistic, idealist or materialist, prefascistic or posttraumatic—I stage an intervention by drawing sustained attention to the extensive historical-philosophical debates of the Weimar era itself. While *crisis* (from the ancient Greek *krísis*, meaning "choice," "decision," "judgment," "separation," etc.) bears a spectrum of meanings and is a ubiquitous metaphor in the modern age, as Reinhart Koselleck has shown, I deploy the term here on the basis of its common usage during the interwar period.[86] Examining films in tandem with the widely diagnosed crisis of historicism, I not only contribute to recent work on the affinities of Weimar cinema, science, and philosophy, but also look to early-twentieth-century debates over historicism for indications of how to situate and understand Weimar culture today.[87] If, as I have argued, New Film History often made recourse to central tenets of nineteenth-century historicism, this book instead interprets films in relation to the mounting *critique of historicism* during the first decades of cinema. In so doing, I propose a more reflexive mode of film and media historiography—one that considers how cinema itself reflects on questions of historicism—as well as an approach to studying moving images in conjunction with enduring historical-philosophical concerns.

2. Things As They Could Have Happened
Siegfried Kracauer and the Historical Film

> How can one be *present* at something that has happened, that is over? And this is as much a question whether the events in question are fictional or are historical; the contrast of fiction and history is irrelevant here.
>
> STANLEY CAVELL

> There is no "historical film" that is not fiction first: how indeed could the past be filmed live? Nor any that, however serious its documentation, does not fictionalize the most referenced historical argument.
>
> JEAN-LOUIS COMOLLI

Although the historicist principle of individuality can be traced back to antiquity, thinkers such as Plato and Aristotle had prioritized eternal forms as objects of rational knowledge, dismissing the particular, contingent, and fleeting phenomena of the historical world as trivial, nonphilosophical matters of inquiry.[1] Gottfried Wilhelm Leibniz restored dignity to the particular in his *Monadology* (*La monadologie*, 1714), but it was in the following century that the classical opposition was widely obfuscated: the emerging historical sciences lent the individuality of things a measure of significance equal to that of their universality, and literature focused on concrete details, producing what Roland Barthes would call "the reality effect."[2] The dividing line that Aristotle had drawn between history and poetry—or, in his words, between "what actually happened" and "the kinds of events that would happen"—was thus blurred, with the two fields becoming increasingly indistinguishable in both content and modes of description.[3] Anticipated by Johann Gustav Droysen, whose *Outline of the Principles of History* (*Grundriss der Historik*, 1858) had analyzed the problems of historical representation, the crisis of historicism exposed a dissolving distinction between empirical reality and fictional construction, the history and the story, and the true (*das Wahre*) and the verisimilar (*das Wahrscheinliche*).[4]

Hailed as the art form of the twentieth century, the medium of film emerged as the relativist implications of the historicist tradition were becoming acutely apparent. As the previous chapter established, the crisis of historicism entailed broad-scale debates on ontological, epistemological, and historiographical questions of the philosophy of history, and cinema was quickly recognized for its potential to reshape historical consciousness and to offer novel modes of engagement with the past. Already in 1895, Thomas Edison noted his Kinetoscope's capacity to reproduce transient, dynamic phenomena faithfully and to *re*-present them for centuries to come, long beyond the lives of those depicted on-screen.[5] Inasmuch as motion-picture technology captured aspects of everyday life—from styles of dress to patterns of gesture, movement, and interaction—it also granted access to an embodied, sensory-affective dimension of historical experience, in contradistinction to what Friedrich Nietzsche had critiqued as the dry antiquarianism of nineteenth-century scholarship.[6] Surpassing written chronicles in its vivid completeness and effortless, impartial precision, film heralded a "new way of recording history," as Edison proclaimed, and early commentators called for the establishment of archives, libraries, and museums to preserve the new medium, especially as it served a documentary function.[7]

At the same time, Edison's Kinetoscope films from 1895 such as *The Execution of Mary Queen of Scots*, *Joan of Arc*, and *Rescue of Capt. John Smith by Pocahontas* (all directed by Alfred Clark) helped inaugurate the prominent, enduring genre of the historical film, defined by the reconstruction of past events or periods and their reenactment with real and/or fictional characters.[8] Pivotal in the transition from one-reelers to feature films and from a "cinema of attractions" to one of "narrative integration," historical spectacles sought artistic recognition (e.g., the French *film d'art The Assassination of the Duke of Guise* [*La mort du duc de Guise*, Charles le Bargy and André Calmettes, 1908]) and distinguished themselves through a mise-en-scène that included extravagant costumes, massive crowds, and monumental sets (as in internationally distributed Italian epics including *Quo Vadis* [Enrico Guazzoni, 1913] and *Cabiria* [Giovanni Pastrone, 1914]).[9] In the hands of D. W. Griffith, whose *The Birth of a Nation* (1915) presented historical facsimiles and cited established sources, the genre also increasingly asserted its authenticity, promising that viewers would "actually see what happened."[10] Such textual and extrafilmic claims would prompt what Philip Rosen has dubbed "Everett's Game," whereby spectators seek to locate erroneous details and thereby outwit historical representations—a dynamic that continues in recurring debates over issues of accuracy and poetic license.[11]

Cinema's dual capacities for documenting and staging history, or presenting images *from* and *of* the past, became the hinge for conflicting understandings of its role in the cultural and aesthetic spheres. While the historical film was crucial in efforts to usher in a more gentrified and respectable cinema on par with the traditional arts, many commentators maintained that the genre betrayed essential properties of the new medium, replicating instead the closed dramaturgy of theater. In a 1921 essay, August Wolf wrote:

> Film is the practice of history in the sense of Xenophon, who went among people, to prostitutes, craftsmen, and whoever came his way. He handpicked his characters from everywhere, while lingering on streets and plazas, wherever it so happened. To him, without arrogance, it seemed possible to see something interesting develop in every area. The anonymous moment in heroic time—that's roughly how he perceived history, as a corroboration of the metaphysical concept of personhood: where I am is what I am. History experienced in wandering.
>
> Film was also invented with a feeling for things in motion. Its memory is the camera with the unrolling image, a memory that records accurately and shows in slow motion the acuteness of observation of which it is capable. And what a felicitous memory! It thinks existentially, shows the tree as tree, without an atmospheric stimulant, in the joy of naïve viewing. The pure fact that I live, which I feel by seeing trees blossoming, branches moving on the street—film also presents this fact as uncomplicated trope by showing me once more how trees blossom and branches move. It does not distract or mediate through interpretation what it has to say. As in life, its decor is once again nature. Film does not need to be agitated, does not need any summoning gesture in order to let nature appear; indeed, nature, just as it is, lives in the image.
>
> Oh felicitous film, which requires no dramatic arts.[12]

For Wolf, the motion-picture camera is thus an ideal practitioner of contemporary history, registering the dynamic occurrences of everyday life with extraordinary precision and an impartiality with regard to subjects and locations. Characterizing cinema in the language of *Lebensphilosophie* (which, ironically, had included the new medium in its critique of industrial modernity), Wolf suggests that the natural world or *physis* returns in filmic images without extraneous mediation or hermeneutic intervention.[13] In this regard, his text anticipates Siegfried Kracauer's *Theory of Film* (1960), which would distinguish photographic media from the traditional arts in leaving the "raw material" of the surrounding world intact.[14] Similarly prioritizing documentation over dramatic artifice, Kracauer argued that cinema fulfills its function when it renders visible external phenomena such as "'the ripple of the leaves stirred by the wind.'"[15]

In this chapter, I will argue that insofar as Kracauer came to define the medium's "basic aesthetic principle" in terms of engagement with the singular and transitory occurrences of physical reality, he further obfuscated Aristotle's distinction between history and poetry, paradoxically locating the *poetics* of film in its potential as a *historian* of contemporary life.[16] Notably, however, the genre of the historical film was problematic for Kracauer, given its efforts to visualize a past that is by definition no longer present. Rather than showing "how it essentially was," the historical film can only envision "things as they *could* have happened."[17] An examination of Kracauer's extensive, largely untranslated writings on the historical film will illuminate significant developments in his thought from Weimar Germany to 1960s New York, as his early criticism of the genre shades into an aesthetics and theory of film as well as a broader philosophy of history. Building on Johannes von Moltke's typology of approaches to classical film theory, I will situate Kracauer's writings in relation to the *critique of historicism* in the early twentieth century and beyond.[18] As a major commentator on both cinema and the crisis of historicism, Kracauer offers a unique perspective on the historical-film genre, viewing its problematics through the lens of philosophical debates extending back to antiquity. Not least, in locating film on the fault lines between history and poetics, or fact and fiction, Kracauer's texts provide an occasion for considering how the medium helped complicate and renegotiate terms that have come under renewed scrutiny in our own "post-truth" era.

KRACAUER'S EARLY FILM AESTHETICS

Although, as Miriam Hansen has justly noted, the historical film is one of the genres for which Kracauer's disapproval "crystallizes quite early on and remains rather persistent throughout his life," he nonetheless endorsed such spectacles in his initial years as a critic for the *Frankfurter Zeitung*, lending his acclaim to the *Großfilme* (large-budget epics) produced en masse by the German film industry during the postwar period of inflation.[19] In his first-ever published film review, from June 1, 1921, Kracauer lauded the Georg Büchner adaptation *All for a Woman* (*Danton*, 1921) for its "masterful scenes from the French Revolution," with breathtaking marvels from director Dimitri Buchowetzki and superlative performances by Emil Jannings, Werner Krauss, and others.[20] Likewise set during a period of mass unrest and sociopolitical turmoil, Carl Theodor Dreyer's *Love One Another* (*Die Gezeichneten*, 1922) was noted for its convincing characterization of figures from czarist Russia as well as the skillfulness of its editing and crowd scenes.[21] A Henny Porten vehicle about the tragic affair between Danish Queen Caroline Matilda and Johann Friedrich Struensee, *The Love* of a Queen (*Die Liebe einer Königin*, Ludwig Wolff, 1923), also received praise for its effective direction, which rendered palpable the contrasts between the intrigues at the magnificent court and the people's calls for freedom.[22]

However attentive Kracauer was to the formal and stylistic features of historical films, he had yet to base his assessments on a specific aesthetic conception of the new medium. Writing in November 1923, the young critic still extolled the images and performances in Peter Paul Felner's adaptation of *The Merchant of Venice* (*Der Kaufmann von Venedig*, 1923), but he now argued that the Shakespearean material was fundamentally unsuited to cinema: "Viewed in terms of content, the whole thing is strictly against the spirit of film; instead of visible, disjointed movements, there are mental transitions and superfluous interconnections; instead of grotesque surface, false depth of soul; instead of surprising improvisation, carefully prepared scenes. In short: not a real film, but bad theater and illustrious revue."[23]

Beginning to advance medium-ontological claims, Kracauer categorically dismissed historical pageants for their elaborate, continuous plots, meticulously staged scenes, and attempts to visualize interior experience. Paradoxically devoted to both nonnaturalist genres and renderings of the transient, quotidian phenomena of the modern world (à la Georg Simmel), Kracauer preferred American slapstick comedies, detective stories, and so-called *Hochstaplerfilme* (impostor films) for their improbable, spontaneous qualities and depictions of "exciting events from everyday life."[24] According to Kracauer's modernist aesthetics, guided by a logic of what Hansen calls "double negation," one could find deeper meaning in the "soulless figures, unreal events, and sentimental endings" of cinematic kitsch than in the sluggish, pompous theatricality of historical spectacles.[25] Underlying these claims was his oft-noted identification of film with the representation of surface life as well as his utopian assumption that cinema (like the detective novel) was capable of exaggerating and exposing the unreality of our current existence—or, as he wrote, "of ironizing its illusoriness and thus pointing to true reality."[26]

In this way, the *Historienfilm* (historical film) came to serve as a key genre against which the film critic defined the medium's aesthetic significance and historic task.[27] That the genre had become an early point of negative identification is further indicated by his review of *Peter the Great* (*Peter der Große*, Dimitri Buchowetzki, 1922), an epic from the same director as *Danton* and again starring Emil Jannings in the title role. Unparalleled in its display of grandeur and its faithful rendering of historical events, the film impressed Kracauer for its contingent of masses, variety of backdrops, and sophisticated arrangement of scenes. For Kracauer, however, these advances in direction had been placed in the service of quintessentially nonfilmic material: "Historical subjects," he wrote, "leave people and things in their natural contexts and offer too little opportunity to represent the improbable and fantastic."[28] The fable or fairy tale, by contrast, elicited this "fantastical" (Georg Lukács) and even utopian element.[29] In Kracauer's view, Ulrich Kayser's *The Little Match Girl* (*Armes kleines Mädchen*, 1924), an adaptation of the Hans Christian Andersen short story, was "one of the few works that is entirely in keeping with the nature of film and can only exist as film compositions."[30] Similarly, Friedrich Wilhelm Murnau's *The Last Laugh* (*Der letzte Mann*, 1924) consisted of a sheer succession of images and featured "a fairy-tale-like epilogue so unbelievable that one can only believe it."[31]

Where *The Last Laugh* revealed the full expressive possibilities of imagistic, nonverbal storytelling (famously deploying one single intertitle), German spectacles of the mid-1920s betrayed the aesthetics of silent film, adapting classic texts to the screen with ever-greater seriousness and pomp. Released alongside Fritz Lang's *Die Nibelungen* (1924), which Kracauer dismissed as a "sacred festival drama [*Weihfestspiel*] that endlessly drags itself across the screen like the dragon," *Helena* (Manfred Noa, 1924) was another two-part, multihour adaptation of an epic poem for which no costs or top actors had been spared, as Kracauer noted, in bringing about "the birth of film out of the spirit of the *Iliad*."[32] Less optimistic than a young Nietzsche about the possible rebirth of pre-Socratic forms, Kracauer argued that *Helena* signified not a reawakening of myth but "its hopeless destruction and, moreover, an embarrassing flight of film from itself."[33] Rather than visualizing epic literature and reanimating its legendary figures, Lang's and Noa's films debased myth into kitsch and summoned only gestural shadows. Reiterating ideas from his rapturous reviews of Karl Grune's *The Street* (*Die Straße*, 1923), Kracauer posited film's sole object as "the illusory, silent exterior of the world" and contended that instead of evoking a soulful unity of action, its narratives should be spliced together just like the filmstrips themselves.[34]

Though founding his claims on the very constituents of the filmic medium, Kracauer also drew from the literary and historical-philosophical arguments of Georg Lukács, who had theorized the shift from the Homeric epic to the modern novel as an irrevocable *Verfallsgeschichte* (narrative of decline) from a "spontaneous totality of being" to an alienated state of "transcendental homelessness."[35] Adopting Lukács's lapsarian narrative, Kracauer's essays from 1926 criticized efforts to lend the fragmentary contemporary world the veneer of organic unity or wholeness, whether via processes of film production or exhibition. In "Calico-World" ("Kaliko-Welt," 1926), he noted the Ufa city in Neubabelsberg for excluding nature while also assembling the macrocosm in a simulated, perfectly controlled form: "Everything guaranteed unnatural and everything exactly like nature."[36] For Kracauer, the studio's use of empty facades, illusory objects, and special effects not only distorted conceptions of space, time, and causality, but also muddled or inverted ontological distinctions between old and new, original and replica, nature and cinematic illusion. At a time of over-budget *Monumentalfilme* (monumental films) produced by Erich Pommer (e.g., Murnau's *Faust* [1926], Lang's *Metropolis* [1927]), Ufa appeared as a chaotic warehouse with set pieces from various epochs, cultures, and styles. Even as these pieces created the appearance of a complete historical world on-screen, they were detached from the realm of temporal development and susceptible to rapid construction, transformation, and demolition.

THE MARXIST TURN

As Kracauer became increasingly Marxist in theoretical outlook in the mid-1920s—further turning from a metaphysically laden account of disintegration to a more unequivocal, if still messianically tinged, materialism—his writings on the historical film shifted to the mode of politically driven ideology critique.[37] This development in his thinking is indicated by his reviews of the popular cycle of Fridericus Rex films (aka "Prussian films"), which evoked a glorious, powerful past under King Frederick the Great as a consoling counterimage to Germany's recent experiences of military defeat, forced disarmament, and postwar destitution.[38] In 1924, Kracauer had initially praised the first two parts of the four-part *Fridericus Rex* (Arzén von Cserépy, 1922–23) for their technical mastery and historical believability, and for the performance of Otto Gebühr, who helped ensure that it "does not degenerate into a *Tendenzstück* [tendentious work], but almost allows us to experience something like the necessary tragedy of the brilliant, heroic man."[39] Two years later, however, Kracauer suspected *The Mill at Sanssouci* (*Die Mühle von Sanssouci*, Siegfried Philippi, 1926) of buttressing right-wing sensibilities, especially as it omitted the less pleasant aspects of Frederick's despotic, absolutist eighteenth-century regime.[40] By the early 1930s, Kracauer was certain that Alfred Hugenberg's Ufa had produced *The Flute Concert of Sanssouci* (*Das Flötenkonzert von Sanssouci*, Gustav Ucicky, 1930) to appeal to nationalist, belligerent instincts (as evidenced by the film's highly contentious, politicized premiere), and he criticized *Yorck*

The four-part *Fridericus Rex* (Arzén von Cserépy, 1922–23) launched the popular cycle of "Prussian films." Credit: Collection Ivo Blom.

(Gustav Ucicky, 1931) for propagating zeal and even military action at a time that instead demanded the utmost reason, restraint, and devotion to republicanism.[41]

While the Fridericus Rex films indeed became more overt in their political motivations during the Weimar period, they also appeared increasingly outmoded and reactionary in relation to works of American and Soviet cinema. Drawing transnational comparisons, Kracauer wrote that John Ford's *The Iron Horse* (1924) cultivated a sense of visual immediacy and excitement, without the lulls commonly found in German historical spectacles, and Sergei Eisenstein's *Battleship Potemkin* (*Bronenosets Potyomkin*, 1925) generated suspense not through empty sensations but rather through a genuine cause:

> The instinct of the social class that gives birth to the glorifications of *Fridericus Rex* prohibits, in Europe as well as America, any overly glaring exposure of the critical facts that still determine our so-called social life.... One stays on this side of the wall, represses the only content that would matter by way of historical costume dramas, private psychological or high-life bagatelles, and even the ultimately formally irrelevant slapstick comedies.... [*Potemkin*] is now being shown in *German* cities, in which there is still a kind of theater being performed that no longer has anything to do with us; that goes as well for the picture palaces. Will

the viewers notice how the film differs from the *Fridericus Rex* films, the psychological interiors, and the pretty diversions? Will they recognize the conditions with which this art is tied up?"[42]

Released in Germany only after extensive censorship battles and cuts, *Potemkin* cast in sharper relief the socioeconomic bases and ideological workings of both European and American productions—including the slapstick comedies that Kracauer had previously celebrated for providing a "grotesque contrast to reality."[43] Extolling Eisenstein's film according to his established aesthetic criteria (e.g., "stick[ing] to the surface," "stringing together optical impressions"), Kracauer also now shifted his critical emphasis from modernist negation to immanent truth value, distinguishing *Potemkin* for its venture into more genuine and substantive territory: "It takes on a subject that is *real*; it refers to a truth that should matter."[44] Focusing unblinkingly on an instance of actual revolution in 1905, Eisenstein's film was remarkable for deploying filmic means to represent a social reality and for showing the self-evident interaction between humans and machines—a dynamic that was inconceivable in Germany, whose bourgeois-idealist culture was still beholden to the separation of spiritual and technological realms.

Though no less propagandistic or ideologically laden than the Fridericus Rex films, *Potemkin* and later Soviet films by Vsevolod Pudovkin and others were distinct not only for their formal qualities, but also for their human substance, collective consciousness, and insight into common struggles. Where many German commentators dismissed *Potemkin* out of hand or sought to distinguish its artistic value from its political tendentiousness, Kracauer argued that the film's aesthetic superiority was inextricably bound to its revolutionary cause, especially as the technique of montage could transform reality and gesture toward a valid social order—a point he famously reiterated in his "Photography" essay of 1927.[45] In his contemporaneous reviews, *Potemkin* served as a frequent measure of comparison for historical dramas, including even the most impressive or uncharacteristic of Western films. Thus, although the grandiose film version of *Ben-Hur* (Fred Niblo, 1925) correctly pursued nontheatrical subjects with the utmost realism and the rhythmic, unified construction of sequences (particularly the chariot race), it still appeared inadequate in relation to *Potemkin*; while the latter is concerned with "reality struck in the aesthetic medium of film," the American spectacle involves "a small private affair rendered large on the basis of world-historical subject matter."[46] And, billed as "the German *Potemkin*," the Gerhart Hauptmann adaptation *The Weavers* (*Die Weber*, Friedrich Zelnik, 1927) was thematically and aesthetically indebted to Soviet films, yet it lacked the formal certainty and, above all, the actuality of Eisenstein's and Pudovkin's work: "Not only does it not seem revolutionary, but on the contrary, it may illustrate how wonderfully times have changed."[47]

The prioritization of long-past battles over current struggles became a key target of Kracauer's celebrated essays of the late 1920s. Reaffirming *Potemkin* as the normative center of his thinking on issues of historical representation, the article series "The Little Shopgirls Go to the Movies" ("Die kleinen Ladenmädchen gehen ins Kino," 1927) critiqued capitalist productions for diverting attention from material conditions and ultimately reaffirming the prevailing society:

> The numerous historical films that merely illustrate the past (rather than showing the present in historical guise, as in *Potemkin*) are attempts at deception according to their own terms. Since one always runs the danger, when picturing current events, of turning easily excitable masses against powerful institutions that are in fact often not appealing, one prefers to direct the camera toward a Middle Ages that the audience will find harmlessly edifying. The further back the story is situated historically, the more audacious filmmakers become. They will risk depicting a successful revolution in historical costumes in order to induce people to forget modern revolutions, and they are happy to satisfy the theoretical sense of justice by filming struggles for freedom that are long past. Douglas Fairbanks, the gallant champion of the oppressed, goes to battle in a previous century against a despotic power whose survival is of no consequence to any American today. The courage of these films declines in direct proportion to their proximity to the present.[48]

For Kracauer, historical films thus disingenuously turned to a past safely removed from current powers and struggles, defusing a contemporary sense of injustice through a focus on the conflicts of centuries prior. Invoking the Douglas Fairbanks vehicle *The Mask of Zorro* (Fred Niblo, 1920), Kracauer posited a direct relation between the distance of filmic narratives from the present and their willingness to depict counterhegemonic struggles—a claim that he would problematize and even invert in later texts.[49] While Kracauer reissued his critique one year later in "Film 1928" ("Der heutige Film und sein Publikum," 1928), citing fiction films' attempts to escape contemporary social reality through studio sets and "faraway times and places that are completely irrelevant to us," he also recognized that even the prior decade could seem historical according to mechanisms of evasion and forgetting.[50] Much as the "Photography" essay had noted the alienating effect of recently outmoded fashions, his "Film 1928" sardonically suggested that one need not redirect focus to legendary figures such as Frederick the Great, Martin Luther, and Queen Louise, as the latest German biopics had done. On the contrary, "the most recent past is already so distant from us that it can once again be brought closer."[51]

Following the Hegelian-Marxist tradition in postulating a dialectical intermediation between content and form, Kracauer suggested that the inadequacy of most film material necessarily implied deficiencies in the aesthetic realm. For Kracauer, the stabilized production process had led to both the ossification of narrative genres and a systematized, *"ready-made manufacturing technique"* without regard for visual conception and construction.[52] Like the majority of literary and theatrical adaptations, Kracauer wrote, "the average historical films are . . . mere illustrations; what is more, they portray episodes that are usually badly told—history lessons in images, instead of history emerging out of the images."[53] The Zola adaptation *Thérèse Raquin* (Jacques Feyder, 1928) served as a rare exception, given its naturalist approach to milieu as well as its resistance to depicting inner actions that are articulable only in words.[54] By contrast, films such as Georg Wilhelm Pabst's *Don Quixote* (*Don Quichotte*, 1933) followed their source material in a prosaic, noncinematic manner. In Kracauer's account, the Cervantes adaptation "makes no attempt at all to illustrate the essence of the novel with filmic means, but is nothing more than a theater spectacle concerned with the authenticity of local color."[55]

UFA'S ART OF DISTRACTION

As early as 1927, in a discussion of Béla Balázs's *Visible Man* (*Der sichtbare Mensch*, 1924) and other recent film-theoretical books, Kracauer articulated ideas that would become crucial to his own writings on cinema in the decades to come. Kracauer identified certain general conditions to which the medium is subject and—dismissing the universal premises of idealist aesthetics in favor of a materialist approach—he characterized the medium as a "product of the present" whose contents are both historically conditioned and necessarily related to the contemporary world.[56] Three years later, Kracauer emphasized the Marxist viewpoint of Balázs's second book of film theory, *The Spirit of Film* (*Der Geist des Films*, 1930), which proceeded according to a materialist dialectic rather than abstract, empty idealist categories. Much as he had rejected *Visible Man*'s closing argument about the relation between film and capitalist society, however, he here disparaged Balázs's wholesale, unquestioned support for Soviet ideology.[57] Despite these criticisms, Kracauer would adopt insights from Balázs's work, especially as the latter posited the spirit of film as "an object of 'national psychology'" and emphasized that a sociopsychologically oriented analysis of film could yield "a cultural history of our times, a symptomatic index of living ideologies."[58]

Depicting the working class's seizure of power from oppressive forces, *Potemkin* and other Russian films had developed a filmic language for articulating a dialectical theory of history, most explicitly through their use of montage and formal contrasts. Yet Dreyer's *The Passion of Joan of Arc* (*La passion de Jeanne d'Arc*, 1928), which instead focused on a single individual's powerlessness vis-à-vis traditional institutions, was no less based in an anonymous collective and in "purely optical means."[59] For Kracauer, the film had its own dialectic through the constant interplay of small expressive elements. In visualizing a series of "tiny configurations" through close-ups, Kracauer wrote, Dreyer was able to reduce the period costumes and historical trappings to a minimum, avoiding the use of constructed sets whose artificiality would be immediately apparent.[60] Kracauer's review of *Joan of Arc* also indicates that despite his perpetual emphasis on film's relation to contemporary reality, he remained far from dogmatic, finding many exceptions to his categorical dismissal of the historical-film genre.[61]

Less unwavering, however, was Kracauer's condemnation of Ufa's escapist, reactionary fare during a period of global economic crisis—a period during which film bore a broader significance as a prime commodity and ideological medium of the very capitalist system that was on the defensive. For those facing financial hardship, unemployment, and housing shortages, Kracauer argued, the illumination of social conditions was preferable to the proliferation of fantasies that shrouded and repressed reality, upholding hypnotic illusions and profiting from the audience's desire for a better existence (or what Max Horkheimer and Theodor W. Adorno would later deem "enlightenment as mass deception").[62] Ufa's products remained oriented toward diversion and distraction, however, since portrayal of the actual world could disconcert viewers and even lead them to question the existing order, counter to the interests of the film industry.[63] Even as Kracauer's regular reviews and his sociological study *The Salaried Masses* (*Die Angestellten*, 1930) emphasized the importance of examining the commonplace existence of millions of laborers and salaried employees, works dealing with contemporary conditions and issues appeared impossible to produce on account of censorship and the political disunity of the German populace in the late Weimar years. In this context, Kracauer criticized films that not only retreated into distant times, but also distorted and falsified history, neutralizing its political content and presenting anecdotes and hollow pageantry instead of substantive relationalities (Zusammenhänge).[64]

Among the historical representations with which Kracauer took repeated issue were the war films that appeared with increasing frequency in the early 1930s. Having contributed to the recent wave of novels on the Great War with his own semiautobiographical *Ginster* (1928), Kracauer expressed concern with retaining memory of the cataclysmic event, particularly in view of a younger generation without direct experience of the mid-1910s and a film industry intent on repressing antimilitary sentiments. For Kracauer, Pabst's *Westfront 1918* (1930) was unprecedented in its truthful depiction of World War I ("a piece of war reality that no one has yet dared to reconstruct"), while the contested American adaptation of Erich Maria Remarque's *All Quiet on the Western Front* (Lewis Milestone, 1930) likewise showed the unpalatable horrors of war, but failed to lend insight into its "root causes and true consequences."[65] Both works nonetheless proved aesthetically and ideologically preferable to films that espoused heroic action, glorified military life, romanticized prewar times, remained neutral, or even preached pacifism—in all cases, however, obscuring the senseless horrors of war and the powerful forces responsible for it. Observing these trends, Kracauer argued for a broader definition of war films to include those that ostensibly ignore the subject even while normalizing, naturalizing, or mythicizing combat.

With the transition to sound also came screen versions of what Kracauer perceived as an endless series of German musicals and operettas from the past. ("I would never have guessed that there are so many forgotten operettas," he groaned by 1931.)[66] Beginning with one of the very first German sound films, *The Favourite of Schonbrunn* (*Der Günstling von Schönbrunn*, Erich Waschneck, 1929), advances in the technology of sound film threatened an aesthetic regression to dialogue-heavy theatricality, forgoing the expressive means (e.g., camera movement, montage) developed through the visual language of silent film.[67] Rather than depicting conditions and relations that shape public life and considering the struggles of working people, Ufa presented well-trodden, trivial material with little relevance or promise for audiences across the globe: "Like a drug, the good old days are infused into the new ones, which are certainly no better off as a result."[68] Moreover, the ornate splendor of musical comedies such as *The Congress Dances* (*Der Kongreß tanzt*, Erik Charell, 1931)—"a senseless accumulation of decorations; a product of the art of distraction [*Zerstreuungskunst*] that Ufa began propagating some time ago"—served as a means of evading or obscuring reality, anaesthetizing audiences much as Calypso had enchanted and detained Odysseus in Homer's *Odyssey*.[69]

FRENCH EXILIC WORK

Underlying Kracauer's critique of historical films was his investment in the promise of cinema to capture the spontaneous occurrences of the modern-day environment. Recalling August Wolf's paean to film as an ideal chronicler of contemporary history, Kracauer implored filmmakers to position the camera on the street corner rather than amid closed, artificial studio sets: "It's unfathomable why one keeps resorting to dusty court life when every street today is alive."[70] Kracauer reserved particular ire for films that willfully ignored developments in social reality—whether fictional films that present outmoded material and "give the impression of dusty family portraits" or documentaries and newsreels that shield audiences from pressing concerns and important events through inconsequential, repetitive stories.[71] By the late Weimar period, the critic's emphasis on cinema's relationship to the present was accompanied by his reflections on the curious, often-comical historicity of older works and on the role of films as both historical documents and museum objects. Kracauer would continue to cast a retrospective gaze on cinema during his eight years of Parisian exile, most explicitly in the essay series "Reencountering Old Films" ("Wiedersehen mit alten Filmen," 1938–40). In the process, his thinking on film as a "product of the present" gained dimensions of distance and estrangement as the medium itself became historical.

Having left Germany with his wife Lili on February 28, 1933, one day after the Reichstag fire, Kracauer eventually began to review films for the *Neue Zürcher Zeitung* and the *National-Zeitung Basel,* including historical films directed by Ludwig Berger, Marcel L'Herbier, Max Ophüls, Jean Renoir, and Robert Wiene and Robert Siodmak. Kracauer's most sustained form of historical engagement in France, however, was his "social biography" of the composer and fellow German-Jewish émigré Jacques Offenbach. In a 1930 essay, Kracauer had criticized popular literary biographies of established historical figures as "an art form of the new bourgeoisie" that evaded the insignificance of the individual and the relativism of any single frame of reference, as wrought by the Great War along with subsequent sociopolitical shifts and technological advances.[72] Eschewing this "museum of great individuals," his *Jacques Offenbach and the Paris of His Time* (*Jacques Offenbach und das Paris seiner Zeit,* 1937) instead approached Offenbach in dialectical relationship to nineteenth-century French society, foregrounding the material bases of the composer's work and interweaving developments from the aesthetic, economic, and political realms.[73] Offering the chronicle of an entire historical epoch, Kracauer emphasized the unmistakable actuality of the Second Empire's "phantasmagoria" in light of current events, and he argued that Offenbach's operettas—even when set in antiquity—took aim at the present and "laid bare the foundations of contemporary society."[74]

In 1938, upon learning that Metro-Goldwyn-Mayer was interested in filming the American edition of his Offenbach book, Kracauer composed a "motion picture treatment" for a historical film based on his study.[75] While Kracauer's negotiations with the film industry may be attributed to his precarious existence in French exile, I would argue that his endeavors should not be entirely reduced to "desperation."[76] Not only did the Offenbach study itself make numerous references to film and remobilize aesthetic categories from his Weimar essays on cinema and mass culture; the text also thematized media-technological shifts, recognizing their salient effect on our view of the past. Consider Kracauer's discussion of the masked balls that Offenbach attended at the Théâtre des Variétés during the July Monarchy:

> Anyone looking today at illustrations of the masked balls of the time of Louis-Philippe will scarcely understand the enthusiasm and the excitement they aroused. So many outlets for mass excitement have since been exploited that the old prints give the impression of very tame affairs indeed. They were nothing of the sort. They were no tamer than the old stagecoaches, which in some circumstances were very fast. A few years ago a film was produced showing Napoleon hurrying to some distant theater of war in his traveling coach. In miles per hour his speed was certainly very moderate. But what with mounted orderlies continually galloping up to him and galloping away again, and the Emperor himself opening dispatches and reading them and handing out orders without interrupting his journey for a single moment, the spectator received the impression that he was indeed covering the ground at enormous speed.[77]

Positing that modern entertainment forms have made both the subject and representational medium of nineteenth-century illustrations appear insipid by comparison, Kracauer here draws an analogy to older modes of transportation such as the stagecoach, which likewise seem slow in relation to later innovations. Although Kracauer had largely dismissed Abel Gance's *Napoléon* (1927) one decade prior, he references a scene that he had identified as "one of the highlights," in which tracking shots and camera movements from multiple positions convey the extraordinary velocity of Napoleon's coach by the standards of his time.[78] Remarkable in this passage is Kracauer's suggestion—echoing Walter Benjamin's "The Work of Art in the Age of Its Technological Reproducibility" ("Das Kunstwerk im Zeitalter

The extraordinary velocity of Napoleon's coach in Abel Gance's *Napoléon* (1927).

seiner technischen Reproduzierbarkeit," second version, 1936)—that film corresponds to transformations in sensory experience and conceptions of cultural history, raising the historiographical issue of whether and how to depict earlier periods through the media of the present. (Benjamin's essay quoted Gance's "The Era of the Image Has Arrived!" ["Le temps de l'image est venu!," 1927] and cited historical films as the plainest evidence of "the liquidation of the value of tradition in the cultural heritage.")[79]

If the Offenbach book maintained that film has the capacity to convey historical shifts in modes of perception and experience, Kracauer's later work returned to a more orthodox position, as indicated by a short essay that he published on May 9, 1940, in the *National-Zeitung Basel*. Entitled "The Historical Film" ("Der historische Film"), this was Kracauer's first programmatic essay on the historical film and one of many texts that he wrote on particular genres and aesthetic issues as he began to conceive a book on cinema. Tracing the historical film back to early French and Italian productions, Kracauer noted that it had continued uninterrupted through the history of cinema and had remained problematic. For Kracauer, the genre necessarily moved film in the direction of older art forms, recalling theater, opera, and painting in its mise-en-scène. Aside from these external resemblances, however, the historical film faced deeper issues:

> It has to deal with centuries in which film and the world associated with it did not even exist; with time periods that, unlike ours, are static, that regard as fate much that has long since been revealed to us as the work of man, and that, due to their ignorance of natural events and the function of small material elements, are unable to make the turn from general view to detail and back to long shot that is specific to film. A creature of the present, film intrudes into the past as a stranger; with its particular means, it fails to handle fully the existence of the past, which theater constructed in a valid manner.[80]

Beyond the obvious concern with medium specificity, Kracauer here draws a notable division between films depicting events that occurred within the course of film history and ones set before the era of cinema itself. Like the Offenbach book, which had sought to demonstrate "the dependence of every genre of art on specific social conditions," the 1940 essay upholds the Hegelian-Marxist assumption of a link between aesthetic means and world-historical epoch, positing that media-technological shifts correspond to changes in material reality, worldview, and sensory perception, and also come to bear on our relation to history itself.[81] Yet whereas Kracauer's *Offenbach* had celebrated *Napoléon* for conveying the experience of speed from a century prior, his later essay maintained more dogmatically that film is alien to the precinematic world, recalling Hegel's famous claim that any artist's attempt to reconstruct a past period entails an experience of the "foreign" along with a "clash between different ages."[82]

Because historical films necessarily resort to theatrical elements and subjects, Kracauer further wrote, they seek to distinguish themselves through effects that would be impossible onstage, such as the mass scenes of *Cabiria*, the dizzying velocity of *Ben-Hur*'s chariot race, or the facial close-ups in *The Passion of Joan of Arc* that abstract the figures from their historical settings. Echoing "On the Border of Yesterday" ("An der Grenze des Gestern," 1932), where he had described images that "have not yet become fully historical," Kracauer identified one past epoch of singular significance for film: "the one whose contents still impinge on immediate tradition and yet already belong to the inventory of history."[83] Such a liminal temporal position—or what he would later call a "border region"—was explored to great effect by Frank Lloyd's Boer War drama *Cavalcade* (1933), an American epic that held a significance for Kracauer similar to that of *Potemkin* in the mid-1920s.[84] For Kracauer, *Cavalcade*'s shock effect derived from its articulation of "things that are particularly invisible to us today because they rumble in the depths of our being."[85] Linking this effect to the uncanny relation between photographic media and mortality, Kracauer argued that Lloyd's film demonstrates "that what was believed to be dead lives on in us and that our own lives rush toward death."[86]

STUDIES OF PROPAGANDA

Kracauer arrived in New York in April 1941 with a grant from the Rockefeller Foundation and the Oberlaender Trust of the Carl Schurz Memorial Foundation to conduct a project on foreign-film propaganda at the Museum of Modern Art's Film Library. While this project ultimately led to *From Caligari to Hitler* (1947), it also encompassed a number of shorter writings, many of which addressed issues of historical representation. Taking up lines of theoretical inquiry from his unpublished 1938 study of totalitarian propaganda, the pamphlet "Propaganda and the Nazi War Film" (1942) included an analysis of *Victory in the West* (*Sieg im Westen*, Svend Noldan, 1941), a feature-length documentary primarily composed of newsreel footage of the Battle of France. For Kracauer, Noldan's film was characteristic of German war newsreels in distorting reality and presenting warfare as part of a broader political-historical process.[87] Whereas other campaign films such as *Baptism of Fire* (*Feuertaufe*, Hans Bertram, 1940) offered surveys of current global affairs, *Victory in the West* included what

Kracauer described as "an ambitious retrospect which goes back to the Westphalian Peace of 1648."[88] Yet in both cases, the films buttressed Germany's mythical war narrative, suggesting that the Nazi triumph over world powers would be "the fulfillment of an historic mission, metaphysically justified."[89] With their highly arranged "totalitarian panoramas," these propaganda films drew inspiration less from traditional "films of fact" than from 1920s historical epics by Eisenstein and Pudovkin.[90]

In 1942, Kracauer also considered historical spectacles in the brief commentaries on German films that he penned for MoMA Film Library curator Iris Barry. Noting film as a primary medium in which "NS history is being written," Kracauer highlighted the ideological and psychological workings of productions from the 1930s—whether late Weimar films that "plundered the arsenal of the German past to arouse patriotic passions" or early Nazi films depicting World War I, the German Revolution of 1918–19, and the plight of Frisians in Communist Russia.[91] Kracauer also emboldened his critique of the Fridericus Rex films, observing that their propagandistic tendencies had become even more pronounced than before. In a joint review of *The Hymn of Leuthen* (*Der Choral von Leuthen*, Carl Froelich, 1933) and *Fridericus* (Johannes Meyer, 1936) from July 8, 1942, Kracauer remarked on the similarity between Otto Gebühr's portrayal of Frederick the Great in these films and the popular image of Hitler. Recalling his claim that "the Little Miss Typists model themselves after the examples they see on the screen," he went so far as to argue that the screen version of Frederick the Great had served as "the exact model for Hitler's appearance."[92]

Kracauer's analyses of 1930s German productions also maintained his critique of the historical film along aesthetic lines. Writing back-to-back commentaries on August 31 and September 1, 1942, Kracauer disparaged Heinz Paul's *The Legend of William Tell* (*Wilhelm Tell*, 1934) as a "crude history painting with lots of fake beards, childish dialogue, and shots that turn the real Swiss mountains into cheap backdrops," while he was more ambivalent toward Hans Behrendt's *Danton* (1931).[93] In his original review from 1931, Kracauer had deemed the film "a product of the current neutralizing historical distortion," though he had praised Fritz Kortner's rousing performance in the title role along with a scene with an "ensemble effect that has rarely been achieved in sound film."[94] Eleven years later, his perspective was more historically sedimented and grounded in medium-ontological and historical-philosophical claims: "This film was released a year or two before Hitler and is one of the few notable German historical films. Even today, after an eventful decade, it has retained some of its original power. Of course, as in almost all historical films, the ensemble, costumes, and studio sets are reminiscent of grand opera, and there is no depiction of mass, space, and movement that would make one forget the stage, even for a moment. (The omnipresent film camera, closely linked to the dynamic forces of our time, cannot adequately capture the stationary life of past centuries.)"[95]

Reiterating ideas from his programmatic essay of 1940, Kracauer thus emphasized the inevitable theatricality of historical films and the link between film technology and the sensorial regime of the twentieth century, even as he acknowledged the ongoing affective force of Behrendt's period drama. In *From Caligari to Hitler*, by contrast, Kracauer issued a blanket ideological critique of *Danton* and its predecessor: "This picture resembled *All for a Woman*, Buchowetski's Danton film of 1921, in its indifference to the French Revolution and its emphasis on the private life of the revolutionary leaders."[96]

An excessive focus on the private sphere was a common complaint in *From Caligari to Hitler*, where Kracauer devoted an early chapter to the vogue of German historical pageants after World War I. Following the Italian model of monumental spectacles (e.g., *Quo Vadis*, *Cabiria*), postwar films such as Joe May's three-part *Veritas vincit* (1919) and Ernst Lubitsch's *Madame DuBarry* (1919) had served Ufa's aims of elevating the artistry of German cinema and securing its economic and cultural status abroad. In Kracauer's account, however, *DuBarry* "drains the [French] Revolution of its significance," presenting the event as the result of private passions and psychological conflicts rather than economic and political forces—tendencies continued by Lubitsch's *Sumurun* (1920), *Anna Boleyn* (1920), and *The Loves of Pharaoh* (*Das Weib des Pharao*, 1922).[97] Where American reviewers had praised these films for their "sense of authenticity," Kracauer emphasized their pattern of obscuring rather than illuminating historical developments: "The sustained lack of comprehension in the Lubitsch films is significant inasmuch as they emerged at a moment when it would have been in the interest of the new democratic regime to enlighten the people about social and political developments. All these German pageants which the Americans mistook for summits of 'historical realism' instinctively sabotaged any understanding of historic processes, any attempt to explore patterns of conduct in the past."[98] Propagating a cynical vision of global affairs as meaningless and driven by irrational instincts, Lubitsch's films were symptomatic of a widespread disillusionment with history and of antirevolutionary, even antidemocratic, inclinations. In Kracauer's analysis, such nihilistic dispositions found expression in the films' aesthetic innovations, from unconventional shots and camera angles to the effective rendering of crowds.

Ernst Lubitsch's historical pageant *Madame DuBarry* (1919).

Returning to Weimar historical films at later points in his book, Kracauer contended that the Fridericus Rex films had promoted retrogressive, authoritarian behavior. Where the critic had once differentiated between earlier and later films, he now maintained that the initial ones were "pure propaganda for a restoration of the monarchy" and that the entire cycle "more or less adopted the pattern of the first Fridericus film."[99] In disregarding historical truth and glorifying Frederick the Great as a patriarchal leader and national hero, the films "conformed to psychological dispositions widespread among the people."[100] Amid a period of inner dilemma between chaos and tyranny, the films emphasized a process of development from rebellious insurrection to unconditional submission. The Fridericus Rex films of the 1930s further rationalized absolute rule with more "topical allusions," marking "a thorough attempt to familiarize the masses with the idea of a *Führer*."[101]

REALIST AESTHETICS

During his first decade in New York exile, Kracauer also transposed his sociopsychological methodology from the study of interwar German cinema to Hollywood and other national film industries. In the commissioned article "National Types as Hollywood Presents Them," which appeared as a UNESCO brochure and in *Public Opinion Quarterly* in 1949, Kracauer examined the portrayal of British and Russian characters in American fiction films from 1933 onward. Though explicitly bracketing the genres of the historical and literary film, Kracauer sought to explain why postwar Hollywood was eschewing contemporary Britain in favor of the English past:

> In thus combining disregard of the present with uninhibited rendering of the past, Hollywood follows a rule of conduct which it has already practiced before. Nor is this treatment of foreign peoples unknown to other national film industries: at a time when the German pre-Hitler cinema was completely oblivious of Soviet Russia, it elaborated profusely on the blessings of the Czarist regime. I have reason to believe that in all such cases the emergence of films about the past of a people betrays discontent with its present state of affairs. What makes these films into vehicles of indirect criticism is the fact of their appearance at a moment when any direct mention of that people is strictly avoided. They manifest apprehensions not so much through their content as their sheer existence. Only occasionally do they come into the open, picturing past events for the thinly veiled purpose of dealing with present ones. In *Alexander Nevsky*, the eyes that gleam through visors of the Teutonic Knights are unmistakably the eyes of contemporary Nazis.[102]

Whereas "The Little Shopgirls Go to the Movies" had argued that depictions of the past served as a safeguard against challenging present circumstances, Kracauer's 1949 article contended that the very appearance of historical films indexed dissatisfaction with the status quo and could even serve as a roundabout means of critique. And while the 1927 text had identified *Potemkin* as a counterexample, the study of "national types" instead looked to Eisenstein's *Alexander Nevsky* (*Aleksandr Nevskiy*, 1938) for its unequivocal allegorization of Nazi Germany—one that stood in marked contrast to German cinema's own adulatory figuration of the bygone Russian Empire during the early Weimar years.

Yet *Potemkin* continued to serve as a crucial point of comparison in Kracauer's midcentury writings on film aesthetics. In an unpublished typescript from 1948 on Roberto Rossellini's *Paisan* (*Paisà*, 1946), Kracauer noted that despite a common epic scope, documentary style, and use of location shooting and nonprofessional actors, Eisenstein's and Rossellini's films were profoundly different in form: where *Potemkin*'s streamlined story and montage methods advanced a revolutionary cause, *Paisan*'s open, non-Aristotelian structure of six separate episodes deemphasized overarching ideas in favor of the dignity and lived experience of ordinary people across cultural-linguistic barriers.[103] With its realist aesthetic, *Paisan* also diverged from traditional Italian cinema, which had been known for glossy, theatrical spectacles since as far back as Pastrone's *Cabiria*. (In "An Aesthetic of Reality: Neorealism" ["Le Réalisme cinématographique et l'école italienne de la Libération," 1948], Bazin drew a similar lineage from *Quo Vadis* and *Cabiria* up to Carmine Gallone's *Scipio Africanus* [*Scipione l'Africano*, 1937] and Alessandro Blasetti's *The Iron Crown* [*La corona di ferro*, 1941].)[104] For Kracauer, "the sudden emergence of such a film as *Paisan* indicates that many Italians actually loathe the grand-style manner of the past and all that it implied in allegiances and sham beliefs. They have come to realize the futility of Mussolini's conquests and they seem now determined to do without messages and missions—at least for the moment."[105] During a postwar moment of ideological disillusionment, *Paisan*'s nominalist engagement with the particularities of contemporary reality thus served as a welcome antidote to generalized creeds or political doctrines.

Kracauer's appraisal of *Paisan* as "a revelation of the steady flow of humanity beneath the turmoil of sheer ideology" also signaled a broader reorientation from ideology critique and psychosocial analysis to a "curious realism" (Adorno) and humanist phenomenology of history.[106] In contradistinction to Weimar essays such as "Photography," which had critiqued a social order that relegated contingency to the margins, Kracauer's later American writings characterized the complete historical world in terms of contingency, entailing what Inka Mülder-Bach describes as "the *totalization of the periphery*, the transference of its structural features to the entirety of historical reality."[107] And while the 1927 essay looked to human consciousness (along with Franz Kafka's writings and cinematic montage) for establishing the provisionality of the spatial configuration reified by the alienated lens of the camera, now photographic media presented "life in its fullness," bearing a privileged relation to the physical reality from which subjectivity itself was estranged.[108] This revised stance found its most canonical expression in Kracauer's second book on cinema, *Theory of Film* (1960), where he postulated cinema's "inherent affinities" to "the unstaged," "the fortuitous," "endlessness," and "the indeterminate" along with the "flow of life."[109] It is in this context that he offered his most sustained aesthetic critique of the historical-film genre.

Kracauer titled an early chapter of *Theory of Film* "History and Fantasy," a notable pairing that already suggests a challenge to Aristotelian poetics (as well as a significant departure from his earlier juxtaposition of historical films with "the improbable and fantastic").[110] In this chapter, Kracauer argues that whenever films envision historical or fantastical realms, they risk defying the medium's basic properties. Seeking to resurrect a past world that is outside of present-day life and thus inaccessible to the camera, costume films inevitably distract viewers with their labored staginess and anachronistic facial expressions and gestures—discrepancies that Barthes had also theorized in "The Romans in Films" ("Les Romains au cinéma," 1954).[111] Moreover, in attempting to lend a closed, confined set the appearance of a complete world, they arouse the audience's awareness of the camera's limited potential for exploration. To illustrate this point, Kracauer invokes a thought experiment from Élie Faure's "The Art of Cineplastics" ("De la cinéplastique," 1922):

> At this point a science-fiction fantasy of Elie Faure's comes to mind. He dreams of a documentary film made *now* of the Passion of Christ from a far-distant star and sent to the earth by a projectile or rendered accessible to us by means of interplanetary projection. If this dream materialized, we would be eye-witnesses to the Last Supper, the Crucifixion, the agony in Gethsemane. . . . Let us for the sake of argument assume that a historical film about the Passion has been staged which matches his imaginary documentary in every respect. Obviously this ideal production will nevertheless differ from the latter in that it does not convey the impression of probing a universe at the film maker's free disposal. There is no potential endlessness in it. The spectator will admire it for showing things as they *could* have happened, but he will not be convinced, as he would be when watching Faure's documentary, that things actually happened this way.[112]

Faure's text—with a tacit nod to Camille Flammarion's *Lumen* (1872)—had envisaged a cinematographic record of Jesus's crucifixion to exemplify the medium's preservation of events for millennia after their occurrence.[113] Kracauer's hypothetical comparison between Faure's imagined documentary and its precise reconstruction serves to demonstrate the inherent limitations of the historical film. Cognizant that the world shown on-screen is necessarily finite, the spectator associates its depiction of the past with the subjunctive mood that Aristotle ascribed to poetry ("the kinds of events that would happen"), dismissing the historicist pursuit of showing "how it essentially was."[114]

Recalling Hegel's dual poles of presentism and objective fidelity to the past, Kracauer went on to identify a range of strategies developed by filmmakers to mitigate the uncinematic character of historical films, using familiar examples from his earlier writings. At one end of the spectrum were films (e.g., *Intolerance*, *Ben-Hur*) that imbued the past with "camera-life" through cinematic elements such as chases, chariot races, and mass movements. Most radical in this regard was Dreyer's *The Passion of Joan of Arc*, which sought to narrate the historical figure's inquisition through a continual series of facial close-ups, presenting what Kracauer called a "physiognomic documentary."[115] The opposite extreme were films that cultivated a sense of total immersion in a past era by drawing on its own pictorial materials. Nuancing his erstwhile claim that film is alien to the precinematic world, Kracauer now wrote approvingly of the "finite cosmos" evoked by Dreyer's seventeenth-century drama *Day of Wrath* (*Vredens dag*, 1943), which achieved a sense of authenticity by reanimating period paintings—a method also deployed by films including Renato Castellani's *Romeo and Juliet* (1954).[116]

HISTORY AND POETICS

An avowed "direct continuation" of his *Theory of Film*, Kracauer's final, posthumously published book, *History: The Last Things before the Last* (1969), shifted attention from the aesthetic problems of the historical-film genre to those of historiographical method more broadly.[117] In the chapter "General History and the Aesthetic Approach," Kracauer focused on a major, oft-maligned genre of modern historiography: the large-scale, synthetizing narrative or "general history" that covers phenomena across heterogeneous areas of society (e.g., politics, economics, culture) and often encompasses broad expanses of the past. In Kracauer's account, the macrohistorian seeks to lend streamlined consistency and meaningful, cohesive unity to a historical universe or Husserlian *Lebenswelt* (lifeworld) that is itself disjointed, incoherent, and composed of multiple, coexisting temporalities. For this reason, the historian makes recourse to "*manipulative expedients and devices*," obfuscating the classical division between history and poetics: "What the narrator cannot accomplish in the dimension of content he expects to achieve in the aesthetic dimension."[118] Though such aestheticizing tendencies have their counterpart in theatrical films such as Castellani's aforementioned *Romeo and Juliet*, they are nonetheless at odds with modernist art and literature (e.g., Joyce, Proust, Woolf), which are more invested in fragmentation and multiperspectivity than in temporal continuity and harmonious wholeness. (On this final point, Kracauer cited a 1966 essay by Hayden White, who in his *Metahistory* [1973] would turn the issue of historical emplotment into a more generalized thesis.)[119]

Visiting Lindau, West Germany, in September 1966, just two months before his death, Kracauer presented his chapter on general history to the interdisciplinary research group Poetik und Hermeneutik as part of a conference titled "The Aesthetic as Border Phenomenon of History [Das Ästhetische als Grenzerscheinung der Historie]." Kracauer's chapter was paired with Christian Meier's observations on Herodotus and Reinhart Koselleck's remarks on Johann Wilhelm von Archenholz's *The History of the Seven Years War in Germany* (*Geschichte des siebenjährigen Krieges in Deutschland*, 1789). Taken together, the texts generated a far-reaching discussion on the relationship between history and aesthetics, or fact and fiction, from ancient accounts up to critiques of the nineteenth-century German Historical School.[120] In a closing statement, Koselleck offered a brief conceptual history of the terms *Geschichte* (history) and *Geschichtsphilosophie* (philosophy of history), highlighting the crucial intervention of Droysen:

> Droysen then—based on Humboldt—explicitly completed the transcendental turn with his *Principles of History*: history is always only the knowledge of itself. To put it bluntly: the factum as such is exposed as fiction insofar as the factum can never be reconstructed in the sense of how it really and essentially was. And once this position has been reached, the historian is faced with the problem of how to represent the fiction of the factual as (past) reality. The historian is, so to speak, professionally compelled to use aesthetic criteria, at least in terms of representation, in order to make this perverse process, as S. Kracauer described earlier, at all presentable. The aestheticism of so-called historicism and the experience of "history itself," which is always the history of the modern era [*Neuzeit*] since around 1770, thus point to their mutual commonality.[121]

Koselleck placed Kracauer's chapter on historical aesthetics against the backdrop of Droysen's critique of historicism, whereby the historian can never attain the Rankean ideal of showing "how it essentially was" and must therefore employ compositional means to depict the past. For Koselleck, the inevitable aestheticism of historicism is linked to the experience of "history" as a collective singular in the modern era.[122]

Although Kracauer's *History* certainly followed in the lineage of Droysen's *Outline of the Principles of History*, it also pointed forward to later developments in the study of history and literature, particularly as these fields came to engage increasingly with issues of historical truth and representation, counterfactual or speculative history, and the mode of archive-based, subjunctive narrativization that Saidiya Hartman has called "critical fabulation."[123] Moreover, in addressing the modern challenge to Aristotelian poetics, Kracauer's final book prefigured recent work in philosophical aesthetics, most notably the writings of Jacques Rancière. In *The Politics of Aesthetics* (*Le partage du sensible*, 2000), Rancière theorizes an epochal shift from the "poetic" or "representative" to the "aesthetic" regime of art:

> Aristotle established the superiority of poetry, recounting "what could happen" according to the necessity or plausibility of the poetic arrangement of actions, over history, conceived of as the empirical succession of events, of "what happened." The aesthetic revolution drastically disrupts things: testimony and fiction come under the same regime of meaning. . . . The poetic "story" or "history" henceforth links the realism that shows us the poetic traces inscribed directly in reality with the artificialism that assembles complex machines of understanding. This connection was transferred from literature to the new art of narrative, film, which brought to its highest potential the double resource of the silent imprint that speaks and the montage that calculates the values of truth and the potential for producing meaning.[124]

In Rancière's account, nineteenth-century literature (e.g., Balzac, Hugo, Flaubert) adopted descriptive and narrative arrangements commonly employed in the representation of sociohistorical phenomena, thereby dissolving the Aristotelian opposition between empirical reality and fictional construction. Film inherited and radicalized this troubled distinction, bearing the dual capacity for indexical documentation and the production of meaning through the technique of montage.

While Rancière did not reference Kracauer's *Theory of Film* or *History*, he reiterated a key tenet of those books: film emerged from an epoch that had fundamentally upended classical hierarchies, and the medium contributed to challenging and renegotiating Aristotle's elevation of poetry over history. For Kracauer, not only does the *poetics* of film arise from its documentary function as a *historian* of contemporary life; historical films necessarily resort to the subjunctive mood of poetry, even when they reconstruct the past with a meticulous concern for realist detail. Kracauer's writings from across nearly half a century articulate the enduring problematics of the historical-film genre at the nexus of film history, aesthetics, and politics, and they also suggest a particular mode of engagement with film criticism and theory. Building on Johannes von Moltke's heuristic distinction between *"historicist," "ahistorical," "presentist,"* and *"historicizing"* approaches to classical film theory, I have placed Kracauer's writings in relation to the mounting philosophical *critique of historicism*.[125] As this book argues, film emerged concurrently with the crisis of historicism in the early twentieth century, and the new medium figured significantly in intellectual debates on the legacy of the Rankean tradition. Engagement with the crisis of historicism may help film and media scholars move toward a more reflexive and philosophically grounded model of historiography, one that acknowledges that the distinction between history and poetics has been contested since the very advent of cinema.

The crisis of historicism persists into our own "post-truth" era, characterized by an erosion of standard distinctions between fact and fiction, or legitimate decisional politics and media showmanship. In the immediate aftermath of the 2016 US presidential election, one of the former producers of *The Apprentice* (2004–17) remarked: "We are masterful storytellers and we did our job well. What's shocking to me is how quickly and decisively the world bought it.... Now that the lines of fiction and reality have blurred to the horrifying extent that they have, those involved in the media must have their day of reckoning."[126] Notable here is the producer's emphasis on the obfuscation of the boundary between the history and the story, or actuality and appearance, as well as the ease with which Donald Trump could slip in the popular imagination from reality television persona to national political leader—recalling Kracauer's argument that the screen version of Frederick the Great in the Fridericus Rex films had provided the model for Hitler's popular image. In our contemporary media and political environment, public discourse often finds itself caught between generalized skepticism and credulous paranoia about all truth claims.[127] This dialectic of skepticism and paranoia found pointed expression in a classic work of German Expressionist cinema, *The Cabinet of Dr. Caligari* (*Das Cabinet des Dr. Caligari*, Robert Wiene, 1920), the subject of the following chapter.

3. Relativist Perspectivism
The Cabinet of Dr. Caligari

> The madman jumped into their midst and pierced them with his eyes. "Whither is God?" he cried; "I will tell you. *We have killed him*—you and I."
>
> FRIEDRICH NIETZSCHE

> "I give you the right to lock me up; I am giving you the possibility of healing me." This is the meaning of the avowal of madness: avowal signs the asylum contract.
>
> MICHEL FOUCAULT

Despite its antagonism toward all metaphysical claims, the positivism popularized by Auguste Comte in the nineteenth century often expanded into a universalizing scientism, whereby natural-scientific methods were transposed to the examination of human history, culture, and society at large.[1] Given this imperialist tendency, it is both ironic and suitable that one of the major challenges posed to the Baconian epistemology adopted by positivism—namely, Albert Einstein's theory of relativity—seemed to reverberate within all realms of academic study and creative endeavor in the following century. Published in 1905, Einstein's "On the Electrodynamics of Moving Bodies" ("Zur Elektrodynamik bewegter Körper") implied a relativist perspectivism decisively at odds with the empirical mode of observation widely practiced across diverse scholarly and artistic realms—from the natural sciences to the disciplines of history and sociology, and from the "experimental novels" of naturalist authors to the plein air paintings of the Impressionists.[2] Where practitioners in these realms had assumed the position of fixed, detached observers whose viewpoint was separated from the external world, Einstein's theory suggested a more decentered, spatiotemporally dynamic, and nonabsolute relationship between subject and object. Such a relativist form of interaction, as I hope to demonstrate in this chapter, found expression in both the modernist works and historical-philosophical debates of the Weimar era.

Emerging contemporaneously with Einstein's theories, works of aesthetic modernism likewise rejected traditional, widely accepted standards of observation, evoking a new mode of relationality between human subjectivity and the objective world. While the Impressionists had already substituted an apprehensive space for that of ordered, Euclidean geometry, modernist artists abandoned the mimesis of perceived reality altogether, replacing a fragmentary consciousness for the fixed, detached observer and negating rather than faithfully imitating the exterior realm.[3] Most evident in the turn away from figurative painting, the "dehumanization of art" (José Ortega y Gasset) in fact occurred across a broad range of media, finding its corollary in the retreat from the realistic, coherent plot in literature and the dismissal of harmonic tonality in music.[4] In a 1923 manifesto, Russian author Yevgeny Zamyatin rendered explicit the correspondence between scientific paradigms and artistic practices, characterizing bourgeois and socialist-realist forms as "projections along the fixed, plane coordinates of Euclid's world."[5] Emphasizing the proven nonexistence of such a "finite, fixed world," Zamyatin called for a more complex form of literature—a literature with the pioneering, self-reflexive inquisitiveness of Einstein, who "managed to remember that he . . . , observing motion with a watch in hand, was also moving" and thereby succeeded in "looking at the motion of the earth from *outside*."[6]

Among the modernist movements in art and literature that suggested a new worldview along with a more mutable, impermanent order of spatial relations is Expressionism. As Georg Marzynski wrote in a 1920 study, Expressionist painters shifted emphasis from external reality to human subjectivity, constructing works from colors and forms untethered to the realm of sensory experience. In this way, Marzynski argued, Expressionist artists sought to liberate European painting from the representational function it had performed since the Renaissance; whereas earlier art consisted of "subjectivized objects," their works portrayed "objectifications of the subject."[7] Similarly, Walter Sokel later contended that in the dramas of August Strindberg and the Expressionists, the protagonist's physical environment is not "the source of experience," but rather "a structure designed for the purpose of expressing emotions."[8] In Sokel's analysis, Expressionist dramatists rejected the postulate of a fixed, given external nature, envisioning the world instead as "a field of magnetic and gravitational forces radiating from the soul."[9] The theatrical mise-en-scène of Expressionist dramas, according to Sokel, is thus dynamic, serving as a projection of the protagonist's ever-fluctuating interior states: "The scenery of the Expressionist stage changes with the psychic forces whirling about in it, just as in the universe of relativity space is modified by the matter it contains."[10]

For many commentators, however, the art form most capable of representing the dynamics of the Einsteinian universe was film.[11] Perhaps most famously, Sergei Eisenstein, Jean Epstein, and Dziga Vertov invoked the principle of relativity and the fourth dimension in their theoretical writings on cinema's medial properties and aesthetic possibilities.[12] As Annette Michelson has argued, the three filmmakers shared an interest in the power of montage techniques (e.g., freeze-framing; slow, fast, or reverse motion) to reveal, suspend, or even reconfigure spatiotemporal and causal relations, thereby offering a new mode of experiencing and knowing the phenomenal world.[13] Einstein's ideas also found cinematic articulation in the German context—most explicitly in Hanns Walter Kornblum's 1922 educational film *The Fundamentals of the Einsteinian Relativity Theory* (*Die Grundlagen der Einsteinschen Relativitätstheorie*), but also in relation to works of Expressionism, distinct less for their montage techniques and trick sequences than for their distorted mise-en-scène.[14] In a 1920 essay, Herman Scheffauer invoked Einstein while celebrating Expressionist cinema's plastic and dynamic conceptualization of space, which, in his view, lent the medium a "fourth dimension."[15] For Scheffauer, the first film to exemplify this new spatial sensibility was Robert Wiene's *The Cabinet of Dr. Caligari* (*Das Cabinet des Dr. Caligari*, 1920), the sets of which seemed to apply and visualize "Einstein's invasion of the law of gravity."[16]

In this chapter, I will examine *Caligari* in terms of the relativist perspectivism that was widely invoked in the early twentieth century. During this period, the popularization of Einstein's theory of relativity converged with increasing recognition of the relativist implications of historicist thought, and the dissolution of perspective in the visual arts coincided with the emergence of perspectivism in modern philosophy, especially in the wake of Nietzsche. Locating *Caligari* at the nexus of these broadscale developments, I will build on the work of Thomas Elsaesser, who has accounted for the film's unique stylistic and formal features with reference to Weimar cinema's "double 'legitimation crisis'" vis-à-vis German cultural tradition and an increasingly hegemonic American film industry.[17] Where Elsaesser links the film's reflexive qualities to a "meta-critical discourse," I will position the work as a meditation on conceptions of time and history.[18] And while Elsaesser notes *Caligari*'s "radical skepticism as to evidentiary truth in the cinema," I will argue that the film adopts an ironic stance regarding issues of historical ontology, epistemology, and narration more generally.[19] *Caligari*'s legacy, in my analysis, consists not only in introducing aspects of aesthetic modernism to the medium of film, but also in demonstrating the possibilities of an "intellectual" or "cerebral" cinema—one that engages with fundamental questions of the philosophy of history.

THE THEORY OF RELATIVITY

As Einstein succeeded in generalizing and popularizing his theory of relativity, gaining recognition across disciplinary and national contexts, he provoked widespread debates about the roles of science and philosophy in conceptualizing time and history. Henri Bergson confronted the implications of relativity in a meeting with Einstein at the Société française de philosophie on April 6, 1922, and in a series of texts extending from *Duration and Simultaneity* (*Durée et simultanéité*, 1922) to his final volume, *The Creative Mind* (*La pensée et le mouvant*, 1934). Whereas Einstein argued that an understanding of time is restricted to the domains of physics and psychology, Bergson insisted on the continued relevance of philosophical inquiry into the concept and also resisted efforts to transform the theory of relativity into an expansive philosophy.[20] With a similar emphasis on the irreducibility of humanistic to natural-scientific approaches, Martin Heidegger took up the concept of time in his 1915 *Habilitationsvortrag* (habilitation lecture), analyzing the concept's structure in physics and in the discipline of history. In Heidegger's view, the theory of relativity is concerned with "*measuring time*" rather than with "time itself," treating the latter as "homogeneous," "mathematical," and "quantitatively determinable."[21] The physicist's concept of time, Heidegger argued, is thus distinct from that of the historian, who confronts the "qualitative otherness" of different periods—or what Leopold von Ranke had famously characterized as every epoch's immediacy to God.[22]

While Heidegger, in his 1915 lecture, maintained a Diltheyan confidence in the possibility of bridging the "temporal gulf" between historian and object—a confidence that the past "cannot be something *incomparably* other"—he and fellow thinkers would later diagnose and seek to remedy a foundational crisis in history and other fields of scientific inquiry.[23] In a 1925 lecture series, Heidegger argued that while Dilthey had recognized historical being as the fundamental character of human existence, he had failed to inquire into the category of historicity itself.[24] Though still wary of the general validity of Einstein's theory, Heidegger now acknowledged its significance in discovering the local quality of time, thus undermining its conceptualization within Kantian philosophy. Furthermore, Heidegger identified a commonality between Einsteinian relativity and Husserlian phenomenology in their reflexive understanding of time as "the reality of our own selves."[25] For Heidegger, both approaches indicated that one need not conceive of time in a "metaphysical fashion" in order to pursue an "*absolute* knowledge of nature."[26] Edmund Husserl, for his part, invoked Einstein in his final work, *The Crisis of European Sciences and Transcendental Phenomenology* (*Die Krisis der europäischen Wissenschaften und die transzendentale Phänomenologie*, 1936). Citing Einstein's experiences in a common, prescientific *Lebenswelt* (lifeworld) as the basis for theoretical verification, Husserl emphasized the futility of traditional distinctions between "subjective-relative" perceptions and "objective-scientific" veracities.[27]

The new, temporally dynamic mode of subject–object interaction implied by Einstein's theory also found its analogy in literature's shifting relationship to history. In contrast to the epic, with its self-contained, static, and atemporal world, the novel had expressed the emerging historical consciousness of the nineteenth century, sharing with historiographical texts a narrative form, omniscient narrator, interest in synchronic development, and emphasis on the concrete particularities of empirical reality.[28] Furthermore, whereas the epic hero had represented a broader, unified collectivity, the solitary protagonist of the novel symptomatized the irreconcilable split between subject and environment—or what Georg Lukács characterized in 1916 as the state of "transcendental homelessness" within modern society.[29] While traditional novelists had nonetheless upheld the Diltheyan promise of a vicarious reexperiencing (*Nacherleben*) of others' pasts (albeit with imagined rather than real historical figures), modernist works broke with the tenets of historicism, postulating alternatives to continuous, linear progression and focusing on individual subjectivity rather than on a confounding external reality.[30] In 1930, Siegfried Kracauer invoked a "'crisis' of the novel," which he attributed to the assault of scientific discoveries and sociopolitical phenomena on the bourgeois faith in objective meaning and sovereign power: "Just as, thanks to Einstein, our spatio-temporal system has become a limit concept, the self-satisfied subject has become a limit concept thanks to the object lesson of history."[31]

Modernist texts registered and even thematized contemporary developments in conceptions of time and history. Although, as Lukács argued, Bergsonian *durée* was a constitutive principle of novels such as Gustave Flaubert's *Sentimental Education* (*L'éducation sentimentale*, 1869), the notion of a fluid, psychological time first found literary expression in Marcel Proust's *In Search of Lost Time* (*À la recherche du temps perdu*, 1913–27) and in the stream-of-consciousness technique of writers including Dorothy Richardson, James Joyce, and Virginia Woolf.[32] Einsteinian relativity was a salient point of reference for modernist writers, as evidenced most explicitly by Professor Jones's ironic allusion to the "theorics of Winestain" in Joyce's *Finnegans Wake* (1939).[33] As Jane Goldman has argued, Woolf's writings can also be placed in constellation with Einsteinian physics, particularly if one links her reflections on eclipses in her diaries, essays, stories, and novels to the total solar eclipse that occurred on May 29, 1919 (the longest solar eclipse since 1416), which allowed Arthur Eddington to confirm the general theory of relativity.[34] I would add that the fleeting vision of a "black lunar shadow" caused by the 1919 eclipse—a vision characterized as "terrifying" and "horribly menacing" in contemporary accounts—bears affinities with the momentary appearance of a shadow on the screen during a showing of *Caligari* attended by Woolf, for whom it hinted at a new form of "fear" or "terror" as well as the filmic medium's potential for abstract, symbolic expressivity.[35]

Writing about a revival screening of *Caligari* in 1926, Woolf implied that the shadow that accidentally appeared on-screen was scarier than the film itself, which relied on more prosaic and noncinematic forms of horror. Woolf thereby joined a lineage of authors (including Blaise Cendrars and Ezra Pound) who had likewise criticized *Caligari*'s parasitic relationship to other media along with its opportunistic, even impertinent emulation of innovations within aesthetic modernism.[36] Upon its initial German release in 1920, however, *Caligari* was noted by many commentators not for its derivativeness, but rather for its radical, even inconceivable novelty. As Anne Perlmann wrote in *Der Kinematograph* on May 16, 1920, "I—and probably many others—felt the same way about the Caligari film as I initially felt about Einstein's principle of relativity: the more the newspapers wrote about it, the less my idea of it became clear."[37] Perlmann thus drew an analogy between Wiene's film and Einstein's theory, whose official confirmation on November 6, 1919, had similarly garnered sensational and widespread coverage for a curious and often-bewildered mass public. The following sections will pursue this analogy further, interpreting *Caligari* itself as a meditation on the implications of relativity for conceptions of time and history. This line of argumentation will first require an excursus into the crisis of historicism, Expressionist aesthetics, and cinematic realism in the early twentieth century.

THE CRITIQUE OF POSITIVISM

Positivism made an enormous contribution to empirical sciences such as history and sociology in the nineteenth century, offering these emerging disciplines a model of primary-source research, scientific exactitude, and objective, detached neutrality. Nevertheless, the extension of naturalist postulates to the *Geisteswissenschaften* (human sciences) raised many vexing questions for intellectuals in Central and Western Europe: Might not human life and activity bear unique, vital, and dynamic qualities that are obscured when social existence and behavior are treated like objects of natural-scientific scrutiny? Are there dimensions of one's being, interiority, and lived experience that exceed the purview of a phenomenalist epistemology, which relies on sense perception and denies any distinction between appearances and essences? Can one yield genuine knowledge of spiritual-intellectual realms from a passive, disinterested mode of examination, abstaining from value judgments and proceeding strictly according to inductive generalization? And, finally, is it possible to figure the subjectivity and historicity of the observer without thereby sacrificing a claim to universal validity?[38] Such questions fueled a "crisis of science" addressed by Max Weber in his celebrated 1917 lecture "Science as a Vocation" ("Wissenschaft als Beruf"), delivered at a time when many in the younger generation expressed radical skepticism about the ultimate purpose and meaning of specialized intellectual inquiry.[39]

The general rebellion against science at the end of the long nineteenth century also entailed the rejection of a specific tradition of historical thinking. Though not a simple positivist, Leopold von Ranke had upheld a correspondence theory of truth, pursuing the ideal of faithfully and impartially re-creating empirical reality—or, in his well-known words, showing "how it essentially was."[40] Ranke's mode of historiography, involving the rigorous collection of individual facts, was criticized as early as 1874 by Friedrich Nietzsche, for whom it connoted a dry, ascetic antiquarianism as well as the dissolution of all foundations into a ceaseless, Heraclitean flux.[41] Philosophers including Wilhelm Windelband, Heinrich Rickert, and Wilhelm Dilthey later addressed epistemological and methodological issues related to the science of history, seeking to provide a firm basis for historical knowledge and understanding.[42] Their inability to fend off the relativist implications of historicism presaged a crisis of historical thought diagnosed by Ernst Troeltsch in the disorienting postwar years, when a Rankean faith in the meaning and coherence of the historical process seemed to be decisively shattered.[43] In *Historicism and Its Problems* (*Der Historismus und seine Probleme*, 1922), Troeltsch discerned a "historical relativity of values" in the German historicist tradition—one, in his view, with "a certain analogy to the physical theory of relativity, which, with its set of problems so greatly increased by Einstein, concerns the whole world today."[44]

Expressionist artists participated in the early-twentieth-century revolt against science, following a lineage of philosophical reactions to positivism. As Kracauer argued in a 1918 essay, visual and literary works of Expressionism betrayed a Nietzschean vitalism, countering an "Apollonian intellectuality [*Geistigkeit*]" with elementary and instinctually driven being, "irrepressibly moved and suffused with Dionysian fervor."[45] Kracauer attributed the movement's interest in recovering an "*Ur*-ego" to the repressive, hegemonic power of science, which renders the world increasingly objective and converts the individual into "a pure impersonal intellect."[46] Writing sixteen years later, Georg Lukács set Expressionism against the backdrop of the Kaiserreich's "philosophy of life," which, in its attempts to mediate between neo-Kantianism and historicism, tended toward an "extreme relativism" and even "mystical irrationalism."[47] For Lukács, one of the exemplary figures in this context was Hans Vaihinger, whose *The Philosophy of 'As If'* (*Die Philosophie des Als Ob*, 1911) theorized human fictions on the basis of a Kant- and Nietzsche-derived "idealistic positivism."[48] Vaihinger himself hinted at a link between Expressionist aesthetics and the critique of positivism. In his analysis, the skeptic or logical pessimist discredits a naive identity theory of truth, according to which the psyche "portray[s] the objective world truthfully and without alteration," preferring to regard thought instead "as though it distorted reality like a pair of coloured spectacles or a concave mirror."[49]

The Expressionists' rejection of a positivist epistemology—their insistence, in Gottfried Benn's words, that "there was no reality, only, at most, its distorted image"—also implied a challenge to basic historicist tenets.[50] Manifestos by Kasimir Edschmid and others proclaimed a radical break with the past—a break often articulated in terms of cultural iconoclasm, Oedipal rebellion, and revolutionary or eschatological politics.[51] Negating all traditions, norms, and stylistic conventions, the Expressionists strove toward a new reality, which they envisioned not through faithful mimesis of a given external world, but rather through the act of pure, unfettered creation. The artificial universe formed by the Expressionists would be detached or even independent from concrete temporal and historical determinants, reflecting what Wilhelm Worringer identified in 1907 as an "urge to abstraction."[52] In contrast to naturalism, which had presupposed a confident relationship between human and environment, abstract art arose, in Worringer's words, from "a great inner unrest inspired in man by the phenomena of the outside world"—that is, from a loss of faith in history as the site of logos and meaning.[53] Such a disillusioned view found explicit articulation in Georg Kaiser's "Historical Fidelity" ("Historientreue," 1923), in which the writer characterized history as a "succession of incidents that are senseless and purposeless," and described the task of the poet as that of transforming chaos and accident into order and lawful necessity.[54]

In their conception of surface reality as a creation of the intellect, and in their prioritization of nonmimetic art as a link to the eternal, the

Expressionists drew from Arthur Schopenhauer's *The World as Will and Representation* (*Die Welt als Wille und Vorstellung*, 1819). The first prominent irrationalist among Western philosophers, Schopenhauer had presented a pessimistic vision of human life as lacking sense, direction, and meaning. Opposing Hegel's philosophy, Schopenhauer described the material of history not as a source of general knowledge, but rather as "the particular in its particularity and contingency."[55] Much as Schopenhauer had undermined an affirmative, theodicean view of history, likening its movement to "clouds in the wind . . . , often entirely transformed by the most trifling accident," Expressionist theorists Worringer and Wassily Kandinsky dismissed a coherent or teleological *Geschichtsbild* (conception of history), reflecting a sense, in the former's words, that "man is now just as lost and helpless *vis-à-vis* the world picture as primitive man."[56] Bernhard Diebold also alluded to Schopenhauer's aesthetics in his prescient 1916 article "Expressionism and Cinema" ("Expressionismus und Kino"), and the screenwriters of *Caligari*, Carl Mayer and Hans Janowitz, explicitly modeled their title character's appearance after the nineteenth-century philosopher.[57] Upon its release in February 1920, one critic even lauded *Caligari* for departing from a naturalist preoccupation with "'objective facts,'" depicting instead "the world as will and representation of the madman."[58]

THE REJECTION OF REALIST AESTHETICS

Like Worringer, who identified opposing aesthetic drives in the history of art—a mimetic empathy with the vital, organic world and an abstractionist retreat into a realm of tranquil, crystalline form—Kracauer would later observe dual forces at work in the evolution of photographic media. In *Theory of Film* (1960), Kracauer noted the contemporaneous popularization of photographic technology and positivist methodology in the nineteenth century as well as their common promise of accurately and impersonally reproducing physical reality.[59] While realists across scientific and aesthetic fields celebrated photography's ability to record and reveal nature, other commentators and practitioners—particularly those upholding Romantic ideals—emphasized the medium's artistic qualities, as derived from the selective rendering and creative shaping of raw visual material. Kracauer discerned a comparable interplay between "realistic" and "formative" tendencies in the history of film, which was already split in its early years between the Lumière Brothers' *actualités* and the staged fantasies of Georges Méliès. Echoing Erwin Panofsky, who had distinguished film from older representational media in its compositional process "from bottom to top"—a process, Panofsky argued, corresponding to a materialist rather than an idealist worldview—Kracauer postulated a "basic aesthetic principle" of cinema, prioritizing visual engagement with the infinite, transitory, and fortuitous realm of physical existence.[60]

Given the frequent association of realist and Impressionist aesthetics with photographic representation, the relationship between Expressionism and cinema was a contentious issue among film theorists, enmeshed in broader debates about the medium's specific properties and artistic potential. As Rudolf Kurtz wrote in 1926, "Of all art forms, film seems to be the least like art and the most like nature. Even photography, its fundamental tool, is perceived as being basically inartistic."[61] Kurtz argued that while Expressionism in film necessarily entailed compromise, the movement had nonetheless enriched the medium's visual repertoire, conjuring up "effects that lie beyond the photographable."[62] In a 1934 essay, Rudolf Arnheim likewise credited Expressionism with film's artistic development. Though criticizing the blind transference of stylistic principles from graphic art and painting to three-dimensional, cinematic space, Arnheim acknowledged Expressionism's important influence on film, likening it to the movement's impact on other arts: namely, the prioritization and freer application of formal factors, thus ending "a period in which the object was overvalued."[63] Kracauer, whose aforementioned 1918 essay had recognized the movement for creating new artistic means, similarly argued in 1939 that Expressionist films, while overly theatrical, had been fruitful in establishing the necessary distance from outer reality to approach it anew, released from the constraints of inhibition and convention.[64]

Widely identified as the first work of Expressionist cinema, *Caligari* held a central position in classical film-theoretical debates on modes of engagement with physical reality. From its initial release onward, Wiene's film was praised by some for its attempt to redefine cinematic practice apart from naturalist representation—or, as one reviewer wrote in 1920, for lifting the medium "out of the realm of photography and into the pure sphere of the work of art."[65] Among *Caligari*'s numerous detractors, criticisms included the film's disregard for the medium's unique features and devices; its impure combination of naturalistic and stylized elements; excessive, even enervating décor; and, finally, its linkage of Expressionist aesthetics with the theme of insanity. In his 1947 essay, Panofsky argued that insofar as *Caligari* presented an adulterated profilmic space, it avoided the problem of cinema: namely, "to manipulate and shoot unstylized reality in such a way that the result has style."[66] Writing four years later, André Bazin similarly characterized *Caligari* as a failed attempt to depart from film's inalienable spatial realism, replacing "the world of experience" with "a fabricated nature" strongly influenced by theater and painting.[67] Finally, in *Theory of Film*, Kracauer positioned *Caligari* as the earliest cinematic effort to abandon the medium's recording function. For Kracauer, Wiene's work prioritized free and autonomous creation above "camera-realism" in a misguided, even retrogressive quest to attain the legitimacy of the traditional arts.[68]

Caligari thus served as a negative example in numerous mid-twentieth-century theorizations of cinematic ontology and generic aesthetic boundaries. If, however, with a nod to Kracauer, one pursues an analogy between *Caligari's* reworking of "camera reality" and contemporaneous intellectual efforts to rethink the nature and epistemology of "historical reality," one might also interpret the film in terms of historical-philosophical debates—and, more specifically, as a critique of nineteenth-century German historicism.[69] Indeed, the Expressionist mise-en-scène of Wiene's film not only rejects traditional realist aesthetics, but also abandons the historicist quest to establish "how it essentially was" through individualizing observation. *Caligari*'s circular narrative structure also thwarts the historicist stress on evolutionary development, coinciding more with Oswald Spengler's vision of historical cyclicality.[70] Such a correspondence between Expressionist aesthetics and antihistoricism was suggested by Wiene himself in a 1922 text. Writing in the *Berliner Börsen-Courier*, Wiene positioned the Expressionism that emerged in the decade before World War I as a reaction against aesthetic realism, whether in its historicist or naturalist guises. For Wiene, Expressionism marked "an irrepressible countermovement, which turned against the last vestiges of historicism—in short, against all forms of realism," and had since become the goal of film and all other arts in the current era.[71]

Expressionist cinema's visual features and narrative structures are thus interpretable not only within a metacinematic or metacritical discourse—that is, as reflections of/on the properties, possibilities, and cultural-industrial positionality of the filmic medium—but also as *metahistorical* considerations of the philosophical tenets of historicist thought. Furthermore, Expressionist film's oft-noted reflexivity aligns it with what Hayden White has called an "ironic" mode of historiography, or one that inspires doubt about its own truth claims by self-consciously negating that which it affirms on a literal level.[72] Such ironic reflexivity found astute and eloquent articulation in the culture of Weimar Germany—a culture that Helmut Lethen and Peter Sloterdijk have noted for its cool demeanor and disillusioned, cynical reason—and it is also evident in later movements of film history, including the film noirs of the 1940s and 1950s and the mind-game films of more recent decades.[73] More broadly, by examining Weimar cinema's extraordinary innovations in aesthetic and narrative form with regard to developments in early-twentieth-century intellectual history, I hope to demonstrate the significant role of film in engaging with large-scale, seismic shifts in modern philosophy—in particular, the decentering and disintegration of the Cartesian subject as well as the change from subject-object modes of thinking to a more complex, relativist perspectivism. In what follows, I will study these shifts through a closer analysis of Wiene's *Caligari*.

FRAMING *CALIGARI*

Among the major points of contention in scholarship on Wiene's film since *From Caligari to Hitler* (1947) has been the function of the frame narrative, the addition of which, in Kracauer's well-known assessment, transformed "a revolutionary film ... into a conformist one."[74] Kracauer based his appraisal of the film on a 1941 manuscript by Hans Janowitz, who had attributed the narrative device to Wiene, disavowing its presence in the original script.[75] Numerous scholars have since diverged from Kracauer's critique, offering alternative readings of *Caligari*'s politics; most notably, Anton Kaes has characterized the film as "an aggressive diatribe against the murderous practices of war psychiatry," associating it with "Dada's nihilistic attacks on the establishment."[76] While I would agree with those who have emphasized that *Caligari*'s openness and indeterminacy frustrate all ascriptions of direct sociohistorical referentiality and political coherence, I also wish to shift focus to an unexplored area of inquiry: namely, the film's engagement with ontological, epistemological, and historiographical questions of the philosophy of history.[77] In my analysis, *Caligari* marks a challenge to basic historicist tenets, including the objectivity of historical accounts, the reliability and authority of narration, and the alignment of power and ethics. The film, I argue, conveys a radical skepticism regarding the possibility of detached, disinterested observation, suggesting a more perspectivist sense of historical reality as the interplay of finite interpretations.

For Kracauer, *Caligari*'s framing device pathologizes the narrator, Francis, thereby delegitimizing and even reversing his story's implied challenge to state authority. Furthermore, Kracauer views the narrative device itself, with its ambivalent gesture of containment, as the symbol of a collective trend in Weimar Germany toward both solipsistic retreat and inner, "psychological revolution."[78] Apart from its factual errors, internal contradictions, and dubious methodological premises, Kracauer's argument confronts myriad hermeneutical obstacles, most obviously the extension of the film's Expressionist design into the framing scenes and their intertitles. Because the film's concluding episode does not, as Kracauer himself notes, restore "conventional reality," it problematizes the relationship between Expressionist stylization and narrational insanity assumed by many contemporary reviewers.[79] Whereas Kracauer nonetheless maintains that Francis's story is bracketed as a "madman's fantasy," I would emphasize that the film not only ultimately refuses to designate his (and the asylum director's) degree of sanity, but also interrogates the bases upon which the figures' credibility might be evaluated and ascertained.[80] Moreover, in contrast to Kracauer, who associates the film's exclusive use of studio settings with a postwar German withdrawal from the exterior world, I submit that *Caligari* follows Nietzsche in calling into question the very existence and accessibility of a normative historical reality—one external to the subjective perspectives of discrete individuals.

In juxtaposing *Caligari*'s framing scenes with its inner story, Kracauer also discounts the blurring of formal and textual boundaries that characterizes Wiene's film and the Expressionist movement more generally. Distinguishing Expressionist dramaturgy from earlier theatrical practice, Walter Sokel argued that "the physical stage ... ceases to be a fixed frame of a scene or act," and the protagonist's dreamlike vision is no longer placed within an "explanatory frame of reference."[81] Although, as stated, *Caligari*'s Expressionist style is not consistently or unequivocally aligned with one character's psychological state, the film nonetheless disregards the barriers between inner self and external environment, and between enigmatic visions and elucidatory frameworks. In Wiene's film, aspects of characters' appearances, costumes, and props (e.g., the three streaks in the director's hair and gloves; Cesare's slender, angular physique and knife) correspond to patterns in the surrounding décor, and characteristics of the mise-en-scène (e.g., irregular shapes, distorted angles) extend not only to the film's framing scenes, but also beyond the diegesis to include the font and design of the intertitles. The film also obscures the thresholds between word and image, and between textual and paratextual elements; the injunction "You must become Caligari [*Du musst Caligari werden*]," which appears before the asylum director in a famous scene, also featured prominently in the film's 1920 advertising campaign.

The film's obfuscation of conventional borders also applies to its narrative and thematic registers. Drawing from the Romantic and Gothic literary works of Mary Shelley (*Frankenstein*, 1818), E.T.A. Hoffmann ("The Sandman" ["Der Sandmann," 1817]), Edgar Allan Poe ("The System of Doctor Tarr and Professor Fether," 1845), and Robert Louis Stevenson (*The

Three streaks in the director's hair and gloves.

Cesare's slender, angular physique and knife.

Obscured thresholds between word and image.

Strange Case of Dr. Jekyll and Mr. Hyde, 1886), *Caligari* features fantastic, uncanny figures or motifs (e.g., ghosts, somnambulists, doppelgängers) that frustrate basic ontological distinctions, such as those between life and death, sleeping and wakefulness, sanity and insanity, and self and other. Cesare is first hailed for his omniscient and prophetic powers, which extend across temporal horizons ("Cesare knows the past and sees the future"), and he is also revealed to transgress spatial boundaries, repeatedly exiting the fairground area and penetrating into others' private spheres. The central mystery of the story within the story—who is truly responsible for the series of murders in Holstenwall—not only bleeds into and even beyond the frame narrative, resisting unambiguous resolution or closure, but is also complicated by a further question opened up by the concluding episode: namely, whether the murders narrated by Francis in fact occurred, or if the entire inner story was merely his subjective delusion. The film's inverse, mutually incompatible endings, alternately depicting the director and Francis in straitjackets in the insane asylum, pose an irresolvable challenge to viewers' capacity for decisive adjudication.

Caligari thus challenges the Kantian analytic of aesthetic judgment, confounding the delimitation of the work (*ergon*) from its addendum or frame (*parergon*), or the intrinsic from the extrinsic aspects of pictorial representation.[82] Emphasizing the nonabsoluteness of the boundaries between the aesthetic object and its milieu—or, as Georg Simmel wrote in "The Picture Frame" ("Der Bildrahmen," 1902), between the work of art and elements of an unmediated nature—*Caligari* deploys frames not toward the dual ends of external defense and internal integration, but rather toward those of "continuing exosmosis and endosmosis."[83] By reduplicating the inner story's themes of permeability and liminality across stylistic, narrational, and paratextual registers, the film eliminates the distance from the spectator that Simmel, following the Idealist tradition, deemed as essential for an artwork's wholeness, coherence, and self-sufficiency. Countering Simmel's conceptualization of the work of art as an autonomous, self-enclosed unity, the film highlights the indefiniteness of all demarcations or "border regions" as well as the nonfixity of the relationship between object and observer.[84] This new, more dynamic mode of relationality, as the following section will demonstrate, involved the dissolution of the perspectival system of space, which had not only contributed to the autonomy and formal order of the image, but also allowed it to address a single beholder, whose monocular, immobile point of view was separated from the object of representation.

THE DISSOLUTION OF PERSPECTIVE

In his seminal essay "Perspective as 'Symbolic Form'" ("Die Perspektive als 'symbolische Form,'" 1927), Erwin Panofsky modified the approach of Alois Riegl, who had examined the relationship between the artwork and its surrounding world through his concept of the unique *Kunstwollen* (artistic will) of every epoch.[85] Panofsky replaced Riegl's inchoate *Weltanschauungsphilosophie* (philosophy of world views) with a neo-Kantian theory of the "symbolic form"; the latter was Ernst Cassirer's term for the spiritual energy through which human consciousness attributes meaning to sensual signs across the various realms of cultural expression.[86] Observing correspondences between advances in Western philosophy and the evolution of spatial perception, Panofsky argued that much as the idea of an infinite empirical reality had superseded the circumscribed geocentrism of Aristotelian thought, the system of central perspective had envisaged endless extension to a vanishing point, establishing distance between human beings and an objectified world of experience. Panofsky characterized perspective as an ambivalent and versatile method, and one that has served as the target of diametrically opposed critiques over the course of its history. Whereas ancient and medieval artists had largely eschewed perspective, associating it with subjectivism and contingency, the Expressionists had rejected it for preserving empirical, three-dimensional space, and thereby retaining an element of objectivity that constrained the "formative will" of the individual creator.[87]

The Expressionist movement advanced a broader trend in early-twentieth-century visual art toward dispelling perspectival geometry and envisioning new conceptions of space. Impressionist paintings of the 1860s and 1870s had already signaled an increasing dissatisfaction with perspectival conventions; instead of representing solid objects in three-dimensional space, works by Edgar Degas, Édouard Manet, Claude Monet, Pierre-Auguste Renoir, and others had depicted the fleeting, subjective impressions that these objects left on the artists' perceptual apparatuses. However, where works of Impressionism had maintained a connection to physical reality, subsequent art movements (e.g., Postimpressionism, Cubism) blatantly defied the aim of perspectival technique, as identified by Panofsky: "to construct pictorial space, in principle, out of the elements of, and according to the plan of, empirical visual space."[88] This rejection of art's function as a mimesis of external objects—and, with it, a dismissal of the pictorial surface's status as a window to the outer world—troubled the long-standing Cartesian split between the thinking subject (*res cogitans*) and the extended substance (*res extensa*). Emphasizing the untenability of separating the world of objects from a fixed observer, modern artists abandoned what the art historian Carl Einstein, in *Art of the Twentieth Century* (*Die Kunst des 20. Jahrhunderts*, 1926), called the "perspectival calculation of distance," inaugurating "an epoch of technical and formal freedom."[89]

Concurrent with art historians' responses to the innovations of aesthetic modernism, early film theorists recognized cinema for its potential to expand and reconfigure the field of human perception. In *The Photoplay* (1916), Hugo Münsterberg made a plea for film's aesthetic independence on account of unique methods like the close-up, through which "an entirely new perspective was opened."[90] Defending film against negative comparisons to the realist theater, Münsterberg emphasized that art's purpose is "not to imitate life but to reset it in a way which is totally different from reality."[91] Eight years later, Béla Balázs's *Visible Man* (*Der sichtbare Mensch*, 1924) distinguished film from legitimized arts (e.g., painting, theater) through its ability to offer spectators a dynamic point of view and a multiplicity of perspectives. Identifying uniquely cinematic scales and shot distances, Balázs celebrated film's ability to capture the ephemeral, often-invisible phenomena of everyday experience and to abstract them from their spatiotemporal coordinates.[92] Finally, in "The Cinema Seen from Etna" ("Le cinématographe vu de l'Etna," 1926), Jean Epstein argued that cinema contributes an additional element to three-dimensional spatial representation: "To the elements of perspective employed in drawing, the cinema adds a new perspective in time."[93] Epstein highlighted the versatility of this temporal perspective, especially on account of cinematic techniques such as slow and fast motion.

Caligari marked an early demonstration of cinema's potential to offset conventions of perspectival representation. Emphasizing the medium's stylistic above its naturalist capacities—or, in Kracauer's words, its "formative" above its "realistic" tendencies—Wiene's film refuses to create the illusion of solid objects in three-dimensional space.[94] The film thwarts viewers' sense of objects' physical properties and depth relationships through flat, painted studio sets with sharp, oblique angles; irregular, crooked shapes; and often-exaggerated sizes and proportions. Furthermore, whereas perspectival unity had depended on a particular point of observation, Wiene's film creates a highly unstable spectatorial positionality, not least through instances of direct address to the camera, alternation between the first- and third-person voice in the intertitles, and unresolved ambiguities regarding narratorial credibility. Writing in the *Berliner Abendpost* on February 29, 1920, Eugen Tannenbaum argued that Wiene's film does not depict "the perspective from the auditorium," but rather imposes the point of view of a madman: "The viewer is forced to see everything through *his* eyes: bizarre, grotesque, distorted, full of dark secrets and inexplicable connections."[95] Other reviewers similarly noted the film for its "shifting of perspective," abandonment of "all laws of things in space," and representation of the world "from a different viewpoint than that common until now."[96]

Challenging the association of film with the faithful reproduction of three-dimensional space, *Caligari* thus destabilized a linear-perspectival scheme that had reigned from Renaissance art to Impressionist painting. Though not fully exploring the possibilities of montage and camera movement, *Caligari* nonetheless deployed stylistic and narrative devices to enact what Kracauer, in his *Theory of Film*, identified as the "dissolution of traditional perspectives"—a general process that he attributed to photographic media, with their capacity to record and reveal unusual aspects of physical reality.[97] While Kracauer disparagingly categorized German Expressionist films as among those "which neglect the external world in freely composed dreams or visions," it may be more productive, following Friedrich Kittler, to place the films in a trajectory that includes optical devices (e.g., camera obscura, magic lantern, stroboscope), romantic literature (Friedrich

Flat, painted studio sets with sharp, oblique angles.

Often-exaggerated sizes and proportions.

Schiller's *The Ghost-Seer* [*Der Geisterseher*, 1787–89], Novalis's *Heinrich von Ofterdingen* [1802], E.T.A. Hoffmann's *The Devil's Elixirs* [*Die Elixiere des Teufels*, 1815]), and emerging sciences (psychiatry, hypnotism, psychoanalysis), all of which involve illusions, hallucinations, and blurred boundaries between dreams and palpable reality.[98] If, as Kittler argues, the medium of film mobilizes the spectator's gaze and manipulates their "unconscious psychological states," it decenters the transcendental subject and suggests a more finite, relational regime of vision—or what Nietzsche had theorized as perspectivism.[99]

THE ADVENT OF PERSPECTIVISM

In its four-century-long "scopic regime," the technique of linear perspective was metaphorically extended to denote processes of perception and cognition.[100] Etymologically derived from the Latin verb *perspicio* ("to look at/into," "to look/see through," "to examine," "to observe"), the term *perspective* came to designate a particular line of sight on an object as well as a spatial or temporal distance necessary for proper valuation or judgment.[101] From the seventeenth century onward, the metaphor was employed by thinkers including Francis Bacon, François de La Rochefoucauld, Blaise Pascal, and Gottfried Wilhelm Leibniz, the latter of whom first transposed the figure to the realm of metaphysics. Whereas Leibniz assumed a divinely assured, "perfect harmony" among different epistemic points of view, later philosophers confronted the immanence and potential incommensurability of discrete, localized perspectives.[102] The attendant concept of perspectivism, as developed by Gustav Teichmüller in *The Real and the Apparent World* (*Die wirkliche und die scheinbare Welt*, 1882), was theorized most influentially by Nietzsche and was also taken up by twentieth-century thinkers including José Ortega y Gasset, George Herbert Mead, Edmund Husserl, and Maurice Merleau-Ponty. The concept's emergence in modern philosophy thus coincided with the dissolution of perspective in the visual arts, reflecting what Claudio Guillén and Martin Jay have identified as an epochal change in conceiving vision as a possible means of knowledge and understanding.[103]

Across his writings, Nietzsche shifted between semantic registers of perspectivism, moving from an "unbridled" to a more "circumspect" use of the metaphor, as James Conant has argued.[104] In "On Truth and Lies in a Nonmoral Sense" ("Über Wahrheit und Lüge im außermoralischen Sinne," 1873), Nietzsche emphasized the impossibility of "correct perception" or "pure knowledge" of an external object, undistorted by the subject's cognitive perspective.[105] Nietzsche's early work nonetheless presupposed the possibility of *conceptualizing* "the essence of things," unmediated by forms of human subjectivity—a conceptualization, as he later acknowledged, that would itself be unavoidably perspectival in character.[106] Questioning a fatalistic sense of inescapable confinement within subjective consciousness, Nietzsche restricted the scope of the metaphor and argued for the untenability of the antithesis between the noumenon and phenomenon, or the thing-in-itself (*Ding an sich*) and its perspectival appearance. By *On the Genealogy of Morality* (*Zur Genealogie der Moral*, 1887), Nietzsche called for rethinking the entire conceptual opposition between objectivity and subjectivity, emphasizing their necessary admixture and interaction in the quest for truth. Rather than postulating the existence of an endless multitude of perspectives as an indication of humans' untranscendable epistemic constraints, Nietzsche now invoked the possibility of employing "a *variety* of perspectives and affective interpretations in the service of knowledge."[107]

Nietzsche's theorization of perspectivism raised critical issues for the discipline of history. The advent and metaphorization of Renaissance perspective had prompted increasing reflection on the particularity of the historian's viewpoint. Already in the eighteenth century, Johann Martin Chladenius had recognized the historian's perspectival position as a determining factor in their understanding and interpretation of the past.[108] Whereas Hegel's *Lectures on the Philosophy of World History* (*Vorlesungen über die Philosophie der Weltgeschichte*, 1822–30) had adopted an avowedly omniscient view—"the sum total of all possible perspectives"—Ranke had espoused the more modest, self-effacing ideal of impartial, objective representation, or showing the "naked truth without adornment."[109] Critiquing historicism in both guises, Nietzsche not only denied the existence of a transcendent, supraindividual point of view, but also questioned the assumption of a single, actual history that could be methodically reconstructed. Furthermore, dispelling Hegel's affirmative theodicy and Ranke's optimistic faith in the alliance of ethics and power, Nietzsche instead presented historical reality as the interplay of fallible and value-laden interpretations. Thus, although perspectivism has often been conflated with historicism (both of which seem to have relativist implications), it bears emphasis that Nietzsche's writings destabilized and even undermined the latter's basic tenets, anticipating the crisis of historicism widely diagnosed following the German defeat in World War I.

Emerging contemporaneously with the acute crisis of historical thought, *Caligari* enacts the idea of perspectivism through its narrative and aesthetic features. Wiene's film is intensely preoccupied with how historical accounts are mediated and distorted through subjective consciousness. The first scene alone focuses on an act of first-person narration and deploys multiple iris shots, which highlight the incompleteness of the perspective offered by the individual storyteller and by the camera lens. The film's inner story likewise emphasizes forms of visual and cognitive limitation, with multiple secrets, inexplicable occurrences, and instances in which both the film's characters and its viewers are deceived or denied information—an epistemic instability reduplicated through the film's spatiotemporally indeterminate settings and disorienting, postperspectival set design. The final sequence, which discloses the narrator's unreliability but maintains the Expressionist style, offers neither a detached, stable point of view on the action nor narrative clarification and resolution. Refusing insight into the "actual" course of events, the film's concluding scenes instead suggest a proliferation of incommensurable accounts without an external standard of judgment. Furthermore, denying viewers a definite specification of the identities, ethical commitments, and degrees of sanity of both doctor and patient, the film intimates an interchangeability of roles and even an arbitrariness of institutional power structures.

Abandoning the historicist ideal of unbiased, comprehensive representation, *Caligari* instead stresses the invariable partisanship and epistemic limitations of all accounts. In its skepticism regarding the attainability of pure truth, and in its self-reflexive figuration of all human knowledge as bounded, imprecise, and relative, the film recalls Nicholas of Cusa's doctrine of "learned ignorance [*docta ignorantia*]."[110] However, whereas Nicholas postulated the essential incomprehensibility of an Absolute Being who alone "apprehends what He is," *Caligari* instead follows Nietzsche in confronting the philosophical dilemmas accompanying the proverbial death of God—a death, as Martin Jay emphasizes, that also eradicated the "God's-eye view."[111] *Caligari*, in my analysis, takes up Nietzsche's early invocation of a relativist, subjectivist, and even solipsistic perspectivism, as envisaged in the film's final depiction of the insane asylum, where each patient is radically insular and discrete in assumed identity and worldview. Notably, the multiplicity and incommensurability of different perspectives extend beyond the mise-en-scène to interpellate the film's own viewers, faced with a bewildering array of possible interpretations of the work itself. Wiene's work, as I will demonstrate, thus foregrounds problems of hermeneutics following the detranscendalization and dissolution of Cartesian perspectivalism, whereby all cognizing subjects are implicated as finite, locally conditioned participants within the dynamic process of history.

An interchangeability of roles and arbitrariness of institutional power structures.

A subjectivist, even solipsistic perspectivism.

PROBLEMS OF HERMENEUTICS

Recognizing the threat of relativism faced by the historical sciences, Wilhelm Dilthey adapted the interpretive procedures developed by Friedrich Schleiermacher into a methodology for securing knowledge of the past. In "The Rise of Hermeneutics" ("Die Entstehung der Hermeneutik," 1900), Dilthey conceived a process of understanding (*Verstehen*) through an imaginative reexperiencing (*Nacherleben*) of others' psychic states. In this way, Dilthey wrote, the subjective operations of the observer could "be raised to objective validity."[112] Among the many problems with Dilthey's approach was an assumed homogeneity of exegete and author, or subject and object of research. Appealing to "the substratum of a general human nature" as the basis for interpretation, Dilthey neglected historicism's crucial emphasis on the uniqueness of all sociocultural phenomena and values.[113] Thus, although Dilthey sought to resist what he deemed "the inroads of ... skeptical subjectivity," he failed to offer a satisfactory solution to the aporias of historicist thought, as later formulated by Hans-Georg Gadamer: "how objectivity is possible in relativity and how we are to conceive the relation of the finite to the absolute."[114] Taking up Dilthey's hermeneutic theory, Gadamer emphasized the limited range of vision within the present and the unfeasibility of self-transposition into the past. While postulating the inescapability of tradition and prejudice, Gadamer invoked the potential for historical understanding through an ongoing "fusion of horizons."[115]

For Dilthey, hermeneutics promised not only to avert historicism's relativist implications, but also to delineate humanistic inquiry from an imperialist positivism. An innovator of *Lebensphilosophie* (philosophy of life) in the late nineteenth century, Dilthey distinguished the dynamic sphere of human activity from the inanimate objects of natural-scientific research, positing life itself as the foundation of the human sciences. Countering the theory of phenomenalism, which denied the distinction between appearances and essences, Dilthey described the object of the human sciences as "an inner reality, a coherence experienced from within," and he identified the goal of hermeneutics as that of surpassing an author's own self-understanding, as per the "doctrine of unconscious creation."[116] Furthermore, emphasizing the interpreter's immersion in their very sphere of investigation, Dilthey problematized the separation of facts from judgments and also eliminated the distance between the observer and the objective world; whereas the scientific method had facilitated the amassing of facts based on neutral, disinterested apprehension, Dilthey sought meaningful truth through a more holistic, projective act of interpretation. Finally, in contrast to positivism, which lacked reflexivity regarding the observer's subjective consciousness, Dilthey characterized understanding and interpretation as "active in life itself," and he envisaged the process of historical reconstruction (*Nachbildung*) as a means of self-knowledge.[117]

Caligari followed Dilthey and other philosophers of life in critiquing positivism, challenging the privileged relation that it had presumed between vision and knowledge. Wiene's film perpetually reveals the epistemic insufficiency of external signs, featuring figures who deceive sensory perception, assume alternate names or identities, are driven by obsessive ideas, or are even unaware of their own actions. While highlighting modes of observation and surveillance involved in detective work, the film emphasizes the fallibility and manipulability of visual evidence as well as its inadequacy for determining motives—as when a man is wrongfully accused of the murders in Holstenwall due to his possession of a knife (with which he had hoped to divert suspicion for an attempted homicide), or when Francis unwittingly watches Cesare's dummy for hours while the actual somnambulist abducts Jane. The film also confounds basic temporal and ontological boundaries between the researcher and the object of investigation; in a flashback within the inner story, the asylum director reads an eighteenth-century chronicle of Dr. Caligari and is compelled not only to reenact the doctor's murderous experiments, but also to "become Caligari." Though Francis and the asylum's doctors later unmask the director after scrutinizing his book and diary, the film's concluding scenes disclose the dubiousness of Francis's own story, thus undermining spectators' assumptions based on the entire preceding action.

Insofar as *Caligari* unsettles attempts to ascertain knowledge on the basis of written accounts, it also destabilizes central tenets of Dilthey's hermeneutic theory. Much as the narrative's unsolvable mysteries thwart an optimism regarding the ultimate attainability of truth, the film's own vicissitudinous history of distribution and exhibition disrupts a philological concentration on "fixed and relatively permanent expressions of life," revealing contingencies and discontinuities in the passage from a work's creator(s) to its present-day exegete.[118] The century since *Caligari*'s premiere has witnessed the circulation of prints varying significantly in length, music, intertitles, and coloration along with the proliferation of spurious, often-contradictory claims regarding the film's authorship, production process, and political meanings. Important discoveries (e.g., the screenplay, a tinted nitrate copy) over the past decades have dispelled numerous legends about the film and have also facilitated more precise, historically grounded readings. In my analysis, however, the unreflexive historicism of much research on *Caligari* is at odds with the film's own pointed critique of nineteenth-century historical methodology. If, as I have sought to demonstrate, *Caligari* rejects a naive objectivism and abandons the historicist quest for comprehensive representation, the film renders one new film historian's recent encyclopedic effort to document "the true story behind its creation" a rather ironic undertaking.[119]

Caligari emerged at a time when the German historicist tradition was entering a state of acute and widely diagnosed crisis, and the film, I have argued, engaged with contemporaneous metahistorical debates, offering aesthetic responses to ontological, epistemological, and historiographical questions of the philosophy of history. Dismissing the Rankean ideal of faithfully and impartially reconstructing the past, or showing *"wie es eigentlich gewesen," Caligari* instead followed Nietzsche in envisioning historical reality as the interplay of finite, locally conditioned interpretations. This perspectivist view corresponded with the insights of Einstein's theory of relativity, which superseded Newton's ideas of absolute time and space, provoking an epochal shift, as George Herbert Mead later wrote, from assuming "an absolute world of reality of which perspectives are partial presentations" to conceiving another possibility: that of "a universe consisting of perspectives."[120] Einstein's theory implicated individuals as participants in their very realm of observation, suggesting a more interactive, spatiotemporally dynamic relationship between the cognizing subject and the object of cognition. Enacting this new mode of relationality through its unnerving, enigmatic narrative and Expressionist, postperspectival style, Wiene's *Caligari* helped herald an age of self-conscious uncertainty—an age, as Werner Heisenberg would write, aware of the impossibility of any "sharp separation between the world and the I."[121]

4. Metaphysics of Death
Destiny

> But then what does it mean, "the end of metaphysics"? It means the historical moment in which *the essential possibilities* of metaphysics are exhausted.
>
> MARTIN HEIDEGGER

> Death irremediably exceeds the resources of a metaphysics of the subject.
>
> JEAN-LUC NANCY

"Who we are and when we actually live, no one knows to this day. Darker still is how and where we then go; the dying leave, as what?"[1] Ernst Bloch raised these existential questions at the outset of "The Motif of the Gate" ("Das Tor-Motiv"), a text included in his 1930 collection *Traces* (*Spuren*). Because our ultimate destination as humans is both unknown and inconceivable, Bloch wrote, our transition to the realm of death is often represented via doors, gateways, or portals. Bloch observed the peculiar effect of this motif as it appears in images and stories, and he recalled "the tremendous impression that even a pure film could make with the motif of the gate."[2] The film, recognizable as Fritz Lang's *Destiny* (*Der müde Tod*, or "The weary death"), received Bloch's praise for its "deeper direction," which moves beyond "the trivial feat of cinema" and brings "to consciousness the lethal ur-symbol of the *gate*."[3]

Bloch was not the first commentator to distinguish Lang's film for its profound inner workings. In fact, shortly after the film's premiere at Berlin's Mozartsaal and Union Theater Kurfürstendamm on October 6, 1921, a critic for *Vorwärts* wrote, "There is a great line of deep seriousness and philosophical, even religious thinking running through the film."[4] This intellectual strand was similarly observed in France, where Lang's film was released the following year under the title *Les trois lumières* ("The three lights"). A reviewer for *Ciné-Journal* described the film as "a *powerful work*, deeply human and with a truly moving lyricism, in which philosophy happily unites with a world of romantic mysticism."[5] In *Le Matin*, the film was noted for "its exceptional execution and the curious philosophical thesis behind it."[6]

The motif of the gate.

Destiny was thus celebrated in Bloch's text and the initial appraisals for demonstrating film's capacity to serve as a medium of thought. That this capacity was far from axiomatic is evidenced by other commentators' categorical dismissals of the work as well as fellow filmmakers' reflections on its influence and legacy.[7] René Clair wrote in 1922 that *Destiny*, following Robert Wiene's *The Cabinet of Dr. Caligari* (1920), heralded a "cerebral cinema" whose mise-en-scène "forms a whole in the mastery of which the intellect takes delight."[8] And, in a 1937 article, Georges Franju characterized Lang as "constantly . . . dreaming of a higher kind of justice and balance," and identified *Destiny* as a "philosophical work" in which the director "first posed the eternal problem represented by the scales."[9]

If *Destiny* is positioned within Lang's oeuvre as the earliest of the director's fully realized works—or, in Tom Gunning's words, "the first example of Lang's completely developed system"—its status as such cannot be attributed to the film's narrative and aesthetic features alone.[10] *Destiny* certainly synthesized thematic and dramaturgical elements of Lang's initial efforts and continued his collaboration with screenwriter Thea von Harbou, producer Erich Pommer, and actors Lil Dagover and Rudolf Klein-Rogge as well as costume or set designers Walter Röhrig, Heinrich Umlauff, and

Hermann Warm. Yet beyond its "complex meditation on cinematic narration," *Destiny* gained distinction for probing the nexus between film and philosophy.[11]

PHILOSOPHY OF DEATH

"Could the spiritual not be photographed? Could thoughts not be expressed in images?"[12] Raised by Carlo Mierendorff in his programmatic essay "If I Only Had the Cinema!" ("Hätte ich das Kino!," 1920), these questions were increasingly considered in relation to cinema during the Weimar period. As I argued in the previous chapter, Wiene's *Caligari* not only introduced Expressionist aesthetics to film, but also demonstrated the medium's potential to engage with fundamental questions of the philosophy of history. In *The Film till Now* (1930), Paul Rotha distinguished Wiene's film for breaking with photographic realism and, more significantly, for engaging viewers psychologically: "What *The Cabinet of Dr. Caligari* did ... was to attract to the cinema audience many people who had hitherto regarded a film as the low watermark of intelligence."[13] With a common producer (Pommer), actors (Dagover, Klein-Rogge), and set designers (Röhrig, Warm), *Destiny* further explored the ability of film, in Lang's own words, "to photograph *thoughts*, that is, render them visually."[14]

More tenuous in its relation to Expressionism than *Caligari*, *Destiny* also took up a distinct set of philosophical issues linked to the early-twentieth-century crisis of historicism.[15] In "Science as a Vocation" ("Wissenschaft als Beruf," 1919), Max Weber argued that the process of intellectualist rationalization had not only led to the "disenchantment of the world," but also yielded a sense of continuous, infinite progress—one that highlighted the provisional nature of all human phenomena and raised "the problem of whether or not death is a meaningful phenomenon."[16] Such a concern with human transience was common to German-speaking intellectuals such as Bloch, Sigmund Freud, Georg Simmel, Walter Benjamin, and Martin Heidegger, and it gained urgency following a devastating world war and a global influenza pandemic with an even greater death toll than the coronavirus of our own time.[17]

Emerging in the immediate aftermath of these cataclysms, *Destiny* is animated by a series of questions regarding human finitude: Is death a matter of pure contingency, or does it acquire meaning through a sacrificial logic of symbolic redemption? Does death mark the ultimate test of human courage and resolution, or is it driven by fate and thereby unamenable to human control? What is the relation between acknowledging one's own mortality and grappling with the death of another? And how does one link an individual death to the survival of the community: is the death of the one necessary to allow for the regeneration of the many? The responses to these questions in Weimar Germany have informed theorizations of death over the past century. Jean-Luc Nancy would later contend that the community—defined in terms of relational being, or Heideggerian *Mitsein*—reveals itself through, and is calibrated on, the individual member's death, which is otherwise threatened with insignificance in the modern world.[18]

Lang's *Destiny*, as I will argue, is concerned with the status of the singular death in a period at "the end of metaphysics" (Heidegger), in which faith in the meaning and coherence of history had been irrevocably shattered.[19] Whereas nineteenth-century historicism had treated every epoch as "immediate to God," in Leopold von Ranke's famous words, *Destiny* advances a negative philosophy of history, presenting each epoch instead as *immediate to death*.[20] Registering the collapse of historicism into relativism in the postwar years, the film intervened in concurrent philosophical debates by indicating that the very inevitability of death remains an eternal and ubiquitous truth—or, as Nancy would write, that "finitude alone is communitarian."[21] In this way, the film contributed to the theorization of finitude that characterized Weimar intellectual and cultural life, and also anticipated an argument made by Lang's friend Theodor W. Adorno: "That metaphysics is no longer possible becomes the ultimate metaphysics."[22]

POETICS OF ANALOGY

Questions of metaphysics moved to the fore during a period of acute crisis and change. As German intellectuals witnessed a cataclysmic and bewildering succession of early-twentieth-century events, they reexamined the philosophical premises of traditional historiography and historical thought. Whereas German Idealism had upheld a basic optimism regarding the directionality and purposiveness of the historical process, Weimar intellectual currents betrayed disillusionment with the course of history as well as skepticism of history's status as the site of logos and meaning. At the outset of his two-volume *The Decline of the West* (*Der Untergang des Abendlandes*, 1918 and 1922), Oswald Spengler asked: "Is there a logic of history? Is there, beyond all the casual and incalculable elements of the separate events, something that we may call a metaphysical structure of historic humanity, something that is essentially independent of the outward forms—social, spiritual and political—which we see so clearly?"[23] While Spengler's work recalled philosophies of world history from the late eighteenth and early nineteenth centuries, it sharply diverged from their teleological claims and efforts at universal synthesis. In place of a progressive and unified conception of the historical process, Spengler advanced a morphological theory of recurring, organic cycles of cultural development.[24]

Though exerting a massive impact on Weimar thought and culture, Spengler's work—marked as it was by historical determinism and tragic fatalism—was also criticized by an extended lineage of philosophers including Adorno, Heidegger, Georg Lukács, Otto Neurath, Karl Popper, and Siegfried Kracauer.[25] In his posthumously published *History: The Last Things before the Last* (1969), Kracauer argued that while Spengler improved upon nineteenth-century historical thought by dismissing the postulate of a single, unilinear temporal continuum, he failed to conceptualize an alternative medium of time in which diverse cultures might commonly develop and interact. Kracauer also faulted Spengler for perpetuating the deterministic equation of history with a static, lawful nature as well as for forming "irrelevant analogies" between the achievements of various cultures, here detached from their specific contexts.[26] Notably, whereas Spengler developed a Goethean method of analogy to "understand living forms" and to "la[y] bare the organic structure of history," Kracauer drew analogies with photographic media to comprehend a historical reality that he characterized as contingent, seemingly endless, and indeterminate in meaning.[27] Likening historians to photographers and filmmakers in their engagement with the "raw material" of a Husserlian *Lebenswelt* (lifeworld), Kracauer found a counterpart to historiographical narratives in "episodic films," with each segment "emerging from, and again disappearing in, the flow of life."[28]

Lang's *Destiny*, in my analysis, joined Spengler in critiquing the historicist postulation of a continuous and unilinear temporal flow, and also followed the thinker in espousing alternative conceptions of cyclicality and recurrence. In Lang's film, the figure of Death (Bernhard Goetzke) offers a maiden (Lil Dagover) the chance to reconvene with her lover (Walter Janssen) by saving the life of someone in an Arab caliphate, Renaissance Venice, or imperial China. Episodes in these three settings not only depict similar narratives of forbidden love and untimely loss, but also reveal equivalences in length (one reel) and the casting of lead actors (Dagover, Goetzke, Janssen); in their organization around ritual ceremonies or celebrations (Ramadan, Carnival, the Chinese emperor's birthday); and in their use of particular geometrical shapes and structures (pointed arches, bridges, walls, staircases) within the mise-en-scène. Thus, in diametrical opposition

A visual poetics of parallelism and analogy.

to nineteenth-century historicism, which treated each state and epoch as individual and unique ("immediate to God"), Lang's film conveys a visual poetics of parallelism and analogy, emphasizing transhistorical affinities and commonalities rather than distinct inner principles. In its disregard for temporal distinction, the film recalls historical paintings such as Albrecht Altdorfer's *The Battle of Alexander at Issus* (*Die Alexanderschlacht*, 1528–29), which, as Reinhart Koselleck has argued, consciously deployed anachronism and encompassed past and present within a common plane.[29]

With its parallelist narrative form, Lang's film also follows an aesthetic trajectory of episode films (*Episodenfilme*) that includes Luigi Maggi's *Satan* (*Satana*, 1912), D. W. Griffith's *Intolerance* (1916), Joe May's *Veritas vincit* (1918), Friedrich Wilhelm Murnau's *Satan* (*Satanas*, 1920), and Carl Theodor Dreyer's *Leaves from Satan's Book* (*Blade af Satans bog*, 1921). Partitioned into episodes that leap across world-historical space and time, these far-reaching spectacles not only take up early cinema's "encyclopedic ambition" as well as the promise of film to serve as a universal language, but also deploy formal devices and stylistic motifs to articulate broader philosophies of history.[30] In *Destiny*, Death's imposing and impenetrable graveyard wall is both a spatiotemporal and an ontological boundary, and the portal that the maiden enters functions as a passageway into distant and even transcendental realms, with a flight of steps recalling the biblical motif of Jacob's Ladder. Like the Whitmanian tableau of the Woman Who Rocks the Cradle in *Intolerance*, the Grimmian hall of flames into which Death takes the maiden offers an intermediary space for metaphysical and metahistorical meditation, with each burning candle representing an individual life within world history. As with the crosscutting in Griffith's film, the adjacency of the candles establishes homology across different periods, thereby postulating a historical ontology outside the framework of continuous, linear chronology.

TIME AND NARRATIVE

"Can one narrate time—time as such, in and of itself?"[31] Self-reflexively asked in chapter 7 of Thomas Mann's *The Magic Mountain* (*Der Zauberberg*, 1924), this question signaled a new awareness of time as an essential element of both narration and life within Weimar modernism. Advancing a shift away from the Idealist tradition, Heidegger and others posited historicity, finitude, and isolation as basic, inescapable conditions of human existence, exhibiting a mode of thought that Peter Eli Gordon has termed "philosophical expressionism."[32] In section 2, chapter 1, of *Being and Time*, in which Heidegger develops an existential concept of death, he writes that because one's transition from existence (*Dasein*) to death (*Nichtmehrdasein*) is outside one's realm of possible experience and understanding, the death of another is all the more striking. While another's death lends one "objective" access to "an end of Da-sein [*Beendigung des Daseins*]," it nonetheless fails to provide the actual experience of having died (*Zuendegekommensein*).[33] Not only is one thus unable to experience the dying of another in a genuine sense; one also cannot relieve another of their dying, as this self-sacrifice merely defers the other's still-certain death. In this zero-sum game in which no death is substitutable or avoidable, one confronts the ontological constitution of death through "mineness and existence [*Jemeinigkeit und Existenz*]" as well as the limits of comprehension and representability.[34]

As a nonbypassable boundary of one's experience of being in the world, death serves as an organizing principle of both time and narrative. Challenging the emphasis on the mortal individual rather than the enduring community in *Being and Time*, Paul Ricoeur observes that in Heidegger's analytic of time, the act of *Wiederholen* (repetition, recollection) returns historicity to an originary temporal structure, mediating between the finitude of each life and the endlessness of natural and human history. Extending this concept of repetition to questions of narrativity, Ricoeur argues that Odyssean tales, which often involve a return to a point of origin, imbricate two qualities of time: "the circularity of the imaginary travel and the linearity of the quest as such."[35] Writing within a more psychoanalytical framework, Laura Mulvey identifies the trope of death as a common and overdetermined means of bringing filmic narratives to a halt.[36] Since film is a time-based medium that involves the reproduction and repetition of still images—the moving image eternally preserves mortal bodies via a "mummification of change" (Bazin)—narrative closure in death returns both the characters and the filmic form itself to a primary state of inanimacy.[37] In Mulvey's analysis, films that conclude with a "human end" conflate stillness with the loss of life, and thereby mark death as a point "beyond narratability."[38]

Lang's *Destiny* resists the mortal limits of time through patterns of repetition. Alongside films ranging from *Intolerance* to Tom Tykwer's *Run Lola Run* (*Lola rennt*, 1998), *Destiny* dramatizes a woman's effort to avert the severing of her lover's "cord of life"—a suspenseful endeavor that is linked to the possibility of outpacing, ceasing, or even reversing the movement of time. To entertain this revolutionary possibility, Lang (like Griffith and Tykwer) breaks the ceaseless forward motion of cinematic time into successive episodes, thereby shaping a linear temporal continuum into cyclical patterns. In *Destiny*, the maiden attempts to usurp the sovereignty of Death through a suicidal gesture that stops the clock—and, with it, the progression of narrative time—at 11 p.m. The maiden receives three chances to rescue a single life before its flame is extinguished, as well as a final "eleventh hour" to find someone willing to exchange their life for that of her lover. Nevertheless, the three spatiotemporal settings to which she travels become the loci of repeated narratives of separation and loss, and the townspeople whose lives she requests give a common response: "Not one day—Not one hour—Not one breath!!" Furthermore, the figure of Death perpetually appears in threefold repetition, finding triple allegorical-emblematic representation (alongside a skeleton and hourglass) in an early scene at the Golden Unicorn (*Goldenen Einhorn*), and also materializing in each of the film's central episodes. In contrast to Griffith's and Tykwer's films, *Destiny* eliminates the element of contingency from its parallel or alternate narrative scenarios, denying the possibility of repetition with a difference.

While deploying repetitive patterns to engage with the limits of mortal life, *Destiny* also thus emphasizes the abiding, inevitable quality of death. Lang's fairy-tale-like film, which leaves its characters, time, and place

A visual quotation of Gustav Spangenberg's *Der Zug des Todes* (1876).

unidentified ("somewhere and sometime [*irgendwo und irgendwann*]"), draws from a Brothers Grimm *Märchen* entitled "Godfather Death" ("Der Gevatter Tod," 1812), wherein Death introduces itself to a destitute father: "I am Death, and I make all equal [*Ich bin der Tod, der alle gleich macht*]."[39] The film substantiates Death's egalitarian epithet by stressing the common *Todesangst* among townspeople, including the elderly, poor, and infirm, as well as by visually quoting Gustav Spangenberg's painting *The Train of Death* (*Der Zug des Todes*, 1876), in which a grieving widow observes a procession of spirits, with figures of varying age and social rank. In Lang's film, the maiden's quest places her experience of loss into perspective by replaying her story under conditions of rigid social barriers (gender, religion, caste) and unjust imperial rule—a perspective also signified by the film's extreme contrasts of scale, as when the maiden is towered over by the graveyard wall. Similarly, through her encounters with a baby in the hall of flames and the village hospital at the film's close, the maiden considers her fiancé's premature death against an even graver prospect: the loss of one's child. Lang's film, which ultimately denies the possibility of recouping a deceased lover through substitution, upholds a Heideggerian economy of death, wherein mortality is an equalizing and inescapable force. Responding

Natality and mortality.

to the pervasive awareness of death in the early Weimar years, the film consolingly affirms its sovereignty in all historical periods and regimes.

THE WORK OF MOURNING

A ubiquitous awareness of death formed the historical backdrop for Sigmund Freud's diagnosis of the psychic operations of mourning in a series of texts composed during and after the Great War. In "Mourning and Melancholia" ("Trauer und Melancholie," 1917), Freud differentiated mourning from a more unconscious and pathological mode of reacting to loss. According to Freud, the condition of mourning is commonly overcome after "a certain lapse of time," at the end of which one's ego succeeds in releasing the libido from a lost object and displacing it onto another.[40] By contrast, melancholia entails a withdrawal of the libido into the ego as well as an identification of the ego with the lost object; cathectic attachment is thus replaced by identification, and "object-loss" transmutes into "ego-loss."[41] In his later *The Ego and the Id* (*Das Ich und das Es*, 1923), Freud wrote that the process of identification attributed to melancholia may in fact be the only condition under which the id is able to relinquish objects. Revising his earlier assessment of mourning as a discrete and temporary condition, Freud emphasized the frequency and formative influence of the identificatory process, and described the character of the ego as the "precipitate" of relinquished attachments—a repository of the "history" of past object choices.[42]

The relation between mourning and history also figured centrally in Walter Benjamin's study of the German *Trauerspiel* (play of mourning). In *Origin of the German Trauerspiel* (*Ursprung des deutschen Trauerspiels*, 1928), Benjamin criticized aestheticians' tendency to conflate the sixteenth- and seventeenth-century *Trauerspiel* with classical tragedy—a tendency guided by the false assumption that tragedy is not "a historically restricted form."[43] Among the major distinguishing features of the *Trauerspiel*, according to Benjamin, is indeed its engagement with history; unlike Greek tragedy, the object of which is myth, the *Trauerspiel* finds its content in "historical life" (resonating with Ernst Cassirer's differentiation of historical and mythical time in volume 2 of *Philosophy of Symbolic Forms* [*Philosophie der symbolischen Formen*, 1925]).[44] Benjamin associated the baroque *Trauerspiel* with an allegorical form of expression, which he defined in contradistinction to the symbol: "Whereas in the symbol, with the sublimation of downfall, the transfigured countenance of nature reveals itself fleetingly in the light of salvation, in allegory there lies before the eyes of the observer the *facies hippocratica* of history as petrified primal landscape."⁴⁵ In other words, rather than espousing a theodicy of natural destruction, allegory fixates more unforgivingly on the power of death, conveying a saturnine, ruinous vision of history as the locus of eternal transience and inexorable decay. Benjamin observed aspects of baroque spiritual tumult in his own historical moment, and also noted analogies between the *Trauerspiel* and contemporary German Expressionist drama.

Lang's *Destiny* shares with the baroque *Trauerspiel* morbid preoccupations, allegorical-emblematic forms of expression, and exotic and imperial themes. Depicting Death in a black cloak and top hat as well as with a skeleton-adorned scepter (with notable similarities to Victor Sjöström's *The Phantom Carriage* [*Körkarlen*, 1921]), the film references the late-medieval allegory of death as the scythe-bearing Grim Reaper (*Sensenmann, Schnitter Tod*, or *Gevatter Tod*). This anthropomorphic figure, anticipated in ancient mythology by Chronos (the Greek god of time) and Saturn (the Roman god of agriculture), came to connote the finite temporality of one's being in the world—or, in Benjamin's words, "the inexorable passage of every life toward death."⁴⁶ Literalizing the metaphor that "death is after you," the figure of "The Weary Death" in Lang's film halts the woman and her fiancé as they ride into the village, enters their carriage, and follows them into the Golden Unicorn. Positioned vis-à-vis the couple, Death becomes associated with the uncanny vision of an hourglass, an object famously represented in Albrecht Dürer's 1514 engraving *Melencolia I* (itself the subject of a 1923 monograph by Erwin Panofsky and Fritz Saxl).⁴⁷ Emblematizing the relentless movement and finitude of time, the trickling hourglass functions as a memento mori—a function likewise performed in *Destiny* by the ticking clock in the German village, the burning candles in the hall of flames, and the shriveling magic wand in China. As the film's protagonist travels to exotic locales, entering Shakespearean tales of tyrannical rule and courtly intrigue, she is perpetually reminded of the irrevocability of death and the transience of each human life.

In depicting the maiden's confrontation with mortal finitude, Lang's film also reactivates a fifteenth-century motif that regained prominence in Romantic and Expressionist art: that of Death and the Maiden. This erotically charged Renaissance motif, which emerged from the late-medieval allegory of the Dance of Death (*Totentanz*), was also prefigured in Greek mythology by Hades's abduction of Persephone and by the conflict between Eros and Thanatos—figures whom Freud identified with the two classes of human instincts.⁴⁸ As the maiden in Lang's film takes sanctuary in the village apothecary, she encounters a verse from the Song of Solomon that likens these two forces: "Set me as a seal upon thine heart, / As a seal upon thine arm, / For love is strong as death / Passion is cruel as the grave; / It blazes up like blazing fire, / Fiercer than any flame" (8:6). Addressed by a bride to her groom, this biblical verse conveys love's superlative strength through analogy with the personified figure of infernal Death.[49] In Lang's film, the verse fuels the maiden's belief in the triumphant power of Eros and impels her quasi-suicidal attempt to reunite with her fiancé. Throughout her Orphean quest, however, she finds that her beloved's life—like the procession of spirits and the flickering flames—is ephemeral, evanescent, and susceptible to Death's extinguishing power. Only the blazing hospital fire at the film's close becomes the occasion for reconciling Eros and Thanatos in the form of a *Liebestod*.

NEW WORLDVIEWS

The vanishing of stable meaning systems gave rise to the longing for a cohesive *Weltanschauung*, as Hermann Hesse expressed in a 1926 article. Alongside the German academic "mandarins" discussed by Fritz Ringer, including Wilhelm Dilthey, Max Weber, and Ernst Troeltsch, Hesse recognized a primary ramification of the nineteenth-century emphasis on the impermanent and unfixed aspects of life: the threat of relativism.[50] Evoking the social and spiritual upheaval that followed industrialization and modern technological war, Hesse lamented the undermining of cultural foundations that had once seemed enduring and indestructible. In Hesse's analysis, civic and religious ideals had been replaced by fashionable ephemera, and humankind's ongoing metaphysical needs were now exploited by "seers and founders; charlatans and quacks."[51] Nevertheless, Hesse lauded the younger generation's quest to locate new sources of meaning, which ranged from irrational spiritualism to genuine philosophy, from primitive mysticism to newly developing religions. Among these sources, Hesse listed Reformed theology, Catholic revivalism, and neo-Hasidism; American Christian Science and English theosophy; anthroposophy and the School of Wisdom; Mazdaznan and neo-Sufism; and, finally, translations of Buddhist and Chinese texts.

Hesse's own fascination with Eastern sources, which found expression in literary works such as *Fairy Tales* (*Märchen*, 1919) and *Siddhartha* (1922), was shared by Béla Balázs, who published Chinese fairy tales in the collections *Seven Tales* (*Hét mese*, 1918) and *The Cloak of Dreams* (*Der Mantel der Träume*, 1922).[52] However, whereas Hesse celebrated the renewed vitality of spiritual forces in the postwar years, Balázs directed attention to an emergent cultural institution that rivaled or even surpassed religion in the extent of its public appeal. In *Visible Man* (*Der sichtbare Mensch*, 1924), Balázs contended that cinema—"*the popular art* of our century"—now provided the source from which "the spirit of the people arises."[53] Designating his text as an "essay on the *philosophy of the art of film*," Balázs sought to theorize the powerful new medium's unique aesthetic possibilities.[54] While characterizing film as a "surface art" comprising images and gestural language, Balázs nonetheless praised cinematic efforts to achieve "literary 'depth'" through a "third, intellectual dimension"—one that extends beyond the visible action.[55] As exemplars of such efforts, Balázs cited recent films with "parallel plots," in which actors play the same roles across various historical periods or social strata.[56] For Balázs, these combinatory works revealed meaning "at the points of intersection between different destinies" and thus demonstrated the possibility of creating "films with a world view."[57]

Using a grief-stricken maiden as its envoy, Lang's *Destiny* joined Hesse's and Balázs's postwar literary texts in exploring wide-ranging and distant loci of signification. In its opening reels, the film alludes to spiritualist, occultist, and religious discourses, as represented in the mise-en-scène by the procession of spirits, village apothecary, and biblical verse, and it also prominently features the local cemetery and garden, or what Michel Foucault would later classify as "heterotopias" (along with the honeymoon trip and the cinema itself, according to his spatial typology).[58] Outside of the village, exotic locations in the Near East, Italy, and China not only provide grounds for visual attractions, sensual indulgence, and fantastic or uncanny themes, but also offer alternative structures of temporality and narration. Much as the film leaves the spatiotemporal coordinates of the village unspecified, it refuses to contextualize the three settings, thereby frustrating historicist frameworks of chronology and causality. Like Richard Oswald's *Uncanny Stories* (*Unheimliche Geschichten*, 1919) and Paul Leni's later *Waxworks* (*Das Wachsfigurenkabinett*, 1924), Lang's film adopts the nonlinear, episodic form of the *One Thousand and One Nights* (whose fairy tales Balázs envisaged in 1923 as "the most ideal film material"), with a frame narrative that contains a succession of stories.[59] As with the *Arabian Nights,* in which Scheherazade regales the Persian king with serialized tales, the repetitive and self-conscious act of storytelling serves as a means of engaging with tyrannical rule as well as a strategy for deferring and resisting the curse of death.

In addition to offering alternative temporal and narrative frameworks, *Destiny*'s disparate locations evince forces that extend across sociohistorical periods and regimes. The film's broadly and often-offensively caricatured premodern settings—the "old German" village and the three foreign realms—are characterized by constancy and invariance, with long-standing rulers, fixed hierarchies, and habitual ceremonies or religious rituals.[60] In *Destiny*, the static temporality of these powers is undermined through forces (romantic love, mortality) that transgress established social and metaphysical boundaries as well as through modernist techniques that distort the shapes of narrative and cinematic time. Death's initial arrival in the village is represented through a flashback that both precedes the narrative's parameters and reverses its developmental flow, and the maiden's quest to retrieve her lover punctures and dilates the narrative action, pausing the clock at 11 p.m. While such moments mark breaks or even revolutionary ruptures in the narrative frame, the discontinuities themselves become integral to the film's broader historical-philosophical claims. Appearing shortly after a world war and a global pandemic, Lang's film sought to assimilate the anarchic, seemingly nonsensical phenomena of world history into a cohesive vision. The film's spatiotemporal settings served as common sites of suffering and loss, revealing the figure of Death as a universal and enduring force of reckoning.

PERPETUAL STRANGERS

The apparent nonsensicality of history was a key concern of Theodor Lessing, who addressed it in conjunction with the dilemmas of the Jewish people's situation. Writing in 1929, Lessing alluded to pervasive and ongoing forms of persecution faced by the group as well as its unremitting sense of "insecurity and uncertainty."[61] With reference to recent unrest between Arabs and Zionists in Mandatory Palestine, Lessing bemoaned that even a national solution to the perennial "Jewish question" now seemed untenable. Extending the argument of his 1919 book *History as Giving Meaning to the Meaningless* (*Geschichte als Sinngebung des Sinnlosen*), Lessing posited anti-Semitism as an attempt to lend retrospective meaning to the senseless and unjustifiable occurrences of Jewish history, effectively attributing guilt or moral responsibility to Jews for their own "hopeless, irredeemable suffering."[62] In Lessing's view, Jews tended to condone and even encourage this mode of inculpation—a tendency he linked to their abiding belief in fate or providential intentionality as operative forces within an otherwise unbearable *Leidensgeschichte* (history of suffering). Lessing emphasized that the group's pattern of interpreting wrongful injuries as self-incurred penalties was unhealthy and even pathological. Popularizing a term from Anton Kuh's *Jews and Germans* (*Juden und Deutsche*, 1921), he famously diagnosed this phenomenon as "Jewish self-hatred."[63]

Jewish people's contested and even self-negating position within German culture was often negotiated via the topos of the Orient. Regarded as "Asiatic refugees" (Christian Wilhelm von Dohm), Central European Jews actively embraced and perpetuated their Oriental associations in the nineteenth century, most notably in the philological-historical scholarship of Abraham Geiger, Heinrich Graetz, and Ignaz Goldziher as well as in the Moorish architecture of Reform synagogues.[64] In a dialectical turn, these associations became integral to the anti-Semitic discourses propagated by figures such as Heinrich von Treitschke and Werner Sombart, the latter of whom typified the group in 1911 as an "Oriental people among Northern races."[65] While many Jews responded to increasing racism by deemphasizing or even disavowing their Semitic roots, a small minority represented their status as social pariahs through the proxy of Orientalist themes. Distinct from the imperial enterprises and art nouveau exoticism famously analyzed by Edward Said, such "Jewish Orientalism" served instead, in John Efron's words, as "a profound expression of [Jews'] own cultural anxiety and insecurity."[66] This strand of Orientalism figured directly in the cultural Zionist texts of Martin Buber (e.g., "The Spirit of the Orient and Judaism" ["Der Geist des Orients und das Judentum," 1912]), and can also be traced more obliquely in various works of aesthetic modernism. Commenting on the Chinese motifs in Gustav Mahler's *Das Lied von der Erde* (*The Song of the Earth*, 1908–9), Theodor W. Adorno identified the Orient as "a cover for Mahler's Jewish element," his exoticism "a prelude to emigration."[67]

Alongside contemporaneous modernist works, Lang's *Destiny* encodes the fraught positionality of Jews within its broader thematization of alterity and nonbelonging. The film focuses on a plethora of outsider characters, including the couple visiting the German village, the Frank in the Near East, and the figure of Death itself, whom the townspeople identify as "The Stranger [*Der Fremde*]"—an appellation that recalls the eponymous subject of Georg Simmel's 1908 essay.[68] Like the paradigmatic stranger of Simmel's text—the European Jew—Death is a lone traveler, unbound by "established ties of kinship, locality, or occupation," who initially enters the village through an economic transaction (a trope that reappears in other Weimar films, including *Caligari* and Murnau's *Nosferatu* [1922], where foreign, uncanny figures acquire property and cause deaths in premodern German towns).[69] Immediately purchasing a plot of land adjoining the village graveyard, Death follows the historical settling patterns of Jews in provincial Germany, as described by Werner Cahnman: "Wherever Jews came, the first thing which they negotiated, after the terms of settlement had been fixed, was the acquisition of a burial ground."[70] Characterized as weary from extensive traveling and subject to a higher power ("alpha and omega," or Jesus Christ), the personage of the Weary Death in Lang's film bears ironic affinities with the mythical figure of Ahasverus, the Wandering Jew (*Der ewige Jude*), from medieval Christian folklore. In a discussion of Ahasverus in *History: The Last Things before the Last*, Kracauer suggested that only this immortal and unredeemed figure would bear reliable, firsthand knowledge of epochal developments and transitions, his grotesque and ever-transmogrifying face(s) belying the historicist postulate of cross-temporal homogeneity and coherence.[71]

As a means of emphasizing the enduring and uncanny foreignness of Death along with the figure's unboundedness to any particular space or time, *Destiny* also synthesizes German folk tradition with Orientalist motifs. Subtitled *A German Folk Song in Six Verses* (*Ein deutsches Volkslied in sechs Versen*), Lang's film adopts the repetitive patterns and strophic rhythm of a Romantic volkslied, with intertitles written in stanzaic form, idiomatic fonts, and a vernacular tone. In combining this folk element with exotic themes, Lang's film resonates with the late work of Gustav Mahler, who—like Hanns Eisler, Arnold Schönberg, and Anton Webern in subsequent years—composed settings of ancient Far Eastern poems translated into German by Hans Bethge. The film shares with Mahler's *Das Lied von der Erde* a sextuple form, exotic stylistic principle, global scope, and preoccupation with themes of loss, isolation, and mortality. Mahler's six-song cycle concludes with "Der Abschied" ("The Farewell"), in which a lone girl stands outside at dusk, waiting to bid a last farewell to her vanished lover. Much as the balladic intertitles in Lang's film draw an analogy between the cyclical course of human life and the recurrent passage of the seasons, the final words of Mahler's "song-symphony" invoke an eternal nature's omnipresent regeneration: "The beloved earth everywhere blossoms and greens in springtime / Anew. Everywhere and forever the distances brighten blue! / Forever . . . forever . . ."[72]

THE PROBLEM OF FATE

"What fears and hopes swept Germany immediately after World War I?"[73] Kracauer posed this question in the introduction to his influential 1947 book *From Caligari to Hitler*. In a chapter entitled "Destiny," Kracauer argued that the postwar German imagination—exploring only the possibilities of tyranny and anarchy, both of which appeared "pregnant with doom"—made recourse to an "ancient concept of fate," as evidenced by Lang's films from the early 1920s.[74] For Kracauer, Lang's *Destiny* aligned tyrannical actions with the workings of Providence, valorized the maiden's religiously connoted self-renunciation, humanized the figure of Death, and suggested the inaccessibility, unavoidability, and finality of Fate. However much *From Caligari to Hitler* has been targeted for criticism in recent decades, the book continues to inform scholarship on Lang's film. As Patrice Petro has noted, "scholars . . . have often contended that *Destiny* confirms the Weimar cinema's (and Fritz Lang's) general obsession with fate in its various guises."[75]

While often segregated from the *Caligari* book, Kracauer's later works also condemned an *amor fati*, emphasizing instead the role of contingency in both film aesthetics and the historical process. In *Theory of Film*, Kracauer argued that Lang's *Destiny* placed theatrical fantasy on par with a transitory physical reality, thereby violating the medium's "basic aesthetic principle."[76] Consulting the Marseille notebooks in which the book was first outlined, Miriam Hansen writes that for Kracauer, Lang's work typified a "closed dramaturgy of fate or destiny" that marked a historical-philosophical foil to the theorist's modernist concept of chance.[77] Kracauer's posthumous book, *History*, would similarly describe historical reality (like camera reality) as "full of intrinsic contingencies which obstruct its calculability, its subsumption under the deterministic principle."[78]

Following Kracauer's death in 1966, Theodor W. Adorno published an obituary discussing the theorist's defiant relation to aging, finitude, and closure. According to Adorno, Kracauer seemed to disavow the inevitability of death in his late years, finding his own imminent passing "unbelievable."[79] Adorno further noted that in their final conversation, Kracauer had expressed "how much he agreed with those passages from *The Jargon of Authenticity* [*Jargon der Eigentlichkeit*] in which I had criticized the attempt to distill metaphysics from death, the plainly material."[80] In that 1964 book, Adorno had polemicized against the existentialist philosophy of Heidegger, whose *Being and Time*, Adorno argued, turned death into *Dasein*'s essence and identity. Adorno rebuked such an ontologization of death, emphasizing, "the fact that death destroys *Dasein* truly negates it."[81] In his obituary for Kracauer, he likewise invoked a metaphysics "to which death is absolutely opposed and which has its essence in resistance to it."[82]

Lang's *Destiny*, as I have suggested, might similarly be accused of attempting to derive a metaphysics from death, most explicitly in its denouement of self-sacrifice, reunion, and resurrection (with Death's final promise, "Who gives his life away for my sake shall gain it," quoting from the Gospel of Matthew 10:39). Obedient to "alpha and omega," the figure of *"der müde Tod"* serves as a delegate of God in Lang's film, his winged

Slippage between existential ontology and Christian theology.

cloak resembling that of both the Virgin of Mercy and the Angel of Death as he guides the transfigured couple into the beyond. In this way, *Destiny* betrays the slippage between existential ontology and Christian theology that Adorno later discerned in the language of Heidegger and his followers. While the film suggests the extension of the couple's lives beyond their immanent limits, it nonetheless acknowledges the a priori significance of death in both lending form to human life and affecting its contents—a significance, as Georg Simmel wrote in "The Metaphysics of Death" ("Zur Metaphysik des Todes," 1910), that Christianity paradoxically removed in its effort "to place life, from the outset, under the aspect of its own eternity."[83]

Destiny's dual gesture of assenting to and sublating human finitude marks only one of the film's profounder contradictions. In Lang's film, the competing forces of love and death disregard or even revolt against social hierarchies and regimes, but are also naturalized as eternal elements of the human condition. Moreover, while the film interrupts the linear, progressive continuum of history and reveals alternative temporal conceptions (e.g., simultaneity, cyclical recurrence, episodic discontinuity), it also shows the futility of such activism, indicating the perpetual failure of the maiden's death-defying efforts as well as the apparent necessity of her self-sacrifice for the baby's survival and for the reestablishment of community. To whatever extent *Destiny* resorts, as Kracauer claimed, to an "ancient concept of Fate," its privileging of the newborn's life also resonates with Hannah Arendt's notion of natality as the "capacity to begin," suggesting another ontology—one rooted not in inevitable death, but in birth, human freedom, and the faculty to act and start something new.[84] This chance for a new beginning was a key concern of the Weimar avant-garde, as the following chapter will show.

5. The Nonsimultaneity of the Simultaneous
Rhythm 21

> How should one deal with the nonsimultaneity of the simultaneous in history?
>
> SIEGFRIED KRACAUER

> The idea of modernity would like there to be only one meaning and direction in history, whereas the temporality specific to the aesthetic regime of the arts is a co-presence of heterogeneous temporalities.
>
> JACQUES RANCIÈRE

If, as one film scholar has recently argued, the European avant-garde of the 1920s adopted a complex relation to modernity, this complexity ensued in no small part from the temporal dialectics of the concept of modernity itself.[1] In Hans Blumenberg's words, "The modern age was the first and only age that understood itself as an epoch and, in so doing, simultaneously created the other epochs."[2] For Blumenberg, the invention of historical periods and the concomitant sense of temporal discontinuity raised a problem of legitimacy, especially given the discrepancy between modernity's "claim to carry out a radical break with tradition" and "the reality of history, which can never begin entirely anew."[3] Drawing from Blumenberg's work along with Reinhart Koselleck's semantic history of *Neuzeit* (the modern era), Peter Osborne argues that modernity was novel as a periodizing category and a form of historical self-consciousness, defining itself solely in terms of temporal determinants and an assertion of its qualitative newness. In Osborne's analysis, while modernity designates "the presentness of an epoch to the time of its classification," it registers this contemporaneity according to a "self-transcending temporality" that constantly differentiates the present from even the recent past, *neueste Geschichte* (contemporary history) from *neuere Geschichte* (modern history)—both of which are associated with the modern age more generally.[4]

In his recent writings on aesthetics and politics, Jacques Rancière has further problematized the notion of modernity, recasting it in terms of an "aesthetic regime" that inaugurated an equalization of all arts, genres, and subject matter. Rancière identifies the advent of the aesthetic regime with literary realism, which, as he contends, preceded both the science of history and the photographic and filmic arts in its focus on anonymous, ordinary lives and its valorization of commonplace details (or what Arthur Danto called "the transfiguration of the commonplace").[5] Lending a political dimension to Roland Barthes's analysis of texts such as Gustave Flaubert's *Madame Bovary* (1856) and *A Simple Heart* (*Un cœur simple*, 1877), Rancière views the proliferation of superfluous description as the mark of a democratic mode of experience—a mode characterized by a newfound attention to seemingly insignificant events, objects, and feelings as well as a belief in all individuals' capacity for self-determination. Furthermore, diverging from the conventional view of aesthetic modernism as a repudiation of mimetic modes and narrational excesses, Rancière perceives it as continuous with nineteenth-century realist fiction in its challenge to representational hierarchies. For Rancière, modernism—and above all cinematic modernism—established an equivalence of art and life, constructing "a sensorium of radical equality."[6]

Among the problems with Rancière's argument is its homogeneous, undifferentiated conception of realism and modernism, here linked in a broad historical trajectory of democratization. Whereas Barthes emphasized the approximate contemporaneity of literary realism ("what took place"), scholarly history ("what really happened"), and photographic technology ("what was here") in the nineteenth century, Rancière offers a diachronic narrative that suffers from imprecision, as Gertrud Koch has noted: "Rancière of course ignores much that could not be fitted into the historical-philosophical thesis. . . . One must now ask whether the theory of aesthetics, as it is developed here as antipodal to Aristotelian poetics, can be read seamlessly as that of film, or whether a historicization would not be appropriate here."[7] In presenting modernism as the final stage of aesthetic egalitarianism, Rancière also elides the frequent inaccessibility of avant-garde works to mass audiences as well as the unabashed elitism, extremism, and political promiscuity of many early-twentieth-century artists. Finally, insofar as Rancière conceives both historical science and modernism as continuous with literary realism, he leaves open the question of how to approach the *crisis of historicism* that emerged concurrently with the cinematic avant-garde—a question that I will address in this chapter through a focus on Hans Richter's films and publications of the Weimar era.

DIALECTICS OF THE AVANT-GARDE

Scholarship has long defined aesthetic modernism in terms of its enormous hostility to historical styles, cultural traditions, and institutions of art—a hostility perhaps most plainly articulated in the 1909 Futurist Manifesto, in which F.T. Marinetti expressed the intention "to destroy museums, libraries, academies of every sort."[8] Furthermore, modernist works are often noted for opposing linear modes of historical narration, whether in the circular poem-paintings of Guillaume Apollinaire, the simultaneism of Robert Delaunay's Orphic art, the primitivism of Pablo Picasso's paintings, or the atemporal myths and nonclosure of James Joyce's literature. As Carl E. Schorske has argued, such antihistoricism betrayed a loss of faith in the progressive Enlightenment of liberal democracy at the fin de siècle. During this period, artistic and intellectual innovators, in Schorske's words, "broke, more or less deliberately, their ties to the historical outlook central to the nineteenth-century liberal culture in which they had been reared."[9] In the works of Secessionist artists such as Gustav Klimt, Schorske discerned a conscious rebellion against positivist referentiality and the optimistic belief in history as the site of directionality and meaning.

The avant-garde's relationship to the past was not one of simple negation, however, but involved a dialectical interpenetration of history and the contemporary age. Nuancing Charles Baudelaire's and Friedrich Nietzsche's critiques of the prevailing antiquarianism of nineteenth-century European culture, Paul de Man has emphasized that modernism was not only a generative historical force or movement, but also itself a part of the historical process—one with various predecessors in its very gesture of rejecting the past and establishing a new point of origin.[10] With a similar interest in the temporal paradoxes of modernism's insurrectionary rhetoric, Eric Hobsbawm has argued that members of the avant-garde were caught between marking an end to all prior art and legitimating their own artistic endeavors and social positions through an appeal to recognized, time-honored idioms: "They were constantly torn between the conviction that there could be no future to the art of the past—even yesterday's past, or even to any kind of art in the old definition—and the conviction that what they were doing in the old social role of 'artists' and 'geniuses' was important, and rooted in the great tradition of the past."[11]

Such conflictual dynamics symptomatize a broader dialectic in modernity between revolutionary impulses and new modes of engagement with the past. As Rancière has argued, the "aesthetic regime" gave rise to both artistic innovations and novel forms of preservation and interpretation, including archives, museums, and the emerging discipline of art history. Although modernism is often conceived in terms of aesthetic rupture, it nonetheless depends on an idea of art's past and a broader context of historical intelligibility; even the iconoclastic Futurist Manifesto tacitly relies on established institutions as a point of negative identification. In this regard, modernism's avowed break with the past was itself inextricably linked to the historicist paradigm that burgeoned in the nineteenth century. If, as Peter Osborne has contended, historicism replaces tradition as a source of temporal continuity within modernity, serving as an antidote to the epoch's own forms of shock and disruption, it belies Baudelaire's sole identification of the present age with "the ephemeral, the fugitive, the contingent."[12]

THE CONCEPT OF *UNGLEICHZEITIGKEIT*

Modernism is not only marked by its fraught relationship to history, but also beset by multiple, often competing temporalities. Originally referring to the vanguard of an army, the term *avant-garde* was metaphorically transposed to the arts in mid-nineteenth-century France. As Hans Magnus Enzensberger argued in "The Aporias of the Avant-Garde" ("Die Aporien der Avantgarde," 1962), while the temporalization of a spatial category implied a conception of the arts as part of a linear, ever-advancing historical process, it also suggested the coexistence of forerunners and latecomers, and thus the "nonsimultaneity of the simultaneous [*Ungleichzeitigkeit des Gleichzeitigen*]."[13] Among the aporias of the avant-garde, in Enzensberger's analysis, is the question of who decides at any given time what is indeed *en avant*—a judgment that can first be ascertained a posteriori. In his *Theory of the Avant-Garde* (*Theorie der Avantgarde*, 1974), Peter Bürger would likewise take up the concept of *Ungleichzeitigkeit* (variously translated as nonsimultaneity, noncontemporaneity, or nonsynchronicity), associating modernist movements with a challenge to the view of art as a succession of styles and techniques across history. Insofar as avant-garde movements thus evoked "a simultaneity of the radically disparate," as Bürger argues, they negated their own central claim "to be historically more advanced *as art*."[14]

The concept of nonsimultaneity also bears implications for examining the politics of the avant-garde, troubling the standard distinction between progressive and reactionary aesthetic practices. With reference to Ernst Bloch's *Heritage of Our Times* (*Erbschaft dieser Zeit*, 1935) and Bürger's notion of a "full unfolding" of eclectic artistic possibilities under modernism, Andrew Hewitt has argued that the avant-garde shared with fascism a conception of itself as both fulfilling and sublating historical sequentiality within a "metaphysics of presence."[15] Hewitt emphasizes that the idea of *Ungleichzeitigkeit* problematizes basic tenets of scholarship on modernism, including the assumption of an alignment of aesthetic and political radicalism as well as a critical dismissal of all things anachronistic—a category, as he points out, that itself becomes "the most fundamental of anachronisms."[16] Similarly invoking "a co-presence of heterogeneous temporalities," Rancière has identified two discrete conceptions of the avant-garde, which he distinguishes as archipolitical and metapolitical, strategic and aesthetic.[17] While the former conception is that of an advanced, detached force or party that leads on the basis of its capacity for historical interpretation and innovation, the latter is a more Schillerian notion of anticipating and preparing for a future life within the realm of aesthetics.

Notably absent from the aforementioned theories of the avant-garde is a thorough engagement with the intellectual debates about history that occurred alongside the rise of aesthetic modernism. The concept of *Ungleichzeitigkeit* was indeed first widely theorized in the early twentieth century—not only in Bloch's 1935 analysis of fascism, but also in the art-historical and sociological writings of figures including Wilhelm Pinder, Karl Mannheim, Erwin Panofsky, and Henri Focillon. Ironically, then, the avant-garde emerged contemporaneously with an increasing focus on the notion of nonsimultaneity and on problems of historical time and periodization. These historical-philosophical issues, I will argue, need to inform our ways of both historicizing the avant-garde and theorizing its relationship to history. The present chapter will consider the interconnections between the interwar avant-garde and the crisis of historicism, both of which involved a reaction against nineteenth-century practices as well as the postulation of alternative, nonlinear conceptions of time and history. The object of my analysis will be Hans Richter's *Rhythm 21* (*Rhythmus 21*, 1923–25), which I will examine in dialogue with his theoretical texts from the 1920s.

THE HISTORICAL AVANT-GARDE

"History is what is happening today," declared Hans Richter in the April 1926 issue of his avant-garde journal *G: Zeitschrift für elementare Gestaltung* (*G: Journal for Elementary Construction*, 1923–26).[18] Calling for a mode of historiography that serves present-day artistic practice, Richter's manifesto is notably at odds with his later, often-autobiographical writings, including retrospective essays and books chronicling the Dada movement, early documentary and experimental film, and the cinematic avant-garde in Germany—writings that have significantly shaped and informed the scholarship on these topics over the past half century.[19] Apart from its tensions with Richter's subsequent historiographical efforts, however, the 1926 text also raises vexing questions for any reflexive approach to modernism today: How might contemporary scholars best approach an avant-garde that is itself now historical, particularly if, as Bruno Latour argues, "it has been a long time since the very notion of the avant-garde . . . passed away, pushed aside by other forces, moved to the rear guard, or maybe lumped with the baggage train"?[20] How can we historicize the work of artists who radically questioned the very bases and functions of art history, articulating what might be called an antihistoricist presentism? And, finally, how can we address the irony that modernist movements, characterized by an adversarial stance toward the past, have themselves become an integral part of our artistic institutions, cultural traditions, and conceptions of art and film history?

Although the process of canonization has brought with it a sustained interest in the interwar avant-garde, the voluminous scholarship within the field has largely elided the aforementioned problematics. Much of the existing research on Richter is historicist, interested in presenting an accurate, comprehensive account of his life and work; resituating his art within its cultural and political contexts; and documenting the emergence of the Weimar avant-garde, including settling the question of which was the "first" abstract film—a question in which Richter maintained quite a vested interest, for all the pointed antihistoricism of his 1926 text.[21] By contrast, other scholarship has been ahistorical in methodology, especially insofar as it uncritically deploys Richter's midcentury writings to interpret his work from decades prior.[22] Recent research by Michael Cowan, Thomas Elsaesser, Malte Hagener, Yvonne Zimmermann, and others has moved beyond biographical and national paradigms to provide a more holistic sense of the networks, film cultures, and economic conditions of the European avant-garde, focusing in particular on its advertising and commissioned films.[23] In the following, I hope to complement this research through a focus on questions of historicism and the philosophy of history.

Where Zimmermann has conducted groundbreaking research on Richter's later, retrospective historiographical efforts, I will be interested in problems of time and history in his films and publications of the Weimar era—works, in my analysis, that are of interest precisely because of their ostensible efforts to deny the past and establish a temporality of pure presence.[24] While placing Richter's work within a broader intellectual-historical trajectory, I will nonetheless diverge from the set of thinkers and ideas that have repeatedly appeared in the literature on "absolute films," ranging from Leibniz, Goethe, and Schelling to Bergson, Busoni, and Klages, and from concepts of *ars combinatoria*, the *Generalbaß der Malerei* (thoroughbass of painting), and polarity to movement, counterpoint, and rhythm.[25] Analyzing *Rhythm 21* as a response to the crisis of historicism, I will argue that Richter paradoxically relied on various aesthetic and intellectual traditions in the very act of rejecting the past, articulating an antihistoricist presentism that was caught in a performative contradiction even before the avant-garde became historical and institutionalized. Moreover, engaging with early-twentieth-century writings by myriad thinkers on the notion of nonsimultaneity, I will problematize Richter's presentism and also suggest a more reflexive approach to the "historical avant-garde"—one that considers it in conjunction with contemporaneous debates on the philosophy of history.

THE MUSICAL ANALOGY

Aesthetic modernism ensued from nineteenth-century critiques of German Idealism, historicism, and positivist referentiality. In turning to abstraction, modernist artists were anticipated by Arthur Schopenhauer and Friedrich Nietzsche, especially in these philosophers' pessimistic conception of the external world as directionless and meaningless as well as in their rejection of the purpose of art as the imitation of reality. Opposing the Hegelian rationalism and historicism of the early nineteenth century, Schopenhauer had substituted art for history and religion as a locus of truth and redemption, associating art with the suspension of the individual will, the dissolution of the self, and access to a deeper reality beneath surface phenomena. Much as Schopenhauer's work prioritized music among the arts for its sublime, nonrepresentational qualities, Nietzsche's *The Birth of Tragedy from the Spirit of Music* (*Die Geburt der Tragödie aus dem Geiste der Musik*, 1872) attributed to Wagner's music dramas the potential to serve the functions of the chorus in pre-Socratic tragedy: namely, loss of individuated selfhood, the return to an irrational will, ecstatic immersion into a broader unity, and the overcoming of the Cartesian split between mind and body fundamental to conceptual, Idealist thought.

Like Schopenhauer and Nietzsche, modernist artists and theorists often celebrated music as a nonmimetic form of expression. Whereas language bore elements of history and tradition, music facilitated the free play of signifiers detached from their external signifieds. In *Concerning the Spiritual in Art* (*Über das Geistige in der Kunst*, 1912), Wassily Kandinsky observed a general striving across the arts toward the abstract and nonmaterial, for which music served as a primary model: "With few exceptions music has been for some centuries the art which has devoted itself not to the reproduction of natural phenomena, but rather to the expression of the artist's soul."[26] The same year, in "The Relationship to the Text" ("Das Verhältnis zum Text"), Arnold Schoenberg followed Eduard Hanslick in

DER ABSOLUTE FILM

EINMALIGE FILMMATINEE
veranstaltet von der
NOVEMBERGRUPPE
in Gemeinschaft mit der
KULTURABTEILUNG DER UFA

PROGRAMM

Dreiteilige Farbensonatine —————— Hirschfeld-Mack
Reflektorische Farbenspiele   Bauhaus Dessau

Film ist Rhythmus —————— Hans Richter Berlin

Symphonie Diagonale —————— Viking Eggeling Berlin

Opus 2, 3 und 4 —————— Walther Ruttmann Berlin

Images mobiles —————— Fernand Leger
                            und Dudley Murphy, Paris

Entr' Acte —————— Scénario de Francis Picabia
                    adapté et réalisé par René Clair

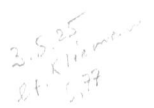

Program for the 1925 film matinee "Der absolute Film," organized by the Novembergruppe in cooperation with Ufa's Kulturabteilung. Credit: Berlinische Galerie.

dismissing the assumption that music must evoke images, citing Schopenhauer's remark that the composer discloses the world's innermost essence and conveys the deepest truth in a language beyond reason.[27] Heralding a diminishing concern with both text and subject matter, Schoenberg praised the nonfigurative paintings of Kandinsky and Oskar

Kokoschka, describing their "objective theme" as "hardly more than an excuse to improvise in colors and forms and to express themselves as only the musician expressed himself."[28]

Schoenberg's analogy to music in describing abstract visual art was common to postwar avant-garde filmmakers including Richter, Viking Eggeling, and Walter Ruttmann, whose films bore titles such as *Rhythm 21*, *Symphonie diagonale*, and *Lichtspiel Opus 1*, respectively. (The crossmedial analogy and formal experimentation also extended to the period's narrative cinema, which often employed musical language and integrated elementary aesthetics, most famously in Ruttmann's animated dream sequence for Lang's *Die Nibelungen* [1924].) Richter, Eggeling, and Ruttmann all began as painters and endeavored to introduce elements of time and movement to their abstract works, thereby creating what Ruttmann described as "an art for the eyes, which differs from painting because it occurs in time (like music)."[29] In so doing, the filmmakers conceived of film as a medium that unites the spatial dimension of painting with the temporal aspect of music, transgressing Gotthold Ephraim Lessing's famous partition of the arts. It was not merely music's temporal development that attracted these directors, however, but also its potential to transcend linguistic and national barriers—especially through what Hanslick had theorized as absolute music, or nonillustrative, nonrepresentational instrumental works. The filmmakers' "absolute films," which were screened at Berlin's Ufa-Palast on May 3 and 10, 1925 (organized by the Novembergruppe in cooperation with Ufa's Kulturabteilung), shared with their musical counterparts an eschewal of narrative and figurative content, visualizing instead the rhythmic play of abstract forms and structures.

THE ABSOLUTE FILM

If cinema promised to realize the dynamization of visual art, it is no coincidence that Richter's *Rhythm 21* begins with a tacit invocation of Kazimir Malevich's *Black Square* (1915), which is immediately set into motion. At the outset of Richter's film, a predominantly black screen gradually turns white, and the reverse then occurs in double succession—a sequence that could be described as a horizontally contracting and dilating black square or as two swelling and shrinking (or shifting and receding) white rectangles, depending on how one perceives the moving picture puzzle (*Vexierbild*).[30] These opening five seconds establish many of the film's basic elements: simple quadrangles that reduplicate the form of the screen and change in shape and size; a black-and-white palette in which the two colors are often

The opening of *Rhythm 21*, with a dynamization of Kazimir Malevich's *Black Square* (1915).

substituted; ambiguous spatial dynamics, particularly with regard to depth relations and the identity of figure and background, solid and void, and interior and exterior areas; a play between fluid and discontinuous motion; and, finally, repetitions, variations, and inversions of action and direction of movement. The film's subsequent three minutes add further components: vertical movement, gray tones, and diagonal figures; the multiplication, disappearance, and overlapping of geometrical forms, often of varying sizes, relative distances, and degrees of mobility and speed; and simultaneous motions that are alternately synchronous and disunified, unilinear and multidirectional.

Lacking narrative development and external referents, *Rhythm 21* challenges the bases of film analysis, including units and categories such as the shot, scene, and profilmic event, and it also frustrates the tools of semantic and iconological interpretation. If, as Ingo Zechner has justly suggested, Richter's work directs attention to the most rudimentary of visual elements (e.g., relations and dynamics of form, space, light, color, rhythm), this should not necessarily delimit discussion of the film to a metacinematic discourse, wherein it appears as "a systematic inventory of filmic possibilities and their conditions ... a zero point of cinema."[31] Instead, I argue, the film can be viewed with regard to conceptions of time and history in early-twentieth-century aesthetic theory and practice. The historical-philosophical implications of abstraction were indeed addressed in Wilhelm Worringer's foundational text on modernism, *Abstraction and Empathy* (*Abstraktion und Einfühlung*, 1908), where he conceived the "urge to abstraction" as the effort to find refuge from an external world of arbitrary, ephemeral, and relative phenomena within a realm of absolute, eternal necessity.[32] Positing a recursive conception of humankind's spiritual evolution, Worringer argued that much as primitive art had conveyed an instinctive sense of spiritual dread and uncertainty within a bewildering universe, modern abstract art now expressed a Schopenhauerian recognition of the limits of reason and knowledge.

Extending the ideas of Worringer and Kandinsky, numerous commentators have noted absolute films for their flight from the historicity and materiality of filmic representation. In "The Visible Symphony" (1924), Herman Scheffauer characterized Ruttmann's early experiments as an attempt "to detach the film from all reality and to infuse it with a new aesthetic, sensuous and spiritual content," thus elevating the medium "into the realm of purely abstract art."[33] Rudolf Kurtz's *Expressionism and Film* (*Expressionismus und Film*, 1926) similarly observed the absence of "history, plot, and events" and of all human figures in Richter's and Eggeling's absolute films; for Kurtz, the interrelation of elementary geometrical forms allowed for the unfolding of "spiritual dramas."[34] Over half a century later, in *Cinéma 1* (1983), Gilles Deleuze would associate Richter's *Rhythm* films with a movement wherein the whole spiritual universe passes through a fire of chaos, "only to break its sensible attachments to the material, the organic, and the human, to detach itself from all the states of the past, and thus to discover the spiritual abstract Form of the future."[35] Most recently, in an essay titled "Abstraction and Empathy in the Early German Avant-Garde" (2000), Christine N. Brinckmann has remarked upon the lack of overall structural progression in Eggeling's *Symphonie diagonale*, characterizing the film in terms of "a time-consuming timelessness."[36]

RICHTER'S PERFORMATIVE CONTRADICTION

Through the rejection of visual and linguistic referentiality, absolute film sought not only to circumvent the historicity of the filmic medium, but also to avoid perceptual conventions and emotional associations on the part of viewers. In "The Badly Trained Soul" ("Die schlecht trainierte Seele,"

1924), Richter argued for a more active and precise understanding of sensory processes than assumed in various realms of contemporary life, and especially in current cinema. Reproaching existing feature films for failing to demonstrate the possibilities of photography and movement, Richter redefined the medium in terms of optical rhythm, as represented through photo-technical means and corresponding to the functions of the human apperceptive apparatus. Furthermore, rather than relying on kitsch images, archetypal figures, and familiar, pathos-laden scenarios, his and Eggeling's absolute films presented sheer organized movement, refusing any "'stopping points' at which one could return into memories."[37] In this way, Richter wrote, the viewer is compelled into a mode of feeling detached from all content and from the powers of recollection. Seeking to cultivate greater awareness of the elementary laws of sensation, Richter dismissed what he called the "ready-to-wear feelings from past or nonexistent centuries"—feelings, he claimed, that both constitute our soul's nature and shape our image of the world (*Weltbild*).[38]

Despite Richter's express wish to present abstract rhythms unbound to long-standing sensorial regimes and visualized through uniquely cinematic means, his absolute films in fact followed a history of media experimentation and theorization. Not only had similar attempts been made by brothers Bruno Corra and Arnaldo Ginna in Italy and by French painter Léopold Survage before World War I; Richter's absolute films also joined an extended trajectory of aesthetic concepts including Friedrich Schlegel's "absolute novel [*absoluter Roman*]," Eduard Hanslick's "absolute music [*absolute Musik*]," Stéphane Mallarmé's "pure poetry [*poésie pure*]," and Rudolf Blümner's "absolute poetry [*absolute Dichtung*]." Furthermore, though ostensibly demonstrations of cinema's specific capabilities, the absolute films paradoxically recalled various synesthetic ideas (e.g., Adalbert Stifter's "music for the eye [*Musik für das Auge*]"), artistic movements (Symbolism, Expressionism, Cubism, Futurism, Suprematism, Dada, Constructivism) and media aesthetics—from music and painting to the scroll, shadow play, color organ, kaleidoscope, and light sculpture.[39] In these regards, the concept of "absolute film" was a performative contradiction, making a claim for cinema's nonreferential autonomy within the established idioms of older media.

These paradoxes were increasingly acknowledged in the late 1920s, as filmmakers and theorists voiced criticism of absolute films and also called for greater engagement with material-historical circumstances. Likely targeting the Gesellschaft Neuer Film, a society for alternative cinema cofounded by Richter, Ruttmann's "The 'Absolute' Fashion" ("Die 'absolute' Mode," 1928)

Hans Richter's avant-garde journal *G: Zeitschrift für elementare Gestaltung*, nos. 5–6 (April 1926). Credit: Berlinische Galerie.

questioned whether film is correctly understood "when one wishes upon it ... the fate of absolute music."[40] For Ruttmann, who had famously turned away from abstract animation with the documentary *Berlin: Symphony of a Metropolis* (*Berlin—Die Sinfonie der Großstadt*, 1927), the quest for pure, autonomous aesthetics reactivated the very ideology of *l'art pour l'art* "from which film had just released us."[41] Shortly thereafter, in a review of the Gesellschaft's screening of abstract films in Frankfurt, Siegfried Kracauer argued that the nonnarrative, nonobjective works of Eggeling, Richter, and others—"seemingly born from the spirit of film itself"—helped envisage new possibilities in cinematic language, but remained empty and meaningless inasmuch as they lacked any relation to reality.[42] At the Congrès international du cinéma indépendant in La Sarraz, Switzerland, in 1929, Béla Balázs emphasized the social role of independent cinema, while Richter defended films that remained abstract and incomprehensible. In *The Spirit of Film* (*Der Geist des Films*, 1930), Balázs would further pursue this line of criticism, characterizing abstract cinema as "an aesthetic escape from the obligations of reality," especially during a period of open class struggle.[43] Further aesthetic and political critiques of abstract films would be voiced in later decades by critical theorists such as Walter Benjamin, Theodor W. Adorno, and Hanns Eisler.[44]

"HISTORY IS WHAT IS HAPPENING TODAY"

While *Rhythm 21* and other absolute films challenged routinized modes of visual representation and sensorial engagement, Richter's theoretical writings of the Weimar era condemned prevailing art-historical methods. The aforementioned manifesto by Richter, "History Is What Is Happening Today," was occasioned by the publication of Rudolf Kurtz's *Expressionism and Film*, the first book-length study of Expressionist cinema. A writer, dramatist, and editor in chief of *Lichtbild-Bühne*, Kurtz surveyed Expressionism across the arts before focusing on the movement's extension to cinema, discussing six feature films by Robert Wiene, Karlheinz Martin, and Paul Leni as well as the absolute works of Eggeling, Richter, Ruttmann, and others. In an excerpt from the book printed alongside Richter's text in the April 1926 issue of *G* and accompanied by frames from Eggeling's *Symphonie diagonale*, Kurtz proclaimed the new art as that which does not passively accept and reproduce everyday life, but rather willfully creates and releases "forms of reality" according to a particular *Weltbild*.[45] Issuing an implicit critique of the theory of empathy (*Einfühlungstheorie*) and psychologism associated with German philosophers such as Robert Vischer and

Theodor Lipps, Kurtz rejected the privileged role of empathy as an artistic means and a basis for knowledge of the existing world, placing emphasis instead on the constructive, volitional elements of the human spirit.

Having already praised *Expressionism and Film* in the prior issue of *G*, Richter now looked to the book as a basis for reflecting more generally on the uses and disadvantages of history for "living art."[46] For Richter, Kurtz's book marked film's appropriation by art history—a discipline, in his view, that was responsible for the "crudest nonsense of our age."[47] Much as Kandinsky's *Concerning the Spiritual in Art* had disparaged aesthetic theory as "the lamp which sheds light on the petrified ideas of yesterday and of the more distant past," Richter's text described art history as an effort to lend retrospective meaning to movements that are now fixed and defunct, serving as "the inscription on gravestones."[48] Heralding Kurtz's book as the first trace of a "creative art history," Richter proclaimed that "*history is what is happening today*," and—with a tacit nod to Nietzsche's concept of affirmation (*Bejahung*)—he contended that the past would become meaningful again only through the "profound and affirmative apprehension of the present."[49] Furthermore, identifying historical reality as a construct rather than a matter of scientific factuality, he enjoined art historians to assume a standpoint, campaign for contemporary art, and signal unexplored creative paths. (Richter's claims ostensibly ignored aspects of the present that deserved to be critiqued rather than affirmed, and also posited a false dichotomy between constructivism and positivism.)

Richter's polemic took aim not only at a dry, objectivist antiquarianism, but also at the atomizing and relativizing effects of historicism, with its emphasis on the development and irreducible uniqueness of individual historical entities. Recalling the "Call for Elementary Art" ("Aufruf zur elementaren Kunst," 1921), in which Raoul Hausmann, Hans Arp, Ivan Puni, and László Moholy-Nagy had urged for a regenerated art that expresses "the forces of an epoch" through formal elements that transcend the individual creator, Richter argued that art history should serve as the "the history of the moving forces of the epoch" and should establish new aesthetic standards, rather than simply amassing biographies and drawing facile comparisons between figures.[50] Moreover, taking up the concept of the *Weltbild* theorized in the early twentieth century by Max Planck, Wilhelm Dilthey, Karl Jaspers, Max Weber, Martin Heidegger, and others, Richter reenvisioned art history as "the creation of a unified world-image on a large scale—so that 'history' may render a world, a world core, for which art is its will and expression."[51] For Richter, Kurtz's study of Expressionist cinema was exemplary both in revealing coherent forces across all realms of human expression and in concerning itself with a *Weltbild* emerging in dynamic relation to contemporary art—a world image in which film would also find its nature.

RICHTER'S INTELLECTUAL INHERITANCES

In a chapter of *The Filming of Modern Life* on Richter's abstract works of the 1920s, Malcolm Turvey argues that the filmmaker allied himself not with "the nihilistic critique of rationality often associated with Nietzsche," but rather with the ideal of harmony espoused by Friedrich Schiller in *On the Aesthetic Education of Man* (*Über die ästhetische Erziehung des Menschen*, 1795).[52] Recalling Rancière's Schillerian account of the "aesthetic regime," Turvey's argument relies on a reductionist view of Nietzsche's philosophy and elides developments in intellectual history since Weimar Classicism. In my analysis, Richter's 1926 manifesto in fact had its most significant antecedents in Nietzsche's early writings. Richter's assertion that "the reality of history is not read off from the 'facts' but is instead—constructed" recalls Nietzsche's aesthetic critique of disinterested positivism as well as his perspectivist notion of historical reality as the interplay of finite, value-laden interpretations (as discussed in chapter 3).[53] Furthermore, Richter's call for a mode of history writing in the service of contemporary art follows the vitalist attack on ascetic, antiquarian historiography in "On the Uses and Disadvantages of History for Life" ("Vom Nutzen und Nachteil der Historie für das Leben," 1874), where Nietzsche—like later philosophers such as Benedetto Croce—sought to extricate natural-scientific approaches from the realm of human activity and contended that all engagement with the past is inseparable from present needs and interests.

In critiquing standard historiographical practices, Richter drew as well from the methodological insights of prominent Central European art historians. Although Alois Riegl upheld Leopold von Ranke's emphasis on the uniqueness of every epoch, he followed Nietzsche in condemning historicism for stifling human creativity and for neglecting humans' active role in interpreting the world according to their standpoint and desires. For Riegl, art historians had adopted empirical and materialist approaches all too zealously in their reaction against Hegelian conceptualism, leading to a "cult of individual facts."[54] Returning to ideas from Hegel's *Lectures on Aesthetics* (*Vorlesungen über die Ästhetik*, 1835), Riegl presented art as concurrent with a period's broader worldview, arguing in the conclusion to *Late Roman Art Industry* (*Spätrömische Kunstindustrie*, 1901) that each age has a single, dynamic *Kunstwollen* (artistic will), which not only governs "all four types of plastic art in the same measure," but is also "identical with the other main forms of expression of the human will."⁵⁵ A quarter century later, Richter evoked the concept of the *Kunstwollen* in praising Kurtz's book for demonstrating "the existence of coherent, driving energies in film as well as in all areas of expression," and he also echoed Riegl in urging for a shift of focus from specific works or styles to broader unifying elements of art history.⁵⁶

With his insistence that art history is not "the amassing of individual artists' biographies," Richter also adopted ideas set forth a decade earlier in Heinrich Wölfflin's *Principles of Art History* (*Kunstgeschichtliche Grundbegriffe*, 1915).⁵⁷ In the preface to the book's first edition, Wölfflin envisioned a mode of historiography that not only chronicles particular artists, but also traces more general developments in style and in pictorial form and imagination—or what he famously deemed an "art history without names."⁵⁸ Moving beyond examining the "personal style" of artists to also consider "*the style of the school, the country, the race*" to which they belonged, Wölfflin conceived artistic styles as expressions of individual, national, and epochal temperament, and he sought to direct attention to the possibilities of representational form available during particular periods as well as historical changes in modes of vision or "imaginative beholding."⁵⁹ Richter's plea for the creation of new art-historical standards recalls Wölfflin's interest in establishing "standards by which the historical transformations (and the national types) can be more exactly defined," and his dismissal of "the art history of taste [*Geschmackskunstgeschichte*]" resonates with Wölfflin's claim that national differences in apprehension exceed "a mere question of taste" to convey "the whole *Weltbild* of a people."⁶⁰

THE CRITERION OF CONTEMPORANEITY

In identifying history with present-day action (à la Thomas Edison's characterization of film as a "new way of recording history," discussed in chapter 2), Richter's manifesto also gestures toward the broader issue of contemporaneity that has been central to modern aesthetic theory, including recent writings by Terry Smith, Giorgio Agamben, Boris Groys, Peter Osborne, Juliane Rebentisch, and others.⁶¹ In his lectures on fine art, Hegel prescribed a relationship of immediate identity between the individual and the worldview of his period as well as between the work of art and the spirit of the people (*Volksgeist*): "Just as every man is a child of his time in every activity, whether political, religious, or scientific, and just as he has the task of bringing out the essential content and the therefore necessary form of that time, so it is the vocation of art to find for the spirit of a people the artistic expression corresponding to it."[62] While, for Hegel, the frequent use of materials (e.g., religion, worldview, customs, laws) from past epochs allowed for a degree of generalization requisite for all art, it also raised the prospect of a lack of both intelligibility and "living and contemporary interest" for the public.[63] Mediating between presentism and faithful, self-effacing antiquarianism—positions that he identified with France and Germany, respectively—Hegel advocated a third mode of artistic portrayal, wherein a direct connection is established between past and current circumstances: "History is only ours when it belongs to the nation to which we belong, or when we can look on the present in general as a consequence of a chain of events in which the characters or deeds represented form an essential link."[64]

Hegel's critique of historical representation would be radicalized in the subsequent decades, when works of art were increasingly defined by their novelty and ability to capture characteristic aspects of the current era. In "The Painter of Modern Life" ("Le peintre de la vie moderne," 1863), Baudelaire argued that the present serves as a source of pleasure not only for its potential beauty, but also for "its essential quality of being present."[65] For Baudelaire, the feature of "modernity" was lacking from the works of many contemporary artists, who tended to cover their subjects in historical facades, thereby sacrificing the originality deriving from "the seal which Time imprints on our sensations."[66] As Paul de Man later noted, Baudelaire's call for "the representation of the present" was blatantly paradoxical, "opening perspectives of distance and difference within the apparent uniqueness of the instant."[67] Yet, whatever the impossibility of immediately capturing the present moment, the demand for contemporaneity would pervade modernist aesthetic discourse, whether in the motto of the Vienna Secession, "To every age its art, to every art its freedom [*Der Zeit ihre Kunst. Der Kunst ihre Freiheit*]"; Kandinsky's claim that "each period of culture produces an art of its own"; Walter Gropius's proclamation that "the new age demands its own meaning"; or Moholy-Nagy's insistence, in *Painting, Photography, Film* (*Malerei, Fotographie, Film*, 1925), that "we, the creators of our own time, should go to work with up-to-date means."[68]

While the criterion of contemporaneity was thus applied across the arts, it was the medium of film that bore the greatest promise of temporal immediacy for many theorists. The 1916 Futurist cinema manifesto by F.T. Marinetti, Bruno Corra, Arnaldo Ginna, and others celebrated film for its capacities, inter alia, to "endow intelligence with a prodigious sense of simultaneity and omnipresence" and to "attain the *polyexpressiveness* toward which all the most modern artistic researches are moving."[69] Much as the Futurists contended that cinema would thereby supplant print media, Béla Balázs argued in *Visible Man* (*Der sichtbare Mensch*, 1924) that the filmic image—existing "only in the present"—allows for forms of simultaneous harmony and polyphony, whereas language remains invariably linear and sequential.[70] Four decades later, in "On the Impression of Reality in the Cinema" ("À propos de l'impression de réalité au cinema," 1965), Christian Metz built on the media-theoretical writings of André Bazin and Roland Barthes, distinguishing motion pictures from still photography in that "the spectator always sees movement as being present (even if it duplicates a past movement)."[71] If, as Mary Ann Doane notes in *The Emergence of Cinematic Time* (2002), the spectator's experience of presence is nonetheless unstable on account of film's archivability and consequent historicity—the medium produces "the sense of a present moment laden with historicity" while also encouraging "a belief in our access to pure presence, instantaneity"—early abstract films such as *Rhythm 21* marked a limit case in the modernist attempt to achieve a cinematic temporality of pure presence, ostensibly eliminating all indexical traces of the past.[72] Yet not only was Richter unable to outrun his historical debts, making a historically overdetermined claim to ahistoricity; his work was also curiously untimely, as I will now show by reading the concept of nonsimultaneity into his film theory and practice of the 1920s.

THE NONSIMULTANEITY OF THE SIMULTANEOUS

Insofar as Richter's absolute film sought to lend expression to "the energies of modern, tangibly contemporary life, as reduced to their simplest form," as Rudolf Kurtz wrote in 1926, this mode of contemporaneity was ironically at odds with temporal concepts emerging concurrently in the discipline of art history.[73] Published the same year as Kurtz's *Expressionism and Film*, Wilhelm Pinder's *The Problem of Generation in European Art History* (*Das Problem der Generation in der Kunstgeschichte Europas*, 1926) invoked a "nonsimultaneity of the simultaneous [*Ungleichzeitigkeit des Gleichzeitigen*]" arising from the copresence of varying generations, each with its separate tasks and goals.[74] In a pointed critique of Wölfflin's work, Pinder argued that stylistic differences between coexisting generations could not be grasped according to an "art history without names"—a concept, he claimed, that relied on a one-dimensional view of time periods and a facile, uniseriate mode of ordering works of art.[75] Dismissing the common assumption of a "'unified time' with its unified 'progress,'" Pinder characterized historical reality instead as multilayered and polyphonic, contending that "simple 'presences' do not exist at all, because every historical 'moment' is experienced by people with their *own*, quite distinct historical durations and means something different for everyone—*even a different time!*"[76] In these regards, as Frederic J. Schwartz has observed, Pinder's book not only contributed to methodological debates within art history during the Weimar era, but also responded to the broader crisis of historicism across the human sciences (*Geisteswissenschaften*), challenging the historicist postulate of a coherent and unilinear temporal flow.[77]

One year following the publication of Pinder's book, Erwin Panofsky would also question the tenability of chronological time as a means of dating artworks and of forging connections between stylistic and broader historical developments. In the appendix to his 1927 article "On the Chronology of the Four Masters of Reims" ("Über die Reihenfolge der vier Meister von Reims"), Panofsky departed from his more immediate concern with the order of architectural work on the Reims cathedral to consider the limitations of marking stylistic changes in art through diachronic series: "One may ask whether it makes any sense at all to assimilate art historical observations into a temporal course of events, given the circumstances in which contemporary works are stylistically so disparate that they appear to have been created at different times."[78] Dismissively alluding to Pinder's book, Panofsky recast its subject in broader terms drawn from Georg Simmel's 1916 essay "The Problem of Historical Time" ("Das Problem der historischen Zeit"), remarking that "the problem of generations is really just a specific instance of historical time, and not even the most important one at that."[79] Furthermore, adopting neo-Kantian categories from Ernst Cassirer's writings, Panofsky distinguished between cultural and natural time, and historical and geographical space, arguing for the interdependence of these coordinates in constituting various frames of reference and, more generally, in lending artistic phenomena a continuous order and "unity of meaning."[80]

While the sociologist Karl Mannheim included a discussion of Pinder's book in his important 1928 essay on issues of generation, it was Ernst Bloch who would most famously expand the concept of *Ungleichzeitigkeit* into a theory of modern culture with *Heritage of Our Times* (1935).[81] Diverging from Pinder, who had advanced a biologically determinist notion of entelechy and became an early supporter of the National Socialist regime, Bloch repurposed the idea of nonsimultaneity within a historical-materialist analysis of the ascendance of fascist politics in Germany. In a central chapter entitled "Nonsimultaneity and Obligation to Its Dialectic" ("Ungleichzeitigkeit und Pflicht zu ihrer Dialektik," dated May 1932), Bloch highlighted the persistence of an unresolved past, writing, "Not all people exist in the same Now. They do so only externally, through the fact that they can be seen today. But they are thereby not yet living at the same time with the others. They rather carry an earlier element with them; this interferes."[82] For Bloch, such forms of nonsimultaneity emerged along lines of location, class, and age, and resulted from the uneven rate of change in and across different societal realms—or what Karl Marx, in the 1857 introduction to his *Contribution to the Critique of Political Economy* (*Zur Kritik der politischen Ökonomie*, 1859), had called the "unequal development of material production and, e.g., that of art."[83] Nonetheless distinguishing Bloch's theory of *Ungleichzeitigkeit* from historical dialectics in the Hegelian-Marxist tradition, Martin Jay has emphasized that the concept of myriad, often-contradictory temporalities eschews a single, progressive narrative as well as the promise of ultimate coherence.[84] In this way, the concept of nonsimultaneity implies a decisive break with Richter's assertion of "coherent, driving energies in film as well as in all areas of human expression."[85]

THE MIGRATION OF EUROPEAN INTELLECTUALS

That the concept of nonsimultaneity was also theorized outside the German-speaking world in the interwar period is indicated by French art historian Henri Focillon's 1934 book *The Life of Forms in Art* (*Vie des formes*). In the chapter titled "Forms in the Realm of Time," Focillon argued that the chronological organization of time not only lends a quasi-mystical power to units of measurement such as the century, but also ascribes a presumed harmony to single dates, thereby homogenizing a vast array of actions and places as well as obfuscating the reality of history as "a conflict among what is precocious, actual or merely delayed."[86] Whereas Hippolyte Taine had postulated an inherent connection between various sociocultural spheres, famously invoking static, determinist ideas of "race, milieu and moment," Focillon differentiated between the evolution of artistic forms and phenomena in other domains of human endeavor: "From the fact that various modes of action are contemporaneous, . . . it does not follow that they all stand at an equal point in their development. At the same date, politics, economics and art do not occupy identical positions on their respective graphs, and the line joining them at any one given moment is more often than not a very irregular and sinuous one."[87] Characterizing historical time as disjointed and asynchronous, Focillon dismissed the presupposition that the artist is necessarily a contemporary of their era, defining every new work of art less as a part of an unbroken continuum than as an event or "phenomenon of *rupture*."[88]

With the migration of European intellectuals to the United States in the 1930s, the idea of nonsimultaneity would enter into American academic discourse. Two years after taking a position at the University of Iowa, Czech literary scholar René Wellek delivered a lecture, titled "The Parallelism between Literature and the Arts" (1941), in which he refuted the existence of a zeitgeist that permeates and unifies the various arts during any given period. Challenging the methodologies of Wölfflin, Oswald Spengler, and other early-twentieth-century thinkers, Wellek argued that the arts evolve individually—"with a different tempo and a different internal structure of elements"—and that similarities in their development "take the form of an intricate pattern of coincidences and divergences rather than parallel lines."[89] Two decades later, the American art historian George Kubler, a former student of Focillon's at Yale University, would similarly question the postulate of a general sensibility shared by writers and artists within a particular sociohistorical context. In *The Shape of Time* (1962), Kubler envisaged the cross section of every moment as "a mosaic of pieces in different developmental states, and of different ages, rather than a radial design conferring its meaning upon all the pieces."[90] Taking up Focillon's argument that the life of forms necessarily implies "the idea of *succession*," Kubler further contended that every work of art joins a chain of solutions to a specific problem.[91] These sequences, he wrote, exist simultaneously across different form classes and represent "independent systems of expression that may occasionally converge."[92]

Having received an advance copy of *The Shape of Time*, Erwin Panofsky immediately recommended the book to fellow German-Jewish émigré Siegfried Kracauer, who was preparing a new project on "some problems of history" in 1962.[93] In an essay of the following year, "Time and History," Kracauer applied Kubler's critique of artistic chronology to historiographical practice more generally, arguing that the occurrences of history might likewise be ordered according to sequences of phenomena in diverse areas: "History consists of events whose chronology tells us but little about their relationships and meanings. Since simultaneous events are more often than not intrinsically asynchronous, it makes no sense indeed to conceive of the historical process as a homogeneous flow. The image of that flow only veils the divergent times in which substantial sequences of historical events materialize. In referring to history, one should speak of the march of times rather than the 'March of Time.' Far from marching, calendric time is an empty vessel."[94]

Kracauer similarly emphasized the purely formal character of linear, chronological time in his posthumously published book, *History: The Last*

Things before the Last (1969). Intervening in myriad debates in the philosophy of history, he used the concept of nonsimultaneity to problematize not only the concept of the zeitgeist, but also the "present-interest" theory of Benedetto Croce and R.G. Collingwood, who had identified the historian's contemporary standpoint as a decisive influence on their rendering of the past.[95] Extending the "basic aesthetic principle" from his *Theory of Film* (1960), Kracauer also drew an analogy between photographic media and modern historiography, citing the works of "the *avant-garde* film artists of the 'twenties" alongside stylized historical chronicles (e.g., Johan Huizinga's *The Autumn of the Middle Ages* [*Herfsttij der Middeleeuwen*, 1919]) as examples of an excessive stress on formative tendencies to the neglect of the "raw material" of the external world.[96]

THIS WILL HAVE BEEN OUR ERA

As I have argued, Richter's claims to a temporality of pure presence in his abstract films and theoretical writings of the 1920s marked a performative contradiction, drawing from a plethora of artistic and intellectual traditions in the very act of dismissing the past. Furthermore, in defining historiography as a chronicle of "the moving forces of the epoch," Richter assumed a notion of temporal coherence that was itself becoming passé in the interwar era, as art historians and philosophers increasingly rejected periodizing topoi (e.g., *Kunstwollen*) that appeared to lend undue homogeneity, dialectical unity, and meaning to the historical process.[97] Ironically, then, Richter's vision of an art history aligned with contemporary creative forces—one demonstrating "the existence of coherent, driving energies in film as well as in all areas of human expression"—appeared at a time when representatives of the discipline were beginning to postulate uneven, asynchronous developments in various domains.[98] Theorizing the copresence of multiple, often-competing temporalities, Pinder, Panofsky, Focillon, and others conceived of each moment as a palimpsest that resists assimilation into any general, synthesizing narrative.

The idea of nonsimultaneity was nonetheless implicit in the self-positioning of Richter and other members of the avant-garde, who assumed the status of leaders and privileged witnesses of their own era. In their quest to express the spirit of the age, these artists and theorists recalled the discourse of Hegel, who had characterized every individual as "*a child of his time*" and thereby deduced his definition of philosophy as "*its own time comprehended in thoughts.*"[99] However, whereas Hegel had argued that humans are unable to surpass their own moment without shifting from the sphere of reason to one of fanciful opinion, avant-gardists claimed a temporal advantage, conceiving of contemporaneity less as a mode of copresence with their time than as the paradoxical capacity to view the present already from the perspective of the future. By this logic, truly contemporary art could gain wider appreciation only ex post facto, and a history of "what is happening today" would be at once proleptic and retroactive; the history of the present (*Zeitgeschichte* or *Gegenwartsgeschichte*) espoused by Richter would be written not in the present tense, but rather in the future perfect, claiming that *this will have been our era.*

The avant-garde's paradoxical rhetoric responded to the crisis of historicism widely diagnosed in the postwar era, at a moment of heightened skepticism of the coherence, meaning, and unilinear directionality of historical time. If time seemed "out of joint" in the Weimar Republic amid both the specters of the past and a contested new political regime, the National Socialist Party would later seek to rectify this sense of *Ungleichzeitigkeit* through a systematic *Gleichschaltung* (coordination) of all realms of German society, forcing Jewish artists and theorists such as Richter into the extraterritoriality of exile—a condition, as Kracauer wrote, in which one's "life history is disrupted."[100] Yet the relationship between the crisis of historicism and the rise of Nazism is itself far from unequivocal. As the following chapter will show, even Arnold Fanck's mountain films of the Weimar period—regarded by Kracauer as "symptomatic of an antirationalism on which the Nazis could capitalize"—signal the copresence of disjunctive, incommensurable temporalities.[101]

6. Natural History
The Holy Mountain

> One can look at history from two sides and divide it into the history of nature and the history of men. The two sides are, however, inseparable; the history of nature and the history of men are dependent on each other so long as men exist.
>
> KARL MARX

> Philosophical nature has to be regarded as history, and history as nature.
>
> THEODOR W. ADORNO

Disputed since the publication of *From Caligari to Hitler* (1947), Siegfried Kracauer's argument that Weimar cinema reveals protofascist psychological dispositions is further problematized when films of "pre-Hitler Germany" are analyzed in relation to the interwar crisis of historicism.[1] The connection between fascism and historicism is vexed and ambiguous, particularly on account of the incongruous, often-contradictory meanings that the latter term has acquired from twentieth-century commentators. If, as Friedrich Meinecke wrote in "On the Crisis of Historicism" ("Von der Krisis des Historismus," 1942), historicism emphasized the development and irreducible uniqueness of historical entities, then the National Socialist understanding of history was historicist to the extent that "nationality, race, and empire are individual entities and subject to the law of individual historical development."[2] In *The Poverty of Historicism* (1957), by contrast, Karl Popper offered an idiosyncratic definition of historicism as a deterministic effort to predict the future course of human history through the identification of underlying patterns of evolution. For Popper, the Third Reich espoused "historicist superstitions," victimizing millions of lives through its totalitarian belief in "Inexorable Laws of Historical Destiny."[3]

At issue in the conflicting definitions of historicism is the relationship between natural and historical processes. Extending back to the early modern philosophy of René Descartes and Giambattista Vico and reconceived by Idealists including G.W.F. Hegel and F.W.J. Schelling, the distinction between nature and history—and, with it, between the natural sciences and humanities—would become a crucial point of contention in the interwar debates over historicism.[4] Taking up Wilhelm Dilthey's efforts to avert the threat of subjectivist relativism, Martin Heidegger's *Being and Time* (*Sein und Zeit*, 1927) attempted to reconcile nature and history by absolutizing historicity as the basic ontological structure of human existence. While Heidegger's work assumed a leading position within German philosophy of the late Weimar period, Theodor W. Adorno contended that its apparent solution to the crisis of historicism merely transfigured history into an ontology—one insufficient in addressing historical contingencies and in interpreting specific empirical phenomena—and also remained trapped in tautologies, owing to its tacit preservation of Idealist elements. In a 1932 lecture to the Frankfurt chapter of the Kant-Gesellschaft, Adorno sought to overcome the traditional antithesis of nature and history through a dialectical concept of natural history (*Naturgeschichte*), emphasizing the two terms' "concrete unity" and "insuperable interwovenness."[5]

Kracauer's own Weimar essays addressed the crisis of historicism and also explored the nexus of history, nature, and photographic media, as I have discussed in previous chapters. Nevertheless, his "psychological history" of German cinema would famously condemn the genre most celebrated in the 1920s for its depiction of the natural realm: the mountain films (*Bergfilme*) pioneered by geologist-turned-director Arnold Fanck. In the present chapter, I will intervene in ongoing debates over this contested genre by engaging with developments in early- to mid-twentieth-century philosophy. Where Kracauer interpreted mountain films as efforts to cope with the vicissitudes of interwar history by regressing into an antirationalist nature idolatry—or, in Eric Rentschler's gloss, as "endeavors ... to take flight from the troubled streets of modernity, from anomie and inflation, to escape into a pristine world of snow-covered peaks and overpowering elements"—I will argue that they participated in rethinking the very dualism of nature and history.[6] Building on Rentschler's work along with more recent reevaluations of the mountain film, I will highlight the genre's contribution to the philosophical critique of historicism during the Weimar era. The object of my analysis will be Fanck's *The Holy Mountain* (*Der heilige Berg*, 1926), which traces the interaction of nonidentical, ultimately irreconcilable human figures and geophysical forces. The film thus suggests a vision of Adornian dialectics and also prefigures contemporary efforts to reconsider the relationship between nature and history against the backdrop of our global ecological crisis.

THE CINEMATIC JARGON OF AUTHENTICITY

Among the central issues in scholarship on the mountain film are the genre's political allegiances and its ideological positions vis-à-vis the modern epoch. Mountain films signal a rejection of bourgeois society and convention as well as a yearning for a restored sense of community, *Heimat*, and autochthonous rootedness in a vital, natural landscape. In this way, they appear to react against modern forms of disenchantment and alienation, evincing key tropes of the "conservative revolution"—a phrase popularized by Hugo von Hofmannsthal in his 1927 speech "Literature as the Spiritual Space of the Nation" ("Das Schrifttum als geistiger Raum der Nation"), and since used by scholars to describe a movement of right-wing, nationalist opposition to the Weimar Republic.[7] In an influential study of conservative-revolutionary German thinkers including Hans Freyer, Ernst Jünger, Carl Schmitt, Werner Sombart, and Oswald Spengler, Jeffrey Herf observes that their repudiation of Enlightenment rationality was paradoxically coupled with an enthusiasm for modern technology. Describing this ideological current as "reactionary modernism," Herf argues that it laid the foundation for the Nazi regime's efforts to forge a cultural synthesis of spiritual inwardness with advanced technology, or what Thomas Mann characterized as "highly technological Romanticism."[8] Moreover, criticizing Max Horkheimer and Adorno's *Dialectic of Enlightenment* (*Dialektik der Aufklärung*, 1944) for its overgeneralized account of the Enlightenment and the rise of fascism, Herf stresses the specificity of the German context as the site of a weak liberal-democratic tradition and rapid industrial modernization.

Numerous commentators have critiqued Herf's study, problematizing its central terms of analysis. For Andrew Hewitt, Herf's opening claim—"There is no such thing as modernity in general. There are only national societies, each of which becomes modern in its own fashion"—is itself paradoxical, ridding "modernity" of its overall meaning while maintaining that the category is lent specific inflections.[9] Peter Osborne further contends that "reactionary modernism" should be regarded not as the conjunction of contradictory stances, as Herf suggests, but rather as an "*integral* form of modernism in its own right."[10] Where Herf associates "modernism" with industrial technology and the aesthetic vanguard, Osborne argues that "reactionary" political forms such as fascism should also be identified with a revolutionary and fundamentally modernist temporality, pushing toward a radically new state of affairs while imagining it as a form of mythical return, conservation, or recovery. Finally, Anson Rabinbach faults Herf's study for obscuring Nazism's distinct phases and eclectic cultural sources along with its competing powers and ideological positions. In Rabinbach's view, while Herf seeks to offer a more differentiated account of German fascism than Horkheimer and Adorno, he nonetheless conveys a monolithic conception of the Nazi discourse on technology, focusing solely on a modernist lineage that was quickly marginalized in the 1930s.[11]

Although excluded from consideration in Herf's study, cinema was a key locus of ambivalence in early-twentieth-century intellectual debates, particularly insofar as the medium fused modern technology and artistic aspiration. As Katharina Loew has demonstrated, theoretical writings on the artistic possibilities of film were underpinned by an effort to reconcile the technologically based medium with established aesthetic categories, especially from the domain of German Idealism.[12] The paradoxes of this "techno-romantic" discourse are evident already in the opening title card of Fanck's *The Holy Mountain*: "The well-known sportspeople who appear in the film *The Holy Mountain* ask the audience not to mistake their achievements for photographic tricks, to which they would not stoop. All of the outdoor shots were really filmed in the mountains, in the most beautiful regions of the Alps, over a period of one and a half years. German, Norwegian, and Austrian champions took part in the big ski race. The screenplay for the placeless and timeless story, which is set in the mountains, emerged from real experiences during a twenty-year existence in the high mountains."[13]

Articulating what I will call a cinematic jargon of authenticity—that is, a reified second nature that falsely asserts privileged representational access to first nature; auratic mystification on film that assumes the ideological guise of a critique of modern alienation—this prefatory text claims multiple forms of realism, including the established mountaineers and skiers, their genuine athletic feats, the location shooting, and the screenplay's basis in actual experience. In emphasizing the extended duration of the filming process and of prior residence in the Alps, the title card suggests an artisanal, nonalienated mode of labor as well as rootedness within the natural landscape—forms of production and existence that are arguably in tension with a quintessentially modern medium (recalling Adorno's claim that "jargon pursues artisanship under the shadow of industry").[14] Through the disavowal of "photographic tricks," the text also implicitly acknowledges the medium's capacities for visual deception through professional actors, special effects, and studio sets. Not only do cinema's aesthetic and technological possibilities thus challenge the very criterion of authenticity to which the title card appeals; they also threaten to exceed viewers' sensory faculty and power of cognitive judgment, such that film adopts the quality of the sublime from the realm of primary nature that it represents.

Fanck's repudiation of "photographic tricks" is notably belied by his film's prominent use of state-of-the-art techniques that both distort the natural flow of time and afford novel views of the human body and its environment. As recent commentators have emphasized, while mountain films contain numerous "signifiers of social, technological, and economic modernization" (e.g., tourists, resort hotels, automobiles, sporting equipment and events), their modernism can also be discerned on a formal level.[15] Beyond Fanck's well-known interest in new camera models, film stock, and lenses as well as his innovations in sports cinematography (e.g., mounting cameras to downhill skiers), this modernism is perhaps most evident in *The Holy Mountain* with regard to time and montage.[16] Fanck deploys a plethora of techniques (e.g., slow-motion shots of *Ausdruckstanz* and of gravity-defying ski jumps; time-lapse photography of cloud formations), which offer manageable images of processes whose actual duration defies human capacities for acute observation. Moreover, his film compacts its main narrative arc into the events of a single day and often disregards sequential chronology—particularly through subjective flashbacks and visions, superimpositions, parallel and overlapping editing, jump cuts, a narratively unintegrated prelude, and many further attractions (e.g., dance performances, a ski race) that arrest the story's forward motion. Rupturing and reconfiguring the natural unfolding of time, these cinematic devices and elements suggest modernist temporalities of acceleration, deceleration, disjuncture, repetition, reversal, and simultaneity.

Evoking both long-term, unbroken rootedness in the landscape and a proliferation of nonlinear temporalities, *The Holy Mountain* adopts a highly ambivalent relationship to nature and human history. Subtitled *A Dramatic Poem in Images from Nature* (*Eine dramatische Dichtung in Bildern aus der Natur*), the film signals this equivocal stance already in the opening title card, identifying the sites and length of production while also untethering the narrative from specific spatiotemporal coordinates ("placeless and timeless [*ort- und zeitlos*]"). This internal schism would factor into the divided reception of the mountain-film genre, with critics increasingly distinguishing between magnificent documentary images of nature and inane fictional story lines, and between authentic, open-air locations and highly contrived, derivative scenarios.[17] Recalling debates among Romantic landscape painters as well as issues in early film theory on the role of narrative and the proper mode of engagement with the external world (e.g., Hermann Häfker's prioritization of "grand images of nature," Béla Balázs's call for the "stylization of nature," Germaine Dulac's interest in instructional films on "natural history"), these dual tendencies would be famously characterized by Kracauer as "realistic" and "formative" in his *Theory of Film* (1960).[18] In Fanck's own writings of the Weimar period, the mountain-film director adopted both positions, claiming "to show nature as it is . . . with the greatest possible reality and liveliness" while also disavowing cinema's task as that of reproducing the phenomena of the physical world without creative *Gestaltung* or artistic intervention.[19]

Finally, although the opening title card abstracts the narrative from the sphere of historical reality into a realm of fairy tale or myth, the film draws generously from a broad range of aesthetic traditions and cultural sources, revealing a historicist eclecticism. Named after the figure in Plato's *Symposium* and Friedrich Hölderlin's *Hyperion*, the female protagonist, Diotima (played by Leni Riefenstahl), performs dances whose titles and gestural vocabulary evoke Friedrich Schiller's "Ode to Joy" ("An die Freude," 1785) and Fidus's paintings and illustrations. By contrast, the leading male character (Luis Trenker), a solitary mountain dweller called "The Friend," bears affinities with Friedrich Nietzsche's Zarathustra along with Parzival from Wolfram von Eschenbach's epic poem and Richard Wagner's opera.[20] The narrative spaces also display a vast array of visual and architectural styles: the Grand Hotel contains Grecian stone columns and modernist elements; images of the natural landscape recall the works of Romantic painters including Carl Gustav Carus, Caspar David Friedrich, Joseph Anton Koch, Ludwig Richter, Philipp Otto Runge, and Karl Friedrich Schinkel; a torch-lit rescue party brings to mind abstract films of the Weimar period; and, lastly, the vision of a Gothic "ice cathedral" suggests the Expressionist designs of German architects such as Wassili Luckhardt, Hans Poelzig, and Bruno Taut.[21] With its range of sources—classical, Teutonic, Christian, Romantic, modernist—the film thus complicates Herf's argument about the conjunction of antirational and technophilic positions in the Weimar and Nazi periods, revealing a more complex, profound heterogeneity in interwar German culture.

TECHNOLOGY AND THE PERCEPTION OF NATURE

Despite their claims to an eternal, unchanging landscape, Fanck's mountain films activated a dialectic between technology and the perception of nature, furthering a centuries-long reappraisal of the Alpine peaks. If, as Marjorie Hope Nicolson famously argued, mountains gradually shifted in signification during the early modern period from foreboding, accursed sites to exemplars of holy nature—or, in her Ruskinian terms, from spaces of "gloom" to "glory"—these dual connotations would nonetheless extend into subsequent centuries.²² While Albrecht von Haller ("The Alps" ["Die Alpen"], 1732) and Jean-Jacques Rousseau (*Julie; or, The New Heloise* [*La Nouvelle Héloïse*], 1761) attributed to the Alps a state of liberty, virtue, and natural grace, another intellectual lineage—inaugurated by John Dennis, Edmund Burke, and Immanuel Kant—presented a sublime vision of the high mountains, which provoked what Kant characterized as "horror," "awesome shudder," and an "astonishment bordering on terror."²³ Romantic artists and writers conferred a constellational harmony on these two discursive strands in their reaction against Enlightenment rationality and the Industrial Revolution, conceiving Alpine travel as both an overwhelming, liminal experience and a healthy, regenerative escape from urban civilization. Whereas Roland Barthes would associate the "Alpine myth" with the nineteenth century, one could thus argue that the overdetermination of physical, moral, and spiritual elements—the "hybrid compound of the cult of nature and of puritanism"—can be traced to the very advent of modernity.²⁴

Petrarch's ascent of Mont Ventoux in 1336 had already pointed forward to the modern epoch, as Hans Blumenberg contended, especially insofar as the Italian poet and scholar was motivated by visual curiosity, or "a desire to see the great height of it."²⁵ Nevertheless, human experience of the Alps would adopt novel features in the mid to late nineteenth century, when sports offered the sensation not only of height, but also of movement and speed. Aside from mountain climbing, which was popularized through societies such as the German Alpine Club (Deutscher Alpenverein, founded in 1869), skiing was introduced from Scandinavia into Central Europe, precipitating competitive athletic events, year-round commercial activity, and expanded railway transport.²⁶ Promising both pristine nature and luxurious adventure, Alpine travel marked a Romantic quest for an elemental, unsullied landscape while also contributing to the transformation and destruction of that very setting; it paradoxically served as a mode of refuge from the demands of bourgeois existence and a symbol of elite educational and class status.²⁷ In this regard, alpinism exemplified the dialectics of tourism theorized by Hans Magnus Enzensberger, whereby relief from the conditions of industrial capitalism is produced in commodity form.²⁸

Alpinism expanded into a mass phenomenon by the early twentieth century, when interest in the mountains reached historic proportions. Apart from canonical works such as Richard Strauss's *An Alpine Symphony* (*Eine Alpensinfonie*, 1915) and Thomas Mann's *The Magic Mountain* (*Der Zauberberg*, 1924), the Alps also figured prominently in popular culture through the *Heimat* literature of Friedrich Lienhard and Ludwig Ganghofer as well as the mountain novels of Theodor Mayer, Karl Springenschmid, and Gustav Renker, whose *Holy Mountains: An Alpine Novel* (*Heilige Berge: Ein Alpenroman*) appeared in 1921.[29] While representations of the Alps proliferated in illustrated magazines, travel brochures, exhibitions, and other visual media, films including Fanck's two-part *The Marvel of the Snowshoe* (*Das Wunder des Schneeschuhs*, 1920 and 1922) distinguished themselves through their dynamism and ability to bring viewers to spaces previously out of reach to cinematic technology.[30] Alongside mass tourism, visual representations increasingly threatened the Alps with vulgarization, especially inasmuch as the region had offered solitude, detachment from society, and a privileged, elevated perspective (most notably in Nietzsche's writings). Whereas Georg Simmel's "Alpine Journeys" ("Alpenreisen," 1895) had ambivalently observed the growing "industry of nature enjoyment," Ernst Bloch asked in 1930 whether the Alps had been irrevocably debased from the sublime to trivial, picture-postcard kitsch on account of their wide accessibility and overfamiliarity through photographic technology.[31]

The Alps thus became a locus for contemplating the loss of "aura"—a term Walter Benjamin defined in relation to the mountain landscape in his famous "Artwork" essay. Distinct from Nietzsche, who had conceived the nimbus around Sils Maria in terms of its place "6,000 feet above sea level and much higher above all human things," Benjamin characterized "aura" as the appearance of distance on a horizontal plane, as when one follows "with the eye—while resting on a summer afternoon—a mountain range on the horizon."[32] For Benjamin, this perceived distance was eliminated in the modern era through the demand for proximity and the relinquishment of uniqueness, as facilitated by technologically based, reproducible media such as film. Inasmuch as mountain films rendered the Alps accessible to the masses while also upholding Romantic conceptions of nature, they anticipated Benjamin's critique of fascism in his "Artwork" essay as well as earlier texts. Writing on Ernst Jünger's *War and Warrior* (*Krieg und Krieger*, 1930), Benjamin argued that the cataclysm of World War I had indicated society's inability to integrate technology into existing relations successfully. For Benjamin, the writings of Jünger and other nationalist, protofascist thinkers represented an anachronistic approach to technology, as symptomatized by their portrayal of the war-ridden landscape through the lens of Idealism, their glorification and mystification of death, and their invocations of the "heroic," "eternal," and "primeval."[33] While such traits can undoubtedly be found in Fanck's films, it bears emphasis that progressive critics of the Weimar era expressed enthusiasm for his work, focusing precisely on the dialectic of nature and technology.

Having published a travel report on the Swiss Alps in the *Frankfurter Zeitung* as early as 1906 ("An Evening in the High Mountains" ["Ein Abend im Hochgebirge"]), Kracauer initially celebrated Fanck's work for offering new perspectives of nature and for expanding and contracting the natural flow of time.[34] In one of his first film reviews, Kracauer praised part 1 of Fanck's *The Marvel of the Snowshoe*, writing: "In images of rare beauty, it reveals to the viewer the wonders of the winter high mountains, which are only directly accessible to experienced alpinists and skiers."[35] Four years later, Kracauer again waxed lyrical about the "glorious images of nature" in Fanck's *Mountain of Destiny* (*Der Berg des Schicksals*, 1924), focusing in particular on the film's fast-motion shots of cloud formations: "Faster than in reality, they rush by and dissipate, cheated of their duration by the time lapse.... Their curious allure derives above all from the fact that processes requiring many hours to unfold in nature are here presented in a few minutes. The cloud events concentrate and the distortion of time produces an enchanting optical intoxication."[36] Although *The Holy Mountain* still drew Kracauer's praise for its nature cinematography upon its release in 1926, the critic dismissed the work as a whole as "a gigantic composition of body culture fantasies, moronic sun idolatry, and cosmic babble."[37] For Kracauer, Fanck's films now seemed to participate in a vague, sentimental nature worship rather than showcasing the medium's capacities to unmask a reified social order—or, as he wrote in his famous "Photography" essay of 1927, "to stir up the elements of nature."[38]

Kracauer's shift in thinking should be attributed not only to the growing prominence of narrative elements in Fanck's mountain films, the first of which bore greater affinities with the travelogues of early cinema.[39] As Kracauer became more Marxist in theoretical orientation by the mid-1920s, Miriam Hansen emphasizes, he also issued an ideology critique of *Naturbilder* (images of nature) and adopted an increasingly negative conception of nature itself, which he posited against reason and truth in texts including "The Mass Ornament" ("Das Ornament der Masse," 1927).[40] Where Kracauer viewed vernacular imagery of the Alps as retreating from contemporary crises into a seemingly unmediated, ahistorical nature, however, fellow film critic and theorist Béla Balázs (and later screenwriter of Riefenstahl's mountain film, *The Blue Light* [*Das blaue Licht*, 1932]) insisted on the importance of recovering a romantic "feeling for nature" for a progressive politics, especially at a time of fierce social struggle.[41] In his foreword to the illustrated book accompanying Fanck's *Storm over Mont Blanc* (*Stürme über dem Montblanc*, 1930), Balázs defended Fanck's mountain films against common reproaches such as the mixture of "grand images of his mountain world" and "stories of petty human destinies."[42] Problematizing the dichotomy upon which this critique was founded, Balázs adopted a more dialectical approach, arguing that natural forces gain grandeur in relation to individual figures, and that mountains become "dramatic elements" or "living beings" when mediated through human experience.[43] Balázs's defense of Fanck recalled his theorization of landscape in *Visible Man* (*Der sichtbare Mensch*, 1924), where he had similarly suggested a dynamic interplay between natural environments and dramatic action on-screen.[44]

SEA AND STONE

Balázs's theorization of the dialectic between grand mountains and individual characters can be viewed in relation to the aesthetic and philosophical writings of his erstwhile teacher Georg Simmel. In his 1911 essay "On the Aesthetics of the Alps" ("Zur Ästhetik der Alpen"), Simmel emphasized the salience of scale in aesthetic impressions, positing a spectrum extending from the Alps to the human form.[45] Where the human body's familiarity allows it to be represented in a wide variety of sizes within works of art, the aesthetic value of the Alps, Simmel suggested, is inextricably linked to their natural dimensions. Repurposing categories from Wilhelm Worringer's *Abstraction and Empathy* (*Abstraktion und Einfühlung*, 1907), Simmel wrote that the mountain landscape marks a form of abstraction from the ceaseless temporal flux of life, in contrast to the sea's mode of empathy and mediation. Much as Simmel had likened the sea to humankind's inner existence in his 1895 essay on the Alps—especially through the "purposeless *circulus vitiosus* of its movement"—he here defined water as a symbol of life in its eternal, restless motion.[46] With their chaotic, diffuse limitlessness, however, the Alps serve as a paradoxical exception to the use of juxtaposition to establish spatial relations. For Simmel, the mountains' true, sublime height comes into view only when unconditioned by life below, gesturing instead to a transcendent absolute.

Simmel also explored the concepts of the relative and the absolute in a 1911 essay on the problem of gender. Here, Simmel identified the basic form of relativity in human life as that of masculinity and femininity—a form wherein the male element had nonetheless become dominant, claiming the status of the absolute, objective, and universally human. While, in Simmel's analysis, men determine the cultural norms and claim an unmarked, generally valid position in society, their hegemony comes at the price of a split between reality and idea, practical limitation and infinite striving, and recognition of autonomous existence and a will toward formation and interpenetration. In this regard, men are paradoxically more relativistic than women, who—despite being relegated to the realm of specificity—remain unified and identical with the basis of life itself, bearing a "self-contained completeness."[47] Perpetuating Otto Weininger's view of women as nondifferentiated beings, Simmel associated them not with the ills of the current era, however, but more benevolently with the transcendence of the modern fragmentation of subject and object, means and ends, and higher and lower.

Taking up Simmel's philosophical concerns, Fanck's film is structured around the opposition between the mountains and the sea, articulating this geological distinction in gendered terms. Opening with an image in which a snowy mountain range is superimposed onto an endless body of water (an image that reappears twice in the prelude as well as at the film's conclusion), *The Holy Mountain* considers the possibility of uniting or "wedding" the two natural elements, here also serving as metaphors for man and woman. Perched on a cliff like the Sirens of Greek mythology or the Lorelei of German folklore, Diotima—at home "where the rock descends steeply and defiantly into the surf"—gazes onto the sea, which is characterized as "her love, wild and boundless." First depicted in low-angle silhouette against the clouds, the allegorically named Friend stands atop a pointed spire and is identified as the object of Diotima's longing ("him, whom she saw atop the highest mountain peak, as if in a dream"). This opposition of both gendered bodies and natural topoi pervades the film's visual and narrative features, most explicitly as the mother figure (Frida Richard) prophetically asserts, "The sea and the stone will never wed." Throughout, the film hints that water erodes and even destroys the banks, threatening the masculinized terrain with ruination. Juxtaposing solid rock formations with a dynamic, fluid femininity, the film recalls postwar German "male fantasies," which, as Klaus Theweleit observes, were "consistently organized around the sharp contrast between summit and valley, height and depth, towering and streaming."[48]

While the film registers nineteenth-century modes of engagement with the Alps, as projected onto the two male protagonists—the solitary, romantic alpinist (the Friend) and the competitive downhill skier (Vigo)—it also differentiates between mountain climbing and dancing as gendered forms of activity and modes of relation to nature.[49] Identified as "the expression of her stormy soul," Diotima's dance in the opening sequence is depicted through slow-motion shots of her body against the rippling water as well as a pattern of crosscutting between her corporeal gestures and the waves, whose movement she seems to conduct with her arms. (Released earlier that year in Germany, Sergei Eisenstein's *Battleship Potemkin* [*Bronenosets Potyomkin*, 1925] begins with similar imagery of the tide hitting the shore, also with an original score by Edmund Meisel.)[50] Recalling the choreography of Mary Wigman and Isadora Duncan, Diotima's "Dance to the Sea" ("Tanz an das Meer") belongs to a broad repertoire of interwar dances in which the sea and waves figured prominently, including Rudolf von Laban's "The Deluded" ("Die Geblendeten," 1922), Edith von Schrenck's "Waves" ("Wellen," 1922), and Loie Fuller's "The Sea" ("La Mer," 1925).[51] By contrast, the Friend represents the cult of mountains in Romantic and modernist work, descending—like Nietzsche's Zarathustra—from the remote Alpine heights to join human society at sea level. His search for a perfect peak for his engagement to Diotima and his final vision of their wedding in an "ice cathedral" also evoke themes from the Parzival legend, following Bruno Taut's utopian vision of mountain chains as "landscapes of Grail-shrines" in his book *Alpine Architecture* (*Alpine Architektur*, 1919).[52]

Juxtaposing what Kant called "the dark and raging sea" with "shapeless mountain masses towering above one another in wild disorder with their pyramids of ice," the film considers these sites of gendered expression in terms of the aesthetic experience of the sublime.[53] At the outset of the film's prologue, Diotima is seen in a soft-focus close-up, which—following Balázs's *Visible Man*—abstracts and dislocates her from spatiotemporal coordinates, opening an affective realm of "any space whatsoever," in Gilles Deleuze's formulation.[54] While the prologue presents her fantasy image of the Friend, the subsequent sequence tracks him and Vigo (Ernst Petersen)—introduced as "two friends from the mountains," suggesting a homosocial codefinition of the men and an ominous asymmetry in the gender dynamic—as they enter the Grand Hotel, encountering Diotima in multiple posters and onstage.[55] Exceeding all aesthetic frames within this reflexive sequence of exhibition and spectatorship, Diotima enraptures the Friend with her appearance and dance performances, compelling him to retreat into the high mountains "in order to master the overpowering impression" (anticipating a later scene where his view of her with another man will provoke a similar flight to the peaks). Whereas Diotima thus initially appears as a sublime entity eliciting both delight and terror, attraction and repulsion, she later views the mountains through her window as a delimited and domesticated aesthetic phenomenon, entering the landscape as an outsider with a tourist perspective or even an ethnographic gaze. During their first conversation, Diotima identifies the peaks with the quality of beauty, while the Friend espouses a Nietzschean vision of the mountains as a site of sublime power, introspection, and self-overcoming. The film will both validate and radicalize the Friend's response, tracing a shifting perception of the Alps from a youthful site of wonder and heroic action to a power that is far more ferocious, dangerous, and even life-threatening.

The film encodes its distinction between summit and sea in metaphors of sexuality, maternity, and birth. In *The Interpretation of Dreams* (*Die Traumdeutung*, 1900), Sigmund Freud linked dream images involving water to "intra-uterine life, or existence in the womb and the act of birth."[56] (Climbing, by contrast, represented sexual intercourse, with the rock and mountain serving as phallic symbols.) At once an erotic femme fatale, a maternal figure, and a religious icon (likened to a "saint" or "Madonna"), Diotima agrees to let the young Vigo rest his head in her lap—a compulsively repeated motif of Weimar cinema—following his victory in a ski race, leading to a tragic misunderstanding with the Friend.[57] Ultimately surviving the two men as an enduring presence, Diotima once again stands atop a cliff overlooking the water at the film's conclusion, recalling Goethe's conception of the "eternal feminine" ("Ewig-Weibliche") in part 2 of *Faust* (1832), in which Thales also proclaims: "All things have their beginning in water!! / Water sustains all things that exist; / may you, Oceanus, rule us forever!"[58] Reproducing essentialist visions of femininity, the film figures Diotima as an ahistorical, natural force—less, however, as "an immovable prehistoric boulder in the landscape of modernity," in Klaus Lichtblau's gloss on Simmel, than as what the film itself characterizes as the "the eternal sea."[59]

ADORNIAN DIALECTICS

Even as the film invokes the "eternal feminine," it suggests the historicity and finitude of the gendered landscape, thereby participating in interwar debates on the bases of historicism. Criticizing Heidegger's essentialization of historicity as the fundamental structure of *Dasein*, Adorno's 1932 lecture posited the idea of "natural history" as a means of overcoming the long-standing Idealist dualism between the dynamic realm of history and a lawful, immutable nature.[60] (Adorno's concept of nature includes both inner and outer nature, the human and nonhuman natural world, designating that which is unchanging or bears timeless, mythical qualities.) For Adorno, nature and history could be viewed as dialectically interrelated, revealing aspects of each other precisely where they appear in their most pronounced form: "If the question of the relation of nature and history is to be seriously posed, then it only offers any chance of solution if it is possible *to comprehend historical being in its most extreme historical determi-*

nacy, where it is most historical, as natural being, or if it were possible to comprehend nature as an historical being where it seems to rest most deeply in itself as nature."[61]

In reconceiving the traditional antithesis of nature and history, Adorno drew from two contemporaneous ideas: the Hegelian-Marxist concept of "second nature," as deployed by Georg Lukács in *The Theory of the Novel* (*Die Theorie des Romans*, 1916) to denote the naturalization of historical phenomena via processes of conventionalization and reification; and, conversely, the transience of nature, which Benjamin discerned in the baroque allegorical mode in his *Origin of the German Trauerspiel* (*Ursprung des deutschen Trauerspiels*, 1928). Where Lukács theorized the naturalization of history, Benjamin invoked a nature turned historical or transient.

For Adorno, Benjamin's emphasis on transience (*Vergänglichkeit*) not only served as a corrective to Heidegger's response to the crisis of historicism, but also challenged Idealist conceptions of nature and history. Adorno would elaborate on his idea of natural history in the decades to come, whether in *Dialectic of Enlightenment* (1944), where he and Horkheimer addressed "the intertwinement . . . of nature and the mastery of nature," or in a chapter of *Negative Dialectics* (*Negative Dialektik*, 1966) entitled "World Spirit and Natural History" ("Weltgeist und Naturgeschichte").[62] In the latter text, Adorno provided his most extensive treatment of the idea of natural history, refuting in particular the theodicean promise of inner coherence, unity, and a totality of meaning in Hegel's philosophy of history. For Adorno, Hegel had mythologized the historical process and absolutized domination, lending chance occurrences a sense of inexorable, fateful necessity and thereby justifying the current social order—tendencies, as Adorno argued, that were perpetuated by Heidegger, who further equated history with an invariable, inescapable nature.[63] Invoking the "eternal transience" that Benjamin had recognized in the German *Trauerspiel*, Adorno sought to develop a critical, non-Idealist theory of history sensitive to the concrete, corporeal suffering brought about by material conditions.[64]

Despite its appeal to a cinematic jargon of authenticity, *The Holy Mountain* arguably challenges the metaphysical presuppositions of both Idealism and existential ontology. Recalling Lukács's and Benjamin's early aesthetic writings, the film suggests a disharmony within human consciousness and nature, with catastrophe and ruinous fragmentation in place of classical balance and universal totality. Consider the aforementioned scene in which the Friend discovers Diotima with another man, as represented by three shots of his recoil through jump cuts and overlapping editing, followed by a dissolve and associative montage with narratively unmotivated

A jump cut, dissolve, and associative montage.

images of mountains exploding—notable violations of conventional editing in this melodrama of jealousy (*Eifersuchtsmelodram*). The Friend's experience of traumatic shock instigates his maniacal quest to conquer the north face of Monte Santo, where Vigo will hang from a rope in climactic scenes of literal suspense. While these scenes uphold the association of the mountain landscape with chaos, horror, and violent calamity, they nonetheless extend the negative, pessimistic moment of the sublime. Rather than evoking "ideas of reason" that diminish the sensible objects of nature, as per Kant's philosophy, the two men's confrontation with overwhelming nature leaves open an abyss into which they ultimately fall.[65] Like Richard Strauss's *An Alpine Symphony*, Fanck's film thus diverges in part from Idealist and Romantic conceptions of the mountains, aligning itself less with the metaphysical sublime than with Nietzsche's late characterizations of the Alpine sublime in terms of an earthly, nontranscendental nature.[66]

Whereas the film opens with Diotima's vision of a unification of water and high mountains, its denouement features the Friend's own fantasy of their marriage ceremony in an "ice cathedral." (Both sequences include a tracking shot of cloud formations, which Kracauer would proleptically link to the opening sequence of Riefenstahl's *Triumph of the Will* [*Triumph des*

The ultimate irreconcilability of the two lovers and the natural elements.

Willens, 1935].)⁶⁷ A mountain-like Gothic cathedral, the "ice cathedral" represents a sanctification of the Alpine landscape, a conflation of first and second nature as well as a synthesis or middle point between the elements of sea and stone (evoking Caspar David Friedrich's painting *The Sea of Ice* [*Das Eismeer*, 1823–24], where a frozen shipwreck appears in the form of large ice floes). With towering halls and giant icicles in place of stone columns, the cathedral features a Grail-like glowing altar that shatters as Diotima and the Friend join hands in union, similar to the mountains that explode in the Friend's prior subjective vision. Marking the ultimate irreconcilability of both the two lovers and the natural elements, the film suggests an Adornian dialectics, with the contradictory forces remaining nonidentical rather than reaching a point of consummation or systematic completion. The film thus rejects Hölderlin's concept of a beauty that synthesizes opposites and unites lovers in divine, endless communion. While Diotima in *Hyperion* exerted a harmonizing influence, the female protagonist of Fanck's film instead leads the Friend to deadly extremes, radicalizing Hölderlin's emphasis on the fragility and potential destructibility of the bond between man and woman.⁶⁸

Indicating irresolvable tensions in the gender economy and natural order, the film nonetheless seeks to mask its negative dialectics through myriad ideological claims, perpetuating a cinematic jargon of authenticity. Fanck attributes socioreligious meanings and even an ethical dignity to the activity of mountaineering, which Simmel had compared with gambling in its reckless, egoistic pleasures.[69] Furthermore, like Wagnerian Romanticism and later fascist doctrine, *The Holy Mountain* mystifies human mortality and ennobles self-sacrifice, appealing to a Christian vision of death as a means of redemption and also obscuring the senselessness of two men's untimely deaths within a credo of friendship and loyalty—a credo reinscribed through the film's own dedication to Fanck's late friend, the mountain climber Hans Rohde. While the opening titles emphasize the authentic physical exertion and suffering of the cast, even differentiating the "sportspeople" from the lone "actress" (Frida Richard) involved in the production, the film depicts a world detached from labor and material considerations, ultimately invoking an "eternal sea" that "rolls tranquilly in long waves over people's anguish and aspiration." Insofar as the film presents a vision of exploding mountains while also positing nature as a timeless, recursive force—conceiving water's erosion of the mountain landscape as part of an "eternal cycle"—it equivocates between historicizing and mythicizing gestures, or between what Leo Löwenthal later called "apparent disorder and happenstance" and "the endless reproduction of natural phenomena, the cyclic order of nature."[70]

In this way, Fanck's film adopts a highly ambivalent relationship to German historicism, which had threatened to dissolve absolute, eternal truths into a subjectivist relativism, provoking debates on the relationship between temporality and ontology, history and nature, during the Weimar era. Where Heidegger's *Being and Time* rendered these terms identical, seeking a moment before the split between subject and object, Adorno's 1932 lecture to the Frankfurt Kant-Gesellschaft conceived the antithetical concept pairs as mutually constitutive and chiasmatically intertwined. Scholarship that has associated *The Holy Mountain* and other mountain films with a flight from the contingencies of contemporary sociopolitical history into a timeless, mythical nature assumes an insufficiently dialectical conception of these terms, which—far from separate and discrete—were being jointly renegotiated during the interwar period. Departing from Idealist metaphysics, Fanck's film rethought the relation between natural and historical elements, appealing to eternal forces while also suggesting the historical mutability of the Alpine landscape. The film's very use of the extended metaphors of sea and stone implies a nonidentity of concept and matter, rejecting Descartes's ideal of a philosophical language articulated purely in clear, well-defined concepts—an ideal, as Hans Blumenberg argued, that would have rendered historicity "null and void."[71] Fanck's work thus serves as an example of film philosophy, demonstrating the intellectual operation of cinematographic images through metaphorical figures.[72]

THE ALPINE ANTHROPOCENE

The association of *The Holy Mountain* and the broader early-twentieth-century cult of mountains with protofascist psychological dispositions is further belied by the significance that the Alps later held in the works of many émigrés. Composed in Palestinian exile, Arnold Zweig's *Dialectic of the Alps* (*Dialektik der Alpen*, 1940) used the history of the Alps as a metonym for European history, from the continent's very beginnings to the Nazi era.[73] Having coauthored a similarly ambitious, historically sweeping account of the rise of fascism with *Dialectic of Enlightenment*, Adorno returned from the United States to Germany following World War II, taking yearly summer vacations with his wife, Gretel, in the Swiss Alps. Their preferred destination was the village of Sils Maria, where Nietzsche had written parts of *Thus Spoke Zarathustra* (*Also sprach Zarathustra*) during his regular visits in the 1880s. In "From Sila Maria" ("Aus Sils Maria," 1966), Adorno recounted his and Herbert Marcuse's conversation with an elderly local salesman who had known Nietzsche as a child.[74] Three years later, Adorno would suffer a fatal heart attack during a summer respite in the Swiss highlands.

The year of Adorno's death also saw the posthumous publication of Kracauer's *History: The Last Things before the Last* (1969). In the first chapter of his study, Kracauer addressed the relationship between human affairs and the events of nature, questioning whether the two are "equally amenable to the establishment of natural, or quasi-natural, laws."[75] While human history—"the realm of contingencies, of new beginnings"—is devoid of immutable forces and fixed patterns, Kracauer argued, the sphere of nature is mostly unchanging and marked by long-term regularities.[76] In thus distinguishing the field of history from the natural sciences, Kracauer critiqued the scientific worldview that had prevailed in the prior century, following the shift away from broad-scale theological speculations and from the universalizing philosophies of history (e.g., Kant, Hegel) that assumed an "invisible hand" at work in the historical process.

The opening chapter of Kracauer's book not only reacted (à la Dilthey) against nineteenth-century positivism, however, but also presciently registered the advent of a computer-based society that might threaten the sphere of human freedom, much like surveillance capitalism today. Nevertheless, his claim that "natural causes will continue to produce their predicted effects for an indeterminate time" appears outdated amid widespread recognition of the destructive impact of industrial civilization and the urgent need for nature preservation—concerns that in fact gained prominence in the early twentieth century, including in German alpine societies.[77] As human influence on the earth's ecosystems intensifies, critical environmental scholars are debating the relation of nature and society, the nonhuman and human—from the concepts of the Anthropocene and Capitalocene to the perspectives of actor-network theory, new materialism, posthumanism, metabolic rift theory, and world ecology.[78] Global ecological crisis is underscoring the mutability of nature, initiating another acute crisis of historical thinking. In the epilogue, I will draw an analogy between the crises of the Weimar era and the global present through the lens of Fritz Lang's *Metropolis* (1927), which also probes the nexus of human, technology, and environment.

EPILOGUE The Weimar Analogy
Metropolis and the Global Present

> I've put in so many enigmas and puzzles that it will keep the professors busy for centuries arguing over what I meant, and that's the only way of insuring one's immortality.
>
> JAMES JOYCE

"This film is the counterpart to *The Holy Mountain*, the hymn to nature; it is a hymn to technology."[1] Such was the contrast drawn by a critic for the trade journal *Reichsfilmblatt*, juxtaposing Arnold Fanck's work with Ufa's latest epic production: Fritz Lang's *Metropolis*. Premiering at Berlin's Ufa-Palast am Zoo on January 10, 1927, less than one month after Fanck's mountain film, *Metropolis* envisaged a futuristic cityscape in which imposing skyscrapers took the place of the Alps as the site of overwhelming spectacle, marking a shift from the natural to the technological sublime, or—in Hegelian-Marxist terms—from first to second nature. A culmination of silent-film aesthetics, *Metropolis* usurped international historical films such as *Cabiria*, *Intolerance*, and *Ben-Hur* in its monumental sets and mass displays. At the same time, Lang's film brought together diverse elements of Weimar cinema: from the uncanny doubles of *The Cabinet of Dr. Caligari* to the religious symbols and exotic locales of *Destiny*, and from the geometric abstraction of "absolute films" to the conservative ideological tendencies of the *Bergfilm* genre. *Metropolis* thus serves as an apt point of focus for this book's epilogue, which will examine the cinema and historical-philosophical debates of the Weimar period in relation to the political, economic, and environmental crises of the global present.

Released following an extended publicity campaign, *Metropolis* quickly became notorious for its megalomaniacal scale along with its colossal incoherence. The film involved over seventeen months of shooting and a skyrocketing, unprecedented budget that exacerbated Ufa's financial woes, which had already resulted in the 1925 Parufamet agreement with Paramount and MGM. Developed in a dependent, highly ambivalent relation to the United States (which Lang and producer Erich Pommer had visited in 1924), *Metropolis* shuttled between Expressionism and New

Objectivity, German romantic idealism and Americanism, and a fear of the chaotic, destructive potential of technology and a fascination with the rational efficiency of Taylorist-Fordist production. Compounding these structuring tensions, the film drew generously from a dizzying proliferation of mythical, religious, literary, pictorial, and other cultural referents. In the hands of set designers Otto Hunte, Erich Kettelhut, and Karl Vollbrecht, *Metropolis* also showcased a wide array of architectural styles, from a classical stadium through a Gothic cathedral up to modernist skyscrapers. Enumerating these disparate sources, commentators have variously characterized the film in terms of baroque excess, historicist eclecticism, and protopostmodern pastiche. Whatever else it might be, the film is a hot mess.

Scholars of Weimar cinema and visual culture have long analyzed *Metropolis* in conjunction with the notion of modernity. In foundational texts, they have approached Lang's film with regard to aspects of modern urban life, from its novel forms of industrial technology and mass-cultural entertainment to its specific modes of spatiality, sociality, and sensory experience.[2] Bracketing older polemics within Cinema and Media Studies against the so-called modernity thesis, the past years have seen thinkers across multiple disciplines interrogate the concept of "modernity" as such.[3] As the prior two chapters have indicated, aesthetic philosophers such as Peter Osborne and Jacques Rancière have emphasized the shortcomings and unacknowledged dialectics of "modernity" as a periodizing category, and environmental scholars have recast the entire modern epoch as the "Anthropocene" or "Capitalocene," among other neologisms.[4] Meanwhile, critical theorists in the social sciences have distanced themselves from the modernization theory of the 1950s and 1960s, reestablishing "capitalism" as a central category for understanding contemporary political developments around the globe. Remarking on the resurgence of interest in Marxism since the 2008 financial crisis, Moishe Postone writes, "[T]he term 'capitalism' has been reintroduced to broader academic as well as general intellectual discussions as a conception that now appears more analytically adequate than that of 'modernity,' which had been more dominant in the postwar decades."[5]

Apart from its ties to modernity, *Metropolis* has often been regarded as the harbinger of a postmodern cultural logic. Thea von Harbou's scenario-turned-novel—an example of the Weimar *Zukunftsroman*—borrowed from the science-fiction literature of Mary Shelley, Jules Verne, H. G. Wells, Edward Bellamy, Auguste Villiers de l'Isle-Adam, Karel Čapek, and Claude Farrère. Half a century after its release, *Metropolis* would become what Thomas Elsaesser called "an *Ur-text* of cinematic postmodernity," figuring into Thomas Pynchon's *Gravity's Rainbow* (1973) as well as numerous science-fiction films and music videos.⁶ Restored and reedited by Giorgio Moroder with a pop soundtrack in 1984, the film offered a wealth of cultural-historical referents that easily became simulacra—or, in Fredric Jameson's words, "emptied of their necessity, and reduced to pretexts for so many glossy images."⁷ Today, however, Jameson's diagnosis of the "perpetual present" of postmodernism itself appears passé. As Andreas Malm has argued, recent years have witnessed a return of historical consciousness as centuries of fossil-fuel combustion increasingly overtake the present.⁸ No longer is the vocation of science fiction, pace Jameson, "to demonstrate and to dramatize our incapacity to imagine the future"; instead, as E. Ann Kaplan emphasizes, the genre often envisions the cataclysmic climate change on our immediate horizon.⁹

Building on current critical trends, this epilogue will interpret Lang's *Metropolis* in relation to critiques of capitalism in the Weimar years and the contemporary moment. Faced with the tumultuous phenomena of the 1910s and 1920s, members of a younger generation—much like Freder, the protagonist of Lang's film—questioned aspects of their liberal bourgeois inheritance, from materialist artifice to capitalist ideologies of success and power, and from what Ernst Troeltsch described as "the suffocating mass of tradition" to "the historicist idea of development."¹⁰ Yet, as I will argue, where Troeltsch maintained the need for a "cultural synthesis [*Kultursynthese*]" in response to the crisis of historicism, Lang's film symptomatized the disunified incoherence of Weimar culture, where "the revolt of the son" assumed a promiscuous set of forms across the realms of aesthetics, religion, politics, and intellectual life.¹¹ In the final sections, I will shift attention to two recent films, *Sorry to Bother You* (Boots Riley, 2018) and *Parasite* (Bong Joon-ho, 2019), that extend and challenge the legacy of *Metropolis* in allegorizing racial capitalism and environmental injustice. Taking up scholarly discussions of the legitimacy and utility of historical analogies, I will explore the actuality of interwar Germany amid the crisis rhetoric of our time and also identify vital questions raised by the "many enigmas and puzzles" of Weimar culture—a culture that, like Joyce's writings, "will keep the professors busy."

HEAD, HEART, AND HANDS

While the filial revolt dramatized by *Metropolis* was an archetype of Weimar culture, it has significant precursors dating back to the nineteenth century. Perhaps most notably, the protagonist of Lang's film recalls Friedrich Engels, whose wealthy father owned large textile mills in German and English cities. Like Freder in *Metropolis*, Engels formed a relationship with a working-class woman, Mary Burns, and drew attention to the miserable conditions of factory laborers, highlighting the frequency of machine-related accidents and explosions.[12] Instances of Oedipal rebellion among young members of the industrial class became increasingly common by the fin de siècle. Across the political spectrum, leaders of new movements in Central Europe (e.g., Social Democracy, Christian Socialism, Pan-Germanism) challenged the liberal bourgeois order from which they had emerged, releasing the energies of the oppressed masses. Exemplary in this regard was the German nationalist and anti-Semitic politician Georg von Schönerer, the son of an eminent railway pioneer in Lang's native Vienna. "As a frustrated pseudo-aristocrat," Carl E. Schorske writes, "Georg prepared himself almost unconsciously to lead those social strata who chafed under the rule of the industrial bourgeoisie from which he himself sprang. Revolting masses and rebellious son would in due course find each other."[13]

Intergenerational conflict would become a recurring motif of the Expressionist theater that informed the narrative and aesthetics of *Metropolis*. Already in the prewar years, Expressionist dramas such as Reinhart Johannes Sorge's *The Beggar* (*Der Bettler*, 1912) staged the tension between youthful vision and patriarchal rule in a mechanistic, bourgeois society. Yet this scenario gained an explicit political coloration in the postwar "fatherless society," especially in the works of Georg Kaiser, Ernst Toller, and Fritz von Unruh.[14] In Kaiser's *Gas I* (1918), a compassionate billionaire's son shares profits with his workers, who slog at their machines for long hours. After a catastrophic explosion, the workers stage a misdirected revolt that fails to remedy the ills of industrialism, whereupon they ultimately follow a technocratic engineer "back to work . . . from explosion to explosion."[15] Emerging from Germany's short-lived period of revolutionary fervor, *Gas* and other Expressionist works conveyed disillusionment with radical activism, underscoring the gap between the artist-intellectual and the proletarian masses whom he hopes to lead toward regenerative transformation. Much like Lang's film, these dramas sought to infuse a cold industrial system with humanistic ideals of brotherhood and love, striving for what Unruh described as a "new covenant of the mind [*Geistes*] with the beating heart."[16]

In calling for a synthesis of head and heart, Expressionists confronted an enduring problem within Marxism that gained acute urgency in the late 1910s. "The head of this emancipation is philosophy, its heart is the proletariat," wrote Marx in the 1844 introduction to his *Critique of Hegel's Philosophy of Right* (*Zur Kritik der Hegelschen Rechtsphilosophie*, 1843), recalling Johann Heinrich Pestalozzi's pedagogical principle of head, heart, and hand.[17] Emphasizing the need for both spiritual-intellectual and material weapons, Marx argued that Germany's liberation from feudal social conditions would mark the realization of philosophy and the abolition of the proletariat, heralding a unification of theory and praxis. In 1918–19, Germany experienced one of its greatest moments of utopian hope for such sociopolitical transformation, as postwar uprisings promised spiritual renewal and an end to capitalist exploitation. For those committed to the Marxist cause, however, the failure of the German Revolution of 1918–19 raised a number of pressing questions: Why had socialism established itself in Russia rather than in the heart of Europe, contrary to Marx's expectations? How could one explain the German proletariat's inability to serve its role as the "subject of history"? And what political function could artists and intellectuals assume under the compromised and turbulent conditions of Weimar democracy, where the plight of the working class remained unresolved?

Lang's *Metropolis*, in my analysis, addressed the problematics of the spiritual-intellectual leadership of the working masses, redeploying Marx's corporeal metaphor in proposing the heart as a "mediator between brain and hands," or between capital and labor. Envisioning, à la Marx and Engels, a polarized society with "two great classes directly facing each other: Bourgeoisie and Proletariat," the film follows Freder—the wealthy son of the city's master, Joh Fredersen—as he joins his love interest, Maria, in championing the cause of destitute laborers, who are subjected to inhumane conditions and often-fatal industrial accidents.[18] Following the machinations of Fredersen and the inventor Rotwang, Maria's rabble-rousing doppelgänger (loosely evoking Rosa Luxemburg) sparks a destructive, Luddite revolt avowedly modeled after the failed German proletarian uprisings of 1918–19.[19] Ending without any change to the hierarchical division between *Kopf- und Handarbeiter* (mental and manual workers), the film's unsatisfying, oft-maligned resolution is symptomatic of what Max Horkheimer later diagnosed as a chasm between theory and praxis in advanced capitalist societies. Diverging from orthodox Marxists such as Georg Lukács, Horkheimer denied any necessary link between radical theory and the proletarian masses, whose situation was "no guarantee of correct knowledge."[20]

While sharing left-wing intellectuals' diminished faith in the revolutionary agency of a unified proletariat—as expressed, inter alia, in Horkheimer's 1927 essay "The Impotence of the German Working Class" ("Die Ohnmacht der deutschen Arbeiterklasse")—*Metropolis* itself drew the ideological scrutiny of the Weimar Republic's film and cultural critics.[21]

Reviewing Lang's film for a cultural-socialist monthly journal, *Kulturwille*, Felix Ziege wrote: "This film is born of bourgeois capitalist ideology and produced with the obtrusively noticeable tendency to propagate the idea of class reconciliation for the greater success of capitalist methods of exploitation. It exposes the bourgeois, worker-friendly phraseology in all its mendacity, for the same capital that financed this film has now ordered the exploitative Working Hours Act (*Arbeitszeitgesetz*)."[22] Referring to the eight-hour workday regulation passed on April 8, 1927 (drafted by the Social Democratic Party [SPD] and pushed forward by Christian trade unions), Ziege emphasized that Lang's film was the unmistakable product of bourgeois consciousness. For Ziege, *Metropolis* offered a trivial, sentimentally laden reconciliation between proletariat and capital without challenging the socioeconomic order and its relations of exploitation. Other reviewers similarly noted the film's disingenuous appeal to both workers and industrialists, Social Democrats and liberal bourgeois parties, reflecting the relative centrism of Weimar-era governmental coalitions. For all of its invocations of classical Marxism, *Metropolis* thus dismissed violent revolution in favor of evolutionary, piecemeal transformation, embracing the modest reforms and conciliatory positions more associated with the Marxist revisionism of Eduard Bernstein and the SPD.

CRISIS THEOLOGY

In *Cinéma 2* (1985), Gilles Deleuze claimed, "From the outset, Christianity and revolution, the Christian faith and revolutionary faith, were the two poles which attracted the art of the masses."[23] *Metropolis* moved in the direction of both poles, appealing to Christian doctrine and Marxist theory, salvation history and economic history. Yet the film appeared during an era of significant developments in the two traditions: while the postwar years witnessed the rise of Protestant neoorthodoxy and Catholic renewal movements amid the crisis of historicism (as initiated by Karl Barth's *The Epistle to the Romans* [*Der Römerbrief*, 1919] and Max Scheler's *On the Eternal in Man* [*Vom Ewigen im Menschen*, 1921], respectively), the failed German Revolution prompted a reexamination of Marxism—most notably in the Institute for Social Research (founded in 1923), which would integrate psychoanalysis into its neo-Marxist critical theory. It is against this broad intellectual-historical backdrop that we might consider the Marxist, Freudian, and Christological archetypes of *Metropolis*. In Lang's film, Freder is not only a workers' advocate and rebellious son, but also a sacrificial, Christlike mediator between father and humanity. The corporeal triad (head, heart, and hands) is thus overdetermined by the Oedipal triangle and the Holy Trinity.[24]

Metropolis is suffused with biblical references that become complexly and even perversely entangled. Most explicit in allegorical sequences depicting Moloch, the Tower of Babel, and the Seven Deadly Sins, the film's Christian iconography extends more generally to its topographical and characterological planes. While the workers gather in catacombs that suggest the places of early Christian worship in ancient Rome, the final reconciliation between capital and labor occurs on the steps of a medieval Gothic cathedral, with a climactic rooftop fight that takes inspiration from *The Hunchback of Notre Dame* (Wallace Worsley, 1923). Freder assumes a Christlike devotion to the poor and oppressed, appearing crucified after trading places with a worker for a ten-hour shift at the factory's dial wheel. Meanwhile, Maria and her machine double occupy multiple roles: as the Virgin of Mercy, surrounded by workers' children in the Eternal Gardens; as John the Baptist, prophesying the coming of a mediator in her subterranean sermons; and as the Whore of Babylon in the Yoshiwara nightclub, holding a golden cup and sitting upon a seven-headed, ten-horned beast. This proliferation of religious roles intertwines with Oedipal dynamics, particularly as Freder glimpses his father embracing the false Maria (paralleling the moment in *The Holy Mountain* when the Friend sees Vigo in the lap of Diotima).

The film's biblically laden story line intersected with the conservative modernist thought of interwar Germany. In the late nineteenth and early twentieth centuries, urban skyscrapers had become the current-day Towers of Babel, often surpassing the heights of medieval cathedrals, and cities such as New York and Berlin—frequently likened to Babylon for their sinful decadence—appeared to cultural critics as sites of monstrous engorgement. (In volume 2 of *The Decline of the West* [*Der Untergang des Abendlandes*, 1922], Oswald Spengler wrote, "The giant city sucks the country dry, insatiably and incessantly demanding and devouring fresh streams of men till it wearies and dies.")[25] Lang's own "imagination of disaster" makes recourse to biblical scenes from the Book of Genesis (e.g., the flood narrative) and the Book of Revelation, which Freder is shown reading in a limited edition by Avalun Press.[26] The film's lapsarian and eschatological imagery prompted one critic to describe *Metropolis* in 1927 as "a vision of the decline of the West, an apparition of the apocalypse, a film about the end-all of technical intelligence."[27] Drawing from Lang's dystopian images of machine civilization in *The Worker* (*Der Arbeiter*, 1932), Ernst Jünger would later write: "In the film *Metropolis* everything concerning the plot, the sets, or the machines is just as captivating as the attempt to develop a social worldview at the same time is tiring."[28]

Whatever its attempt at a worldview, Lang's film revealed an often-syncretic cultural hybridity, with title cards quoting from Omar Khayyam and Oscar Wilde; narrative sources as disparate as Greek and Norse mythology and Arthurian legend; images that cite artworks by Hieronymus Bosch, Pieter Brueghel, Auguste Rodin, Arnold Böcklin, Kurt Schmidt, and Oskar Schlemmer; and a score by Gottfried Huppertz that integrates "Dies Irae" and "La Marseillaise" and follows the late Romantic music of Richard Wagner, Richard Strauss, Giacomo Puccini, and Eugen d'Albert. For all of this indiscriminate eclecticism, however, *Metropolis* shows a sustained interest in the long tradition of magic and witchcraft. According to Harbou's novel, Rotwang's house was originally built by "a magician who had come from the East," with doors stamped with "the seal of Solomon, the pentagram"—a magical sign or talisman that figured in medieval Muslim, Jewish, and Christian sources and assumed significance in alchemy and occultism, including in a scene of Goethe's *Faust*.[29] Created in front of a reversed pentagram (an occult symbol of evil), the false Maria is ultimately burned at the stake, in the manner of early modern witch hunts. Both atavistic and ultramodern, Rotwang and his machine-human are at the juncture of magic and technology, sorcery and science, Faustian and Edisonian innovation.

The film's combination of archaic and pioneering elements was itself a matter of contention. Despite his debt to monumental films in the lineage of *Cabiria*, Lang distinguished his futuristic film from historical epics for its lack of an established model from which to build a cinematic world. Yet critics observed that *Metropolis* lacked a vision of the future, serving as an incoherent and ultimately empty revue of literary, theatrical, and filmic precedents. As Kurt Pinthus wrote, "Lang's *Metropolis* film wants to show the humanity of the future, the state of the future, the technology of the future, and hope for the future, and yet it leads into the past."[30] For such critics, the film not only synthesized familiar science-fiction fantasies, but also revealed an outdated and banal conception of complex socioeconomic problems, as filtered through biblical allusions, Romantic tropes, and bourgeois sentimentality. The film's Janus-faced split between antiquated and forward-looking impulses was mirrored by its often-contradictory appeal to both spirituality and technology, organic and mechanical rhythms, and mythical and historical time. The futuristic metropolis of Lang's film is more akin to the Eternal City of Sigmund Freud's *Civilization and Its Discontents* (*Das Unbehagen in der Kultur*, 1930): a palimpsestic composite of past and present structures, displaying a heterogeneous nonsimultaneity that breaks with the historicist postulate of a coherent and unilinear temporal flow.[31]

FALSE RECONCILIATION

The multiple, nonsynchronous temporalities of *Metropolis* are linked to the film's ambivalent evocation and containment of alterity. After Freder trades places with the worker Georgy, the latter is tempted by print ads for Yoshiwara, named after the red-light district established in early-seventeenth-century Japan. The allure of Yoshiwara is first envisaged via rapid montage, with superimposed images of alcohol, jazz music, dancing, queerness, sensuality, gambling, "Apache" violence, and the faces of white, Asian, and Black women. (This concern with racial physiognomy and intermingling is also explicit in the novel, where Harbou describes the face of Yoshiwara's owner in terms of a "complex racial mixture.")[32] The false Maria makes her eroticized dance debut on an ornamental pedestal held by seminude Black men who later turn to stone, recalling the treasure-bearing dwarfs in Lang's previous film, *Die Nibelungen* (1924). Like Alberich in *Die Nibelungen*, Rotwang is tacitly coded as Semitic, and his mechanical hand serves as an obstacle to the goal of an organic union of head, heart, and hands. Scapegoated alongside his robotic vamp, Rotwang falls from the parapets of the cathedral in the film's penultimate scene. His elimination allows for the formation of the couple and the rebirth of the spiritual-religious community, freed from nefarious Jewish influence and unfettered sexuality.[33]

It is now a commonplace that *Metropolis* displaces anxieties regarding mechanization onto women, homologizing technology and female sexuality as potential threats to male authority. While men's bodies become increasingly machinelike due to factory labor, only Maria is literally hybridized with technology, à la the artificial Hadaly in Villiers de l'Isle-Adam's *The Future Eve* (*L'Eve future*, 1886). Congruent with the film's general relegation of women to the domestic and erotic spheres—as mothers or prostitutes, sources of procreation or pleasure—the doubling of Maria evokes a misogynistic Madonna-whore complex: where Maria is a nurturing virgin mother who preaches messianic patience to the exploited male workers, her robotic counterpart is a seductive *femme machine* who incites a frenzied Luddite riot. Inexplicably excluded from the film's scenes of industrial labor, working-class women first appear as part of a raging, irrational mob that destroys the city's machinery and unleashes an all-engulfing flood. Only the burning of the soulless, witchlike machine-woman allows for the reestablishment of patriarchal order and industrial productivity, with clear boundaries reasserted between man and woman, human and machine. In the film's closing scene in front of the Gothic cathedral, sexuality and technology are both spiritualized rather than menacingly uncontrolled.

Having opened with images of moving machine parts, the film ends as the laborers march to the steps of the cathedral, led by their foreman, Grot. The only woman present, Maria looks to Freder as a mediator who can facilitate a symbolic handshake between Grot and Fredersen, or between the guardian and the owner of the machines. Analyzing the scene, Patrice Petro writes:

> Just as the real Maria's sexuality is drained to fuel the erotic deceptions of the Robot-machine, so, too, are the workers drained of energy, affect, and will. They emerge in the film's closing moments as an ornamental, hierarchical wedge, an aesthetically pleasing part of the mise-en-scène, organized to witness the formation of the couple and the healing of the breach between capital and labor. But ironically, in destroying the machine, it is they who have become machinelike, deceived by the deception of this pseudo-unity and community. In what would appear to be the absolute limit case of cynical reasoning, the final sequence of *Metropolis* leaves us with the image of a faceless mass whose revolutionary impulses have been purged, just as the real Maria is purged of sexuality, volition, and control.[34]

Susceptible to the sexually charged machinations of Rotwang throughout the film, Maria has shifted from a strong-willed, passionate leader to a passive damsel in distress. Misguided into violent insurrection by her robotic double, the workers are quickly expunged of any revolutionary instinct, remaining fickle and easily manipulable to the very end. Dressed in uniform and seen only from behind, the obedient laborers appear machinelike in their anonymous, lockstep marching. With a nod to Peter Sloterdijk, Petro views the film's ending as an extreme instance of cynical reason, with the harmonious resolution occurring at the expense of any political agency on the part of women and the working class.[35] Whatever its Expressionist pretenses to renewed community and a union of head and hands, the film tacitly reestablishes a technocratic ethos, signaling the pyramidal power structure of Taylorist-Fordist production through the rigidly triangular arrangement of the proletarian men.[36]

While the film's ending appeals to a broad audience through its noncommittal, incoherent politics (with vague elements of utopian socialism, social democracy, Manchester liberalism, and patriarchal conservatism), it has nonetheless drawn near-unanimous condemnation. Weimar critics noted that the film leaves intact the oppressive ruling structure, proposing milquetoast reforms such as a Parzival-like sense of compassion on the part of the newly benevolent elite. The film's conciliatory, comic ending—

overlaying romance, the restoration of family, and broader social peace—unconvincingly insists on possibilities for overcoming class conflict and the ills of industrialism without deposing management or unsettling the capitalist order. Seizing on these glaring contradictions, Kracauer and subsequent commentators would deem the film's ending authoritarian, with its pompous, ornamental mass procession toward an omnipotent leader.[37] Referencing Kracauer's analysis, Peter Gay viewed *Metropolis* as symptomatic of a rightward political turn among German youth in the latter half of the 1920s, as the Expressionist "revolt of the son" gave way to New Objectivity's "revenge of the father." In Gay's account, a regressive, politically promiscuous "hunger for wholeness" shaped Weimar cultural life, often assuming the form of "the urge for direct action or for surrender to a charismatic leader."[38]

For present purposes, I am less interested in relitigating the matter of Weimar cinema's protofascism than in reexamining *Metropolis* through a contemporary lens, mobilizing ongoing debates in critical theory to think both *with* and *beyond* the film. How can we reinterpret the film's figuration of political economy following the shift from state-centric Fordism to global financializing neoliberal capital? How does our perspective shift when we move past the film's ambivalent and highly problematic engagement with alterity to consider racial capitalism, including histories of colonialism and enslavement? And, finally, how might *Metropolis* be understood in relation to issues of environmental injustice and climate displacement? In the following section, I will take up these questions by placing *Metropolis* in conversation with two recent works of global cinema that continue and extend the thematization of issues of class, race, and environment. My focus will be on films that display the "new verticality" that Kristen Whissel has identified as a key feature of early-twenty-first century popular cinema—a trope, in Whissel's account, that films often use "to acknowledge extremism, economic polarization, and thwarted upward mobility as significant aspects of their global audience's condition of existence."[39] Tracing this visual trope across periods and geopolitical regimes (à la Lang's *Destiny*, discussed in chapter 4), I will also contribute to current scholarly discussions of the potential for drawing analogies between the Weimar Republic and our own historical moment.

THE TROPE OF VERTICALITY

Metropolis schematizes class relations and hierarchical power structures through a vertically organized cityscape. Employing the common science-fiction device of "world reduction," the film's opening scenes and stylized,

The luxurious upper world of the capitalist bourgeoisie.

variably scrolling intertitles establish a strong separation between the luxurious upper world of the capitalist bourgeoisie and the dark, dystopian underworld of the working masses.[40] Where the wealthy inhabit an elevated utopia of soaring skyscrapers and a "Sons' Club" (with lecture halls, libraries, theaters, stadiums, and pleasure gardens), the exploited laborers are confined to inhumane factories, subterranean tenements, and ancient catacombs, hidden from the purview of the ruling elite in what Seth Peabody describes as "the often-invisible infrastructural layers of the city."[41] Although the trope of verticality can be analyzed with regard to debates in Weimar Germany over monumental and high-rise architecture, as Dietrich Neumann has shown, the physical division of the city along this axis also harks back to the late-nineteenth-century writings of H. G. Wells.[42] In a scathing review of *Metropolis* from 1927, Wells accused the film of plagiarizing elements of his own early novel *The Sleeper Awakes* (1899). For Wells, Lang's film appeared anachronistic for envisioning urban space and population distribution in terms of centripetal concentration rather than centrifugal, horizontal sprawl: "This vertical social stratification is stale old stuff."[43]

Wells's polemic aside, recent cinematic allegories of capitalism continue to visualize class disparities through vertical architectural relations, attesting to

The dark, dystopian underworld of the working masses.

Industrial smoke in the machine room.

The flooding of the workers' quarters.

the ongoing resonance and enduring global legacy of Lang's film. Take Boots Riley's *Sorry to Bother You* (2018): the low-wage telemarketers work in the dingy, cramped basement of the RegalView company building in Oakland, California, while the "Power Callers" ride a golden elevator up to the sleek and spacious top floor. Adopting a "white voice," the Black protagonist, Cassius "Cash" Green, quickly ascends the ranks and is recruited by RegalView's client Worryfree, a corporation that propagates slave labor. Much as Fredersen deploys Maria's robotic double to foment a self-destructive workers' rebellion in *Metropolis*, Worryfree's CEO, Steve Lift, offers Cassius the role of false leader of the "equisapiens," a hybrid species of horse-humans engineered to maximize profits (recalling Frederick Winslow Taylor's infamous claim that "it would be possible to train an intelligent gorilla so as to become a more efficient ... handler than any man can be").[44] Yet Riley's film is decidedly more radical and satisfying in its ending than *Metropolis*: where Lang shows the workers returning to a state of machinelike docility following their Luddite revolt, here the equisapiens harness technology to break into Lift's home in a final scene of violent, revolutionary confrontation.

Described by Riley as "an absurdist dark comedy with magical realism and science fiction," *Sorry to Bother You* can be further located in multiple aesthetic, political, and philosophical traditions—from dystopian satire and surrealism to Black speculative fiction and Afrofuturism (e.g., Sun Ra, Octavia E. Butler), and from socialism to the existential absurdism of Franz Kafka and Albert Camus.[45] Commenting on the film, Robin D.G. Kelley writes, "Life is not *inherently* absurd; instead its absurdities are produced by capitalism, racism, and patriarchy. The point of dialectical analysis is not to find the meaning of life but to reveal the fundamental antagonisms in the material world. For Riley, as for Marx, only by remolding the world can we begin to resolve its philosophical contradictions. *Sorry to Bother You* chooses revolution over the lone Camusian rebel, suggesting that our survival as a species and as a planet depends on the overthrow of capitalism, the redistribution of wealth, and a complete reordering of society based on collective needs."[46]

In contradistinction to *Metropolis*, Riley's film thus affirms collective revolutionary struggle as a necessary means of abolishing capitalism and realizing a more equitable and sustainable global order. Developed amid the horizontally organized Occupy and Black Lives Matter movements, *Sorry to Bother You* aligns itself with Black Marxist accounts of the racialism that permeates capitalism's highly stratified organization of labor.[47] Drawing attention to the ongoing history of slavery, Riley's work—like Janelle Monáe's concept series *Metropolis* (2007–)—encourages us to reenvision the architectonic social hierarchies of Lang's film as structured by colonial relations.[48] (In "The Skyscraper" ["Der Wolkenkratzer," 1934], Max Horkheimer imagined the high-rise building as a cross section of capitalist society, emphasizing its underlying basis in "the horrible exploitation apparatus at work in the partly or fully colonial territories.")[49]

Appearing one year after Riley's film, Bong Joon-ho's *Parasite* (*Gisaengchung*, 2019) is another allegory of capitalism that figures class stratification through vertical hierarchies.[50] The destitute Kim family dwells in a bleak semibasement *banjiha* apartment on a squalid side street in Seoul, subsisting on precarious, low-paying gigs. By contrast, the affluent Park family owns a sequestered and architecturally significant modernist home in a quiet and elevated neighborhood (recalling Kingo Gondo's hilltop house in Akira Kurosawa's *High and Low* [*Tengoku to jigoku*, 1963]). Like *Metropolis*, *Parasite* is structured around the motif of uncannily doubled and mistaken identity, as the Kim family gradually infiltrates the Park household by taking on a series of domestic roles (English tutor, art therapist, chauffeur, housekeeper) under false pretenses. Their charade is threatened by the sudden reappearance of the previous housekeeper, whose husband has spent years hiding from loan sharks in the house's

The dingy, cramped basement and the sleek and spacious top floor in Boots Riley's *Sorry to Bother You* (2018).

secret, subterranean bunker. As with Freder in Lang's film, the Park family's pampered son, Da-song, is traumatized by his exposure to the horrific underworld of unrecognized misery subtending his haut bourgeois existence of luxury and privilege. Repressed class antagonisms ultimately rise to the surface, culminating in a violent uprising that fails to alter the socioeconomic order.

In allegorizing the rigid class divides and rampant wealth inequality in South Korean society—site of recent corruption scandals, rising unemployment and costs of living, and intensifying air pollution and monsoon floods—*Parasite* compels viewers to consider the nexus of economic and environmental injustice. In *Metropolis*, the upper class lives with sunlight, clean air, and luscious gardens filled with plants and animals, while the workers down below exist in a state of dark confinement, with industrial smoke and a dearth of forms of natural life. Similarly, in *Parasite*, the Park family estate includes a landscaped yard, whereas the Kims' living

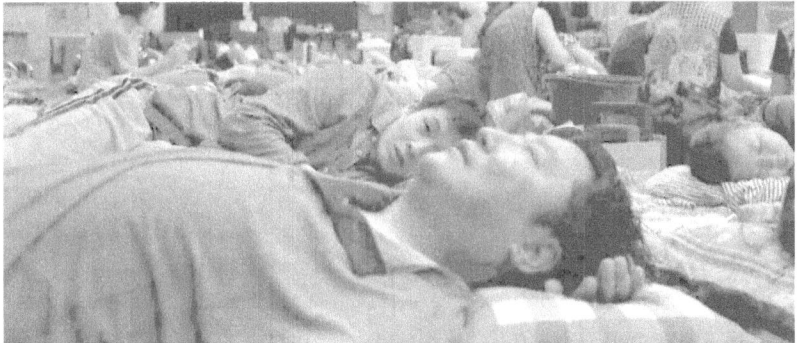

The Kims' apartment is submerged with sewer water, turning them into climate refugees, in Bong Joon-ho's *Parasite* (2019).

conditions are grimy and abject, including bug infestations and a moldy smell that becomes a source of ridicule and stigma. Much as the workers' quarters are flooded during the misbegotten revolt in *Metropolis*, the Kims' apartment is submerged with sewer water during a severe rainstorm that turns them into climate refugees, forced to shelter in a crowded gymnasium alongside other displaced families. Taking up themes from Bong's earlier film *Snowpiercer* (2013), *Parasite* thus suggests the imbrication of capitalism and climate catastrophe: the wealthy—disproportionately responsible for carbon emissions—remain secure and only minorly inconvenienced, while the impoverished bear the brunt of environmental disaster.

THE POLITICS OF ANALOGY

As I have maintained in this closing chapter, a critical theory of capitalism provides a fitting lens for analyzing the metastasizing crises of the Weimar years and the global present. Yet while a Marxist interpretive framework allows us to understand both periods in terms of capitalism's deep-seated contradictions and inherent crisis tendencies, we still need to attend to the historically specific phases of this overarching social order. When placed in constellation, the films by Lang, Riley, and Bong indeed illuminate a broad-scale, globally uneven shift from an industrial age to a service economy, and from the physical labor of factory workers to the affective labor of telemarketers and domestic workers. Where the figure of Joh Fredersen in *Metropolis* evokes Henry Ford—known for the standardizing efficiency of assembly-line mass production and for the five-day, forty-hour workweek—Steve Lift in *Sorry to Bother You* and Park Dong-ik in *Parasite* are tech CEOs associated with a neoliberal ideology of flexibility, deregulation, and the dissolution of boundaries between work and life, or labor and leisure. In examining *Metropolis* in conjunction with the two contemporary films, we thus confront broader philosophical questions regarding analogical reasoning and the uses and disadvantages of historical comparisons. As Kracauer asked in *History: The Last Things before the Last* (1969), "What is the good of indulging in analogies? Why dote on a subject only to jilt it for a similar subject?"[51]

Recent years have witnessed a staggering proliferation of analogies to Weimar Germany, as commentators have analyzed political developments via parallels with interwar Europe—from the socioeconomic turmoil wrought by global capitalist crisis to the rise of right-wing, authoritarian-populist regimes. Cultural and intellectual historians have disputed the legitimacy and utility of such analogies as well as their capacity to emphasize both similarity and uniqueness, commonality and distinctiveness, continuity and novelty.[52] In an eloquent exchange in the *New York Review of Books* during the final year of the Trump administration, Peter Eli Gordon defends usage of the term *concentration camps* with reference to US migrant detention centers, distinguishing historical difference from incommensurability, while Samuel Moyn contends that comparisons to fascism and National Socialism are often misleading, abnormalizing Trump and obscuring local histories of genocide, slavery, and state violence.[53] At stake in the debate are enduring dilemmas of the German historicist tradition: the historicist stress on the development and irreducible individuality of historical entities (or what Wilhelm Windelband characterized as a particularizing, "idiographic" method of understanding) comes into tension with an interpretive interconnection and moral judgment informed by present-day values and concerns.[54]

Issues of difference and rupture occupy a central position in research on the Weimar Republic and twentieth-century Germany, shaped by debates over the *Sonderweg* (special path) versus common European processes of modernization, a "shattered past" versus the longer-term "continuities of German history."[55] Writing amid the *Historikerstreit* (historians' dispute) of the 1980s, Detlev Peukert examined the Weimar Republic in its own right as the "crisis of classical modernity," underscoring the era's tensions and intensifying contradictions rather than its traumatic beginnings or ultimate collapse into what Friedrich Meinecke termed the "German catastrophe."[56] While eschewing Peukert's overarching theory of modernity, contemporary scholars have maintained his emphasis on the complex pluralism and manifold potentiality of Germany's first democracy, calling attention to the era's historical openness and contingency. Drawing from Reinhart Koselleck, Rüdiger Graf studies the ubiquitous narratives of crisis in the Weimar Republic and subsequent historiography, arguing that the term *crisis* denoted a time of decision, action, and either-or possibility for the future instead of a pessimistic or fatalistic sense of doom.[57] Jochen Hung challenges the common dichotomy between innovative cultural achievement and political-economic instability, as epitomized by Peter Gay's oft-repurposed image of "a dance on the edge of a volcano."[58]

Positing a more dialectical relation between modernist cultural experimentation and broad-scale social and spiritual-intellectual upheaval, this epilogue has demonstrated that for all of Weimar culture's "hunger for wholeness," there was no return from atomized fragmentation to unified totality, or from relativist skepticism to absolute values, transcendental norms, and eternal, universal truths. While symptomatizing what Ernst Troeltsch identified as a widespread longing for "synthesis, system, worldview, structure, and position," *Metropolis* betrayed the promiscuous, often-polarized forms assumed by a younger generation's revolt against the liberal bourgeois worldview—from "communist and pacifist ideals to completely romantic and folkloristic, religious, and national ones."[59] Where Troeltsch's *Historicism and Its Problems* (*Der Historismus und seine Probleme*, 1922) concluded with an appeal to a "cultural synthesis" based on the selective retrieval of Europe's constitutive values, *Metropolis* sought to unify heterogeneous elements of cultural history, including the achievements of German silent cinema. Yet in drawing the formal and aesthetic innovations of Weimar cinema into one grand vortex—the Expressionism of *Caligari*, metaphysical allegory of *Destiny*, formalist abstraction of the "absolute film," and conservative tendencies of the mountain film—the film succumbs to an incoherent plot and inane temporal resolution.

Metropolis thus marks at once the summa and the reductio ad absurdum of the cinematic experiments in nonlinear time examined in this book.

Over the course of this study, I have offered a reassessment of pioneering works of Weimar cinema in light of the crisis of historicism diagnosed by Troeltsch and other German intellectuals in the interwar period. Diverging from interpretations of Weimar filmmaking as overdetermined by the trauma of World War I or as teleologically prefiguring the rise of Nazism— that is, as a "shell shock cinema" or as sociopsychological sensors of "pre-Hitler Germany"—I have focused on the period's own vital, extensive debates on the theory and practice of history.[60] If, as Graf writes, "convincing historical explanation must scrutinize the ways in which crises were diagnosed and used by various historical actors," I have sought to elucidate myriad facets of the crisis of historicism through the prism of disparate thinkers and films.[61] Tracking the question of history across a broad spectrum of film styles, modes, and genres, I have positioned Weimar films as philosophical texts that meditated on the diverse problems of the German historicist tradition. In the process, I have explored the historiographical implications of the filmic medium, developing a loose typology of thinking about time and history through the moving image.

A WAY A LONE A LAST A LOVED A LONG THE

Where intellectual histories of the crisis of historicism have commonly neglected the sphere of audiovisual culture, this book has focused on the emergence of film as a crucial medium for registering a shattered faith in the meaning and coherence of history in the early twentieth century. Challenging the logocentrism of prior accounts, I have emphasized the concurrence of the Weimar debates over historicism and the increasing recognition of cinema's capacity to figure and engage with complex ideas. In probing the interconnections between cinema and the crisis of historicism, I have not only historicized contemporary interest in film philosophy, excavating a vast archive of writings that long predates the work of Cavell and Deleuze; I have also contributed to critical reflection on the import and legacy of the "historical turn" in Cinema and Media Studies, drawing sustained attention to the philosophical critiques of historicism that accompanied the first decades of moving-image culture. Not least, I have looked to interwar Germany to shed fresh light on our own moment of pervasive narratives of "crisis," understanding the term less as a cause for despair than as a signal of mutability and Joycean, open-ended indeterminacy. For if there is a key meaning to be gleaned from the "many enigmas and puzzles" of Weimar culture today, it is the . . .

Notes

INTRODUCTION

Epigraphs: Siegfried Kracauer, *History: The Last Things before the Last* (Princeton, NJ: Markus Wiener, 1995), 3–4; Pauline Kael, "Is There a Cure for Film Criticism? Or, Some Unhappy Thoughts on Siegfried Kracauer's *Theory of Film: The Redemption of Physical Reality*," in *I Lost It at the Movies: Film Writings, 1954–1965* (London and New York: Marion Boyars, 2002), 291.

1. Thomas Elsaesser, "Beyond the New Film History" (remarks presented at the Histories of Film History: Materials & Methods conference, University of Marburg, December 14, 2018).

2. Thomas Elsaesser, "The New Film History," *Sight and Sound* 55, no. 4 (1986): 247.

3. See Mark Lynn Anderson, *Twilight of the Idols: Hollywood and the Human Sciences in 1920s America* (Berkeley: University of California Press, 2011); Mark Lynn Anderson, "Anger Management, or the Dream of a Falsifiable Film-Historical Past," *NECSUS: European Journal of Media Studies* 11, no. 1 (Spring 2022): 67–87; Jane M. Gaines, "Why We Took the 'Historical Turn': The Poisons and Antidotes Version," in *At the Borders of (Film) History: Temporality, Archaeology, Theories*, ed. Alberto Beltrame, Giuseppe Fidotta, and Andrea Mariani (Udine: Forum, 2015), 179–90; Jane M. Gaines, *Pink-Slipped: What Happened to Women in the Silent Film Industries?* (Urbana: University of Illinois Press, 2018); Katherine Groo, *Bad Film Histories: Ethnography and the Early Archive* (Minneapolis: University of Minnesota Press, 2019); Katherine Groo, "Let It Burn: Film Historiography in Flames," *Discourse* 41, no. 1 (Winter 2019): 3–36; Priya Jaikumar, *Where Histories Reside: India as Filmed Space* (Durham, NC, and London: Duke University Press, 2019); and Samantha N. Sheppard, "Changing the Subject: Lynn Nottage's *By the Way, Meet Vera Stark* and the Making of Black Women's Film History," *Feminist Media Histories* 8, no. 2 (Spring 2022): 14–42.

4. David Bordwell and Noël Carroll, eds., *Post-Theory: Reconstructing Film Studies* (Madison: University of Wisconsin Press, 1996); D.N. Rodowick, "An Elegy for Theory," *October* 122 (Fall 2007): 91–109.

5. See, e.g., Patrice Petro, "Classical Feminist Film Theory: Then and (Mostly) Now," in *The Routledge Companion to Cinema and Gender*, ed. Kristin Lené Hole, Dijana Jelača, E. Ann Kaplan, and Patrice Petro (London: Routledge, 2017), 15–24; and Nico Baumbach, *Cinema/Politics/Philosophy* (New York: Columbia University Press, 2019).

6. Philip Rosen, *Change Mummified: Cinema, Historicity, Theory* (Minneapolis: University of Minnesota Press, 2001); Mary Ann Doane, *The Emergence of Cinematic Time: Modernity, Contingency, the Archive* (Cambridge, MA: Harvard University Press, 2002); Laura Mulvey, *Death 24x a Second: Stillness and the Moving Image* (London: Reaktion Books, 2006).

7. Leo Löwenthal and Siegfried Kracauer, *In steter Freundschaft: Briefwechsel 1921–1966*, ed. Peter-Erwin Jansen and Christian Schmidt (Springe: Zu Klampen, 2003), 38. See also "Geschichtsschreibung und Geschichtsphilosophie," in Kracauer, *Werke*, vol. 5.1, ed. Inka Mülder-Bach (Berlin: Suhrkamp, 2011), 404–8.

8. Kracauer to Leo Löwenthal, February 10, 1961; quoted in "Siegfried Kracauer 1889–1966," ed. Ingrid Belke and Irina Renz, *Marbacher Magazin* 47 (1988): 118.

9. See, e.g., Ivan Ross, "Mediating the Historical Imagination: Visual Media and the U.S. Civil War, 1861–2011" (PhD diss., University of Chicago, 2012); and Peter Geimer, "Einführung: Verfahren der Historisierung," in *Komplexität und Einfachheit: DFG-Symposion 2015*, ed. Albrecht Koschorke (Stuttgart: J. B. Metzler, 2017), 449–57.

10. See Siegfried Kracauer, *From Caligari to Hitler: A Psychological History of the German Film*, ed. Leonardo Quaresima (Princeton, NJ: Princeton University Press, 2004); and Anton Kaes, *Shell Shock Cinema: Weimar Culture and the Wounds of War* (Princeton, NJ: Princeton University Press, 2009).

11. E. C. Kenyon, *Thomas Alva Edison: The Telegraph-Boy Who Became a Great Inventor* (London: W. & R. Chambers, 1895), 112.

12. Leopold von Ranke, "Preface to the First Edition of *Histories of the Latin and Germanic Peoples*," in *The Theory and Practice of History*, ed. Georg G. Iggers, trans. Wilma A. Iggers (London and New York: Routledge, 2011), 86; Siegfried Kracauer, *Theory of Film: The Redemption of Physical Reality* (Princeton, NJ: Princeton University Press, 1997), 78. On the proper translation of *"wie es eigentlich gewesen,"* see Georg G. Iggers, introduction to Ranke, *Theory and Practice of History*, xiv: "It is not factuality, but the emphasis on the essential that makes an account historical." On shifting interpretations (and misinterpretations) of Ranke in the United States and Germany, see also Georg G. Iggers, "The Image of Ranke in American and German Historical Thought," *History and Theory* 2, no. 1 (1962): 17–40.

13. Fritz Lang, "The Future of the Feature Film in Germany," trans. Don Reneau, in *The Weimar Republic Sourcebook*, ed. Anton Kaes, Martin Jay, and Edward Dimendberg (Berkeley: University of California Press, 1994), 623.

14. Leopold von Ranke, "On Progress in History," trans. Wilma A. Iggers, in Ranke, *Theory and Practice of History*, 21.

15. Hans Richter, "History Is What Is Happening Today," in *G: An Avant-Garde Journal of Art, Architecture, Design, and Film, 1923–1926*, ed. Detlef Mertins and Michael W. Jennings, trans. Steven Lindberg with Margareta Ingrid Christian (Los Angeles: Getty Research Institute, 2010), 228–29.
16. Ernst Troeltsch, "Die geistige Revolution: Berliner Brief," in *Kunstwart und Kulturwart* 34, no. 4 (January 1921): 231.
17. Kracauer, *History*, 216.
18. Frank Ankersmit, "Historicism: An Attempt at Synthesis," *History and Theory* 34, no. 3 (1995): 161.

CHAPTER 1

Epigraphs: Carl Heinrich Becker, "Der Wandel im geschichtlichen Bewußtsein," *Die neue Rundschau* 38, no. 1 (1927): 113; Frank Ankersmit, "Historicism: An Attempt at Synthesis," *History and Theory* 34, no. 3 (1995): 161.
1. Wilhelm Dilthey, *Einleitung in die Geisteswissenschaften: Versuch einer Grundlegung für das Studium der Gesellschaft und der Geschichte*, vol. 1 (Leipzig: Duncker & Humblot, 1883), v.
2. Wilhelm Dilthey, preface to *Introduction to the Human Sciences*, trans. Michael Neville, in *Introduction to the Human Sciences*, ed. Rudolf A. Makkreel and Frithjof Rodi (Princeton, NJ: Princeton University Press, 1989), 50.
3. Charles R. Bambach, *Heidegger, Dilthey, and the Crisis of Historicism* (Ithaca, NY, and London: Cornell University Press, 1995), 141.
4. On this point, see, e.g., Tom Gunning, "'Now You See It, Now You Don't': The Temporality of the Cinema of Attractions," in *The Silent Cinema Reader*, ed. Lee Grieveson and Peter Krämer (London and New York: Routledge, 2004), 41–50.
5. This point was recognized by Philip Beck already in 1985: "The 'revisionist' movement in film history has positioned itself for the most part not in relation to theories of history and historical practice, but rather in relation to past film historical work that is now, for a variety of reasons, judged deficient or methodologically unsound." Philip Beck, "Historicism and Historism in Recent Film Historiography," *Journal of Film and Video* 37, no. 1 (1985): 5.
6. Jane M. Gaines, *Pink-Slipped: What Happened to Women in the Silent Film Industries?* (Urbana: University of Illinois Press, 2018), 12. For further reconsiderations of the "historical turn," see Alison Butler, "New Film Histories and the Politics of Location," *Screen* 33, no. 4 (1992): 413–26; Katherine Groo, "Cut, Paste, Glitch, and Stutter: Remixing Film History," *Frames Cinema Journal* 1, no. 1 (2012), https://framescinemajournal.com/article/cut-paste-glitch-and-stutter/; and Jane M. Gaines, "What Happened to the Philosophy of Film History?," *Film History* 25, nos. 1–2 (2013): 70–80. Gaines identifies three major dossiers devoted to the theory or philosophy of film history: see D. N. Rodowick, "Historical Knowing in Film," *Iris* 2, no. 2 (1984): 2–4; Paolo Cherchi Usai, "The Philosophy of Film History," *Film History* 6, no. 1 (1994): 3–5; and Sumiko Higashi, "Film History, or a Baedeker Guide to the Historical Turn," *Cinema Journal* 44, no. 1 (2004): 94–100.

7. See Jay Leyda, "Toward a New Film History," *Cinema Journal* 14, no. 2 (1974): 40–41; and James Harvey Robinson, *The New History: Essays Illustrating the Modern Historical Outlook* (New York: Macmillan Company, 1912), 8, 47.

8. See Robert C. Allen and Douglas Gomery, *Film History: Theory and Practice* (New York: Alfred A. Knopf, 1985), 3–23; and Charles A. Beard, "That Noble Dream," *American Historical Review* 41, no. 1 (1935): 74–87.

9. On this point, see, e.g., André Gaudreault and Tom Gunning, "Early Cinema as a Challenge to Film History," trans. Joyce Goggin and Wanda Strauven, in *The Cinema of Attractions Reloaded*, ed. Wanda Strauven (Amsterdam: Amsterdam University Press, 2006), 376–77; Philip Rosen, *Change Mummified: Cinema, Historicity, Theory* (Minneapolis: University of Minnesota Press, 2001), xxi; and Katherine Groo, *Bad Film Histories: Ethnography and the Early Archive* (Minneapolis: University of Minnesota Press, 2019), 11–12. For summaries of New Film History and the New Cinema History (focused on the social and cultural history of cinema), see also Annette Kuhn and Jackie Stacey, "Screen Histories: An Introduction," in *Screen Histories: A Screen Reader*, ed. Annette Kuhn and Jackie Stacey (Oxford: Clarendon Press, 1998), 1–10; James Chapman, Mark Glancy, and Sue Harper, introduction to *The New Film History: Sources, Methods, Approaches*, ed. James Chapman, Mark Glancy, and Sue Harper (New York: Palgrave Macmillan, 2007), 1–10; and Richard Maltby, "New Cinema Histories," in *Explorations in New Cinema History: Approaches and Case Studies*, ed. Richard Maltby, Daniel Biltereyst, and Philippe Meers (Malden, MA, and Oxford: Blackwell, 2011), 3–40.

10. Thomas Elsaesser, "The New Film History," *Sight and Sound* 55, no. 4 (1986): 251.

11. See Thomas Elsaesser, "The New Film History as Media Archaeology," in *CiNéMAS* 14, nos. 2–3 (2004): 75–117. Elsaesser used the term "media archaeology" as early as 1990; see Thomas Elsaesser, "Early Cinema: From Linear History to Mass Media Archaeology," in *Early Cinema: Space, Frame, Narrative*, ed. Thomas Elsaesser with Adam Barker (London: BFI, 1990), 1–8.

12. On media archaeology, see, e.g., Jussi Parikka, *What Is Media Archaeology?* (Cambridge: Polity Press, 2012); Erkki Huhtamo and Jussi Parikka, eds., *Media Archaeology: Approaches, Applications, and Implications* (Berkeley: University of California Press, 2011); Wanda Strauven, "Media Archaeology: Where Film History, Media Art, and New Media (Can) Meet," in *Preserving and Exhibiting Media Art: Challenges and Perspectives*, ed. Julia Noordegraaf, Cosetta Saba, Barbara Le Maitre, and Vinzenz Hediger (Amsterdam: Amsterdam University Press, 2013), 59–79; and Erkki Huhtamo and Doron Galili, "The Pasts and Prospects of Media Archaeology," *Early Popular Visual Culture* 18, no. 4 (2020): 333–39.

13. Thomas Elsaesser, *Film History as Media Archaeology: Tracking Digital Cinema* (Amsterdam: Amsterdam University Press, 2016), 46. On the relation between media archaeology and early cinema history, see also Doron Galili, "Early Cinema and the Emergence of Television: An Archaeology of Intertwined

Media," in *The Oxford Handbook of Silent Cinema*, ed. Rob King and Charlie Keil (New York: Oxford University Press, 2024), 38–54.

14. See *Oxford English Dictionary Online*, s.v. "historicism," www.oed.com/view/Entry/87304?redirectedFrom=historicism&; and Karl Popper, *The Poverty of Historicism* (London and New York: Routledge, 2002). On the conceptual history of historicism, see also Otto Gerhard Oexle, "'Historismus': Überlegungen zur Geschichte des Phänomens und des Begriffs," in *Jahrbuch 1986 der Braunschweigischen Wissenschaftlichen Gesellschaft* (Göttingen: Erich Goltze, 1986), 119–55; and Georg G. Iggers, "Historicism: The History and Meaning of the Term," *Journal of the History of Ideas* 56, no. 1 (1995): 129–52.

15. Friedrich Meinecke, *Historism: The Rise of a New Historical Outlook*, trans. J. E. Anderson (London: Routledge and Kegan Paul, 1972), lv.

16. Meinecke, lv; Georg G. Iggers, *The German Conception of History: The National Tradition of Historical Thought from Herder to the Present* (Middletown, CT: Wesleyan University Press, 1983).

17. Frederick C. Beiser, *The German Historicist Tradition* (Oxford: Oxford University Press, 2011).

18. Ernst Troeltsch, "Die Krisis des Historismus," *Die neue Rundschau* 33 (1922): 573. See also Max Weber, "Science as a Vocation," in *Essays in Sociology*, ed. and trans. H. H. Gerth and C. Wright Mills (New York: Oxford University Press, 1946), 129–56; and Troeltsch's response to the debate sparked by Weber's lecture in Troeltsch, *Die Revolution in der Wissenschaft* (Munich and Leipzig: Duncker & Humblot, 1921).

19. Friedrich Nietzsche, "On the Uses and Disadvantages of History for Life," in *Untimely Meditations*, ed. Daniel Breazeale, trans. R. J. Hollingdale (Cambridge: Cambridge University Press, 1997), 108.

20. Ernst Troeltsch, *Der Historismus und seine Probleme* (Tübingen: J. C. B. Mohr, 1922). For more extensive accounts of Troeltsch's late writings on the problems of historicism and its links to ethics, see Brent Sockness, "Geschichte durch Ethik überwinden? Ernst Troeltsch, Moral Consciousness, and the Crisis of Historicism," in *Praktische Theologie und protestantische Kultur*, ed. Wilhelm Gräb and Birgit Weyel (Gütersloh: Christian Kaiser, 2002), 200–217; and Brent W. Sockness, "Historicism and Its Unresolved Problems: Ernst Troeltsch's Last Word," in *Historisierung: Begriff—Geschichte—Praxisfelder*, ed. Moritz Baumstark and Robert Forkel (Stuttgart: J. B. Metzler, 2016), 210–30.

21. Oswald Spengler, *The Decline of the West*, trans. Charles Francis Atkinson (New York: Alfred A. Knopf, 1926); Friedrich Meinecke, "Ernst Troeltsch und das Problem des Historismus" [1923], in Meinecke, *Staat und Persönlichkeit* (Berlin: E. S. Mittler & Sohn, 1933), 54–64; Karl Mannheim, "Historicism" [1924], in *Essays on the Sociology of Knowledge*, ed. Paul Kecskemeti (London: Routledge & Kegan Paul, 1952), 84–133; Otto Hintze, "Troeltsch und die Probleme des Historismus: Kritische Studien," *Historische Zeitschrift* 135, no. 2 (1927): 188–239. See also Paul Tillich, "E. Troeltsch: Historismus und seine Probleme" [1924], reprinted in *Journal for the Scientific Study of Religion* 1, no. 1 (1961): 109–14;

and Fritz-Joachim von Rintelen, "Der Versuch einer Überwindung des Historismus bei Ernst Troeltsch," *Deutsche Vierteljahrsschrift für Literaturwissenschaft und Geistesgeschichte* 8 (1930): 324–72. On the Weimar "historicism debate," see also Wolfgang Bialas and Gérard Raulet, eds., *Die Historismusdebatte in der Weimarer Republik* (Frankfurt am Main: Peter Lang, 1996); and Lothar Köhn, "Überwindung des Historismus: Zu Problemen einer Geschichte der deutschen Literatur zwischen 1918 und 1933," pts. 1 and 2, *Deutsche Vierteljahrsschrift für Literaturwissenschaft und Geistesgeschichte* 48, no. 4 (1974): 704–66; 49, no. 1 (1975): 94–165.

22. For contemporary takes on the crisis of historicism, see Bambach, *Heidegger, Dilthey, and the Crisis of Historicism*; Ankersmit, "Historicism"; Allan Megill, "Why Was There a Crisis of Historicism?," *History and Theory* 36, no. 3 (1997): 416–29; David N. Myers, *Resisting History: Historicism and Its Discontents in German-Jewish Thought* (Princeton, NJ, and Oxford: Princeton University Press, 2003); Ulrich Kittstein, *"Mit Geschichte will man etwas": Historisches Erzählen in der Weimarer Republik und im Exil (1918–1945)* (Würzburg: Königshausen & Neumann, 2006); and Peter E. Gordon, "Weimar Theology: From Historicism to Crisis," in *Weimar Thought: A Contested Legacy*, ed. Peter E. Gordon and John P. McCormick (Princeton, NJ: Princeton University Press, 2013), 150–78.

23. Leopold von Ranke, "On Progress in History," trans. Wilma A. Iggers, in *The Theory and Practice of History*, ed. Georg G. Iggers (London and New York: Routledge, 2011), 21.

24. On this point, see Karl Heussi, *Die Krisis des Historismus* (Tübingen: J. C. B. Mohr, 1932), 37; and Friedrich Meinecke, "Von der Krisis des Historismus," *Aphorismen und Skizzen zur Geschichte* (Leipzig: Koehler & Amelang, 1942), 121.

25. Heussi, *Die Krisis des Historismus*, 69, 56.

26. Meinecke, "Von der Krisis des Historismus," 119. Meinecke had reviewed Heussi's book in 1934; see Meinecke, *"Die Krisis des Historismus," Historische Zeitschrift* 149, no. 2 (1934): 303–5.

27. On Meinecke's ambivalence toward the Hitler regime, see, e.g., Amy R. Sims, "Intellectuals in Crisis: Historians under Hitler," *Virginia Quarterly Review* 54, no. 2 (Spring 1978): 246–62.

28. Siegfried Kracauer, *Soziologie als Wissenschaft*, in Kracauer, *Werke*, vol. 1, ed. Inka Mülder-Bach (Frankfurt am Main: Suhrkamp, 2006), 9–101.

29. Siegfried Kracauer, "The Crisis of Science: On the Foundational Writings of Max Weber and Ernst Troeltsch," in *The Mass Ornament: Weimar Essays*, ed. and trans. Thomas Y. Levin (Cambridge, MA: Harvard University Press, 1995), 213; translation modified.

30. Siegfried Kracauer, "Photography," in Kracauer, *The Mass Ornament*, 59; translation modified.

31. Kracauer, 49–50; translation modified. I base my modifications on the original 1927 version of the essay. The reference to Dilthey was omitted from the version printed in *Das Ornament der Masse* (1963).

32. Kracauer, 61, 63.
33. Siegfried Kracauer, *History: The Last Things before the Last* (Princeton, NJ: Markus Wiener, 1995), 3–4.
34. Kracauer, *History*, 4.
35. Kracauer, 47.
36. Walter Benjamin, "Eduard Fuchs, Collector and Historian," trans. Howard Eiland and Michael W. Jennings, in Benjamin, *Selected Writings*, vol. 3, ed. Howard Eiland and Michael W. Jennings (Cambridge, MA: Harvard University Press, 2002), 260–302; Walter Benjamin, "On the Concept of History," trans. Harry Zohn, in Benjamin, *Selected Writings*, vol. 4, ed. Howard Eiland and Michael W. Jennings (Cambridge, MA, and London: Harvard University Press, 2003), 389–400.
37. Benjamin, "On the Concept of History," 392; translation modified.
38. Kracauer, "Photography," 62; Benjamin, "On the Concept of History," 396.
39. Benjamin, "On the Concept of History," 390.
40. See Walter Benjamin, "The Work of Art in the Age of Its Technological Reproducibility: Second Version," trans. Edmund Jephcott and Harry Zohn, in Benjamin, *Selected Writings*, vol. 3, 131n31; Benjamin, "Doctrine of the Similar," trans. Michael Jennings, in Benjamin, *Selected Writings*, vol. 2, pt. 2, ed. Michael W. Jennings, Howard Eiland, and Gary Smith (Cambridge, MA, and London: Harvard University Press, 1999), 694–98; Benjamin, "On the Mimetic Faculty," trans. Edmund Jephcott, in Benjamin, *Selected Writings*, vol. 2, pt. 2, 720–22; Benjamin, "The Paris of the Second Empire in Baudelaire," trans. Harry Zohn, in Benjamin, *Selected Writings*, vol. 4, ed. Howard Eiland and Michael W. Jennings (Cambridge, MA, and London: Harvard University Press, 2003), 62; Benjamin, "Central Park," trans. Edmund Jephcott and Howard Eiland, in Benjamin, *Selected Writings*, vol. 4, 183; and Benjamin, *The Arcades Project*, trans. Howard Eiland and Kevin McLaughlin (Cambridge, MA, and London: Harvard University Press, 1999), 473 (fragment N9,7). Sigmund Freud described perception in terms of the "flickering-up [*Aufleuchten*] and passing-away [*Vergehen*] of consciousness"; see Freud, "A Note upon the 'Mystic Writing-Pad,'" in Freud, *The Standard Edition of the Complete Psychological Works of Sigmund Freud*, vol. 19, ed. and trans. James Strachey (London: Hogarth Press, 1961), 231.
41. Theodor W. Adorno, "Prologue to Television," in Adorno, *Critical Models: Interventions and Catchwords*, trans. Henry W. Pickford (New York: Columbia University Press, 2005), 55. See also Adorno, "The Schema of Mass Culture," in Adorno, *The Culture Industry: Selected Essays on Mass Culture*, ed. J. M. Bernstein (London and New York: Routledge, 1991), 93; and Adorno, *Aesthetic Theory*, ed. Gretel Adorno and Rolf Tiedemann, trans. Robert Hullot-Kentor (London and New York: Continuum, 2002), 81.
42. Benjamin, "On the Concept of History," 395; translation modified. On the nexus of history and photography in Benjamin's work, see also Eduardo Cadava, *Words of Light: Theses on the Photography of History* (Princeton, NJ: Princeton University Press, 1997); and Humberto Beck, *The Moment of*

Rupture: Historical Consciousness in Interwar German Thought (Philadelphia: University of Pennsylvania Press, 2019).

43. Roland Barthes, "The Discourse of History," in Barthes, *The Rustle of Language*, trans. Richard Howard (Berkeley: University of California Press, 1989), 127–40; Hayden White, *Metahistory: The Historical Imagination in Nineteenth-Century Europe* (Baltimore and London: Johns Hopkins University Press, 1973); Michel Foucault, *The Archaeology of Knowledge*, trans. A.M. Sheridan Smith (New York: Vintage, 1972); Michel Foucault, "Nietzsche, Genealogy, History," in *Language, Counter-Memory, Practice: Selected Essays and Interviews*, ed. Donald F. Bouchard, trans. Donald F. Bouchard and Sherry Simon (Ithaca, NY: Cornell University Press, 1977), 139–64; and Reinhart Koselleck, *The Practice of Conceptual History: Timing History, Spacing Concepts*, trans. Todd Samuel Presner and others (Stanford, CA: Stanford University Press, 2002).

44. Saul Friedlander, ed., *Probing the Limits of Representation: Nazism and the "Final Solution"* (Cambridge, MA, and London: Harvard University Press, 1992); Cathy Caruth, *Unclaimed Experience: Trauma, Narrative, and History* (Baltimore: Johns Hopkins University Press, 1996); Dominick LaCapra, *Writing History, Writing Trauma* (Baltimore: Johns Hopkins University Press, 2001); Martin Jay, "Historical Explanation and the Event: Reflections on the Limits of Contextualization," *New Literary History* 42, no. 4 (2011): 557–71; Martin Jay, "Historicism and the Event," in *Against the Grain: Jewish Intellectuals in Hard Times*, ed. Ezra Mendelsohn, Stefani Hoffman, and Richard I. Cohen (New York and Oxford: Berghahn, 2014), 143–67; Frank Ankersmit, *Sublime Historical Experience* (Stanford, CA: Stanford University Press, 2005); and Eelco Runia, "Presence," *History and Theory* 45, no. 1 (2006): 1–29. See also Jouni-Matti Kuukkanen, ed., *Philosophy of History: Twenty-First-Century Perspectives* (London and New York: Bloomsbury Academic, 2020).

45. Bonnie G. Smith, *The Gender of History: Men, Women, and Historical Practice* (Cambridge, MA: Harvard University Press, 1998); Dipesh Chakrabarty, *Provincializing Europe: Postcolonial Thought and Historical Difference* (Princeton, NJ: Princeton University Press, 2000).

46. Dipesh Chakrabarty, *The Climate of History in a Planetary Age* (Chicago: University of Chicago Press, 2021).

47. Andreas Fickers, "Towards a New Digital Historicism? Doing History in the Age of Abundance," *Journal of European History and Culture* 1, no. 1 (2012): 19–26.

48. Tom Eyers, "The Perils of the 'Digital Humanities': New Positivisms and the Fate of Literary Theory," *Postmodern Culture* 23, no. 2 (2013), https://muse.jhu.edu/article/537059. On "distant reading" and "algorithmic criticism," see Franco Moretti, *Distant Reading* (London and New York: Verso, 2013); and Stephen Ramsay, *Reading Machines: Toward an Algorithmic Criticism* (Urbana: University of Illinois Press, 2011).

49. Rita Felski, *The Limits of Critique* (Chicago: University of Chicago Press, 2015), 155. See also, e.g., Allen Dunn and Thomas F. Haddox, eds., *The*

Limits of Literary Historicism (Knoxville: University of Tennessee Press, 2011); and Jennifer Fleissner, "Historicism Blues," *American Literary History* 25, no. 4 (2013): 699–717.

50. Reinhart Koselleck, "'Space of Experience' and 'Horizon of Expectation': Two Historical Categories," in Koselleck, *Futures Past: On the Semantics of Historical Time*, trans. Keith Tribe (New York: Columbia University Press, 2004), 255–75; and François Hartog, *Regimes of Historicity: Presentism and Experiences of Time*, trans. Saskia Brown (New York: Columbia University Press, 2015), 17–18.

51. Enzo Traverso, *Left-Wing Melancholia: Marxism, History, and Memory* (New York: Columbia University Press, 2016). See also Ernst Bloch, *The Principle of Hope*, trans. Neville Plaice, Stephen Plaice, and Paul Knight (Cambridge, MA: MIT Press, 1986); and Hans Jonas, *The Imperative of Responsibility: In Search of an Ethics for the Technological Age*, trans. Hans Jonas and David Herr (Chicago: University of Chicago Press, 1984).

52. Hans Ulrich Gumbrecht, *Our Broad Present: Time and Contemporary Culture* (New York: Columbia University Press, 2014), 71.

53. See Kracauer, "Photography," 50; translation modified; Kracauer, *History*, 108, 182; and Kracauer, *Theory of Film: The Redemption of Physical Reality* (Princeton, NJ: Princeton University Press, 1997), 63–64.

54. Kracauer explicitly engages with Bergson and Proust in his essay "Sound-Image Film," trans. Nicholas Baer, in *The Promise of Cinema: German Film Theory, 1907–1933*, ed. Anton Kaes, Nicholas Baer, and Michael Cowan (Oakland: University of California Press, 2016), 556–58. For a Bergsonian analysis of Facebook, see Lewis Goodings and Ian Tucker, "Social Media and the Co-production of Bodies Online: Bergson, Serres and Facebook's Timeline," *Media, Culture & Society* 36, no. 1 (2014): 37–51.

55. Roland Barthes, *Camera Lucida: Reflections on Photography*, trans. Richard Howard (New York: Hill and Wang, 1981).

56. Stephen Bann, *Romanticism and the Rise of History* (New York: Twayne, 1995).

57. Wolfgang Ernst, "Let There Be Irony: Cultural History and Media Archaeology in Parallel Lines," in *Digital Memory and the Archive*, ed. Jussi Parikka (Minneapolis and London: University of Minnesota Press, 2013), 48–49.

58. See Jacques Rancière, "Die Geschichtlichkeit des Films," trans. Stefan Barmann, in *Die Gegenwart der Vergangenheit: Dokumentarfilm, Fernsehen und Geschichte*, ed. Eva Hohenberger and Judith Keilbach (Berlin: Verlag Vorwerk 8, 2003), 230–46.

59. Antoine de Baecque, *Camera Historica: The Century in Cinema*, trans. Ninon Vinsonneau and Jonathan Magidoff (New York: Columbia University Press, 2012), 20.

60. Marc Ferro, *Cinema and History*, trans. Naomi Greene (Detroit: Wayne State University Press, 1988); Pierre Sorlin, *The Film in History: Restaging the Past* (Totowa, NJ: Barnes & Noble Books, 1980); Hayden White, "Historiography

and Historiophoty," *American Historical Review* 93, no. 5 (December 1988): 1193. On the relationship between history and film, see also Vinzenz Hediger, "Aufhebung: Geschichte im Zeitalter des Films," in *Essays zur Film-Philosophie*, ed. Lorenz Engell, Oliver Fahle, Vinzenz Hediger, and Christiane Voss (Paderborn: Wilhelm Fink, 2015), 169–249.

61. See Robert A. Rosenstone, *Visions of the Past: The Challenge of Film to Our Idea of History* (Cambridge, MA: Harvard University Press, 1995); and Robert A. Rosenstone, *History on Film/Film on History* (Harlow, UK: Pearson, 2006).

62. See Alison Landsberg, *Prosthetic Memory: The Transformation of American Remembrance in the Age of Mass Culture* (New York: Columbia University Press, 2004); Steve F. Anderson, *Technologies of History: Visual Media and the Eccentricity of the Past* (Hanover, NH: Dartmouth College Press, 2011); Sven Lütticken, *History in Motion: Time in the Age of the Moving Image* (Berlin: Sternberg, 2013), and Alison Landsberg, *Engaging the Past: Mass Culture and the Production of Historical Knowledge* (New York: Columbia University Press, 2015).

63. Natalie Zemon Davis, *Slaves on Screen: Film and Historical Vision* (Cambridge, MA: Harvard University Press, 2000), 12, 14; Natalie Zemon Davis, "'Any Resemblance to Persons Living or Dead': Film and the Challenge of Authenticity," *Historical Journal of Film, Radio and Television* 8, no. 3 (1988): 269–83; Vivian Sobchack, "'Surge and Splendor': A Phenomenology of the Hollywood Historical Epic," *Representations*, no. 29 (Winter 1990): 24–49; Vivian Sobchack, "The Insistent Fringe: Moving Images and Historical Consciousness," *History and Theory* 36, no. 4 (December 1997): 4–20.

64. Robert Burgoyne, *Film Nation: Hollywood Looks at U.S. History* (Minneapolis: University of Minnesota Press, 1997); Robert Burgoyne, *The Hollywood Historical Film* (Oxford: Blackwell, 2008).

65. Rosen, *Change Mummified*, 147–99; Eleftheria Thanouli, *History and Film: A Tale of Two Disciplines* (New York: Bloomsbury, 2018).

66. Gustav Benkwitz, "Der Beirat für Geschichte," *Der Kinematograph*, no. 746 (June 5, 1921); Paul Eller, "Geschichtsstudium und Film," *Der Kinematograph*, no. 752 (June 17, 1921); Oskar Kalbus, "Zeit- und Kulturgeschichte," in *Der deutsche Lehrfilm in der Wissenschaft und im Unterricht* (Berlin: Heymann, 1922), 161–73; Gustav Würtenberg, "Geschichtsunterricht und Kino," *Vergangenheit und Gegenwart* 18, no. 6 (1928): 361–66.

67. Mason Kamana Allred, *Weimar Cinema, Embodiment, and Historicity: Cultural Memory and the Historical Films of Ernst Lubitsch* (New York and London: Routledge, 2017).

68. Lotte H. Eisner, *The Haunted Screen: Expressionism in the German Cinema and the Influence of Max Reinhardt*, trans. Roger Greaves (London: Thames and Hudson, 1969), 73.

69. Christian Rogowski, "Introduction: Images and Imaginaries," in *The Many Faces of Weimar Cinema: Rediscovering Germany's Filmic Legacy*, ed. Christian Rogowski (Rochester, NY: Camden House, 2010), 7.

70. Gilles Deleuze, *Cinema 1: The Movement-Image*, trans. Hugh Tomlinson and Barbara Habberjam (Minneapolis: University of Minnesota Press, 1986), 149.

71. On the parallelist or combinatory narrative form, see also Armin Loacker and Ines Steiner, eds., *Imaginierte Antike: Österreichische Monumental-Stummfilme* (Vienna: Filmarchiv Austria, 2002).

72. Miriam Hansen, *Babel and Babylon: Spectatorship in American Silent Film* (Cambridge, MA: Harvard University Press, 1991), 168. For a critique of Deleuze's remarks on Nietzsche and the historical film, see also Nicholas Baer, "The Rebirth of a Nation: Cinema, Herzlian Zionism, and Emotion in Jewish History," *Leo Baeck Institute Year Book* 59 (2014): 233–48.

73. See, e.g., Daniel Frampton, *Filmosophy* (London: Wallflower, 2006); Paisley Livingston, *Cinema, Philosophy, Bergman: On Film as Philosophy* (Oxford: Oxford University Press, 2009); Stephen Mulhall, "Film as Philosophy: The Very Idea," *Proceedings of the Aristotelian Society* 107 (2007): 279–94; John Mullarkey, *Refractions of Reality: Philosophy and the Moving Image* (New York: Palgrave Macmillan, 2009); Patricia Pisters, *The Neuroimage: A Deleuzian Film-Philosophy of Digital Screen Culture* (Stanford, CA: Stanford University Press, 2012); Robert Sinnerbrink, *New Philosophies of Film: Thinking Images* (London: Continuum, 2011); and Thomas E. Wartenberg, *Thinking on Screen: Film as Philosophy* (London: Routledge, 2007).

74. Sinnerbrink, *New Philosophies of Film*, 117–35.

75. Livingston, *Cinema, Philosophy, Bergman*, 11–38.

76. D.N. Rodowick, *Philosophy's Artful Conversation* (Cambridge, MA: Harvard University Press, 2015), 307.

77. For a reconsideration of the periodization of film theory and film philosophy, see also Nico Baumbach, "Metz with Deleuze: From Film-Philosophy to Film Theory and Back Again," in *Christian Metz and the Codes of Cinema: Film Semiology and Beyond*, ed. Margrit Tröhler and Guido Kirsten (Amsterdam: Amsterdam University Press, 2018), 415–32.

78. Rodowick, *Philosophy's Artful Conversation*, 297–98.

79. Eduard Bäumer, "Cinematograph and Epistemology," trans. Sara Hall, in Kaes, Baer, and Cowan, *The Promise of Cinema*, 79.

80. Siegfried Kracauer, *From Caligari to Hitler: A Psychological History of the German Film*, ed. Leonardo Quaresima (Princeton, NJ: Princeton University Press, 2004), li.

81. See., e.g., Barry Salt, "From Caligari to Who?," *Sight and Sound* 48, no. 2 (1979): 119–23; Patrice Petro, *Joyless Streets: Women and Melodramatic Representation in Weimar Germany* (Princeton, NJ: Princeton University Press, 1989), 9–17, 140–45; Dietrich Scheunemann, "Activating the Differences: Expressionist Film and Early Weimar Cinema," in *Expressionist Film: New Perspectives*, ed. Dietrich Scheunemann (Rochester, NY: Camden House, 2003), 1–31; and Rogowski, "Introduction: Images and Imaginaries," 1–2.

82. Thomas Elsaesser, *Weimar Cinema and After: Germany's Historical Imaginary* (London: Routledge, 2000), 438.

83. Elsaesser, 5, 82, 95.

84. Anton Kaes, *Shell Shock Cinema: Weimar Culture and the Wounds of War* (Princeton, NJ: Princeton University Press, 2009).

85. Bambach, *Heidegger, Dilthey, and the Crisis of Historicism*, 49. See also Troeltsch, "Die Krisis des Historismus," 584; Heussi, *Die Krisis des Historismus*, 25; Megill, "Why Was There a Crisis of Historicism?," 426; and Sockness, "Geschichte durch Ethik überwinden?," 205.

86. See Reinhart Koselleck, "Crisis," trans. Michaela Richter, *Journal of the History of Ideas* 67, no. 2 (2006): 357–400. On crisis in film history, see, e.g., Rick Altman, *Silent Film Sound* (New York: Columbia University Press, 2004), 15–23; Michael Wedel, *Filmgeschichte als Krisengeschichte: Schnitte und Spuren durch den deutschen Film* (Bielefeld: transcript, 2011); and Malte Hagener, "Das Medium in der Krise: Der Film, das Kinematographische und der Wert von instabilem Wissen," *AugenBlick: Marburger Hefte zur Medienwissenschaft*, no. 52 (2012): 30–46.

87. For pathbreaking recent work on Weimar cinema, science, and philosophy, see Steve Choe, *Afterlives: Allegories of Film and Mortality in Early Weimar Germany* (New York: Bloomsbury, 2014); Scott Curtis, *The Shape of Spectatorship: Art, Science, and Early Cinema in Germany* (New York: Columbia University Press, 2015); Andreas Killen, *Homo Cinematicus: Science, Motion Pictures, and the Making of Modern Germany* (Philadelphia: University of Pennsylvania Press, 2017); Inga Pollmann, *Cinematic Vitalism: Film Theory and the Question of Life* (Amsterdam: Amsterdam University Press, 2018); and Paul Dobryden, *The Hygienic Apparatus: Weimar Cinema and Environmental Disorder* (Evanston, IL: Northwestern University Press, 2022).

CHAPTER 2

Epigraphs: Stanley Cavell, *The World Viewed: Reflections on the Ontology of Film*, enl. ed. (Cambridge, MA: Harvard University Press, 1979), 210. Copyright © 1971, 1974, 1979 by Stanley Cavell. Used by permission. All rights reserved. Jean-Louis Comolli, "Historical Fiction: A Body Too Much," trans. Ben Brewster, *Screen* 19, no. 2 (1978): 42. Used by permission of Oxford University Press.

1. See Frederick C. Beiser, *The German Historicist Tradition* (Oxford: Oxford University Press, 2011).

2. Roland Barthes, "The Reality Effect," in *The Rustle of Language*, trans. Richard Howard (Berkeley: University of California Press, 1989), 141–48.

3. Aristotle, *Poetics* 9, 1451b2–3.

4. See Johann Gustav Droysen, *Outline of the Principles of History*, trans. E. Benjamin Andrews (Boston: Ginn & Company, 1893). Also see Daniel Fulda, *Wissenschaft aus Kunst: Die Entstehung der modernen deutschen Geschichtsschreibung 1760–1860* (Berlin and New York: Walter de Gruyter, 1996).

5. E. C. Kenyon, *Thomas Alva Edison: The Telegraph-Boy Who Became a Great Inventor* (London: W. & R. Chambers, 1895), 113.

6. See Friedrich Nietzsche, "On the Uses and Disadvantages of History for Life," in *Untimely Meditations*, ed. Daniel Breazeale, trans. R.J. Hollingdale (Cambridge: Cambridge University Press, 1997), 59–123.

7. Kenyon, *Thomas Alva Edison*, 112. See also, e.g., Boleslas Matuszewski, "A New Source of History," trans. Laura U. Marks and Diane Koszarski, *Film History* 7, no. 3 (Autumn 1995): 322–24; and Ludwig Brauner, "Cinematographic Archives," trans. Alex H. Bush, in *The Promise of Cinema: German Film Theory, 1907–1933*, ed. Anton Kaes, Nicholas Baer, and Michael Cowan (Oakland: University of California Press, 2016), 74–77.

8. See Roberta Pearson, "Historical Films," in *Encyclopedia of Early Cinema*, ed. Richard Abel (London: Routledge, 2005), 299–301. See also Gertrud Koch, "Der Historienfilm als Mythos des Alltags," *Journal Geschichte*, no. 2 (April 1989): 13–19; and Christoph Brecht and Ines Steiner, "Film," in *Historismus und literarische Moderne*, ed. Moritz Baßler, Christoph Brecht, Dirk Niefanger, and Gotthart Wunberg (Tübingen: Max Niemeyer, 1996), 333–51.

9. See Tom Gunning, "The Cinema of Attraction: Early Film, Its Spectator and the Avant-Garde," *Wide Angle* 8, nos. 3–4 (1986): 63–70; and Tom Gunning, *D.W. Griffith and the Origins of American Narrative Film: The Early Years at Biograph* (Urbana: University of Illinois Press, 1991).

10. Richard Barry, "Five Dollar Movies Prophesied," *New York Times*, March 28, 1915, 16.

11. Philip Rosen, *Change Mummified: Cinema, Historicity, Theory* (Minneapolis: University of Minnesota Press, 2001), 156.

12. August Wolf, "Film as Historian," trans. Nicholas Baer, in Kaes, Baer, and Cowan, *The Promise of Cinema*, 94–95.

13. See Henri Bergson, *Creative Evolution*, trans. Arthur Mitchell (New York: Henry Holt and Company, 1911), 306.

14. Siegfried Kracauer, *Theory of Film: The Redemption of Physical Reality* (Princeton, NJ: Princeton University Press, 1997), l.

15. Kracauer, xlix, 31, 303. The quote ("le frémissement des feuilles sous l'action du vent") comes from Henri de Parville; see Georges Sadoul, *L'invention du cinéma 1832–1897* (Paris: Denoël, 1973), 290.

16. Kracauer, *Theory of Film*, 12–13.

17. Leopold von Ranke, "Preface to the First Edition of *Histories of the Latin and Germanic Peoples*," in *The Theory and Practice of History*, ed. Georg G. Iggers, trans. Wilma A. Iggers (London and New York: Routledge, 2011), 86; Kracauer, *Theory of Film*, 78.

18. Johannes von Moltke, "Out of the Past: Classical Film Theory," *Screen* 55, no. 3 (Autumn 2014): 399; Johannes von Moltke, *The Curious Humanist: Siegfried Kracauer in America* (Oakland: University of California Press, 2016), 17.

19. Miriam Bratu Hansen, *Cinema and Experience: Siegfried Kracauer, Walter Benjamin, and Theodor W. Adorno* (Berkeley: University of California Press, 2012), 13.

20. Siegfried Kracauer, "Großfilm 'Danton,'" *Frankfurter Zeitung* (hereafter *FZ*), June 1, 1921, in *Werke*, vol. 6.1, ed. Inka Mülder-Bach (Frankfurt am Main: Suhrkamp, 2004), 10.

21. Siegfried Kracauer, "[Alemannia-Lichtspiele]," *FZ*, November 19, 1922, in *Werke*, 6.1:18.

22. Siegfried Kracauer, "Neue Lichtbühne," *FZ*, October 28, 1923, in *Werke*, 6.1:34.

23. Siegfried Kracauer, "Der Kaufmann von Venedig," *FZ*, November 24, 1923, in *Werke*, 6.1:38.

24. Siegfried Kracauer, "Hochstaplerfilme," *FZ*, November 17, 1923, in *Werke*, 6.1:37.

25. Hansen, *Cinema and Experience*, 8; Kracauer, "Hochstaplerfilme," 37.

26. Siegfried Kracauer, "Wetter und Retter," *FZ*, December 16, 1923, in *Werke*, 6.1:43.

27. I thus diverge from Peter Geimer's recent claim that Kracauer's "discontent with the historical film ostensibly did not afflict him until he became a theorist and systematist of film"; see Peter Geimer, "Verstellte Zeit: Kracauers Unbehagen am Historienfilm," in *Siegfried Kracauers Grenzgänge: Zur Rettung des Realen*, ed. Sabine Biebl, Helmut Lethen, and Johannes von Moltke (Frankfurt am Main: Campus, 2019), 108.

28. Siegfried Kracauer, "Peter der Große," *FZ*, December 28, 1923, in *Werke*, 6.1:46.

29. Georg Lukács, "Thoughts toward an Aesthetic of the Cinema," trans. Janelle Blankenship, in Kaes, Baer, and Cowan, *The Promise of Cinema*, 378, 380.

30. Siegfried Kracauer, "Niddy Impekoven im Film," *FZ*, November 29, 1924, in *Werke*, 6.1:104.

31. Siegfried Kracauer, "Der letzte Mann," *FZ*, February 11, 1925, in *Werke*, 6.1:121.

32. Siegfried Kracauer, "Der Mythos im Großfilm," *FZ*, May 7, 1924, in *Werke*, 6.1:79, 80.

33. Kracauer, 80.

34. Kracauer, 80.

35. Georg Lukács, *The Theory of the Novel: A Historico-Philosophical Essay on the Forms of Great Epic Literature*, trans. Anna Bostock (Cambridge, MA: MIT Press, 1971), 38, 41.

36. Siegfried Kracauer, "Calico-World: The Ufa City in Neubabelsberg," in *The Mass Ornament: Weimar Essays*, ed. and trans. Thomas Y. Levin (Cambridge, MA: Harvard University Press, 1995), 281.

37. On this shift, see Hansen, *Cinema and Experience*, 20, 43.

38. See Siegfried Kracauer, "Kriegs- und Militärfilme in Deutschland," typescript, 1931, in *Werke*, vol. 6.2, ed. Inka Mülder-Bach (Frankfurt am Main: Suhrkamp, 2004), 496–97.

39. Siegfried Kracauer, "Fridericus Rex [Teil II]," *FZ*, June 1, 1924, in *Werke*, 6.1:83.

40. Siegfried Kracauer, "Friedrich der Große im Film," *FZ*, February 20, 1926, in *Werke*, 6.1:203.

41. Siegfried Kracauer, "Der bejubelte Fridericus Rex," *FZ*, December 23, 1930, in *Werke*, 6.2:430–31; Siegfried Kracauer, "Der Film im Dezember," *FZ*, December 30, 1931, in *Werke*, 6.2:572n15; Siegfried Kracauer, "Tonfilm von heute," *Kunst und Künstler*, January/February 1932, in *Werke*, vol. 6.3, ed. Inka Mülder-Bach (Frankfurt am Main: Suhrkamp, 2004), 32–33.

42. Siegfried Kracauer, "The Klieg Lights Stay On: The Frankfurt Screening of *Potemkin*," trans. Miriam Bratu Hansen, in Kaes, Baer, and Cowan, *The Promise of Cinema*, 353–55. See also Siegfried Kracauer, "Das Feuerroß," *FZ*, March 10, 1926, in *Werke*, 6.1:215–16. Kracauer's dismissive remarks about German theater elided the innovations of experimental stage directors such as Erwin Piscator, who was already incorporating slide and film projections into his Marxist productions by the mid-1920s.

43. Kracauer, "Das Feuerroß," 216.

44. Kracauer, "The Klieg Lights Stay On," 354, 353; see also Siegfried Kracauer, "Matrosen-Regiment Nr. 17," *FZ*, April 3, 1927, in *Werke*, 6.1: 326. The following year, Kracauer would lament, "It's a pity that the inclination of the audience and, following it, that of the directors, is nowadays so strongly directed toward glossy historical films that are ultimately unable to work through the material"; Siegfried Kracauer, "Auferstehung," *FZ*, November 4, 1927, in *Werke*, 6.1:406. On the "positivization of truth" in Kracauer's thinking, see also Hansen, *Cinema and Experience*, 38; and Miriam Hansen, "'Of Lightning Rods, Prisms, and Forgotten Scissors': *Potemkin* and German Film Theory," *New German Critique*, no. 95 (Spring–Summer 2005): 172.

45. See Kracauer, "Photography," in *The Mass Ornament*, 62–63.

46. Siegfried Kracauer, "Ben Hur: Zur Aufführung in Frankfurt," *FZ*, October 23, 1926, in *Werke*, 6.1:266.

47. Siegfried Kracauer, "Die verfilmten 'Weber,'" *FZ*, May 30, 1927, in *Werke*, 6.1:351.

48. Siegfried Kracauer, "The Little Shopgirls Go to the Movies," in *The Mass Ornament*, 293.

49. Reviewing Luis Trenker's *Der Rebell* (1932), Kracauer wrote, "The discomfort that the film creates obviously arises from the fact that it does not place a historical event at the necessary historical distance, but rather, just the other way around, wants to *force it onto today* with all its might." Siegfried Kracauer, "Idyll, Volkserhebung, Charakter," *FZ*, January 24, 1933, in *Werke*, 6.3:134–35.

50. Siegfried Kracauer, "Film 1928," in *The Mass Ornament*, 308.

51. Kracauer, 308; see also Kracauer, "Photography," 55.

52. Kracauer, "Film 1928," 312–13.

53. Kracauer, 313.

54. Siegfried Kracauer, "Thérèse Raquin," *FZ*, March 29, 1928, in *Werke*, 6.2:53.

55. Siegfried Kracauer, "Zwei deutsche Filmregisseure im Ausland," *FZ*, April 7, 1933, in *Werke*, 6.3:161. See also Siegfried Kracauer, "Die Abenteuer einer schönen Kurtisane," *FZ*, February 17, 1929, in *Werke*, 6.2:208.

56. Siegfried Kracauer, "Bücher vom Film," *FZ*, July 10, 1927, in *Werke*, 6.1:370.

57. See Kracauer, 371–72; and Siegfried Kracauer, "Ein neues Filmbuch," *FZ*, November 2, 1930, in *Werke*, 6.2:413–14.

58. Béla Balázs, *The Spirit of Film*, in Balázs, *Early Film Theory: "Visible Man" and "The Spirit of Film,"* ed. Erica Carter, trans. Rodney Livingstone (New York: Berghahn, 2010), 211.

59. Siegfried Kracauer, "Johanna von Orléans: Anmerkungen zum Film," *FZ*, December 22, 1928, in *Werke*, 6.2:177.

60. Kracauer, 176.

61. Exceptions also included *The Night of Love*, George Fitzmaurice's 1927 adaptation of a dramatic poem by Calderón ("Not really a film, but a film after all, as strikingly and visually as the scenes are strung together"), and Frank Lloyd's 1929 *The Divine Lady* ("Of the historical films, this one . . . is not the worst. It works with a tremendous amount of splendor, but does not get lost in it."). Siegfried Kracauer, "Das Recht der ersten Nacht," *FZ*, October 27, 1927, in *Werke*, 6.1:403; Siegfried Kracauer, "Die ungekrönte Königin," *FZ*, February 27, 1929, in *Werke*, 6.2:214.

62. See Max Horkheimer and Theodor W. Adorno, *Dialectic of Enlightenment: Philosophical Fragments*, ed. Gunzelin Schmid Noerr, trans. Edmund Jephcott (Stanford, CA: Stanford University Press, 2002), 94–136.

63. That Kracauer's critique could extend to a condemnation of racism is indicated by his review of Harry A. Pollard's *Uncle Tom's Cabin* (1927): "As long as the Black race is seen as inferior over there, it is hypocrisy of the highest order to simply blind today's viewers with days gone by." Siegfried Kracauer, "Onkel Tom's Hütte," *FZ*, May 6, 1928, in *Werke*, 6.2:76.

64. Such films included *Waterloo* (Karl Grune, 1928), *Danton* (Hans Behrendt, 1931), and *Goethe Lives . . . !* (*Goethe lebt . . . !*, Eberhard Frowein, 1932). See Siegfried Kracauer, "Waterloo," *FZ*, March 16, 1929, in *Werke*, 6.2:226–27; Siegfried Kracauer, "Der blaue Engel," *Die neue Rundschau*, June 1930, in *Werke*, 6.2:375; Siegfried Kracauer, "Fußball, Vorkriegsliebe und Revolution," *FZ*, February 2, 1931, in *Werke*, 6.2:448; Siegfried Kracauer, "Schluß mit dem Klamauk! Zu einer Rundfrage des Reichsfilmblattes," *FZ*, January 10, 1932, in *Werke*, 6.3:10, 12; and Siegfried Kracauer, "Goethe im Film," *FZ*, March 22, 1932, in *Werke*, 6.3:42–43.

65. Siegfried Kracauer, "Westfront 1918," *FZ*, May 27, 1930, in *Werke*, 6.2:361; Siegfried Kracauer, "*All Quiet on the Western Front*: On the Remarque Sound Film," trans. Jon Cho-Polizzi, in Kaes, Baer, and Cowan, *The Promise of Cinema*, 286.

66. Siegfried Kracauer, "Zur Lage des Tonfilms," *Die neue Rundschau*, February 1931, in *Werke*, 6.2:462.

67. Siegfried Kracauer, "Der erste deutsche Tonfilm," *FZ*, November 5, 1929, in *Werke*, 6.2:290. Katharina Loew has challenged the view that the introduction of synchronized sound led to the disappearance of expressive means; see Katharina Loew, "Expressive Visual Effects from Silent to Sound Film," in *Aesthetics of Early Sound Film: Media Change around 1930*, ed. Daniel Wiegand (Amsterdam: Amsterdam University Press, 2023), 49–66.

68. Siegfried Kracauer, "Neue Filmware," *FZ*, April 14, 1931, in *Werke* 6.2:480.

69. Siegfried Kracauer, "Kunst und Dekoration," *FZ*, October 28, 1931, in *Werke*, 6.2:551. Also see Siegfried Kracauer, "Film-Notizen," *FZ*, June 3, 1932, in *Werke*, 6.3:66; and Siegfried Kracauer, "Zur Ideologie des deutschen Tonfilms," typescript, July 4, 1932, in *Werke*, 6.3:70.

70. Siegfried Kracauer, "Die Königin seines Herzens," *FZ*, August 14, 1928, in *Werke*, 6.2:112.

71. Siegfried Kracauer, "Aus der Vorkriegszeit," *FZ*, July 8, 1928, in *Werke*, 6.2:99.

72. Siegfried Kracauer, "The Biography as an Art Form of the New Bourgeoisie," in *The Mass Ornament*, 102.

73. Kracauer, 105.

74. Siegfried Kracauer, *Jacques Offenbach and the Paris of His Time*, trans. Gwenda David and Eric Mosbacher (New York: Zone Books, 2016), 24, 206; see also 153–55, 159, 212, 225, 277, 324, and 330.

75. Siegfried Kracauer, "Jacques Offenbach: Motion Picture Treatment," in *Werke*, vol. 8, ed. Ingrid Belke (Frankfurt am Main: Suhrkamp, 2005), 485–502.

76. Martin Jay, "The Extraterritorial Life of Siegfried Kracauer," *Salmagundi*, nos. 31/32 (Fall 1975–Winter 1976): 68. Gerd Gemünden places Kracauer's motion-picture treatment in the context of the revisionist Hollywood biopics spearheaded by William Dieterle in the mid and late 1930s; see Gemünden, *Continental Strangers: German Exile Cinema, 1933–1951* (New York: Columbia University Press, 2014), 49–50.

77. Kracauer, *Jacques Offenbach*, 54.

78. Siegfried Kracauer, "Der Napoleon-Film," *FZ*, December 4, 1927, in *Werke*, 6.1:420.

79. Walter Benjamin, "The Work of Art in the Age of Its Technological Reproducibility: Second Version," trans. Edmund Jephcott and Harry Zohn, in *Selected Writings*, vol. 3, ed. Howard Eiland and Michael W. Jennings (Cambridge, MA, and London: Harvard University Press, 2002), 104. Both Benjamin and Adorno were harshly critical of Kracauer's *Offenbach* book, with Adorno noting sardonically that "the piece is so irredeemably terrible that it could easily become a best-seller"; see Theodor W. Adorno and Walter Benjamin, *The Complete Correspondence, 1928–1940*, ed. Henri Lonitz, trans. Nicholas Walker (Cambridge, MA: Harvard University Press, 1999), 184.

80. Siegfried Kracauer, "Der historische Film," *National-Zeitung Basel*, May 9, 1940, in *Werke*, 6.3:314. Kracauer's text served as a supplement to an essay by Christoph Dunker that had appeared in the *National-Zeitung Basel* in

two parts in April 1940 (see *Werke*, 6.3:315n1), and it also anticipated Kracauer's remarks in *Theory of Film* (p. 9). See also Siegfried Kracauer, *History: The Last Things before the Last* (Princeton, NJ: Markus Wiener, 1995), 122: "[T]he big can be adequately rendered only by a permanent movement from the whole to some detail, then back to the whole, etc."

81. Kracauer, *Jacques Offenbach*, 24. André Bazin would similarly argue that photographic media changed the very status of "historical facts"; see André Bazin, "On *Why We Fight*: History, Documentation, and the Newsreel," trans. Bert Cardullo, *Film & History* 31, no. 1 (2001): 62.

82. G.W.F. Hegel, *Aesthetics: Lectures on Fine Art*, vol. 1, trans. T.M. Knox (Oxford: Oxford University Press, 1975), 264–65.

83. Siegfried Kracauer, "On the Border of Yesterday: On the Berlin Film and Photo Exhibition," trans. Michael Cowan, in Kaes, Baer, and Cowan, *The Promise of Cinema*, 608; Kracauer, "Der historische Film," 315.

84. Kracauer, *Theory of Film*, 57.

85. Kracauer, "Der historische Film," 315.

86. Kracauer, 315.

87. Siegfried Kracauer, "Propaganda and the Nazi War Film," in *From Caligari to Hitler: A Psychological History of the German Film*, ed. Leonardo Quaresima (Princeton, NJ: Princeton University Press, 2004), 276, 282.

88. Kracauer, 287.

89. Kracauer, 288.

90. Kracauer, 288, 289–92.

91. Siegfried Kracauer, "Um das Menschenrecht," June 12, 1942, in *Werke*, vol. 2.2, ed. Christian Fleck and Bernd Stiegler (Berlin: Suhrkamp, 2012), 412; Siegfried Kracauer, "Theodor Körner (1932)," typescript, July 15, 1942, in *Werke*, 2.2:426.

92. Siegfried Kracauer, "The Little Shopgirls," 292; Siegfried Kracauer, "Der Choral von Leuthen (7. März 1933) und Fredericus Rex (1934)," typescript, July 8, 1942, in *Werke*, 2.2:422. See also Kracauer's "The Hitler Image" (1944).

93. Siegfried Kracauer, "Wilhelm Tell: Das Freiheitsdrama eines Volkes," typescript, September 1, 1942, in *Werke*, 2.2:439.

94. Kracauer, "Fußball, Vorkriegsliebe und Revolution," 448.

95. Siegfried Kracauer, "Dantons Tod," typescript, August 31, 1942, in *Werke*, 2.2:438.

96. Kracauer, *From Caligari to Hitler*, 253.

97. Kracauer, 49.

98. Kracauer, 51, 52.

99. Kracauer, 115, 116.

100. Kracauer, 117.

101. Kracauer, 267, 268. Fridericus Rex films of the 1930s included *The Flute Concert of Sanssouci*, *The Dancer of Sanssouci* (*Die Tänzerin von Sanssouci*, Friedrich Zelnik, 1932), *Trenck* (Heinz Paul and Ernst Neubach, 1932), *The Hymn of Leuthen*, and *Fridericus*.

102. Siegfried Kracauer, "National Types as Hollywood Presents Them," in *Siegfried Kracauer's American Writings: Essays on Film and Popular Culture*,

ed. Johannes von Moltke and Kristy Rawson (Berkeley: University of California Press, 2012), 96.

103. See Aristotle, *Poetics* 9, 1451b35–37. On Rossellini's *Paisan* and its relation to Eisenstein's work, see also Kracauer, "National Types as Hollywood Presents Them," 102. In *Theory of Film*, Kracauer would further comment on *Potemkin* and *Paisan*, comparing the approaches of Eisenstein and Rossellini; see Kracauer, *Theory of Film*, 98, 204.

104. André Bazin, "An Aesthetic of Reality: Neorealism," in Bazin, *What Is Cinema?*, vol. 2, trans. Hugh Gray (Berkeley: University of California Press, 1971), 18.

105. Siegfried Kracauer, "Paisan," in *Siegfried Kracauer's American Writings*, 155.

106. Kracauer, 156. See Theodor W. Adorno, "The Curious Realist: On Siegfried Kracauer," trans. Shierry Weber Nicholsen, *New German Critique*, no. 54 (Autumn 1991): 159–77; and von Moltke, *The Curious Humanist*.

107. Inka Mülder-Bach, "History as Autobiography: The Last Things Before the Last," trans. Gail Finney, *New German Critique*, no. 54 (Autumn 1991): 152.

108. Kracauer, *Theory of Film*, 134, 169, 232.

109. Kracauer, 60–74.

110. Kracauer, "Peter der Große," 46.

111. Roland Barthes, "The Romans in Films," in *Mythologies*, trans. Annette Lavers (New York: Farrar, Straus & Giroux, 1972), 24–26.

112. Kracauer, *Theory of Film*, 78–79. See also Edgar Morin, *The Cinema, or The Imaginary Man*, trans. Lorraine Mortimer (Minneapolis: University of Minnesota Press, 2005): "Élie Faure develops an analogous vision when he imagines the inhabitants of a distant planet, living at the time of the crucifixion of Jesus, sending us by missile a film that would make us actual witnesses" (60).

113. Élie Faure, "The Art of Cineplastics," trans. Walter Pach, in *French Film Theory and Criticism: A History/Anthology*, ed. Richard Abel (Princeton, NJ: Princeton University Press, 1988), 1:265.

114. Aristotle, *Poetics* 9, 1451b2–3; Ranke, "Preface to the First Edition of *Histories of the Latin and Germanic Peoples*," 86.

115. Kracauer, *Theory of Film*, 79.

116. Kracauer, 81. Other examples included Jacques Feyder's *Carnival in Flanders* (*La kermesse héroïque*, 1935), Martin Frič's *The Emperor and the Golem* (*Císařův pekař—Pekařův císař*, 1952), and Teinosuke Kinugasa's *Gate of Hell* (*Jigokumon*, 1953).

117. Kracauer to Leo Löwenthal, February 10, 1961; quoted in "Siegfried Kracauer 1889–1966," ed. Ingrid Belke and Irina Renz, special issue, *Marbacher Magazin* 47 (1988): 118.

118. Kracauer, *History*, 168, 175. Leopold von Ranke had written, "One cannot demand of a historical work the same free development which at least in theory is sought in a poetic work"; see Ranke, "Preface to the First Edition of *Histories of the Latin and Germanic Peoples*," 86.

119. Hayden V. White, "The Burden of History," *History and Theory* 5, no. 2 (1966): 111–34; Hayden White, *Metahistory: The Historical Imagination in Nineteenth-Century Europe* (Baltimore and London: Johns Hopkins University Press, 1973).

120. These critiques included Paul Yorck von Wartenburg's 1886 contention that Ranke had "veiled the truth in poetry [*die Wahrheit zur Dichtung verschleiert*]"; see "Diskussion: Das Ästhetische als Grenzerscheinung der Historie," in Siegfried Kracauer, *Werke*, vol. 4, ed. Ingrid Belke (Frankfurt am Main: Suhrkamp, 2009), 413.

121. "Diskussion: Das Ästhetische als Grenzerscheinung der Historie," 429. See Droysen, *Outline of the Principles of History*, 49: "History is Humanity's knowledge of itself, its certainty about itself."

122. Koselleck would elaborate on these themes in his 1976 lecture "Fiction and Historical Reality"; see Reinhart Koselleck, *Sediments of Time: On Possible Histories*, ed. and trans. Sean Franzel and Stefan-Ludwig Hoffmann (Stanford, CA: Stanford University Press, 2018), 10–23.

123. Saidiya Hartman, "Venus in Two Acts," *Small Axe*, no. 26 (June 2008): 11.

124. Jacques Rancière, *The Politics of Aesthetics: The Distribution of the Sensible*, trans. Gabriel Rockhill (London: Continuum, 2004), 37–38.

125. See von Moltke, "Out of the Past," 399; and von Moltke, *The Curious Humanist*, 17.

126. Bill Pruitt, "A Former *Apprentice* Producer Responds to Donald Trump Being Elected President," *Vanity Fair*, December 21, 2016, www.vanityfair.com/hollywood/2016/12/apprentice-producer-donald-trump-president.

127. Ernst Troeltsch describes the crisis of historicism in terms of "eine seltsame Mischung von historischer Skepsis und leichtgläubiger Mystik"; see Troeltsch, "Die Krisis des Historismus," *Die neue Rundschau* 33 (1922): 579.

CHAPTER 3

Epigraphs: Friedrich Nietzsche, *The Gay Science*, trans. Walter Kaufmann (New York: Vintage, 1974), 181; Michel Foucault, *Wrong-Doing, Truth-Telling: The Function of Avowal in Justice*, ed. Fabienne Brion and Bernard E. Harcourt, trans. Stephen W. Sawyer (Chicago: University of Chicago Press, 2014), 13. Used by permission of University of Chicago Press.

1. Leszek Kolakowski, *The Alienation of Reason: A History of Positivist Thought*, trans. Norbert Guterman (Garden City, NY: Doubleday & Co., 1968), 9–10.

2. Albert Einstein, "On the Electrodynamics of Moving Bodies," in *The Principle of Relativity*, trans. George Barker Jeffery and Wilfrid Perrett (New York: Dover, 1952), 35–65.

3. See Linda Dalyrimple Henderson, *The Fourth Dimension and Non-Euclidean Geometry in Modern Art* (Princeton, NJ: Princeton University Press, 1983).

4. José Ortega y Gasset, "The Dehumanization of Art," in *The Dehumanization of Art and Other Writings on Art and Culture* (Garden City, NY: Doubleday & Co., 1956), 1–50.

5. Yevgeny Zamyatin, "On Literature, Revolution, Entropy, and Other Matters," in *A Soviet Heretic: Essays by Yevgeny Zamyatin*, ed. and trans. Mirra Ginsberg (Chicago: University of Chicago Press, 1970), 112.

6. Zamyatin, 111–12.

7. Georg Marzynski, *Die Methode des Expressionismus: Studien zu seiner Psychologie* (Leipzig: Klinkhardt & Biermann, 1920), 34.

8. Walter H. Sokel, *The Writer in Extremis: Expressionism in Twentieth-Century German Literature* (Stanford, CA: Stanford University Press, 1959), 39.

9. Sokel, 38.

10. Sokel, 38.

11. On Einstein and the emergence of cinema, see Harro Segeberg, "'Is Everything Relative?': Cinema and the Revolution of Knowledge around 1900," in *Film 1900: Technology, Perception, Culture*, ed. Annemone Ligensa and Klaus Kreimeier (New Barnet, UK: John Libbey Publishing, 2009), 67–76.

12. See Sergei Eisenstein, "The Fourth Dimension in Cinema," in *Selected Works*, vol. 1, *Writings, 1922–34*, ed. and trans. Richard Taylor (London: BFI, 1988), 185; Jean Epstein, *Jean Epstein: Critical Essays and New Translations*, ed. Sarah Keller and Jason N. Paul (Amsterdam: Amsterdam University Press, 2012), 294, 312–14, 319, 324, 348–49, 367, 400; and Dziga Vertov, *Kino-Eye: The Writings of Dziga Vertov*, ed. Annette Michelson, trans. Kevin O'Brien (Berkeley: University of California Press, 1984), 9, 41, 78, 131.

13. Annette Michelson, "Reading Eisenstein Reading 'Capital,'" *October* 2 (Summer 1976): 32; Annette Michelson, "The Wings of Hypothesis: On Montage and the Theory of the Interval," in *Montage and Modern Life, 1919–1942*, ed. Matthew Teitelbaum (Cambridge, MA: MIT Press, 1992), 65.

14. A notable filmic exception is *From Morn to Midnight* (*Von morgens bis mitternachts*, Karlheinz Martin, 1920), which features tricks.

15. Herman George Scheffauer, "The Vivifying of Space," in *The New Vision in the German Arts* (New York: B.W. Huebsch, 1924), 46.

16. Scheffauer, 47.

17. Thomas Elsaesser, *Weimar Cinema and After: Germany's Historical Imaginary* (London: Routledge, 2000), 95.

18. Elsaesser, 5.

19. Elsaesser, 103n54.

20. See Jimena Canales, *The Physicist and the Philosopher: Einstein, Bergson, and the Debate That Changed Our Understanding of Time* (Princeton, NJ: Princeton University Press, 2015). Because of Bergson's challenge to the theory of relativity, the Nobel Prize in Physics in 1921 was granted to Einstein for his other services and discoveries.

21. Martin Heidegger, "The Concept of Time in the Science of History," trans. Harry S. Taylor, Hans W. Uffelmann, and John van Buren, in *Supplements:*

From the Earliest Essays to "Being and Time" and Beyond, ed. John van Buren (Albany: SUNY Press, 2002), 55.

22. Heidegger, 57; Leopold von Ranke, "On Progress in History," in *The Theory and Practice of History*, ed. Georg G. Iggers, trans. Wilma A. Iggers (London and New York: Routledge, 2011), 21.

23. Heidegger, "Concept of Time," 57.

24. Martin Heidegger, "Wilhelm Dilthey's Research and the Struggle for a Historical Worldview," trans. Charles Bambach, in *Supplements: From the Earliest Essays to "Being and Time" and Beyond*, ed. John van Buren (Albany: SUNY Press, 2002), 163, 173.

25. Heidegger, 172.

26. Heidegger, 171–72.

27. Edmund Husserl, *The Crisis of European Sciences and Transcendental Phenomenology*, trans. David Carr (Evanston, IL: Northwestern University Press, 1970), 125–26; see also Husserl's criticisms of Einstein in his 1935 lecture "Philosophy and the Crisis of European Humanity," reprinted in Husserl, 295.

28. See Georg Lukács, *The Historical Novel*, trans. Hannah Mitchell and Stanley Mitchell (Lincoln: University of Nebraska Press, 1983).

29. Georg Lukács, *The Theory of the Novel: A Historico-Philosophical Essay on the Forms of Great Epic Literature*, trans. Anna Bostock (Cambridge, MA: MIT Press, 1971), 41. See also Lukács's remarks on crime and madness as "objectivations of transcendental homelessness" in Lukács, 61.

30. Martin Jay, *Songs of Experience: Modern American and European Variations on a Universal Theme* (Berkeley: University of California Press, 2005), 231–32.

31. Siegfried Kracauer, "The Biography as an Art Form of the New Bourgeoisie," in *The Mass Ornament: Weimar Essays*, ed. and trans. Thomas Y. Levin (Cambridge, MA: Harvard University Press, 1995), 102.

32. Lukács, *Theory of the Novel*, 121, 124; Shiv K. Kumar, *Bergson and the Stream of Consciousness Novel* (New York: New York University Press, 1963).

33. James Joyce, *Finnegans Wake* (Oxford: Oxford University Press, 2012), 149.

34. Jane Goldman, *The Feminist Aesthetics of Virginia Woolf: Modernism, Post-Impressionism and the Politics of the Visual* (Cambridge: Cambridge University Press, 1998), 26.

35. Quoted in Goldman, 28, 213n8; see also Virginia Woolf, "The Movies and Reality," *New Republic*, August 4, 1926, 308–10; reprinted in *Authors on Film*, ed. Harry M. Geduld (Bloomington: Indiana University Press, 1972), 89.

36. Blaise Cendrars, "On *The Cabinet of Doctor Caligari*," trans. Stuart Liebman, in *French Film Theory and Criticism: A History/Anthology*, ed. Richard Abel (Princeton, NJ: Princeton University Press, 1988), 1:271; Ezra Pound, "Paris Letter," in *Ezra Pound and the Visual Arts*, ed. Harriet Zinnes (New York: New Directions, 1980), 175–77.

37. Anne Perlmann, "Das Kabinett des Dr. Caligari—Declafilm: Pressevorführung in den Schadow-Lichtspielen," *Der Kinematograph* 14, no. 696 (May 16, 1920): n.p.

38. Kolakowski, *Alienation of Reason*, 1–10; H. Stuart Hughes, *Consciousness and Society* (New Brunswick, NJ: Transaction Publishers, 2002), 33–66.
39. Max Weber, "Science as a Vocation," in *Essays in Sociology*, ed. and trans. H.H. Gerth and C. Wright Mills (New York: Oxford University Press, 1946), 129–56.
40. Leopold von Ranke, "Preface to the First Edition of *Histories of the Latin and German Peoples*," in *The Theory and Practice of History*, ed. Georg G. Iggers, trans. Wilma A. Iggers (London and New York: Routledge, 2011), 86.
41. Friedrich Nietzsche, "On the Uses and Disadvantages of History for Life," in *Untimely Meditations*, ed. Daniel Breazeale, trans. R.J. Hollingdale (Cambridge: Cambridge University Press, 1997), 108.
42. See Charles R. Bambach, *Heidegger, Dilthey, and the Crisis of Historicism* (Ithaca, NY, and London: Cornell University Press, 1995).
43. Ernst Troeltsch, "Die Krisis des Historismus," *Die neue Rundschau* 33 (1922): 572–90.
44. Ernst Troeltsch, *Der Historismus und seine Probleme* (Tübingen: J.C.B. Mohr, 1922), 219. See also Otto Hintze, "Troeltsch und die Probleme des Historismus: Kritische Studien," *Historische Zeitschrift* 135, no. 2 (1927): 227: "An die Stelle der Beurteilung nach einem absoluten Wertsystem war die lebendige Beziehung zu einer für den Betrachter geltenden, aber historisch bedingten Wertwelt getreten. Es war eine ähnliche Wendung wie die, die in der Naturwissenschaft durch die Einsteinsche Relativitätslehre hervorgebracht worden ist."
45. Siegfried Kracauer, "Über den Expressionismus: Wesen und Sinn einer Zeitbewegung: Abhandlung," in *Werke*, vol. 9.2, ed. Ingrid Belke (Frankfurt am Main: Suhrkamp, 2004), 47, 46.
46. Kracauer, 49, 63.
47. Georg Lukács, "Expressionism: Its Significance and Decline," in *Essays on Realism*, ed. Rodney Livingstone, trans. David Fernbach (Cambridge, MA: MIT Press, 1981), 80.
48. Hans Vaihinger, *The Philosophy of 'As If': A System of the Theoretical, Practical and Religious Fictions of Mankind*, trans. C.K. Ogden (London: Routledge & Kegan Paul, 1935).
49. Vaihinger, 163.
50. Gottfried Benn, "Bekenntnis zum Expressionismus," *Deutsche Zukunft*, November 5, 1933, quoted in Lukács, *Theory of the Novel*, 18.
51. Kasimir Edschmid, *Über den Expressionismus in der Literatur und die neue Dichtung* (Berlin: Erich Reiß, 1919), 31.
52. Wilhelm Worringer, *Abstraction and Empathy: A Contribution to the Psychology of Style*, trans. Michael Bullock (Chicago: Ivan R. Dee, 1997), 4.
53. Worringer, 15.
54. Georg Kaiser, "Historientreue: Am Beispiel der Flucht nach Venedig," in *Werke*, vol. 4, ed. Walther Huder (Frankfurt am Main: Propyläen, 1971), 577.
55. Arthur Schopenhauer, *The World as Will and Idea*, vol. 3, trans. R.B. Haldane and J. Kemp (London: Kegan Paul, Trench, Trübner & Co., 1909), 224.

56. Schopenhauer, 224; Worringer, *Abstraction and Empathy*, 18; and Wassily Kandinsky, *Concerning the Spiritual in Art*, trans. M.T.H. Sadler (New York: Dover, 1977).

57. Bernhard Diebold, "Expressionism and Cinema," trans. Alex H. Bush, in *The Promise of Cinema: German Film Theory, 1907–1933*, ed. Anton Kaes, Nicholas Baer, and Michael Cowan (Oakland: University of California Press, 2016), 416; Carl Mayer and Hans Janowitz, "Das Cabinett des Dr. Calligari: Phantastischer Filmroman in 6 Akten," in *Das Cabinet des Dr. Caligari: Drehbuch von Carl Mayer und Hans Janowitz zu Robert Wienes Film von 1919/20* (Munich: edition text + kritik, 1995), 52–53.

58. Eugen Tannenbaum, "Expressionismus im Film," *Berliner Abendpost*, February 29, 1920.

59. See Siegfried Kracauer, *Theory of Film: The Redemption of Physical Reality* (Princeton, NJ: Princeton University Press, 1997).

60. Erwin Panofsky, "Style and Medium in the Motion Pictures," in *Film Theory and Criticism: Introductory Readings*, ed. Gerald Mast and Marshall Cohen (London: Oxford University Press, 1974), 168; Kracauer, *Theory of Film*, 38.

61. Rudolf Kurtz, *Expressionism and Film*, ed. Christian Kiening and Ulrich Johannes Beil, trans. Brenda Benthien (New Barnet, UK: John Libbey Publishing, 2016), 51.

62. Kurtz, 86.

63. Rudolf Arnheim, "Expressionist Film," in *Film Essays and Criticism*, trans. Brenda Benthien (Madison: University of Wisconsin Press, 1997), 85.

64. Kracauer, "Über den Expressionismus," 77; Siegfried Kracauer, "Wiedersehen mit alten Filmen: Der expressionistische Film," in *Werke*, vol. 6.3, ed. Inka Mülder-Bach (Frankfurt am Main: Suhrkamp, 2004), 269.

65. Balthasar [Roland Schacht], "Caligari," *Freie Deutsche Bühne* 29 (March 14, 1920): 695–98.

66. Panofsky, "Style and Medium," 169.

67. André Bazin, "Theater and Cinema," in *What Is Cinema?*, vol. 1, trans. Hugh Gray (Berkeley: University of California Press, 1967), 109.

68. Kracauer, *Theory of Film*, 37, 39, 61, 84–85.

69. Siegfried Kracauer, *History: The Last Things before the Last* (Princeton, NJ: Markus Wiener, 1995), 3–4.

70. Oswald Spengler, *The Decline of the West*, trans. Charles Francis Atkinson (New York: Alfred A. Knopf, 1926).

71. Robert Wiene, "Expressionism in Film," trans. Eric Ames, in Kaes, Baer, and Cowan, *The Promise of Cinema*, 437.

72. Hayden White, *Metahistory: The Historical Imagination in Nineteenth-Century Europe* (Baltimore and London: Johns Hopkins University Press, 1973), 37–38. See also Martin Jay, "Intention and Irony: The Missed Encounter between Hayden White and Quentin Skinner," *History and Theory* 52, no. 1 (2013): 32–48.

73. Helmut Lethen, *Cool Conduct: The Culture of Distance in Weimar Germany*, trans. Don Reneau (Berkeley: University of California Press, 2002),

36; Peter Sloterdijk, *Critique of Cynical Reason*, trans. Michael Eldred (Minneapolis: University of Minnesota Press, 1987), 546. On *Caligari* as a mind-game film *avant la lettre*, see Thomas Elsaesser, review of *Dr. Caligari's Francis: A Sane Reading*, by Alan Blanchard, *[in]Transition: Journal of Videographic Film & Moving Image Studies* 6, no. 3 (2019), https://mediacommons.org/intransition/dr-caligaris-francis-sane-reading.

74. Siegfried Kracauer, *From Caligari to Hitler: A Psychological History of the German Film*, ed. Leonardo Quaresima (Princeton, NJ: Princeton University Press, 2004), 67.

75. Hans Janowitz, "*Caligari*—The Story of a Famous Story," in *The Cabinet of Dr. Caligari: Texts, Contexts, Histories*, ed. Mike Budd (New Brunswick, NJ: Rutgers University Press, 1990), 221–39.

76. Anton Kaes, *Shell Shock Cinema: Weimar Culture and the Wounds of War* (Princeton, NJ: Princeton University Press, 2009), 53.

77. See Stefan Andriopoulos, "Suggestion, Hypnosis, and Crime: Robert Wiene's *The Cabinet of Dr. Caligari* (1920)," in *Weimar Cinema: An Essential Guide to Classic Films of the Era*, ed. Noah Isenberg (New York: Columbia University Press, 2009), 24; and Elsaesser, *Weimar Cinema and After*, 63, 76, 79, 92, 95.

78. Kracauer, *From Caligari to Hitler*, 67.

79. Kracauer, 70.

80. Kracauer, 67.

81. Sokel, *The Writer in Extremis*, 38, 45.

82. Immanuel Kant, *Critique of the Power of Judgment*, ed. Paul Guyer, trans. Paul Guyer and Eric Matthews (Cambridge: Cambridge University Press, 2000), 110–11. See also Jacques Derrida, *The Truth in Painting*, trans. Geoffrey Bennington and Ian McLeod (Chicago: University of Chicago Press, 1987), 54–73.

83. Georg Simmel, "The Picture Frame: An Aesthetic Study," trans. Mark Ritter, *Theory, Culture & Society* 11 (1994): 11.

84. On "border regions," see Till Dembeck, *Texte rahmen: Grenzregionen literarischer Werke im 18. Jahrhundert* (Berlin: Walter de Gruyter, 2007), 1, 11.

85. Alois Riegl, "The Main Characteristics of the Late Roman *Kunstwollen*," trans. Christopher S. Wood, in *The Vienna School Reader: Politics and Art Historical Method in the 1930s*, ed. Christopher S. Wood (New York: Zone Books, 2003), 87–103.

86. Erwin Panofsky, *Perspective as Symbolic Form*, trans. Christopher S. Wood (New York: Zone Books, 1991), 41; see also Wood's introduction to Panofsky, 7–24.

87. Panofsky, 71.

88. Panofsky, 71.

89. Carl Einstein, *Die Kunst des 20. Jahrhunderts*, ed. Tanja Frank (Leipzig: Reclam, 1988), 12, 17.

90. Hugo Münsterberg, *The Film: A Psychological Study* (Mineola, NY: Dover, 1970), 15–16.

91. Münsterberg, 67.

92. Béla Balázs, *Early Film Theory: "Visible Man" and "The Spirit of Film,"* ed. Erica Carter, trans. Rodney Livingstone (New York: Berghahn, 2010), 41, 62, 63, 71.

93. Jean Epstein, "The Cinema Seen from Etna," trans. Tom Milne, in Epstein, *Critical Essays and New Translations*, 294.

94. Kracauer, *Theory of Film*, 33–36.

95. Tannenbaum, "Expressionismus im Film."

96. Martin Proskauer, "'Das Kabinett des Dr. Caligari'—Ein Nachwort und eine Prophezeiung," *Film-Kurier* 2, no. 51 (February 29, 1920): 2; Christian Flüggen, "Das Kabinet des Dr. Caligari," *Deutsche Lichtspiel-Zeitung* 8, nos. 12/13 (March 27, 1920): 2; and J.P.M., "Ein Film von Eigenart," *Vorwärts* 134 (March 13, 1920): 2.

97. Kracauer, *Theory of Film*, 9.

98. Kracauer, 37; Friedrich Kittler, *Optical Media: Berlin Lectures 1999*, trans. Anthony Enns (Cambridge: Polity Press, 2010), 98–189.

99. Kittler, *Optical Media*, 175.

100. Martin Jay, *Downcast Eyes: The Denigration of Vision in Twentieth-Century French Thought* (Berkeley: University of California Press, 1993), 187.

101. James Conant, "The Dialectic of Perspectivism, I," in *Sats—Nordic Journal of Philosophy* 6, no. 2 (2005): 14; Claudio Guillén, "On the Concept and Metaphor of Perspective," in *Literature as System: Essays toward the Theory of Literary History* (Princeton, NJ: Princeton University Press, 1971), 284–85, 312–13, 310, 328, 336, 338.

102. Gottfried Wilhelm Leibniz, *Theodicy*, trans. E.M. Huggard (New Haven, CT: Yale University Press, 1952), sec. 357.

103. Guillén, "Concept and Metaphor of Perspective," 326, 358; Jay, *Downcast Eyes*, 188–89.

104. Conant, "Dialectic of Perspectivism, I," 8.

105. Friedrich Nietzsche, "On Truth and Lies in a Nonmoral Sense," in *Philosophy and Truth: Selections from Nietzsche's Notebooks of the Early 1870's*, ed. and trans. Daniel Breazeale (Atlantic Highlands, NJ: Humanities Press, 1979), 85, 86.

106. Conant, "Dialectic of Perspectivism, I," 46; James Conant, "The Dialectic of Perspectivism, II," in *Sats—Nordic Journal of Philosophy* 7, no. 1 (2006): 34.

107. Friedrich Nietzsche, *On the Genealogy of Morals & Ecce Homo*, ed. Walter Kaufmann, trans. Walter Kaufmann and R.J. Hollingdale (New York: Random House, 1967), 119.

108. Reinhart Koselleck, "Perspective and Temporality: A Contribution to the Historiographical Exposure of the Historical World," in *Futures Past: On the Semantics of Historical Time*, trans. Keith Tribe (New York: Columbia University Press, 2004), 133–34.

109. G.W.F. Hegel, *Lectures on the Philosophy of World History: Introduction*, trans. H.B. Nisbet (Cambridge: Cambridge University Press,

1975), 30; Leopold von Ranke, *Zur Kritik neuerer Geschichtsschreiber* (Leipzig and Berlin: Reimer, 1824), 28. Yet Ranke also postulated an omniscient God in his *Weltgeschichte*: "I imagine the Deity—if I may allow myself to make this observation—as seeing the whole of historical humanity in its totality (since no time lies before the Deity), and finding it all equally valuable" (quoted in Hans-Georg Gadamer, *Truth and Method*, trans. Joel Weinsheimer and Donald G. Marshall [London and New York: Continuum, 2004], 207).

110. Nicholas of Cusa, *On Learned Ignorance*, trans. Jasper Hopkins (Minneapolis: Arthur J. Banning Press, 1981).

111. Nicholas of Cusa, 25; Jay, *Downcast Eyes*, 190.

112. Wilhelm Dilthey, "The Rise of Hermeneutics," trans. Fredric Jameson, *New Literary History* 3, no. 2 (Winter 1972): 231.

113. Dilthey, 243. See also Jay, *Songs of Experience*, 222–34.

114. Dilthey, "The Rise of Hermeneutics," 244; Gadamer, *Truth and Method*, 230.

115. Gadamer, *Truth and Method*, 305.

116. Dilthey, "The Rise of Hermeneutics," 231, 244.

117. Dilthey, 241, 231.

118. Dilthey, 232. Dilthey claimed that only written documents could be the objects of generally valid interpretation (pp. 233, 244).

119. Olaf Brill, *Der Caligari-Komplex* (Munich: Belleville, 2012), 7. For an extended version of my critique, see Nicholas Baer, "Der Caligari-Komplex," *Historical Journal of Film, Radio and Television* 33, no. 2 (2013): 309–11.

120. George Herbert Mead, *The Philosophy of the Act*, ed. Charles W. Morris (Chicago: University of Chicago Press, 1938), 118–19.

121. Werner Heisenberg, *Physics and Philosophy: The Revolution in Modern Science* (Amherst, MA: Prometheus Books, 1999), 81.

CHAPTER 4

Epigraphs: Martin Heidegger, *Nietzsche*, vol. 4, *Nihilism*, ed. David Farrell Krell, trans. Frank A. Capuzzi (San Francisco: Harper Collins, 1991), 148; Jean-Luc Nancy, *The Inoperative Community*, ed. and trans. Peter Connor (Minneapolis: University of Minnesota Press, 1991), 14.

1. Ernst Bloch, "Das Tor-Motiv," in *Spuren* (Frankfurt am Main: Suhrkamp, 1969), 152.

2. Bloch, 152.

3. Bloch, 154.

4. "Filmschau: Der müde Tod," *Vorwärts* 38, no. 481 (October 12, 1921): 6.

5. G.D., "Der müde Tod," *Ciné-Journal*, June 17, 1922; reprinted in *Lichtbildbühne* 15, no. 30 (July 22, 1922): n.p.

6. "Les Trois Lumières," *Le Matin* 39, no. 13967 (June 16, 1922): 5.

7. See., e.g., G., "Der müde Tod," *Berliner Börsen-Courier* 54, no. 473 (October 9, 1921): 6; and Kurt Pinthus, "Sehenswerte Filme," *Das Tagebuch* 2, no. 42 (October 22, 1921): 1288–89.

8. René Clair, *Cinema Yesterday and Today*, ed. R.C. Dale, trans. Stanley Appelbaum (New York: Dover, 1972), 42.

9. Georges Franju, "Franju on Lang," trans. Diane Matias, *Monthly Film Bulletin* 43, no. 509 (June 1976): 140.

10. Tom Gunning, *The Films of Fritz Lang: Allegories of Vision and Modernity* (London: BFI, 2000), 16.

11. Gunning, 16.

12. Carlo Mierendorff, "If I Only Had the Cinema!," trans. Jeffrey Timon, in *The Promise of Cinema: German Film Theory, 1907–1933*, ed. Anton Kaes, Nicholas Baer, and Michael Cowan (Oakland: University of California Press, 2016), 431.

13. Paul Rotha, *The Film till Now: A Survey of World Cinema* (New York: Twayne Publishers, 1960), 99.

14. Fritz Lang, "The Future of the Feature Film in Germany," trans. Don Reneau, in *The Weimar Republic Sourcebook*, ed. Anton Kaes, Martin Jay, and Edward Dimendberg (Berkeley: University of California Press, 1994), 623.

15. *Destiny* draws from a repertoire of sources that far exceeds Expressionism, as I demonstrate in this chapter, but the film nonetheless exhibits many of its characteristic devices and themes. As with many Expressionist plays, the protagonists in Lang's film lack names and individual features, thereby lending the narrative a general, allegorical quality. Furthermore, following works such as Jakob Wassermann's *The Goose Man* (*Das Gänsemännchen*, 1915), the film traces a shift from anguished isolation to empathetic communitarianism, as the main character comes to understand her personal tragedy in terms of the universal experience of suffering.

16. Max Weber, "Science as a Vocation," in *Essays in Sociology*, ed. and trans. H.H. Gerth and C. Wright Mills (New York: Oxford University Press, 1946), 155, 139.

17. Steve Choe has explored the temporality of life and the moving image in *Destiny*, placing the film in conversation with the writings of early-twentieth-century thinkers who approached life and death as philosophical concepts. See Steve Choe, *Afterlives: Allegories of Film and Mortality in Early Weimar Germany* (New York: Bloomsbury, 2014), 101–36.

18. Jean-Luc Nancy, *The Inoperative Community*, ed. and trans. Peter Connor (Minneapolis: University of Minnesota Press, 1991), 1, 14–15.

19. Martin Heidegger, *Nietzsche*, vol. 4, *Nihilism*, ed. David Farrell Krell, trans. Frank A. Capuzzi (San Francisco: Harper Collins, 1991), 148.

20. Leopold von Ranke, "On Progress in History," in *The Theory and Practice of History*, ed. Georg G. Iggers, trans. Wilma A. Iggers (London and New York: Routledge, 2011), 21.

21. Nancy, *Inoperative Community*, 27.

22. Theodor W. Adorno, *Mahler: A Musical Physiognomy*, trans. Edmund Jephcott (Chicago: University of Chicago Press, 1992), 154. For an interview with Lang and Adorno on *Destiny*, see also Hartmut Birett and Herbert Birett,

"Fritz Lang im Gespräch zum Film *Der müde Tod*," *Filmblatt* 6, no. 16 (Summer 2001): 61–64.

23. Oswald Spengler, *The Decline of the West*, trans. Charles Francis Atkinson (New York: Alfred A. Knopf, 1926), 3.

24. For discussions of Spengler, see Rüdiger Graf, *Die Zukunft der Weimarer Republik: Krisen und Zukunftsaneignungen in Deutschland 1918–1933* (Munich: Oldenbourg, 2008), 104–11; and Charles Bambach, "Weimar Philosophy and the Crisis of Historical Thinking," in *Weimar Thought: A Contested Legacy*, ed. Peter E. Gordon and John P. McCormick (Princeton, NJ: Princeton University Press, 2013), 133–49.

25. See, e.g., Theodor W. Adorno, "Spengler after the Decline," in *Prisms*, trans. Samuel Weber and Shierry Weber (Cambridge, MA: MIT Press, 1983), 51–72; Martin Heidegger, *Nietzsche*, vol. 1, *The Will to Power as Art*, ed. and trans. David Farrell Krell (San Francisco: Harper Collins, 1991), 101; Georg Lukács, *The Destruction of Reason*, trans. Peter Palmer (London and Brooklyn: Verso, 2021); Otto Neurath, "Anti-Spengler," in *Empiricism and Sociology*, ed. Marie Neurath and Robert S. Cohen, trans. Paul Foulkes and Marie Neurath (Dordrecht and Boston: D. Reidel, 1973), 158–213; and Karl Popper, *The Poverty of Historicism* (London and New York: Routledge, 2002), 101.

26. Siegfried Kracauer, *History: The Last Things before the Last* (Princeton, NJ: Markus Wiener, 1995), 40. See also Siegfried Kracauer, *Theory of Film: The Redemption of Physical Reality* (Princeton, NJ: Princeton University Press, 1997), 288.

27. Spengler, *Decline of the West*, 4–5.

28. Kracauer, *History*, 57–58, 181.

29. Reinhart Koselleck, "Modernity and the Planes of Historicity," in *Futures Past: On the Semantics of Historical Time*, trans. Keith Tribe (New York: Columbia University Press, 2004), 9–25.

30. See Tom Gunning, "Early Cinema as Global Cinema: The Encyclopedic Ambition," in *Early Cinema and the "National,"* ed. Richard Abel, Giorgio Bertellini, and Rob King (New Barnet, UK: John Libbey Publishing, 2008), 11–16; and Miriam Hansen, *Babel and Babylon: Spectatorship in American Silent Film* (Cambridge, MA: Harvard University Press, 1991).

31. Thomas Mann, *The Magic Mountain*, trans. John E. Woods (New York: Alfred A. Knopf, 2005), 641.

32. Peter Eli Gordon, *Rosenzweig and Heidegger: Between Judaism and German Philosophy* (Berkeley: University of California Press, 2003), 26.

33. Martin Heidegger, *Being and Time*, trans. Joan Stambaugh (Albany: SUNY Press, 1996), 221.

34. Heidegger, 223.

35. Paul Ricoeur, "Narrative Time," *Critical Inquiry* 7, no. 1 (Autumn 1980): 185.

36. Laura Mulvey, *Death 24x a Second: Stillness and the Moving Image* (London: Reaktion Books, 2006).

37. André Bazin, "Ontology of the Photographic Image," in *What Is Cinema?*, trans. Timothy Barnard (Montreal: Caboose, 2009), 9. See also Gertrud Koch, "Der unsterbliche Körper—Kino und Todesangst," in *Den Körper im Blick*, ed. Beat Wyss and Markus Buschhaus (Munich: Fink, 2008), 35–50.

38. Mulvey, *Death 24x a Second*, 79.

39. Jacob Grimm and Wilhelm Grimm, "Der Gevatter Tod," in *Kinder- und Hausmärchen*, ed. Herman Grimm (Berlin: Wilhelm Hertz, 1895), 124.

40. Sigmund Freud, "Mourning and Melancholia," in *The Standard Edition of the Complete Psychological Works of Sigmund Freud*, vol. 14, ed. and trans. James Strachey (London: Hogarth Press, 1971), 244.

41. Freud, 249.

42. Sigmund Freud, *The Ego and the Id*, ed. James Strachey, trans. Joan Riviere (New York: W.W. Norton & Company, 1960), 24.

43. Walter Benjamin, *Origin of the German Trauerspiel*, trans. Howard Eiland (Cambridge, MA: Harvard University Press, 2019), 16.

44. Benjamin, 46; Ernst Cassirer, *The Philosophy of Symbolic Forms*, vol. 2, *Mythical Thought*, trans. Ralph Manheim (New Haven, CT: Yale University Press, 1955), 106.

45. Benjamin, *German Trauerspiel*, 174.

46. Benjamin, 155.

47. Erwin Panofsky and Fritz Saxl, *Dürers "Melencolia I": Eine quellen- und typengeschichtliche Untersuchung* (Leipzig and Berlin: Teubner, 1923).

48. See Sigmund Freud, *Beyond the Pleasure Principle*, ed. and trans. James Strachey (New York: W.W. Norton & Company, 1961).

49. Marvin H. Pope, *The Anchor Bible: Song of Songs* (Garden City, NY: Doubleday & Company, 1977), 668.

50. Fritz K. Ringer, *The Decline of the German Mandarins: The German Academic Community, 1890–1933* (Hanover, NH: University Press of New England, 1990).

51. Hermann Hesse, "The Longing of Our Time for a Worldview," trans. Don Reneau, in Kaes, Jay, and Dimendberg, *Weimar Republic Sourcebook*, 366.

52. See Béla Balázs, *The Cloak of Dreams: Chinese Fairy Tales*, trans. Jack Zipes (Princeton, NJ: Princeton University Press, 2010).

53. Béla Balázs, *Early Film Theory: "Visible Man" and "The Spirit of Film,"* ed. Erica Carter, trans. Rodney Livingstone (New York: Berghahn, 2010), 4.

54. Balázs, 3. Erica Carter and Hanno Loewy have highlighted the links between Balázs's film theory and his fairy tales and other literary works. See Erica Carter, introduction to Balázs, xxx–xxxi; and Hanno Loewy, *Béla Balázs – Märchen, Ritual und Film* (Berlin: Verlag Vorwerk 8, 2003), 336–38.

55. Balázs, *Early Film Theory*, 19–20.

56. Balázs, 20.

57. Balázs, 20.

58. Michel Foucault, "Of Other Spaces," trans. Jay Miskowiec, *Diacritics* 16, no. 1 (Spring 1986): 22–27.

59. Béla Balázs, "Arabische Nächte," in *Schriften zum Film*, vol. 1, ed. Helmut H. Diederichs (Munich: Carl Hanser, 1982), 181.

60. In "The Mass Ornament" (1927), Siegfried Kracauer invoked the natural powers with which bourgeois revolutions had "settled scores," attributing revolutions of the past 150 years to a rationality derived in part from the utopian "reason of fairy tales"; see Siegfried Kracauer, "The Mass Ornament," in *The Mass Ornament: Weimar Essays*, ed. and trans. Thomas Y. Levin (Cambridge, MA: Harvard University Press, 1995), 80–81.

61. Theodor Lessing, *Jewish Self-Hate*, ed. Benton Arnovitz, trans. Peter C. Appelbaum (New York: Berghahn, 2021), 4.

62. Lessing, 5.

63. See also Paul Reitter, *On the Origins of Jewish Self-Hatred* (Princeton, NJ: Princeton University Press, 2012).

64. Christian Wilhelm Dohm, *Über die bürgerliche Verbesserung der Juden* (Berlin: Friedrich Nicolai, 1781), 8.

65. Werner Sombart, *The Jews and Modern Capitalism*, trans. M. Epstein (Kitchener, ON: Batoche Books, 2001), 225.

66. John M. Efron, *German Jewry and the Allure of the Sephardic* (Princeton, NJ: Princeton University Press, 2016), 15. See also Edward Said, *Orientalism* (New York: Vintage, 1979).

67. Adorno, *Mahler*, 148–49.

68. On the figure of the stranger, see also June J. Hwang, *Lost in Time: Locating the Stranger in German Modernity* (Evanston, IL: Northwestern University Press, 2014).

69. Georg Simmel, "The Stranger," in *On Individuality and Social Forms: Selected Writings*, ed. Donald N. Levine (Chicago: University of Chicago Press, 1971), 145.

70. Werner J. Cahnman, "Village and Small-Town Jews in Germany: A Typological Study," *Leo Baeck Institute Year Book* 19 (1974): 117.

71. Kracauer, *History*, 157.

72. Gustav Mahler, *Das Lied von der Erde in Full Score* (Mineola, NY: Dover, 1988), ix.

73. Siegfried Kracauer, *From Caligari to Hitler: A Psychological History of the German Film*, ed. Leonardo Quaresima (Princeton, NJ: Princeton University Press, 2004), 8.

74. Kracauer, 88.

75. Patrice Petro, *Aftershocks of the New: Feminism and Film History* (New Brunswick, NJ: Rutgers University Press, 2002), 107.

76. Kracauer, *Theory of Film*, 84.

77. Miriam Hansen, introduction to Kracauer, xxii.

78. Kracauer, *History*, 45.

79. Theodor W. Adorno, "Nach Kracauers Tod," in Siegfried Kracauer, *Werke*, vol. 4, ed. Ingrid Belke (Frankfurt am Main: Suhrkamp, 2009), 431. Kracauer wrote to Adorno on November 8, 1963: "It is not as if I were concerned with appearing young or younger; it is merely the aversion to being torn away

from chronological anonymity by the fixing of the date and the inevitable connotations of such fixing." See Theodor W. Adorno and Siegfried Kracauer, *Correspondence 1923–1966*, ed. Wolfgang Schopf, trans. Susan Reynolds and Michael Winkler (Cambridge and Medford, MA: Polity, 2020), 424.

80. Adorno, "Nach Kracauers Tod," 432.

81. Theodor W. Adorno, *The Jargon of Authenticity*, trans. Knut Tarnowski and Frederic Will (Evanston, IL: Northwestern University Press, 1973), 138.

82. Adorno, "Nach Kracauers Tod," 432.

83. Georg Simmel, "The Metaphysics of Death," trans. Ulrich Teucher and Thomas M. Kemple, *Theory, Culture & Society* 24, nos. 7–8 (2007): 74. See also Balázs's essay "The Aesthetics of Death" ("Halálesztétika," 1908), which he dedicated to Simmel after participating in Simmel's private seminar in Berlin. Béla Balázs, "Todesästhetik," trans. Anna Bak-Gara and Marina Gschmeidler, *Mitteilungen des Filmarchiv Austria*, no. 2 (2004): 65–85.

84. Hannah Arendt, *The Origins of Totalitarianism* (Cleveland: Meridian, 1958), 473.

CHAPTER 5

Epigraphs: "Diskussion: Das Ästhetische als Grenzerscheinung der Historie," in Siegfried Kracauer, *Werke*, vol. 4, ed. Ingrid Belke (Frankfurt am Main: Suhrkamp, 2009), 411; Jacques Rancière, *The Politics of Aesthetics: The Distribution of the Sensible*, trans. Gabriel Rockhill (London: Continuum, 2004), 26.

1. See Malcolm Turvey, *The Filming of Modern Life: European Avant-Garde Film of the 1920s* (Cambridge, MA: MIT Press, 2011), 12–15.

2. Hans Blumenberg, *The Legitimacy of the Modern Age*, trans. Robert M. Wallace (Cambridge, MA: MIT Press, 1983), 116.

3. Blumenberg, 116.

4. Peter Osborne, *The Politics of Time: Modernity and Avant-Garde* (London and New York: Verso, 1995), 9, 14.

5. Jacques Rancière, *The Politics of Aesthetics: The Distribution of the Sensible*, trans. Gabriel Rockhill (London: Continuum, 2004), 32–33, 36; Arthur Danto, *The Transfiguration of the Commonplace: A Philosophy of Art* (Cambridge, MA: Harvard University Press, 1981).

6. Jacques Rancière, "Der Wirklichkeitseffekt und die Politik der Fiktion," trans. Mario Horta, in *Realismus in den Künsten der Gegenwart*, ed. Dirck Linck, Michael Lüthy, Brigitte Obermayr, and Martin Vöhler (Zurich: Diaphanes, 2010), 156.

7. Roland Barthes, "The Reality Effect," in *The Rustle of Language*, trans. Richard Howard (Berkeley: University of California Press, 1989), 146; Gertrud Koch, "Nachträgliche Vorwegnahme," in *Kunst, Fortschritt, Geschichte*, ed. Christoph Menke and Juliane Rebentisch (Berlin: Kulturverlag Kadmos, 2006), 92–93.

8. F.T. Marinetti, "The Founding and Manifesto of Futurism," trans. Lawrence Rainey, in *Futurism: An Anthology*, ed. Lawrence Rainey, Christine Poggi, and Laura Wittman (New Haven, CT: Yale University Press, 2009), 51.

9. Carl E. Schorske, *Fin-de-Siècle Vienna: Politics and Culture* (New York: Vintage Books, 1981), xviii.

10. Paul de Man, "Literary History and Literary Modernity," *Daedalus* 99, no. 2 (Spring 1970): 384–404.

11. Eric Hobsbawm, *Behind the Times: The Decline and Fall of the Twentieth-Century Avant-Gardes* (New York: Thames and Hudson, 1998), 25.

12. Charles Baudelaire, "The Painter of Modern Life," in *The Painter of Modern Life and Other Essays*, ed. and trans. Jonathan Mayne (London: Phaidon, 1964), 13.

13. Hans Magnus Enzensberger, "Die Aporien der Avantgarde," in *Einzelheiten II: Poesie und Politik* (Frankfurt am Main: Suhrkamp, 1964), 257.

14. Peter Bürger, *Theory of the Avant-Garde*, trans. Michael Snow (Minneapolis: University of Minnesota Press, 1984), 63.

15. Bürger, *Theory of the Avant-Garde*, 17; Andrew Hewitt, *Fascist Modernism: Aesthetics, Politics, and the Avant-Garde* (Stanford, CA: Stanford University Press, 1993), 7.

16. Hewitt, *Fascist Modernism*, 80.

17. Rancière, *Politics of Aesthetics*, 26.

18. Hans Richter, "History Is What is Happening Today," in *G: An Avant-Garde Journal of Art, Architecture, Design, and Film, 1923–1926*, ed. Detlef Mertins and Michael W. Jennings, trans. Steven Lindberg with Margareta Ingrid Christian (Los Angeles: Getty Research Institute, 2010), 228–29. In its first two issues, the journal was known as *G: Material zur elementaren Gestaltung*.

19. See, e.g., Hans Richter, "The Avant-Garde Film Seen from Within," *Hollywood Quarterly* 4, no. 1 (Autumn 1949): 34–41; Hans Richter, "Dada XYZ...," in *The Dada Painters and Poets: An Anthology*, ed. Robert Motherwell (New York: Wittenborn & Schultz, 1951), 285–89; Hans Richter, "The Film as an Original Art Form," *College Art Journal* 10, no. 2 (Winter 1951): 157–61; Hans Richter, "Easel–Scroll–Film," *Magazine of Art*, February 1952, 78–86; Hans Richter, "Dada und Film," in *Dada: Monographie einer Bewegung*, ed. Willy Verkauf (Teufen: Niggli, 1957), 57–66; Hans Richter, "Hans Richter on the Function of Film History Writing," *Film Culture* 3, no. 18 (April 1958): 25–26; Hans Richter, "Avant-Garde Film in Germany," in *Experiment in the Film*, ed. Roger Manvell (New York: Arno, 1970), 219–33; Hans Richter, "A History of the Avant-Garde," in *Art in Cinema*, ed. Frank Stauffacher (New York: Arno Press, 1971), 8–21; Hans Richter, *The Struggle for the Film: Towards a Socially Responsible Cinema*, ed. Jürgen Römhild, trans. Ben Brewster (New York: St. Martin's Press, 1986); Hans Richter, *Dada: Art and Anti-Art*, trans. David Britt (London: Thames & Hudson, 1997); and Hans Richter, *Encounters from Dada till Today*, trans. Christopher Middleton (Los Angeles: Los Angeles

County Museum of Art; Munich: Prestel, 2013). See also Richter's *Filmgegner von heute—Filmfreunde von morgen* (Berlin: Hermann Reckendorf, 1929).

20. Bruno Latour, "Why Has Critique Run out of Steam? From Matters of Fact to Matters of Concern," *Critical Inquiry* 30, no. 2 (Winter 2004): 226.

21. For important research along these lines, see, e.g., Stephen C. Foster, ed., *Hans Richter: Activism, Modernism, and the Avant-Garde* (Cambridge, MA: MIT Press, 1998); Jeanpaul Goergen, "Hans Richter, Filme bis 1933: Annotierte Filmografie," in *Hans Richter: Film ist Rhythmus*, ed. Jeanpaul Goergen (Berlin: Freunde der Deutschen Kinemathek e.V., 2003), 85–114; Marion von Hofacker, "Kunsthistoriker gegen Künstler," in *Hans Richter: Malerei und Film*, Hilmar Hoffmann and Walter Schobert (Frankfurt am Main: Deutsches Filmmuseum, 1989), 155–67; Walter Schobert, "'Painting in Time' and 'Visual Music': On German Avant-Garde Films of the 1920s," in *Expressionist Film: New Perspectives*, ed. Dietrich Scheunemann (Rochester, NY: Camden House, 2003), 237–49; and Holger Wilmesmeier, "Entstehungsgeschichte: Le Film 100 Titres," in *Hans Richters "Rhythmus 21": Schlüsselfilm der Moderne*, ed. Christoph Bareither et al. (Würzburg: Königshausen & Neumann, 2012), 33–44.

22. Turvey, *The Filming of Modern Life*, 17–45.

23. See, e.g., Michael Cowan, *Walter Ruttmann and the Cinema of Multiplicity: Avant-Garde—Advertising—Modernity* (Amsterdam: Amsterdam University Press, 2014); Malte Hagener, *Moving Forward, Looking Back: The European Avant-Garde and the Invention of Film Culture, 1919–1939* (Amsterdam: Amsterdam University Press, 2007); Yvonne Zimmermann, "Advertising and Avant-Gardes: A History of Concepts, 1930–1940," in *Advertising and the Transformation of Screen Cultures*, ed. Bo Florin, Patrick Vonderau, and Yvonne Zimmermann (Amsterdam: Amsterdam University Press, 2021), 77–111; and Thomas Elsaesser and Malte Hagener, "The Optical Wave: Walter Ruttmann in 1929," in Elsaesser, *Film History as Media Archaeology: Tracking Digital Cinema* (Amsterdam: Amsterdam University Press, 2016), 155–87.

24. See Malte Hagener and Yvonne Zimmermann, "Viking Eggeling and European Avant-Garde Cinema," in *A Cultural History of the Avant-Garde in the Nordic Countries 1925–1950*, ed. Benedikt Hjartarson, Andrea Kollnitz, Per Stounbjerg, and Tania Ørum (Leiden: Brill, 2019), 82–101; Yvonne Zimmermann, "Hans Richter and the *Filmessay*: A Media Archaeological Case Study of Documentary Film History and Historiography," in *A Companion to Documentary Film History*, ed. Joshua Malitsky (Hoboken, NJ: Wiley-Blackwell, 2021), 367–89; and Yvonne Zimmermann, "Hans Richter and the 'Struggle for the Film History,'" in *How Film Histories Were Made: Materials, Methods, Discourses*, ed. Malte Hagener and Yvonne Zimmermann (Amsterdam: Amsterdam University Press, 2024), 209–34. On Richter's later historiographical efforts and his view of film history, see also Ludger Derenthal, "Hans Richter—der Künstler als Kunsthistoriker," in *Hans Richter: Malerei und Film*, ed. Hilmar Hoffmann and Walter Schobert (Frankfurt am Main:

Deutsches Filmmuseum, 1989), 146–54; and Noël Carroll, "Hans Richter's Struggle for Film," in *Theorizing the Moving Image* (New York: Cambridge University Press, 1996), 305–12.

25. On the discourses running through *Rhythm 21*, see Bareither et al., *Hans Richters "Rhythmus 21."*

26. Wassily Kandinsky, *Concerning the Spiritual in Art*, trans. M.T.H. Sadler (New York: Dover, 1977), 19.

27. See Arthur Schopenhauer, *The World as Will and Idea*, vol. 1, trans. R.B. Haldane and J. Kemp (London: Kegan Paul, Trench, Trübner & Co., 1909), 336.

28. Arnold Schoenberg, "The Relationship to the Text," in *Style and Idea*, ed. and trans. Dika Newlin (New York: Philosophical Library, 1950), 5.

29. Walter Ruttmann, "Painting with Time," trans. Michael Cowan, in *The Promise of Cinema: German Film Theory, 1907–1933*, ed. Anton Kaes, Nicholas Baer, and Michael Cowan (Oakland: University of California Press, 2016), 451. See also Joel Westerdale, "The Musical Promise of Abstract Film," in *The Many Faces of Weimar Cinema: Rediscovering Germany's Filmic Legacy*, ed. Christian Rogowski (Rochester, NY: Camden House, 2010), 153–66.

30. On this point, see Ingo Zechner, "Elementares Kino: Fünf Notizen zu Hans Richters *Rhythmus 21*," in Bareither et al., *Hans Richters "Rhythmus 21,"* 91–92, 96.

31. Zechner, 99, 101.

32. Wilhelm Worringer, *Abstraction and Empathy: A Contribution to the Psychology of Style*, trans. Michael Bullock (Chicago: Ivan R. Dee, 1997), 14.

33. Herman George Scheffauer, "The Visible Symphony," in *The New Vision in the German Arts* (New York: B.W. Huebsch, 1924), 141–42.

34. Rudolf Kurtz, *Expressionism and Film*, ed. Christian Kiening and Ulrich Johannes Beil, trans. Brenda Benthien (New Barnet, UK: John Libbey Publishing, 2016), 96; translation modified.

35. Gilles Deleuze, *Cinema 1: The Movement-Image*, trans. Hugh Tomlinson and Barbara Habberjam (Minneapolis: University of Minnesota Press, 1986), 54–55.

36. Christine N. Brinckmann, "Abstraction and Empathy in the Early German Avant-Garde," in *Color and Empathy: Essays on Two Aspects of Film* (Amsterdam: Amsterdam University Press, 2014), 156.

37. Hans Richter, "The Badly Trained Soul," in Mertins and Jennings, G, 147.

38. Richter, 148.

39. On the history of media experimentation and theorization preceding absolute film, see Christian Kiening and Heinrich Adolf, afterword to *Der absolute Film: Dokumente der Medienavantgarde (1912–1936)*, ed. Christian Kiening and Heinrich Adolf (Zurich: Chronos, 2012), 419–500.

40. Walter Ruttmann, "The 'Absolute' Fashion: Film as an End in Itself; Beware of the *Art pour l'art* Position," trans. Nicholas Baer, in Kaes, Baer, and Cowan, *Promise of Cinema*, 465.

41. Ruttmann, 465.

42. Siegfried Kracauer, "Abstract Film: On the Screening by the Gesellschaft Neuer Film," trans. Michael Cowan, in Kaes, Baer, and Cowan, *Promise of Cinema*, 466.

43. Béla Balázs, *Early Film Theory: "Visible Man" and "The Spirit of Film,"* ed. Erica Carter, trans. Rodney Livingstone (New York: Berghahn, 2010), 227.

44. See Walter Benjamin, *The Arcades Project*, trans. Howard Eiland and Kevin McLaughlin (Cambridge, MA, and London: Harvard University Press, 1999), 396; and Theodor W. Adorno and Hanns Eisler, *Composing for the Films* (London and New York: Continuum, 2005), 64.

45. Rudolf Kurtz, "Posing the Problem," in Mertins and Jennings, *G*, 230. Kurtz draws here from Alois Riegl, "The Main Characteristics of the Late Roman *Kunstwollen*," trans. Christopher S. Wood, in *The Vienna School Reader: Politics and Art Historical Method in the 1930s*, ed. Christopher S. Wood (New York: Zone Books, 2003), 95.

46. Richter, "History Is What Is Happening Today," 229. See also Hans Richter, "*Expressionismus und Film* by Rudolf Kurtz," in Mertins and Jennings, *G*, 198.

47. Richter, "History Is What Is Happening Today," 228.

48. Kandinsky, *Concerning the Spiritual in Art*, 12; Richter, "History Is What Is Happening Today," 228.

49. Richter, "History Is What Is Happening Today," 228.

50. Raoul Hausmann, Hans Arp, Ivan Puni, and László Moholy-Nagy, "A Call for Elemental Art," trans. Michael W. Jennings, in Mertins and Jennings, *G*, 241; Richter, "History Is What Is Happening Today," 229.

51. Richter, "History Is What Is Happening Today," 229.

52. Turvey, *Filming of Modern Life*, 27.

53. Richter, "History Is What Is Happening Today," 229.

54. Alois Riegl, *Gesammelte Aufsätze*, ed. Karl Maria Swoboda (Augsburg: Filser, 1929), 63. See also Margaret Iversen, *Alois Riegl: Art History and Theory* (Cambridge, MA: MIT Press, 1993), 4.

55. Riegl, "Late Roman *Kunstwollen*," 94–95.

56. Richter, "History Is What Is Happening Today," 228.

57. Richter, 229.

58. Heinrich Wölfflin, *Kunstgeschichtliche Grundbegriffe: Das Problem der Stilentwicklung in der neueren Kunst* (Munich: Hugo Bruckmann, 1917), vii.

59. Heinrich Wölfflin, *Principles of Art History: The Problem of the Development of Style in Later Art*, trans. M. D. Hottinger (Mineola, NY: Dover, 1950), 6, vii.

60. Wölfflin, vii, 237; Richter, "History Is What Is Happening Today," 229.

61. See Terry Smith, "Contemporary Art and Contemporaneity," *Critical Inquiry* 32, no. 4 (Summer 2006): 681–707; Okwui Enwezor, Nancy Condee, and Terry Smith, eds., *Antinomies of Art and Culture: Modernity, Postmodernity, Contemporaneity* (Durham, NC: Duke University Press, 2008); Giorgio Agamben, "What Is the Contemporary?," in *"What Is an Apparatus?" and Other Essays*, trans. David Kishik and Stefan Pedatella (Stanford, CA:

Stanford University Press, 2009), 39–54; Boris Groys, "Comrades of Time," in *What Is Contemporary Art?*, ed. Julieta Aranda, Anton Vidokle, and Brian Kuan Wood (Berlin: Sternberg, 2010), 22–39; Peter Osborne, *Anywhere or Not at All: Philosophies of Contemporary Art* (London and Brooklyn: Verso, 2013); and Juliane Rebentisch, "The Contemporaneity of Contemporary Art," *New German Critique* 42, no. 1 (February 2015): 223–37.

62. G.W.F. Hegel, *Aesthetics: Lectures on Fine Art*, vol. 1, trans. T.M. Knox (Oxford: Oxford University Press, 1975), 603.

63. Hegel, 608.

64. Hegel, 272.

65. Baudelaire, "Painter of Modern Life," 1.

66. Baudelaire, 14.

67. Baudelaire, 1; de Man, "Literary History and Literary Modernity," 396.

68. Kandinsky, *Concerning the Spiritual in Art*, 1; Walter Gropius, "Die Entwicklung moderner Industriebaukunst," in *Die Kunst in Industrie und Handel: Jahrbuch des Deutschen Werkbundes* (Jena: Eugen Diederichs, 1913), 19; László Moholy-Nagy, *Painting, Photography, Film*, trans. Janet Seligman (London: Lund Humphries, 1967), 9.

69. F.T. Marinetti, Bruno Corra, Emilio Settimelli, Arnaldo Ginna, Giacomo Balla, and Remo Chiti, "The Futurist Cinema," trans. Lawrence Rainey, in Rainey, Poggi, and Wittman, *Futurism: An Anthology*, 230.

70. Balázs, *Early Film Theory*, 48, 67.

71. Christian Metz, "On the Impression of Reality in the Cinema," in *Film Language: A Semiotics of the Cinema*, trans. Michael Taylor (Chicago: University of Chicago Press, 1991), 8.

72. Mary Ann Doane, *The Emergence of Cinematic Time: Modernity, Contingency, the Archive* (Cambridge, MA: Harvard University Press, 2002), 104.

73. Kurtz, *Expressionism and Film*, 105.

74. Wilhelm Pinder, *Das Problem der Generation in der Kunstgeschichte Europas* (Berlin: Frankfurter Verlags-Anstalt, 1926), 22.

75. Pinder's critique of Wölfflin is not entirely fair, given the latter's acknowledgment of problems of periodization and forms of nonsynchronicity in his *Principles of Art History*, viii, 235.

76. Pinder, *Das Problem der Generation*, 13, 15.

77. Frederic J. Schwartz, *Blind Spots: Critical Theory and the History of Art in Twentieth-Century Germany* (New Haven, CT: Yale University Press, 2005), 109–10.

78. Erwin Panofsky, "Reflections on Historical Time," trans. Johanna Bauman, *Critical Inquiry* 30, no. 4 (Summer 2004): 694.

79. Panofsky, 694.

80. Panofsky, 695.

81. See Karl Mannheim, "The Problem of Generations," in *Essays on the Sociology of Knowledge*, ed. and trans. Paul Kecskemeti (London: Routledge & Kegan Paul, 1952), 276–322.

82. Ernst Bloch, *Heritage of Our Times*, trans. Neville Plaice and Stephen Plaice (Berkeley: University of California Press, 1991), 97.

83. Karl Marx, "Introduction to a Critique of Political Economy," in *The German Ideology*, by Karl Marx and Friedrich Engels, ed. C.J. Arthur (New York: International Publishers, 1970), 149.

84. Martin Jay, "1990: Straddling a Watershed?," in *Essays from the Edge: Parerga & Paralipomena* (Charlottesville: University of Virginia Press, 2011), 180.

85. Richter, "History Is What Is Happening Today," 228.

86. Henri Focillon, *The Life of Forms in Art*, trans. Charles Beecher Hogan and George Kubler (New York: Zone Books, 1992), 140.

87. Hippolyte Taine, *History of English Literature*, vol. 1, trans. Henry van Laun (Edinburgh: Edmonston and Douglas, 1871), 10–14; Focillon, *Life of Forms in Art*, 140.

88. Focillon, *Life of Forms in Art*, 155.

89. René Wellek, "The Parallelism between Literature and the Arts," in *Literary Criticism—Idea and Act: The English Institute, 1939–1972; Selected Essays*, ed. W.K. Wimsatt (Berkeley: University of California Press, 1974), 63–64.

90. George Kubler, *The Shape of Time: Remarks on the History of Things* (New Haven, CT: Yale University Press, 2008), 25.

91. Focillon, *Life of Forms in Art*, 137.

92. Kubler, *Shape of Time*, 25.

93. Kracauer to Panofsky, March 3, 1962, in *Siegfried Kracauer / Erwin Panofsky: Briefwechsel 1941–1966*, ed. Volker Breidecker (Berlin: Akademie, 1996), 65.

94. Siegfried Kracauer, "Time and History," *History and Theory* 6 (1966): 68–69. This essay was first published in *Zeugnisse: Theodor W. Adorno zum 60. Geburtstag*, ed. Max Horkheimer (Frankfurt am Main: Europäische Verlagsanstalt, 1963), 50–64, and would also become chapter 6 ("Ahasuerus, or the Riddle of Time") of Kracauer's *History: The Last Things before the Last*.

95. Kracauer, *History*, 62–79.

96. Kracauer, 53–55.

97. Richter, "History Is What Is Happening Today," 229.

98. Richter, 228.

99. G.W.F. Hegel, *Elements of the Philosophy of Right*, ed. Allen W. Wood, trans. H.B. Nisbet (Cambridge: Cambridge University Press, 1991), 21.

100. Kracauer, *History*, 83.

101. Siegfried Kracauer, *From Caligari to Hitler: A Psychological History of the German Film*, ed. Leonardo Quaresima (Princeton, NJ: Princeton University Press, 2004), 112.

CHAPTER 6

Epigraphs: Karl Marx and Friedrich Engels, *The German Ideology*, trans. W. Lough, in *The Collected Works of Karl Marx and Friedrich Engels*, vol. 5, *1845–*

47 (New York: International Publishers, 1976), 28; Theodor W. Adorno, *The Jargon of Authenticity*, trans. Knut Tarnowski and Frederic Will (Evanston, IL: Northwestern University Press, 1973), 98–99.

1. Siegfried Kracauer, *From Caligari to Hitler: A Psychological History of the German Film*, ed. Leonardo Quaresima (Princeton, NJ: Princeton University Press, 2004), li.

2. Friedrich Meinecke, "Von der Krisis des Historismus," *Aphorismen und Skizzen zur Geschichte* (Leipzig: Koehler & Amelang, 1942), 124.

3. Karl Popper, *The Poverty of Historicism* (London and New York: Routledge, 2002), ix.

4. See Karl Löwith, "Nature, History, and Existentialism," *Social Research* 19, no. 1 (March 1952): 79–81.

5. Theodor W. Adorno, "The Idea of Natural History," trans. Bob Hullot-Kentor, *Telos*, no. 60 (Summer 1984): 117.

6. Kracauer, *From Caligari to Hitler*, 112; Eric Rentschler, "Mountains and Modernity: Relocating the *Bergfilm*," *New German Critique*, no. 51 (Autumn 1990): 139.

7. Hugo von Hofmannsthal, *Das Schrifttum als geistiger Raum der Nation* (Munich: Bremer Presse, 1927).

8. Jeffrey Herf, *Reactionary Modernism: Technology, Culture, and Politics in Weimar and the Third Reich* (Cambridge: Cambridge University Press, 1984), 2; Thomas Mann, "Germany and the Germans," in *Thomas Mann's Addresses Delivered at the Library of Congress, 1942–1949* (Washington: Library of Congress, 1963), 62.

9. Herf, *Reactionary Modernism*, 1; Andrew Hewitt, *Fascist Modernism: Aesthetics, Politics, and the Avant-Garde* (Stanford, CA: Stanford University Press, 1993), 44.

10. Peter Osborne, *The Politics of Time: Modernity and Avant-Garde* (London and New York: Verso, 1995), 163.

11. Anson Rabinbach, "Nationalsozialismus und Moderne: Zur Technik-Interpretation im Dritten Reich," in *Der Technikdiskurs in der Hitler-Stalin-Ära*, ed. Wolfgang Emmerich and Carl Wege (Stuttgart and Weimar: Metzler, 1995), 111–12.

12. Katharina Loew, *Special Effects and German Silent Film: Techno-Romantic Cinema* (Amsterdam: Amsterdam University Press, 2021).

13. I am using the restored version of the film included in the "Masters of Cinema" DVD series released by Eureka Entertainment in 2004. Here and below, I have often modified the English translations found on the DVD.

14. Theodor W. Adorno, *The Jargon of Authenticity*, trans. Knut Tarnowski and Frederic Will (Evanston, IL: Northwestern University Press, 1973), 108.

15. Johannes von Moltke, *No Place Like Home: Locations of Heimat in German Cinema* (Berkeley: University of California Press, 2005), 46.

16. On the nexus of nature and modern temporality in the *Bergfilm*, see Alex Bush, "Moving Mountains: Glacial Contingency and Modernity in the *Bergfilm*," *Journal of Cinema and Media Studies* 59, no. 1 (Fall 2019): 1–22. On

sports cinematography and embodied camera operation, see Katie Bird, "Sporting Sensations: Béla Balázs and the *Bergfilm* Camera Operator," *Journal of Cinema and Media Studies* 60, no. 3 (Spring 2021): 9–36.

17. See, e.g., Kracauer, *From Caligari to Hitler*, 110–11.

18. Hermann Häfker, "*Cinema and Geography*: Introduction," trans. Nicholas Baer, in *The Promise of Cinema: German Film Theory, 1907–1933*, ed. Anton Kaes, Nicholas Baer, and Michael Cowan (Oakland: University of California Press, 2016), 51; Béla Balázs, *Early Film Theory: "Visible Man" and "The Spirit of Film,"* ed. Erica Carter, trans. Rodney Livingstone (New York: Berghahn, 2010), 52; Germaine Dulac, *Writings on Cinema (1919–1937)*, ed. Prosper Hillairet, trans. Scott Hammen (Paris: Paris Expérimental, 2018), 92, 209, 236, 238; Siegfried Kracauer, *Theory of Film: The Redemption of Physical Reality* (Princeton, NJ: Princeton University Press, 1997), 30–37.

19. Arnold Fanck, "Die Zukunft des Naturfilms," in *Berge, Licht und Traum: Dr. Arnold Fanck und der deutsche Bergfilm*, ed. Jan-Christopher Horak and Gisela Pichler (Munich: Bruckmann, 1997), 143.

20. On Fanck's views of Nietzsche, see Arnold Fanck, *Er führte Regie mit Gletschern, Stürmen und Lawinen: Ein Filmpionier erzählt* (Munich: Nymphenburger, 1973), 52.

21. On the iconographic sources, see, e.g., Thomas Brandlmeier, "Arnold Fanck," in *CineGraph: Lexikon zum deutschsprachigen Film*, installment 4, ed. Hans-Michael Bock (Munich: edition text + kritik, 1984), E1; and Thomas Jacobs, "Visuelle Traditionen des Bergfilms: Von Fidus zu Friedrich oder Das Ende bürgerlicher Fluchtbewegungen im Faschismus," *Film und Kritik*, no. 1 (June 1992): 31.

22. Marjorie Hope Nicolson, *Mountain Gloom and Mountain Glory: The Development of the Aesthetics of the Infinite* (Seattle: University of Washington Press, 1997).

23. Immanuel Kant, *Critique of the Power of Judgment*, ed. Paul Guyer, trans. Paul Guyer and Eric Matthews (Cambridge: Cambridge University Press, 2000), 152.

24. Roland Barthes, "The *Blue Guide*," in *Mythologies*, trans. Annette Lavers (New York: Farrar, Straus & Giroux, 1972), 74.

25. Francesco Petrarch, *Letters on Familiar Matters*, vol. 1, *Books I–VIII*, trans. Aldo S. Bernardo (New York: Italica Press, 2005), 172; Hans Blumenberg, *The Legitimacy of the Modern Age*, trans. Robert M. Wallace (Cambridge, MA: MIT Press, 1983), 341.

26. See Andrew Denning, *Skiing into Modernity: A Cultural and Environmental History* (Oakland: University of California Press, 2015).

27. A counter to this elitism was the organization Naturfreunde (Friends of Nature), which was founded by Austrian socialists in 1895.

28. Hans Magnus Enzensberger, "A Theory of Tourism," trans. Gerd Gemünden and Kenn Johnson, *New German Critique*, no. 68 (Spring/Summer 1996): 129. See also Jonathan Culler, "Semiotics of Tourism," *American Journal of Semiotics* 1, nos. 1–2 (1981): 127–40; and Nancy P. Nenno, "'Postcards from the Edge': Education to Tourism in the German Mountain Film," in *Light

Motives: German Popular Film in Perspective, ed. Randall Halle and Margaret McCarthy (Detroit: Wayne State University Press, 2003), 61–84.

29. See Seth Peabody, *Film History for the Anthropocene: The Ecological Archive of German Cinema* (Rochester, NY: Camden House, 2023), 122–24.

30. On the figuration of mountains on-screen, see Cornelia Klecker and Christian Quendler, "Cinematic Figurations of Mountains," *New Review of Film and Television Studies* 21, no. 1 (2023): 1–18. Fanck and Hannes Schneider also published an illustrated instructional book on skiing, *Wunder des Schneeschuhs: Ein System des richtigen Skilaufens und seine Anwendung im alpinen Geländelauf* (Hamburg: Enoch, 1925).

31. Georg Simmel, "Alpine Journeys," trans. Jens Klenner, in *Mountains and the German Mind: Translations from Gessner to Messner, 1541–2009*, ed. Sean Ireton and Caroline Schaumann (Rochester, NY: Camden House, 2020), 184; Ernst Bloch, "Alpen ohne Photographie," in *Literarische Aufsätze* (Frankfurt am Main: Suhrkamp, 1965), 488–98.

32. Quoted in Martin Heidegger, *Nietzsche*, vol. 2, *The Eternal Recurrence of the Same*, ed. and trans. David Farrell Krell (San Francisco: Harper Collins, 1991), 75; Walter Benjamin, "The Work of Art in the Age of Its Technological Reproducibility: Second Version," trans. Edmund Jephcott and Harry Zohn, in *Selected Writings*, vol. 3, ed. Howard Eiland and Michael W. Jennings (Cambridge, MA, and London: Harvard University Press, 2002), 105.

33. Walter Benjamin, "Theories of German Fascism: On the Collection of Essays *War and Warrior*, edited by Ernst Jünger," trans. Jerolf Wikoff, in *Selected Writings*, vol. 2, pt. 1, ed. Michael W. Jennings, Howard Eiland, and Gary Smith (Cambridge, MA, and London: Harvard University Press, 1999), 314, 319.

34. Siegfried Kracauer, "Ein Abend im Hochgebirge," *FZ*, August 23, 1906, in *Werke*, vol. 5.1, ed. Inka Mülder-Bach (Berlin: Suhrkamp, 2011), 9–11. See also Kracauer's 1933 sketch for a film adaptation of Alphonse Daudet's *Tartarin on the Alps* (*Tartarin sur les Alpes*, 1885): "Ideen-Entwurf zu einer 'großen Filmkomödie' nach dem berühmten Roman: 'Tartarin sur les Alpes' von Alphonse Daudet," typescript, October 1933, in *Werke*, vol. 6.3, ed. Inka Mülder-Bach (Frankfurt am Main: Suhrkamp, 2004), 518–22.

35. Siegfried Kracauer, "Das Wunder des Schneeschuhs," *FZ*, June 16, 1921, in *Werke*, vol. 6.1, ed. Inka Mülder-Bach (Frankfurt am Main: Suhrkamp, 2004), 11.

36. Siegfried Kracauer, "Mountains, Clouds, People," trans. Nicholas Baer, in Kaes, Baer, and Cowan, *The Promise of Cinema*, 97.

37. Siegfried Kracauer, "Der 'heilige' Berg," *FZ*, March 4, 1927, in *Werke*, 6.1:298.

38. Siegfried Kracauer, "Photography," in *The Mass Ornament: Weimar Essays*, ed. and trans. Thomas Y. Levin (Cambridge, MA: Harvard University Press, 1995), 62.

39. On early travelogues, see Jennifer Lynn Peterson, *Education in the School of Dreams: Travelogues and Early Nonfiction Film* (Durham, NC: Duke University Press, 2013).

40. See Siegfried Kracauer, "The Mass Ornament," in *The Mass Ornament*, 75–86; and Miriam Bratu Hansen, *Cinema and Experience: Siegfried Kracauer, Walter Benjamin, and Theodor W. Adorno* (Berkeley: University of California Press, 2012), 15–16, 71.

41. Béla Balázs, "The Case of Dr. Fanck," trans. Alex H. Bush, in Kaes, Baer, and Cowan, *The Promise of Cinema*, 70.

42. Balázs, 68.

43. Balázs, 69.

44. See Balázs, *Early Film Theory*, 53.

45. Georg Simmel, "On the Aesthetics of the Alps," trans. Jens Klenner, in *Mountains and the German Mind: Translations from Gessner to Messner, 1541–2009*, ed. Sean Ireton and Caroline Schaumann (Rochester, NY: Camden House, 2020), 187–92.

46. Simmel, "Alpine Journeys," 187.

47. Georg Simmel, "The Relative and the Absolute in the Problem of the Sexes," in *On Women, Sexuality, and Love*, trans. Guy Oakes (New Haven, CT: Yale University Press, 1984), 130. On Simmel's social theory, see also Elizabeth S. Goodstein, *Georg Simmel and the Disciplinary Imaginary* (Stanford, CA: Stanford University Press, 2017).

48. Klaus Theweleit, *Male Fantasies*, vol. 1, *Women, Floods, Bodies, History*, trans. Stephen Conway, Erica Carter, and Chris Turner (Minneapolis: University of Minnesota Press, 1987), 249.

49. On this point, see also Christian Rapp, *Höhenrausch: Der deutsche Bergfilm* (Vienna: Sonderzahl, 1997), 108.

50. On Meisel's score for *Der heilige Berg*, see Christopher Morris, *Modernism and the Cult of Mountains: Music, Opera, Cinema* (Farnham, Surrey: Ashgate, 2012), 79–114; and Fiona Ford, "Edmund Meisel's Score to *Der heilige Berg* (1926): Prefiguring Hollywood's 'Golden Age' Narrative-Scoring Practices in Live Performance," in *Music and Sound in Silent Film: From the Nickelodeon to "The Artist,"* ed. Ruth Barton and Simon Trezise (New York: Routledge, 2019), 124–45.

51. On silent cinema and modern dance, see Kristina Köhler, *Der tänzerische Film: Frühe Filmkultur und moderner Tanz* (Marburg: Schüren, 2017).

52. Quoted in Steven E. Aschheim, *The Nietzsche Legacy in Germany, 1890–1990* (Berkeley: University of California Press, 1992), 35.

53. Kant, *Critique of the Power of Judgment*, 139.

54. Balázs, *Early Film Theory*, 134; Gilles Deleuze, *Cinema 1: The Movement-Image*, trans. Hugh Tomlinson and Barbara Habberjam (Minneapolis: University of Minnesota Press, 1986), 97.

55. The allegorical name of the central male character, "The Friend," suggests the impossibility of his marriage to Diotima without destruction of himself and the friendship by which he is defined. *Nomen est omen.*

56. Sigmund Freud, *The Interpretation of Dreams*, trans. James Strachey (New York: Avon, 1965), 435.

57. On this trope, see Kracauer, *From Caligari to Hitler*, 112.

58. Johann Wolfgang von Goethe, *Faust I & II*, ed. and trans. Stuart Atkins (Princeton, NJ: Princeton University Press, 2014), 214. Carl Schmitt would similarly posit water and the sea as "the secret originary ground of all life"; Carl Schmitt, *Land and Sea: A World-Historical Meditation*, ed. Russell A. Berman and Samuel Garrett Zeitlin, trans. Samuel Garrett Zeitlin (Candor, NY: Telos, 2015), 7.

59. See Klaus Lichtblau, "Eros and Culture: Gender Theory in Simmel, Tönnies and Weber," trans. Guenther Roth, *Telos*, no. 82 (Winter 1989–90): 93.

60. Adorno would later cite a passage from *Das Kapital* in which Marx had used the term "natural history"; see Theodor W. Adorno, *Negative Dialectics*, trans. E. B. Ashton (London and New York: Routledge, 1973), 354. See also Peter E. Gordon, *Adorno and Existence* (Cambridge, MA, and London: Harvard University Press, 2016).

61. Adorno, "Idea of Natural History," 117.

62. Max Horkheimer and Theodor W. Adorno, *Dialectic of Enlightenment: Philosophical Fragments*, ed. Gunzelin Schmid Noerr, trans. Edmund Jephcott (Stanford, CA: Stanford University Press, 2002), xviii; Adorno, *Negative Dialectics*, 300–360.

63. See Adorno, *Negative Dialectics*, 358.

64. Walter Benjamin, *Origin of the German Trauerspiel*, trans. Howard Eiland (Cambridge, MA, and London: Harvard University Press, 2019), 190. On the idea of natural history in Adorno's work, see Susan Buck-Morss, *The Origin of Negative Dialectics: Theodor W. Adorno, Walter Benjamin, and the Frankfurt Institute* (New York: Macmillan, 1977), 43–62; Beatrice Hanssen, *Walter Benjamin's Other History: Of Stones, Animals, Human Beings, and Angels* (Berkeley: University of California Press, 1998), 9–102; and Max Pensky, "Natural History: The Life and Afterlife of a Concept in Adorno," *Critical Horizons* 5, no. 1 (2004): 227–58.

65. Kant, *Critique of the Power of Judgment*, 129, 141, 143, 156.

66. For an analysis of Strauss's symphony and its relation to Nietzsche's writings, see Morris, *Modernism and the Cult of Mountains*, 11, 49–78.

67. Kracauer, *From Caligari to Hitler*, 258.

68. See Gabriele von Bassermann-Jordan, *"Schönes Leben! du lebst, wie die zarten Blüthen im Winter...": Die Figur der Diotima in Hölderlins Lyrik und im "Hyperion"-Projekt: Theorie und dichterische Praxis* (Würzburg: Königshausen & Neumann, 2004), 153.

69. Simmel, "Alpine Journeys," 187.

70. Leo Löwenthal, "Knut Hamsun, 1860–1952," in *Literature and the Image of Man* (New Brunswick, NJ: Transaction Books, 1986), 194. On these dual historicizing and mythicizing gestures, see also Herbert Marcuse, "The Struggle against Liberalism in the Totalitarian View of the State," in *Negations: Essays in Critical Theory*, trans. Jeremy J. Shapiro (Boston: Beacon Press, 1968), 5, 23–25.

71. Hans Blumenberg, *Paradigms for a Metaphorology*, trans. Robert Savage (Ithaca, NY: Cornell University Press, 2010), 2.

72. See Gilles Deleuze, *Cinema 2: The Time-Image*, trans. Hugh Tomlinson and Robert Galeta (Minneapolis: University of Minnesota Press, 1989), 158–61.

73. Arnold Zweig, *Dialektik der Alpen: Fortschritt und Hemmnis* (Berlin: Aufbau, 1997). One of Fanck's cameramen for *Der heilige Berg*, Helmar Lerski, also emigrated to Palestine.

74. Theodor W. Adorno, "Aus Sils Maria," in *Ohne Leitbild: Parva Aesthetica* (Frankfurt am Main: Suhrkamp, 1967), 48–51.

75. Siegfried Kracauer, *History: The Last Things before the Last* (Princeton, NJ: Markus Wiener, 1995), 20.

76. Kracauer, 31.

77. Kracauer, 21.

78. For key texts, see, e.g., John Bellamy Foster, *Marx's Ecology: Materialism and Nature* (New York: Monthly Review Press, 2000); Jason W. Moore, *Capitalism in the Web of Life: Ecology and the Accumulation of Capital* (London: Verso, 2015); Donna J. Haraway, *Staying with the Trouble: Making Kin in the Chthulucene* (Durham, NC: Duke University Press, 2016); Bruno Latour, *Facing Gaia: Eight Lectures on the New Climatic Regime*, trans. Catherine Porter (Cambridge: Polity Press, 2017); Andreas Malm, *The Progress of This Storm: Nature and Society in a Warming World* (London: Verso, 2018); and Dipesh Chakrabarty, *The Climate of History in a Planetary Age* (Chicago: University of Chicago Press, 2021).

EPILOGUE

Epigraph: James Joyce, interview with Jacques Benoist-Méchin, 1956; quoted in Richard Ellmann, *James Joyce* (Oxford: Oxford University Press, 1982), 521.

1. c–c., "Filmkritik: Berliner Uraufführungen: *Metropolis*," *Reichsfilmblatt*, no. 2 (January 15, 1927): 42.

2. See, e.g., Anton Kaes, "*Metropolis*: Cinema, City, Modernity," in *Expressionist Utopias: Paradise, Metropolis, Architectural Fantasy*, ed. Timothy O. Benson (Los Angeles: Los Angeles County Museum of Art, 1993), 146–65; Janet Lungstrum, "*Metropolis* and the Technosexual Woman of German Modernity," in *Women in the Metropolis: Gender and Modernity in Weimar Culture*, ed. Katharina von Ankum (Berkeley: University of California Press, 1997), 128–44; and Tom Gunning, *The Films of Fritz Lang: Allegories of Vision and Modernity* (London: BFI, 2000), 52–83.

3. See, e.g., David Bordwell, *On the History of Film Style* (Cambridge, MA: Harvard University Press, 1997), 141–47.

4. See Peter Osborne, *The Politics of Time: Modernity and Avant-Garde* (London and New York: Verso, 1995); and Jacques Rancière, *The Politics of Aesthetics: The Distribution of the Sensible*, trans. Gabriel Rockhill (London: Continuum, 2004), 20–30. See also Clive Hamilton, Christophe Bonneuil, and François Gemenne, eds., *The Anthropocene and the Global Environmental Crisis: Rethinking Modernity in a New Epoch* (London and New York:

Routledge, 2015); and Jason W. Moore, ed., *Anthropocene or Capitalocene? Nature, History, and the Crisis of Capitalism* (Oakland, CA: PM Press, 2016).

5. Moishe Postone, "The Current Crisis and the Anachronism of Value: A Marxian Reading," *Continental Thought & Theory* 1, no. 4 (2017): 38.

6. Thomas Elsaesser, *Metropolis* (London: BFI, 2000), 7.

7. Fredric Jameson, "Progress versus Utopia: or, Can We Imagine the Future?," *Science Fiction Studies* 9, no. 2 (July 1982): 150.

8. Andreas Malm, *The Progress of This Storm: Nature and Society in a Warming World* (London: Verso, 2018).

9. Jameson, "Progress versus Utopia," 153; E. Ann Kaplan, *Climate Trauma: Foreseeing the Future in Dystopian Film and Fiction* (New Brunswick, NJ: Rutgers University Press, 2016).

10. Ernst Troeltsch, "Die geistige Revolution: Berliner Brief," *Kunstwart und Kulturwart* 34, no. 4 (January 1921): 231.

11. Ernst Troeltsch, *Der Historismus und seine Probleme* (Tübingen: J. C. B. Mohr, 1922); Peter Gay, *Weimar Culture: The Outsider as Insider* (New York and London: W. W. Norton & Company, 2001).

12. See Frederick Engels, *The Condition of the Working-Class in England in 1844*, trans. Florence Kelley Wischnewetzky (London: George Allen & Unwin, 1892); and Steven Marcus, *Engels, Manchester, and the Working Class* (New York: Random House, 1974). Karl Marx also invoked "danger to life and limb among the thickly crowded machinery, which, with the regularity of the seasons, issues its list of the killed and wounded in the industrial battle"; Marx, *Capital: A Critique of Political Economy*, vol. 1, ed. Frederick Engels, trans. Samuel Moore and Edward Aveling (Chicago: Charles H. Kerr & Company, 1912), 465.

13. Carl E. Schorske, *Fin-de-Siècle Vienna: Politics and Culture* (New York: Vintage Books, 1981), 124–25.

14. See Paul Federn, *Zur Psychologie der Revolution: Die vaterlose Gesellschaft* (Leipzig and Vienna: Anzengruber, 1919).

15. Georg Kaiser, *Gas: A Play in Five Acts*, trans. Herman Scheffauer (Boston: Small, Maynard & Co., 1924), 83–84.

16. Fritz von Unruh, "Stirb und Werde: Eine Ansprache zur Frankfurter Goethewoche," in *Reden* (Frankfurt am Main: Frankfurter Societäts-Druckerei, 1924), 29.

17. Karl Marx, *Critique of Hegel's "Philosophy of Right,"* ed. Joseph O'Malley, trans. Annette Jolin and Joseph O'Malley (Cambridge: Cambridge University Press, 1970), 142. See also Johann Heinrich Pestalozzi, "Weltweib und Mutter," in *Sämtliche Werke*, vol. 16, ed. Walter Feilchenfeld and Herbert Schönebaum (Berlin and Leipzig: Walter de Gruyter & Co., 1935), 360.

18. Karl Marx and Friedrich Engels, *The Communist Manifesto*, trans. Samuel Moore (London: Penguin, 2002), 220.

19. In Erich Pommer's account, "The uprising of the workers was patterned after the communist attempt to take over Bavaria"; quoted in George A. Huaco, *The Sociology of Film Styles* (New York: Basic Books, 1965), 63.

20. Max Horkheimer, "Traditional and Critical Theory," in *Critical Theory: Selected Essays*, trans. Matthew J. O'Connell (New York: Continuum, 2002), 213.

21. Max Horkheimer, "The Impotence of the German Working Class," in *Dawn & Decline: Notes 1926–1931 and 1950–1969*, trans. Michael Shaw (New York: Seabury Press, 1978), 61–65.

22. Felix Ziege, "Metropolis und wir," *Kulturwille* 4, no. 6 (1927): 125.

23. Gilles Deleuze, *Cinema 2: The Time-Image*, trans. Hugh Tomlinson and Robert Galeta (Minneapolis: University of Minnesota Press, 1989), 171.

24. On this point, see R.L. Rutsky, "The Mediation of Technology and Gender: *Metropolis*, Nazism, Modernism," in *Fritz Lang's "Metropolis": Cinematic Visions of Technology and Fear*, ed. Michael Minden and Holger Bachmann (Rochester, NY: Camden House, 2000), 219–20.

25. Oswald Spengler, *The Decline of the West*, vol. 2, trans. Charles Francis Atkinson (New York: Alfred A. Knopf, 1928), 102.

26. Susan Sontag, "The Imagination of Disaster," *Commentary*, October 1965, 42–48; *Die Offenbarung Sankt Johannis* (Hellerau: Avalun-Verlag, 1923), with ten woodcuts by Bruno Goldschmitt.

27. E.S.P., "Metropolis," *Lichtbildbühne* 20, no. 9 (January 11, 1927).

28. Ernst Jünger, introduction to *Die veränderte Welt: Eine Bilderfibel unserer Zeit*, ed. Edmund Schultz (Breslau: W.G. Korn, 1933), 6.

29. Thea von Harbou, *Metropolis*, ed. Herbert W. Franke (Frankfurt am Main: Ullstein, 1984), 68. See also Gershom Scholem, *Das Davidschild: Geschichte eines Symbols*, trans. Gerold Necker (Frankfurt am Main: Suhrkamp, 1963).

30. Kurt Pinthus, "Lemberg und Metropolis," *Das Tagebuch* 8, no. 3 (January 15, 1927): 98.

31. See Sigmund Freud, *Civilization and Its Discontents*, ed. and trans. James Strachey (New York: W.W. Norton & Company, 1961), 16–17.

32. Harbou, *Metropolis*, 111.

33. On this point, see Kaes, "*Metropolis*," 162.

34. Patrice Petro, *Aftershocks of the New: Feminism and Film History* (New Brunswick, NJ: Rutgers University Press, 2002), 109–10.

35. See Peter Sloterdijk, *Critique of Cynical Reason*, trans. Michael Eldred (Minneapolis: University of Minnesota Press, 1987).

36. On the hierarchical division of men into "brains" and "hands," see Henry Ford, *My Life and Work* (Garden City, NY: Doubleday, Page & Company, 1923), 5.

37. Siegfried Kracauer, *From Caligari to Hitler: A Psychological History of the German Film*, ed. Leonardo Quaresima (Princeton, NJ: Princeton University Press, 2004), 164.

38. Gay, *Weimar Culture*, 96.

39. Kristen Whissel, *Spectacular Digital Effects: CGI and Contemporary Cinema* (Durham, NC: Duke University Press, 2014), 26.

40. Fredric Jameson, "World-Reduction in Le Guin: The Emergence of Utopian Narrative," *Science Fiction Studies* 2, no. 3 (November 1975): 221–30.

41. Seth Peabody, *Film History for the Anthropocene: The Ecological Archive of German Cinema* (Rochester, NY: Camden House, 2023), 103.

42. Dietrich Neumann, "The Urbanistic Vision in Fritz Lang's *Metropolis*," in *Dancing on the Volcano: Essays on the Culture of the Weimar Republic*, ed. Thomas W. Kniesche and Stephen Brockmann (Columbia, SC: Camden House, 1994), 143–62; Dietrich Neumann, ed., *Film Architecture: From Metropolis to Blade Runner* (Munich: Prestel, 1996). On the trope of verticality in modernism, see Paul Haacke, *The Vertical Imagination and the Crisis of Transatlantic Modernism* (Oxford: Oxford University Press, 2021).

43. H.G. Wells, "Mr. Wells Reviews a Current Film," *New York Times Magazine*, April 17, 1927, 4.

44. Frederick Winslow Taylor, *The Principles of Scientific Management* (New York and London: Harper & Brothers, 1915), 40.

45. Quoted in Robin D.G. Kelley, "Sorry, Not Sorry," *Boston Review*, September 13, 2018, http://bostonreview.net/race-literature-culture-arts-society/robin-d-g-kelley-sorry-not-sorry.

46. Kelley, "Sorry, Not Sorry."

47. See Cedric J. Robinson, *Black Marxism: The Making of the Black Radical Tradition* (Chapel Hill: University of North Carolina Press, 2000). Robinson would later develop the concept of racial capitalism in the context of American film history; see Cedric J. Robinson, *Forgeries of Memory and Meaning: Blacks and the Regimes of Race in American Theater and Film before World War II* (Chapel Hill: University of North Carolina Press, 2007).

48. On Janelle Monáe and *Metropolis*, see Erik Steinskog, "Metropolis 2.0: Janelle Monáe's Recycling of Fritz Lang," in *The Black Speculative Arts Movement: Black Futurity, Art+Design*, ed. Reynaldo Anderson and Clinton R. Fluker (Lanham, MD: Lexington Books, 2019), 173–88.

49. Max Horkheimer, "The Skyscraper," in *Dawn & Decline: Notes 1926–1931 and 1950–1969*, trans. Michael Shaw (New York: Seabury Press, 1978), 66.

50. For an analysis of *Parasite* in terms of "South Korean modalities of racial capitalism" in conjunction with "US militarist settler imperialism," see Jodi Kim, *Settler Garrison: Debt Imperialism, Militarism, and Transpacific Imaginaries* (Durham, NC, and London: Duke University Press, 2022), 1–16.

51. Siegfried Kracauer, *History: The Last Things before the Last* (Princeton, NJ: Markus Wiener, 1995), 59.

52. See, e.g., Daniel Bessner and Udi Greenberg, "The Weimar Analogy," *Jacobin*, December 17, 2016, www.jacobinmag.com/2016/12/trump-hitler-germany-fascism-weimar-democracy/.

53. Peter E. Gordon, "Why Historical Analogy Matters," *New York Review of Books*, January 7, 2020, www.nybooks.com/daily/2020/01/07/why-historical-analogy-matters; Samuel Moyn, "The Trouble with Comparisons," *New York Review of Books*, May 19, 2020, www.nybooks.com/daily/2020/05/19/the-trouble-with-comparisons/.

54. Wilhelm Windelband, "History and Natural Science," trans. Guy Oakes, *History and Theory* 19, no. 2 (February 1980): 169–85.

55. Konrad H. Jarausch and Michael Geyer, *Shattered Past: Reconstructing German Histories* (Princeton, NJ: Princeton University Press, 2003); Helmut Walser Smith, *The Continuities of German History: Nation, Religion, and Race across the Long Nineteenth Century* (Cambridge: Cambridge University Press, 2008).

56. Detlev J.K. Peukert, *The Weimar Republic: The Crisis of Classical Modernity*, trans. Richard Deveson (New York: Hill and Wang, 1992); Friedrich Meinecke, *The German Catastrophe: Reflections and Recollections*, trans. Sidney B. Fay (Cambridge, MA: Harvard University Press, 1950).

57. Rüdiger Graf, "Either-Or: The Narrative of 'Crisis' in Weimar Germany and in Historiography," *Central European History* 43, no. 4 (December 2010): 592–615.

58. Jochen Hung, "'Bad' Politics and 'Good' Culture: New Approaches to the History of the Weimar Republic," *Central European History* 49, nos. 3–4 (2016): 441–53; Gay, *Weimar Culture*, xiv.

59. Troeltsch, "Die geistige Revolution," 231.

60. Anton Kaes, *Shell Shock Cinema: Weimar Culture and the Wounds of War* (Princeton, NJ: Princeton University Press, 2009); Kracauer, *From Caligari to Hitler*.

61. Graf, "Either-Or," 593–94.

Bibliography

Adorno, Theodor W. *Aesthetic Theory*. Edited by Gretel Adorno and Rolf Tiedemann. Translated by Robert Hullot-Kentor. London and New York: Continuum, 2002.
———. *Critical Models: Interventions and Catchwords*. Translated by Henry W. Pickford. New York: Columbia University Press, 2005.
———. *The Culture Industry: Selected Essays on Mass Culture*. Edited by J. M. Bernstein. London and New York: Routledge, 1991.
———. "The Curious Realist: On Siegfried Kracauer." Translated by Shierry Weber Nicholsen. *New German Critique*, no. 54 (Autumn 1991): 159–77.
———. "The Idea of Natural History." Translated by Bob Hullot-Kentor. *Telos*, no. 60 (Summer 1984): 111–24.
———. *The Jargon of Authenticity*. Translated by Knut Tarnowski and Frederic Will. Evanston, IL: Northwestern University Press, 1973.
———. *Mahler: A Musical Physiognomy*. Translated by Edmund Jephcott. Chicago: University of Chicago Press, 1992.
———. "Nach Kracauers Tod." In Siegfried Kracauer, *Werke*, vol. 4, edited by Ingrid Belke, 431–34. Frankfurt am Main: Suhrkamp, 2009.
———. *Negative Dialectics*. Translated by E. B. Ashton. London and New York: Routledge, 1973.
———. *Ohne Leitbild: Parva Aesthetica*. Frankfurt am Main: Suhrkamp, 1967.
———. *Prisms*. Translated by Samuel Weber and Shierry Weber. Cambridge, MA: MIT Press, 1983.
Adorno, Theodor W., and Walter Benjamin. *The Complete Correspondence, 1928–1940*. Edited by Henri Lonitz. Translated by Nicholas Walker. Cambridge, MA: Harvard University Press, 1999.
Adorno, Theodor W., and Hanns Eisler. *Composing for the Films*. London and New York: Continuum, 2005.
Adorno, Theodor W., and Siegfried Kracauer. *Correspondence 1923–1966*. Edited by Wolfgang Schopf. Translated by Susan Reynolds and Michael Winkler. Cambridge and Medford, MA: Polity, 2020.

Agamben, Giorgio. "What Is the Contemporary?" In *"What Is an Apparatus?" and Other Essays*, translated by David Kishik and Stefan Pedatella, 39–54. Stanford, CA: Stanford University Press, 2009.
Allen, Robert C., and Douglas Gomery. *Film History: Theory and Practice*. New York: Alfred A. Knopf, 1985.
Allred, Mason Kamana. *Weimar Cinema, Embodiment, and Historicity: Cultural Memory and the Historical Films of Ernst Lubitsch*. New York and London: Routledge, 2017.
Altman, Rick. *Silent Film Sound*. New York: Columbia University Press, 2004.
Anderson, Mark Lynn. "Anger Management, or the Dream of a Falsifiable Film-Historical Past." *NECSUS: European Journal of Media Studies* 11, no. 1 (Spring 2022): 67–87.
———. *Twilight of the Idols: Hollywood and the Human Sciences in 1920s America*. Berkeley: University of California Press, 2011.
Anderson, Steve F. *Technologies of History: Visual Media and the Eccentricity of the Past*. Hanover, NH: Dartmouth College Press, 2011.
Andriopoulos, Stefan. "Suggestion, Hypnosis, and Crime: Robert Wiene's The Cabinet of Dr. Caligari (1920)." In *Weimar Cinema: An Essential Guide to Classic Films of the Era*, edited by Noah Isenberg, 13–32. New York: Columbia University Press, 2009.
Ankersmit, Frank. "Historicism: An Attempt at Synthesis." *History and Theory* 34, no. 3 (1995): 143–61.
———. *Sublime Historical Experience*. Stanford, CA: Stanford University Press, 2005.
Arendt, Hannah. *The Origins of Totalitarianism*. Cleveland: Meridian, 1958.
Aristotle. *Poetics*. Translated by Anthony Kenny. Oxford: Oxford University Press, 2013.
Arnheim, Rudolf. *Film Essays and Criticism*. Translated by Brenda Benthien. Madison: University of Wisconsin Press, 1997.
Aschheim, Steven E. *The Nietzsche Legacy in Germany, 1890–1990*. Berkeley: University of California Press, 1992.
Baecque, Antoine de. *Camera Historica: The Century in Cinema*. Translated by Ninon Vinsonneau and Jonathan Magidoff. New York: Columbia University Press, 2012.
Baer, Nicholas. "Der Caligari-Komplex." *Historical Journal of Film, Radio and Television* 33, no. 2 (2013): 309–11.
———. "The Rebirth of a Nation: Cinema, Herzlian Zionism, and Emotion in Jewish History." *Leo Baeck Institute Year Book* 59 (2014): 233–48.
Balázs, Béla. "The Case of Dr. Fanck." In Kaes, Baer, and Cowan, *The Promise of Cinema*, 68–70.
———. *The Cloak of Dreams: Chinese Fairy Tales*. Translated by Jack Zipes. Princeton, NJ: Princeton University Press, 2010.
———. *Early Film Theory: "Visible Man" and "The Spirit of Film."* Edited by Erica Carter. Translated by Rodney Livingstone. New York: Berghahn, 2010.

———. *Schriften zum Film*. Vol. 1. Edited by Helmut H. Diederichs. Munich: Carl Hanser, 1982.
———. "Todesästhetik." Translated by Anna Bak-Gara and Marina Gschmeidler. *Mitteilungen des Filmarchiv Austria*, no. 2 (2004): 65–85.
Balthasar [Roland Schacht]. "Caligari." *Freie Deutsche Bühne* 29 (March 14, 1920): 695–98.
Bambach, Charles R. *Heidegger, Dilthey, and the Crisis of Historicism*. Ithaca, NY, and London: Cornell University Press, 1995.
———. "Weimar Philosophy and the Crisis of Historical Thinking." In *Weimar Thought: A Contested Legacy*, edited by Peter E. Gordon and John P. McCormick, 133–49. Princeton, NJ: Princeton University Press, 2013.
Bann, Stephen. *Romanticism and the Rise of History*. New York: Twayne, 1995.
Bareither, Christoph, Kurt Beals, Michael Cowan, Paul Dobryden, Karin Fest, Klaus Müller-Richter, and Birgit Nemec, eds. *Hans Richters "Rhythmus 21": Schlüsselfilm der Moderne*. Würzburg: Königshausen & Neumann, 2012.
Barry, Richard. "Five Dollar Movies Prophesied." *New York Times*, March 28, 1915, 16.
Barthes, Roland. *Camera Lucida: Reflections on Photography*. Translated by Richard Howard. New York: Hill and Wang, 1981.
———. *Mythologies*. Translated by Annette Lavers. New York: Farrar, Straus & Giroux, 1972.
———. *The Rustle of Language*. Translated by Richard Howard. Berkeley: University of California Press, 1989.
Bassermann-Jordan, Gabriele von. *"Schönes Leben! du lebst, wie die zarten Blüthen im Winter . . .": Die Figur der Diotima in Hölderlins Lyrik und im "Hyperion"-Projekt: Theorie und dichterische Praxis*. Würzburg: Königshausen & Neumann, 2004.
Baudelaire, Charles. *The Painter of Modern Life and Other Essays*. Edited and translated by Jonathan Mayne. London: Phaidon, 1964.
Baumbach, Nico. *Cinema/Politics/Philosophy*. New York: Columbia University Press, 2019.
———. "Metz with Deleuze: From Film-Philosophy to Film Theory and Back Again." In *Christian Metz and the Codes of Cinema: Film Semiology and Beyond*, edited by Margrit Tröhler and Guido Kirsten, 415–32. Amsterdam: Amsterdam University Press, 2018.
Bäumer, Eduard. "Cinematograph and Epistemology." Translated by Sara Hall. In Kaes, Baer, and Cowan, *The Promise of Cinema*, 78–81.
Bazin, André. "On *Why We Fight*: History, Documentation, and the Newsreel." Translated by Bert Cardullo. *Film & History* 31, no. 1 (2001): 60–62.
———. *What Is Cinema?* Translated by Timothy Barnard. Montreal: Caboose, 2009.
———. *What Is Cinema?* Vol. 1, translated by Hugh Gray. Berkeley: University of California Press, 1967.
———. *What Is Cinema?* Vol. 2, translated by Hugh Gray. Berkeley: University of California Press, 1971.

Beard, Charles A. "That Noble Dream." *American Historical Review* 41, no. 1 (1935): 74–87.
Beck, Humberto. *The Moment of Rupture: Historical Consciousness in Interwar German Thought*. Philadelphia: University of Pennsylvania Press, 2019.
Beck, Philip. "Historicism and Historism in Recent Film Historiography." *Journal of Film and Video* 37, no. 1 (1985): 5–20.
Becker, Carl Heinrich. "Der Wandel im geschichtlichen Bewußtsein." *Die neue Rundschau* 38, no. 1 (1927): 113–21.
Beiser, Frederick C. *The German Historicist Tradition*. Oxford: Oxford University Press, 2011.
Belke, Ingrid, and Irina Renz, eds. "Siegfried Kracauer 1889–1966." Special issue, *Marbacher Magazin* 47 (1988).
Benjamin, Walter. *The Arcades Project*. Translated by Howard Eiland and Kevin McLaughlin. Cambridge, MA, and London: Harvard University Press, 1999.
———. *Origin of the German Trauerspiel*. Translated by Howard Eiland. Cambridge, MA, and London: Harvard University Press, 2019.
———. *Selected Writings*. Vol. 2, pt. 1, edited by Michael W. Jennings, Howard Eiland, and Gary Smith. Cambridge, MA, and London: Harvard University Press, 1999.
———. *Selected Writings*. Vol. 2, pt. 2, edited by Michael W. Jennings, Howard Eiland, and Gary Smith. Cambridge, MA, and London: Harvard University Press, 1999.
———. *Selected Writings*. Vol. 3, edited by Howard Eiland and Michael W. Jennings. Cambridge, MA, and London: Harvard University Press, 2002.
———. *Selected Writings*. Vol. 4, edited by Howard Eiland and Michael W. Jennings. Cambridge, MA, and London: Harvard University Press, 2003.
Benkwitz, Gustav. "Der Beirat für Geschichte." *Der Kinematograph*, no. 746 (June 5, 1921): n.p.
Bergson, Henri. *Creative Evolution*. Translated by Arthur Mitchell. New York: Henry Holt and Company, 1911.
Bessner, Daniel, and Udi Greenberg. "The Weimar Analogy." *Jacobin*, December 17, 2016. www.jacobinmag.com/2016/12/trump-hitler-germany-fascism-weimar-democracy/.
Bialas, Wolfgang, and Gérard Raulet, eds. *Die Historismusdebatte in der Weimarer Republik*. Frankfurt am Main: Peter Lang, 1996.
Bird, Katie. "Sporting Sensations: Béla Balázs and the *Bergfilm* Camera Operator." *Journal of Cinema and Media Studies* 60, no. 3 (Spring 2021): 9–36.
Birett, Hartmut, and Herbert Birett. "Fritz Lang im Gespräch zum Film *Der müde Tod*." *Filmblatt* 6, no. 16 (Summer 2001): 61–64.
Bloch, Ernst. *Heritage of Our Times*. Translated by Neville Plaice and Stephen Plaice. Berkeley: University of California Press, 1991.
———. *Literarische Aufsätze*. Frankfurt am Main: Suhrkamp, 1965.
———. *The Principle of Hope*. Translated by Neville Plaice, Stephen Plaice, and Paul Knight. Cambridge, MA: MIT Press, 1986.

———. *Spuren*. Frankfurt am Main: Suhrkamp, 1969.
Blumenberg, Hans. *The Legitimacy of the Modern Age*. Translated by Robert M. Wallace. Cambridge, MA: MIT Press, 1983.
———. *Paradigms for a Metaphorology*. Translated by Robert Savage. Ithaca, NY: Cornell University Press, 2010.
Bordwell, David. *On the History of Film Style*. Cambridge, MA: Harvard University Press, 1997.
Bordwell, David, and Noël Carroll, eds. *Post-Theory: Reconstructing Film Studies*. Madison: University of Wisconsin Press, 1996.
Brandlmeier, Thomas. "Arnold Fanck." In *CineGraph: Lexikon zum deutschsprachigen Film*, installment 4, edited by Hans-Michael Bock, E1–E4. Munich: edition text + kritik, 1984.
Brauner, Ludwig. "Cinematographic Archives." Translated by Alex H. Bush. In Kaes, Baer, and Cowan, *The Promise of Cinema*, 74–77.
Brecht, Christoph, and Ines Steiner. "Film." In *Historismus und literarische Moderne*, edited by Moritz Baßler, Christoph Brecht, Dirk Niefanger, and Gotthart Wunberg, 333–51. Tübingen: Max Niemeyer, 1996.
Brill, Olaf. *Der Caligari-Komplex*. Munich: Belleville, 2012.
Brinckmann, Christine N. *Color and Empathy: Essays on Two Aspects of Film*. Amsterdam: Amsterdam University Press, 2014.
Buck-Morss, Susan. *The Origin of Negative Dialectics: Theodor W. Adorno, Walter Benjamin, and the Frankfurt Institute*. New York: Macmillan, 1977.
Bürger, Peter. *Theory of the Avant-Garde*. Translated by Michael Snow. Minneapolis: University of Minnesota Press, 1984.
Burgoyne, Robert. *Film Nation: Hollywood Looks at U.S. History*. Minneapolis: University of Minnesota Press, 1997.
———. *The Hollywood Historical Film*. Oxford: Blackwell, 2008.
Bush, Alex. "Moving Mountains: Glacial Contingency and Modernity in the Bergfilm." *Journal of Cinema and Media Studies* 59, no. 1 (Fall 2019): 1–22.
Butler, Alison. "New Film Histories and the Politics of Location." *Screen* 33, no. 4 (1992): 413–26.
c–c. "Filmkritik: Berliner Uraufführungen: *Metropolis*." *Reichsfilmblatt*, no. 2 (January 15, 1927): 42.
Cadava, Eduardo. *Words of Light: Theses on the Photography of History*. Princeton, NJ: Princeton University Press, 1997.
Cahnman, Werner J. "Village and Small-Town Jews in Germany: A Typological Study." *Leo Baeck Institute Year Book* 19 (1974): 107–30.
Canales, Jimena. *The Physicist and the Philosopher: Einstein, Bergson, and the Debate That Changed Our Understanding of Time*. Princeton, NJ: Princeton University Press, 2015.
Carroll, Noël. *Theorizing the Moving Image*. New York: Cambridge University Press, 1996.
Carter, Erica. Introduction to *Early Film Theory: "Visible Man" and "The Spirit of Film,"* by Béla Balázs, edited by Erica Carter, translated by Rodney Livingstone, xv–xlvi. New York: Berghahn, 2010.

Caruth, Cathy. *Unclaimed Experience: Trauma, Narrative, and History*. Baltimore: Johns Hopkins University Press, 1996.
Cassirer, Ernst. *The Philosophy of Symbolic Forms*. Vol. 2, *Mythical Thought*, translated by Ralph Manheim. New Haven, CT: Yale University Press, 1955.
Cavell, Stanley. *The World Viewed: Reflections on the Ontology of Film*. Enl. ed. Cambridge, MA: Harvard University Press, 1979.
Cendrars, Blaise. "On *The Cabinet of Doctor Caligari*." Translated by Stuart Liebman. In *French Film Theory and Criticism: A History/Anthology*, ed. Richard Abel, 1:271. Princeton, NJ: Princeton University Press, 1988.
Chakrabarty, Dipesh. *The Climate of History in a Planetary Age*. Chicago: University of Chicago Press, 2021.
———. *Provincializing Europe: Postcolonial Thought and Historical Difference*. Princeton, NJ: Princeton University Press, 2000.
Chapman, James, Mark Glancy, and Sue Harper, eds. *The New Film History: Sources, Methods, Approaches*. New York: Palgrave Macmillan, 2007.
Choe, Steve. *Afterlives: Allegories of Film and Mortality in Early Weimar Germany*. New York: Bloomsbury, 2014.
Clair, René. *Cinema Yesterday and Today*. Edited by R. C. Dale. Translated by Stanley Appelbaum. New York: Dover, 1972.
Comolli, Jean-Louis. "Historical Fiction: A Body Too Much." Translated by Ben Brewster. *Screen* 19, no. 2 (1978): 41–54.
Conant, James. "The Dialectic of Perspectivism." Pts. 1 and 2. *Sats—Nordic Journal of Philosophy* 6, no. 2 (2005): 5–50; 7, no. 1 (2006): 6–57.
Cowan, Michael. *Walter Ruttmann and the Cinema of Multiplicity: Avant-Garde—Advertising—Modernity*. Amsterdam: Amsterdam University Press, 2014.
Culler, Jonathan. "Semiotics of Tourism." *American Journal of Semiotics* 1, nos. 1–2 (1981): 127–40.
Curtis, Scott. *The Shape of Spectatorship: Art, Science, and Early Cinema in Germany*. New York: Columbia University Press, 2015.
D., G. "Der müde Tod." *Ciné-Journal*, June 17, 1922. Reprinted in *Lichtbildbühne* 15, no. 30 (July 22, 1922): n.p.
Danto, Arthur. *The Transfiguration of the Commonplace: A Philosophy of Art*. Cambridge, MA: Harvard University Press, 1981.
Davis, Natalie Zemon. "'Any Resemblance to Persons Living or Dead': Film and the Challenge of Authenticity." *Historical Journal of Film, Radio and Television* 8, no. 3 (1988): 269–83.
———. *Slaves on Screen: Film and Historical Vision*. Cambridge, MA: Harvard University Press, 2000.
Deleuze, Gilles. *Cinema 1: The Movement-Image*. Translated by Hugh Tomlinson and Barbara Habberjam. Minneapolis: University of Minnesota Press, 1986.
———. *Cinema 2: The Time-Image*. Translated by Hugh Tomlinson and Robert Galeta. Minneapolis: University of Minnesota Press, 1989.

de Man, Paul. "Literary History and Literary Modernity." *Daedalus* 99, no. 2 (Spring 1970): 384–404.
Dembeck, Till. *Texte rahmen: Grenzregionen literarischer Wekre im 18. Jahrhundert*. Berlin: Walter de Gruyter, 2007.
Denning, Andrew. *Skiing into Modernity: A Cultural and Environmental History*. Oakland: University of California Press, 2015.
Derenthal, Ludger. "Hans Richter—der Künstler als Kunsthistoriker." In *Hans Richter: Malerei und Film*, edited by Hilmar Hoffmann and Walter Schobert, 146–54. Frankfurt am Main: Deutsches Filmmuseum, 1989.
Derrida, Jacques. *The Truth in Painting*. Translated by Geoffrey Bennington and Ian McLeod. Chicago: University of Chicago Press, 1987.
Diebold, Bernhard. "Expressionism and Cinema." Translated by Alex H. Bush. In Kaes, Baer, and Cowan, *The Promise of Cinema*, 415–20.
Dilthey, Wilhelm. *Einleitung in die Geisteswissenschaften: Versuch einer Grundlegung für das Studium der Gesellschaft und der Geschichte*. Vol. 1. Leipzig: Duncker & Humblot, 1883.
———. *Introduction to the Human Sciences*. Edited by Rudolf A. Makkreel and Frithjof Rodi. Princeton, NJ: Princeton University Press, 1989.
———. "The Rise of Hermeneutics." Translated by Fredric Jameson. *New Literary History* 3, no. 2 (Winter 1972): 229–44.
Doane, Mary Ann. *The Emergence of Cinematic Time: Modernity, Contingency, the Archive*. Cambridge, MA: Harvard University Press, 2002.
Dobryden, Paul. *The Hygienic Apparatus: Weimar Cinema and Environmental Disorder*. Evanston, IL: Northwestern University Press, 2022.
Dohm, Christian Wilhelm. *Über die bürgerliche Verbesserung der Juden*. Berlin: Friedrich Nicolai, 1781.
Droysen, Johann Gustav. *Outline of the Principles of History*. Translated by E. Benjamin Andrews. Boston: Ginn & Company, 1893.
Dulac, Germaine. *Writings on Cinema (1919–1937)*. Edited by Prosper Hillairet. Translated by Scott Hammen. Paris: Paris Expérimental, 2018.
Dunn, Allen, and Thomas F. Haddox, eds. *The Limits of Literary Historicism*. Knoxville: University of Tennessee Press, 2011.
Edschmid, Kasimir. *Über den Expressionismus in der Literatur und die neue Dichtung*. Berlin: Erich Reiß, 1919.
Efron, John M. *German Jewry and the Allure of the Sephardic*. Princeton, NJ: Princeton University Press, 2016.
Einstein, Albert. *The Principle of Relativity*. Translated by George Barker Jeffery and Wilfrid Perrett. New York: Dover, 1952.
Einstein, Carl. *Die Kunst des 20. Jahrhunderts*. Edited by Tanja Frank. Leipzig: Reclam, 1988.
Eisenstein, Sergei. *Selected Works*. Vol. 1, *Writings, 1922–34*, edited and translated by Richard Taylor. London: BFI, 1988.
Eisner, Lotte H. *The Haunted Screen: Expressionism in the German Cinema and the Influence of Max Reinhardt*. Translated by Roger Greaves. London: Thames and Hudson, 1969.

Eller, Paul. "Geschichtsstudium und Film." *Der Kinematograph*, no. 752 (June 17, 1921): n.p.
Ellmann, Richard. *James Joyce*. Oxford: Oxford University Press, 1982.
Elsaesser, Thomas. "Beyond the New Film History." Remarks presented at the Histories of Film History: Materials & Methods conference, University of Marburg, December 14, 2018.
———. "Early Cinema: From Linear History to Mass Media Archaeology." In *Early Cinema: Space, Frame, Narrative*, edited by Thomas Elsaesser with Adam Barker, 1–8. London: BFI, 1990.
———. *Film History as Media Archaeology: Tracking Digital Cinema*. Amsterdam: Amsterdam University Press, 2016.
———. *Metropolis*. London: BFI, 2000.
———. "The New Film History." *Sight and Sound* 55, no. 4 (1986): 246–51.
———. "The New Film History as Media Archaeology." *CiNéMAS* 14, nos. 2–3 (2004): 75–117.
———. Review of *Dr. Caligari's Francis: A Sane Reading*, by Alan Blanchard. *[in]Transition: Journal of Videographic Film & Moving Image Studies* 6, no. 3 (2019). https://mediacommons.org/intransition/dr-caligaris-francis-sane-reading.
———. *Weimar Cinema and After: Germany's Historical Imaginary*. London: Routledge, 2000.
Engels, Frederick. *The Condition of the Working-Class in England in 1844*. Translated by Florence Kelley Wischnewetzky. London: George Allen & Unwin, 1892.
Enwezor, Okwui, Nancy Condee, and Terry Smith, eds. *Antinomies of Art and Culture: Modernity, Postmodernity, Contemporaneity*. Durham, NC: Duke University Press, 2008.
Enzensberger, Hans Magnus. *Einzelheiten II: Poesie und Politik*. Frankfurt am Main: Suhrkamp, 1964.
———. "A Theory of Tourism." Translated by Gerd Gemünden and Kenn Johnson. *New German Critique*, no. 68 (Spring/Summer 1996): 117–35.
Epstein, Jean. *Jean Epstein: Critical Essays and New Translations*. Edited by Sarah Keller and Jason N. Paul. Amsterdam: Amsterdam University Press, 2012.
Ernst, Wolfgang. *Digital Memory and the Archive*. Edited by Jussi Parikka. Minneapolis and London: University of Minnesota Press, 2013.
Eyers, Tom. "The Perils of the 'Digital Humanities': New Positivisms and the Fate of Literary Theory." *Postmodern Culture* 23, no. 2 (2013). https://muse.jhu.edu/article/537059.
Fanck, Arnold. *Er führte Regie mit Gletschern, Stürmen und Lawinen: Ein Filmpionier erzählt*. Munich: Nymphenburger, 1973.
———. "Die Zukunft des Naturfilms." In *Berge, Licht und Traum: Dr. Arnold Fanck und der deutsche Bergfilm*, edited by Jan-Christopher Horak and Gisela Pichler, 143–46. Munich: Bruckmann, 1997.

Fanck, Arnold, and Hannes Schneider. *Wunder des Schneeschuhs: Ein System des richtigen Skilaufens und seine Anwendung im alpinen Geländelauf.* Hamburg: Enoch, 1925.
Faure, Élie. "The Art of Cineplastics." Translated by Walter Pach. In *French Film Theory and Criticism: A History/Anthology,* ed. Richard Abel, 1:258–68. Princeton, NJ: Princeton University Press, 1988.
Federn, Paul. *Zur Psychologie der Revolution: Die vaterlose Gesellschaft.* Leipzig and Vienna: Anzengruber, 1919.
Felski, Rita. *The Limits of Critique.* Chicago: University of Chicago Press, 2015.
Ferro, Marc. *Cinema and History.* Translated by Naomi Greene. Detroit: Wayne State University Press, 1988.
Fickers, Andreas. "Towards a New Digital Historicism? Doing History in the Age of Abundance." *Journal of European History and Culture* 1, no. 1 (2012): 19–26.
"Filmschau: Der müde Tod." *Vorwärts* 38, no. 481 (October 12, 1921): 6.
Fleissner, Jennifer. "Historicism Blues." *American Literary History* 25, no. 4 (2013): 699–717.
Flüggen, Christian. "Das Kabinet des Dr. Caligari." *Deutsche Lichtspiel-Zeitung* 8, nos. 12/13 (March 27, 1920): 2.
Focillon, Henri. *The Life of Forms in Art.* Translated by Charles Beecher Hogan and George Kubler. New York: Zone Books, 1992.
Ford, Fiona. "Edmund Meisel's Score to *Der heilige Berg* (1926): Prefiguring Hollywood's 'Golden Age' Narrative-Scoring Practices in Live Performance." In *Music and Sound in Silent Film: From the Nickelodeon to "The Artist,"* edited by Ruth Barton and Simon Trezise, 124–45. New York: Routledge, 2019.
Ford, Henry. *My Life and Work.* Garden City, NY: Doubleday, Page & Company, 1923.
Foster, John Bellamy. *Marx's Ecology: Materialism and Nature.* New York: Monthly Review Press, 2000.
Foster, Stephen C., ed. *Hans Richter: Activism, Modernism, and the Avant-Garde.* Cambridge, MA: MIT Press, 1998.
Foucault, Michel. *The Archaeology of Knowledge.* Translated by A. M. Sheridan Smith. New York: Vintage, 1972.
———. *Language, Counter-Memory, Practice: Selected Essays and Interviews.* Edited by Donald F. Bouchard. Translated by Donald F. Bouchard and Sherry Simon. Ithaca, NY: Cornell University Press, 1977.
———. "Of Other Spaces." Translated by Jay Miskowiec. *Diacritics* 16, no. 1 (Spring 1986): 22–27.
———. *Wrong-Doing, Truth-Telling: The Function of Avowal in Justice.* Edited by Fabienne Brion and Bernard E. Harcourt. Translated by Stephen W. Sawyer. Chicago: University of Chicago Press, 2014.
Frampton, Daniel. *Filmosophy.* London: Wallflower, 2006.
Franju, Georges. "Franju on Lang." Translated by Diane Matias. *Monthly Film Bulletin* 43, no. 509 (June 1976): 140.

Freud, Sigmund. *Beyond the Pleasure Principle*. Edited and translated by James Strachey. New York: W.W. Norton & Company, 1961.

———. *Civilization and Its Discontents*. Edited and translated by James Strachey. New York: W.W. Norton & Company, 1961.

———. *The Ego and the Id*. Edited by James Strachey. Translated by Joan Riviere. New York: W.W. Norton & Company, 1960.

———. *The Interpretation of Dreams*. Translated by James Strachey. New York: Avon, 1965.

———. *The Standard Edition of the Complete Psychological Works of Sigmund Freud*. Vol. 14, edited and translated by James Strachey. London: Hogarth Press, 1971.

———. *The Standard Edition of the Complete Psychological Works of Sigmund Freud*. Vol. 19, edited and translated by James Strachey. London: Hogarth Press, 1961.

Friedlander, Saul, ed. *Probing the Limits of Representation: Nazism and the "Final Solution."* Cambridge, MA, and London: Harvard University Press, 1992.

Fulda, Daniel. *Wissenschaft aus Kunst: Die Entstehung der modernen deutschen Geschichtsschreibung 1760–1860*. Berlin and New York: Walter de Gruyter, 1996.

G. "Der müde Tod." *Berliner Börsen-Courier* 54, no. 473 (October 9, 1921): 6.

Gadamer, Hans-Georg. *Truth and Method*. Translated by Joel Weinsheimer and Donald G. Marshall. London and New York: Continuum, 2004.

Gaines, Jane M. *Pink-Slipped: What Happened to Women in the Silent Film Industries?* Urbana: University of Illinois Press, 2018.

———. "What Happened to the Philosophy of Film History?" *Film History* 25, nos. 1–2 (2013): 70–80.

———. "Why We Took the 'Historical Turn': The Poisons and Antidotes Version." In *At the Borders of (Film) History: Temporality, Archaeology, Theories*, edited by Alberto Beltrame, Giuseppe Fidotta, and Andrea Mariani, 179–90. Udine: Forum, 2015.

Galili, Doron. "Early Cinema and the Emergence of Television: An Archaeology of Intertwined Media." In *The Oxford Handbook of Silent Cinema*, edited by Rob King and Charlie Keil, 38–54. New York: Oxford University Press, 2024.

Gaudreault, André, and Tom Gunning. "Early Cinema as a Challenge to Film History." Translated by Joyce Goggin and Wanda Strauven. In *The Cinema of Attractions Reloaded*, edited by Wanda Strauven, 365–80. Amsterdam: Amsterdam University Press, 2006.

Gay, Peter. *Weimar Culture: The Outsider as Insider*. New York and London: W.W. Norton & Company, 2001.

Geimer, Peter. "Einführung: Verfahren der Historisierung." In *Komplexität und Einfachheit: DFG-Symposion 2015*, edited by Albrecht Koschorke, 449–57. Stuttgart: J.B. Metzler, 2017.

———. "Verstellte Zeit: Kracauers Unbehagen am Historienfilm." In *Siegfried Kracauers Grenzgänge: Zur Rettung des Realen*, edited by Sabine Biebl, Helmut Lethen, and Johannes von Moltke, 101–16. Frankfurt am Main: Campus, 2019.

Gemünden, Gerd. *Continental Strangers: German Exile Cinema, 1933–1951*. New York: Columbia University Press, 2014.

Goergen, Jeanpaul. "Hans Richter, Filme bis 1933: Annotierte Filmografie." In *Hans Richter: Film ist Rhythmus*, edited by Jeanpaul Goergen, 85–114. Berlin: Freunde der Deutschen Kinemathek e.V., 2003.

Goethe, Johann Wolfgang von. *Faust I & II*. Edited and translated by Stuart Atkins. Princeton, NJ: Princeton University Press, 2014.

Goldman, Jane. *The Feminist Aesthetics of Virginia Woolf: Modernism, Post-Impressionism and the Politics of the Visual*. Cambridge: Cambridge University Press, 1998.

Goodings, Lewis, and Ian Tucker. "Social Media and the Co-production of Bodies Online: Bergson, Serres and Facebook's Timeline." *Media, Culture & Society* 36, no. 1 (2014): 37–51.

Goodstein, Elizabeth S. *Georg Simmel and the Disciplinary Imaginary*. Stanford, CA: Stanford University Press, 2017.

Gordon, Peter E. *Adorno and Existence*. Cambridge, MA, and London: Harvard University Press, 2016.

———. *Rosenzweig and Heidegger: Between Judaism and German Philosophy*. Berkeley: University of California Press, 2003.

———. "Weimar Theology: From Historicism to Crisis." In *Weimar Thought: A Contested Legacy*, edited by Peter E. Gordon and John P. McCormick, 150–78. Princeton, NJ: Princeton University Press, 2013.

———. "Why Historical Analogy Matters." *New York Review of Books*, January 7, 2020. www.nybooks.com/daily/2020/01/07/why-historical-analogy-matters.

Graf, Rüdiger. "Either-Or: The Narrative of 'Crisis' in Weimar Germany and in Historiography." *Central European History* 43, no. 4 (December 2010): 592–615.

———. *Die Zukunft der Weimarer Republik: Krisen und Zukunftsaneignungen in Deutschland 1918–1933*. Munich: Oldenbourg, 2008.

Grimm, Jacob, and Wilhelm Grimm. "Der Gevatter Tod." In *Kinder- und Hausmärchen*, edited by Herman Grimm, 123–25. Berlin: Wilhelm Hertz, 1895.

Groo, Katherine. *Bad Film Histories: Ethnography and the Early Archive*. Minneapolis: University of Minnesota Press, 2019.

———. "Cut, Paste, Glitch, and Stutter: Remixing Film History." *Frames Cinema Journal* 1, no. 1 (2012). https://framescinemajournal.com/article/cut-paste-glitch-and-stutter.

———. "Let It Burn: Film Historiography in Flames." *Discourse* 41, no. 1 (Winter 2019): 3–36.

Gropius, Walter. *Die Kunst in Industrie und Handel: Jahrbuch des Deutschen Werkbundes.* Jena: Eugen Diederichs, 1913.
Groys, Boris. "Comrades of Time." In *What Is Contemporary Art?*, edited by Julieta Aranda, Anton Vidokle, and Brian Kuan Wood, 22–39. Berlin: Sternberg, 2010.
Guillén, Claudio. *Literature as System: Essays toward the Theory of Literary History.* Princeton, NJ: Princeton University Press, 1971.
Gumbrecht, Hans Ulrich. *Our Broad Present: Time and Contemporary Culture.* New York: Columbia University Press, 2014.
Gunning, Tom. "The Cinema of Attraction: Early Film, Its Spectator and the Avant-Garde." *Wide Angle* 8, nos. 3–4 (1986): 63–70.
———. *D. W. Griffith and the Origins of American Narrative Film: The Early Years at Biograph.* Urbana: University of Illinois Press, 1991.
———. "Early Cinema as Global Cinema: The Encyclopedic Ambition." In *Early Cinema and the "National,"* edited by Richard Abel, Giorgio Bertellini, and Rob King, 11–16. New Barnet, UK: John Libbey Publishing, 2008.
———. *The Films of Fritz Lang: Allegories of Vision and Modernity.* London: BFI, 2000.
———. "'Now You See It, Now You Don't': The Temporality of the Cinema of Attractions." In *The Silent Cinema Reader*, edited by Lee Grieveson and Peter Krämer, 41–50. London and New York: Routledge, 2004.
Haacke, Paul. *The Vertical Imagination and the Crisis of Transatlantic Modernism.* Oxford: Oxford University Press, 2021.
Häfker, Hermann. "*Cinema and Geography*: Introduction." Translated by Nicholas Baer. In Kaes, Baer, and Cowan, *The Promise of Cinema*, 51–52.
Hagener, Malte. "Das Medium in der Krise: Der Film, das Kinematographische und der Wert von instabilem Wissen." *AugenBlick: Marburger Hefte zur Medienwissenschaft*, no. 52 (2012): 30–46.
———. *Moving Forward, Looking Back: The European Avant-Garde and the Invention of Film Culture, 1919–1939.* Amsterdam: Amsterdam University Press, 2007.
Hagener, Malte, and Yvonne Zimmermann. "Viking Eggeling and European Avant-Garde Cinema." In *A Cultural History of the Avant-Garde in the Nordic Countries 1925–1950*, edited by Benedikt Hjartarson, Andrea Kollnitz, Per Stounbjerg, and Tania Ørum, 82–101. Leiden: Brill, 2019.
Hamilton, Clive, Christophe Bonneuil, and François Gemenne, eds. *The Anthropocene and the Global Environmental Crisis: Rethinking Modernity in a New Epoch.* London and New York: Routledge, 2015.
Hansen, Miriam Bratu. *Babel and Babylon: Spectatorship in American Silent Film.* Cambridge, MA: Harvard University Press, 1991.
———. *Cinema and Experience: Siegfried Kracauer, Walter Benjamin, and Theodor W. Adorno.* Berkeley: University of California Press, 2012.
———. Introduction to *Theory of Film: The Redemption of Physical Reality*, by Siegfried Kracauer, vii–xlv. Princeton, NJ: Princeton University Press, 1997.

---. "'Of Lightning Rods, Prisms, and Forgotten Scissors': *Potemkin* and German Film Theory," *New German Critique*, no. 95 (Spring–Summer 2005): 162–79.
Hanssen, Beatrice. *Walter Benjamin's Other History: Of Stones, Animals, Human Beings, and Angels*. Berkeley: University of California Press, 1998.
Haraway, Donna J. *Staying with the Trouble: Making Kin in the Chthulucene*. Durham, NC: Duke University Press, 2016.
Harbou, Thea von. *Metropolis*. Edited by Herbert W. Franke. Frankfurt am Main: Ullstein, 1984.
Hartman, Saidiya. "Venus in Two Acts." *Small Axe*, no. 26 (June 2008): 1–14.
Hartog, François. *Regimes of Historicity: Presentism and Experiences of Time*. Translated by Saskia Brown. New York: Columbia University Press, 2015.
Hausmann, Raoul, Hans Arp, Ivan Puni, and László Moholy-Nagy. "A Call for Elemental Art." Translated by Michael W. Jennings. In Mertins and Jennings, *G*, 241.
Hediger, Vinzenz. "Aufhebung: Geschichte im Zeitalter des Films." In *Essays zur Film-Philosophie*, edited by Lorenz Engell, Oliver Fahle, Vinzenz Hediger, and Christiane Voss, 169–249. Paderborn: Wilhelm Fink, 2015.
Hegel, G.W.F. *Aesthetics: Lectures on Fine Art*. Vol. 1. Translated by T.M. Knox. Oxford: Oxford University Press, 1975.
---. *Elements of the Philosophy of Right*. Edited by Allen W. Wood. Translated by H.B. Nisbet. Cambridge: Cambridge University Press, 1991.
---. *Lectures on the Philosophy of World History: Introduction*. Translated by H.B. Nisbet. Cambridge: Cambridge University Press, 1975.
Heidegger, Martin. *Being and Time*. Translated by Joan Stambaugh. Albany: SUNY Press, 1996.
---. *Nietzsche*. Vol. 1, *The Will to Power as Art*. Edited and translated by David Farrell Krell. San Francisco: Harper Collins, 1991.
---. *Nietzsche*. Vol. 2, *The Eternal Recurrence of the Same*. Edited and translated by David Farrell Krell. San Francisco: Harper Collins, 1991.
---. *Nietzsche*. Vol. 4, *Nihilism*. Edited by David Farrell Krell. Translated by Frank A. Capuzzi. San Francisco: Harper Collins, 1991.
---. *Supplements: From the Earliest Essays to "Being and Time" and Beyond*, edited by John van Buren. Albany: SUNY Press, 2002.
Heisenberg, Werner. *Physics and Philosophy: The Revolution in Modern Science*. Amherst, MA: Prometheus Books, 1999.
Henderson, Linda Dalyrimple. *The Fourth Dimension and Non-Euclidean Geometry in Modern Art*. Princeton, NJ: Princeton University Press, 1983.
Herf, Jeffrey. *Reactionary Modernism: Technology, Culture, and Politics in Weimar and the Third Reich*. Cambridge: Cambridge University Press, 1984.
Hesse, Hermann. "The Longing of Our Time for a Worldview." Translated by Don Reneau. In Kaes, Jay, and Dimendberg, *Weimar Republic Sourcebook*, 365–68.
Heussi, Karl. *Die Krisis des Historismus*. Tübingen: J.C.B. Mohr, 1932.

Hewitt, Andrew. *Fascist Modernism: Aesthetics, Politics, and the Avant-Garde*. Stanford, CA: Stanford University Press, 1993.
Higashi, Sumiko. "Film History, or a Baedeker Guide to the Historical Turn." *Cinema Journal* 44, no. 1 (2004): 94–100.
Hintze, Otto. "Troeltsch und die Probleme des Historismus: Kritische Studien." *Historische Zeitschrift* 135, no. 2 (1927): 188–239.
Hobsbawm, Eric. *Behind the Times: The Decline and Fall of the Twentieth-Century Avant-Gardes*. New York: Thames and Hudson, 1998.
Hofacker, Marion von. "Kunsthistoriker gegen Künstler." In *Hans Richter: Malerei und Film*, edited by Hilmar Hoffmann and Walter Schobert, 155–67. Frankfurt am Main: Deutsches Filmmuseum, 1989.
Hofmannsthal, Hugo von. *Das Schrifttum als geistiger Raum der Nation*. Munich: Bremer Presse, 1927.
Horkheimer, Max. *Critical Theory: Selected Essays*. Translated by Matthew J. O'Connell. New York: Continuum, 2002.
———. *Dawn & Decline: Notes 1926–1931 and 1950–1969*. Translated by Michael Shaw. New York: Seabury Press, 1978.
Horkheimer, Max, and Theodor W. Adorno. *Dialectic of Enlightenment: Philosophical Fragments*. Edited by Gunzelin Schmid Noerr. Translated by Edmund Jephcott. Stanford, CA: Stanford University Press, 2002.
Huaco, George A. *The Sociology of Film Styles*. New York: Basic Books, 1965.
Hughes, H. Stuart. *Consciousness and Society*. New Brunswick, NJ: Transaction Publishers, 2002.
Huhtamo, Erkki, and Doron Galili. "The Pasts and Prospects of Media Archaeology." *Early Popular Visual Culture* 18, no. 4 (2020): 333–39.
Huhtamo, Erkki, and Jussi Parikka, eds. *Media Archaeology: Approaches, Applications, and Implications*. Berkeley: University of California Press, 2011.
Hung, Jochen. "'Bad' Politics and 'Good' Culture: New Approaches to the History of the Weimar Republic." *Central European History* 49, nos. 3–4 (2016): 441–53.
Husserl, Edmund. *The Crisis of European Sciences and Transcendental Phenomenology*. Translated by David Carr. Evanston, IL: Northwestern University Press, 1970.
Hwang, June J. *Lost in Time: Locating the Stranger in German Modernity*. Evanston, IL: Northwestern University Press, 2014.
Iggers, Georg G. *The German Conception of History: The National Tradition of Historical Thought from Herder to the Present*. Middletown, CT: Wesleyan University Press, 1983.
———. "Historicism: The History and Meaning of the Term." *Journal of the History of Ideas* 56, no. 1 (1995): 129–52.
———. "The Image of Ranke in American and German Historical Thought." *History and Theory* 2, no. 1 (1962): 17–40.
Iversen, Margaret. *Alois Riegl: Art History and Theory*. Cambridge, MA: MIT Press, 1993.

Jacobs, Thomas. "Visuelle Traditionen des Bergfilms: Von Fidus zu Friedrich oder Das Ende bürgerlicher Fluchtbewegungen im Faschismus." *Film und Kritik*, no. 1 (June 1992): 28–38.
Jaikumar, Priya. *Where Histories Reside: India as Filmed Space*. Durham, NC, and London: Duke University Press, 2019.
Jameson, Fredric. "Progress versus Utopia: or, Can We Imagine the Future?" *Science Fiction Studies* 9, no. 2 (July 1982): 147–58.
———. "World-Reduction in Le Guin: The Emergence of Utopian Narrative." *Science Fiction Studies* 2, no. 3 (November 1975): 221–30.
Janowitz, Hans. "*Caligari*—The Story of a Famous Story." In *The Cabinet of Dr. Caligari: Texts, Contexts, Histories*, edited by Mike Budd, 221–39. New Brunswick, NJ: Rutgers University Press, 1990.
Jarausch, Konrad H., and Michael Geyer. *Shattered Past: Reconstructing German Histories*. Princeton, NJ: Princeton University Press, 2003.
Jay, Martin. *Downcast Eyes: The Denigration of Vision in Twentieth-Century French Thought*. Berkeley: University of California Press, 1993.
———. *Essays from the Edge: Parerga & Paralipomena*. Charlottesville: University of Virginia Press, 2011.
———. "The Extraterritorial Life of Siegfried Kracauer," *Salmagundi*, nos. 31/32 (Fall 1975–Winter 1976): 49–106.
———. "Historical Explanation and the Event: Reflections on the Limits of Contextualization." *New Literary History* 42, no. 4 (2011): 557–71.
———. "Historicism and the Event." In *Against the Grain: Jewish Intellectuals in Hard Times*, edited by Ezra Mendelsohn, Stefani Hoffman, and Richard I. Cohen, 143–67. New York and Oxford: Berghahn, 2014.
———. "Intention and Irony: The Missed Encounter between Hayden White and Quentin Skinner." *History and Theory* 52, no. 1 (2013): 32–48.
———. *Songs of Experience: Modern American and European Variations on a Universal Theme*. Berkeley: University of California Press, 2005.
Jonas, Hans. *The Imperative of Responsibility: In Search of an Ethics for the Technological Age*. Translated by Hans Jonas and David Herr. Chicago: University of Chicago Press, 1984.
Joyce, James. *Finnegans Wake*. Oxford: Oxford University Press, 2012.
Jünger, Ernst. Introduction to *Die veränderte Welt: Eine Bilderfibel unserer Zeit*, edited by Edmund Schultz, 5–9. Breslau: W.G. Korn, 1933.
Kael, Pauline. *I Lost It at the Movies: Film Writings, 1954–1965*. London and New York: Marion Boyars, 2002.
Kaes, Anton. "*Metropolis*: Cinema, City, Modernity." In *Expressionist Utopias: Paradise, Metropolis, Architectural Fantasy*, edited by Timothy O. Benson, 146–65. Los Angeles: Los Angeles County Museum of Art, 1993.
———. *Shell Shock Cinema: Weimar Culture and the Wounds of War*. Princeton, NJ: Princeton University Press, 2009.
Kaes, Anton, Nicholas Baer, and Michael Cowan, eds. *The Promise of Cinema: German Film Theory, 1907–1933*. Oakland: University of California Press, 2016.

Kaes, Anton, Martin Jay, and Edward Dimendberg, eds. *The Weimar Republic Sourcebook*. Berkeley: University of California Press, 1994.

Kaiser, Georg. *Gas: A Play in Five Acts*. Translated by Herman Scheffauer. Boston: Small, Maynard & Co., 1924.

———. "Historientreue: Am Beispiel der Flucht nach Venedig." In *Werke*, vol. 4, edited by Walther Huder, 576–79. Frankfurt am Main: Propyläen, 1971.

Kalbus, Oskar. *Der deutsche Lehrfilm in der Wissenschaft und im Unterricht*. Berlin: Heymann, 1922.

Kandinsky, Wassily. *Concerning the Spiritual in Art*. Translated by M.T.H. Sadler. New York: Dover, 1977.

Kant, Immanuel. *Critique of the Power of Judgment*. Edited by Paul Guyer. Translated by Paul Guyer and Eric Matthews. Cambridge: Cambridge University Press, 2000.

Kaplan, E. Ann. *Climate Trauma: Foreseeing the Future in Dystopian Film and Fiction*. New Brunswick, NJ: Rutgers University Press, 2016.

Kelley, Robin D.G. "Sorry, Not Sorry." *Boston Review*, September 13, 2018. http://bostonreview.net/race-literature-culture-arts-society/robin-d-g-kelley-sorry-not-sorry.

Kenyon, E.C. *Thomas Alva Edison: The Telegraph-Boy Who Became a Great Inventor*. London: W. & R. Chambers, 1895.

Kiening, Christian, and Heinrich Adolf. Afterword to *Der absolute Film: Dokumente der Medienavantgarde (1912–1936)*, edited by Christian Kiening and Heinrich Adolf, 419–500. Zurich: Chronos, 2012.

Killen, Andreas. *Homo Cinematicus: Science, Motion Pictures, and the Making of Modern Germany*. Philadelphia: University of Pennsylvania Press, 2017.

Kim, Jodi. *Settler Garrison: Debt Imperialism, Militarism, and Transpacific Imaginaries*. Durham, NC, and London: Duke University Press, 2022.

Kittler, Friedrich. *Optical Media: Berlin Lectures 1999*. Translated by Anthony Enns. Cambridge: Polity, 2010.

Kittstein, Ulrich. *"Mit Geschichte will man etwas": Historisches Erzählen in der Weimarer Republik und im Exil (1918–1945)*. Würzburg: Königshausen & Neumann, 2006.

Klecker, Cornelia, and Christian Quendler. "Cinematic Figurations of Mountains." *New Review of Film and Television Studies* 21, no. 1 (2023): 1–18.

Koch, Gertrud. "Der Historienfilm als Mythos des Alltags." *Journal Geschichte*, no. 2 (April 1989): 13–19.

———. "Nachträgliche Vorwegnahme." In *Kunst, Fortschritt, Geschichte*, edited by Christoph Menke and Juliane Rebentisch, 87–96. Berlin: Kulturverlag Kadmos, 2006.

———. "Der unsterbliche Körper—Kino und Todesangst." In *Den Körper im Blick*, edited by Beat Wyss and Markus Buschhaus, 35–50. Munich: Fink, 2008.

Köhler, Kristina. *Der tänzerische Film: Frühe Filmkultur und moderner Tanz*. Marburg: Schüren, 2017.

Köhn, Lothar. "Überwindung des Historismus: Zu Problemen einer Geschichte der deutschen Literatur zwischen 1918 und 1933." Pts. 1 and 2. *Deutsche Vierteljahrsschrift für Literaturwissenschaft und Geistesgeschichte* 48, no. 4 (1974): 704–66; 49, no. 1 (1975): 94–165.

Kolakowski, Leszek. *The Alienation of Reason: A History of Positivist Thought*. Translated by Norbert Guterman. Garden City, NY: Doubleday & Co., 1968.

Koselleck, Reinhart. "Crisis." Translated by Michaela Richter. *Journal of the History of Ideas* 67, no. 2 (2006): 357–400.

———. *Futures Past: On the Semantics of Historical Time*. Translated by Keith Tribe. New York: Columbia University Press, 2004.

———. *The Practice of Conceptual History: Timing History, Spacing Concepts*. Translated by Todd Samuel Presner and others. Stanford, CA: Stanford University Press, 2002.

———. *Sediments of Time: On Possible Histories*. Edited and translated by Sean Franzel and Stefan-Ludwig Hoffmann. Stanford, CA: Stanford University Press, 2018.

Kracauer, Siegfried. "Abstract Film: On the Screening by the Gesellschaft Neuer Film." Translated by Michael Cowan. In Kaes, Baer, and Cowan, *The Promise of Cinema*, 465–67.

———. "*All Quiet on the Western Front*: On the Remarque Sound Film." Translated by Jon Cho-Polizzi. In Kaes, Baer, and Cowan, *The Promise of Cinema*, 284–86.

———. *From Caligari to Hitler: A Psychological History of the German Film*. Edited by Leonardo Quaresima. Princeton, NJ: Princeton University Press, 2004.

———. *History: The Last Things before the Last*. Princeton, NJ: Markus Wiener, 1995.

———. *Jacques Offenbach and the Paris of His Time*. Translated by Gwenda David and Eric Mosbacher. New York: Zone Books, 2016.

———. "The Klieg Lights Stay On: The Frankfurt Screening of *Potemkin*." Translated by Miriam Bratu Hansen. In Kaes, Baer, and Cowan, *The Promise of Cinema*, 353–55.

———. *The Mass Ornament: Weimar Essays*. Edited and translated by Thomas Y. Levin. Cambridge, MA: Harvard University Press, 1995.

———. "Mountains, Clouds, People." Translated by Nicholas Baer. In Kaes, Baer, and Cowan, *The Promise of Cinema*, 97–98.

———. "On the Border of Yesterday: On the Berlin Film and Photo Exhibition." Translated by Michael Cowan. In Kaes, Baer, and Cowan, *The Promise of Cinema*, 607–12.

———. *Siegfried Kracauer's American Writings: Essays on Film and Popular Culture*. Edited by Johannes von Moltke and Kristy Rawson. Berkeley: University of California Press, 2012.

———. "Sound-Image Film." Translated by Nicholas Baer. In Kaes, Baer, and Cowan, *The Promise of Cinema*, 556–58.

———. *Theory of Film: The Redemption of Physical Reality*. Princeton, NJ: Princeton University Press, 1997.
———. "Time and History." *History and Theory* 6 (1966): 65–78.
———. *Werke*. Vol. 1, edited by Inka Mülder-Bach. Frankfurt am Main: Suhrkamp, 2006.
———. *Werke*. Vol. 2.2, edited by Christian Fleck and Bernd Stiegler. Berlin: Suhrkamp, 2012.
———. *Werke*. Vol. 4, edited by Ingrid Belke. Frankfurt am Main: Suhrkamp, 2009.
———. *Werke*. Vol. 5.1, edited by Inka Mülder-Bach. Berlin: Suhrkamp, 2011.
———. *Werke*. Vol. 6.1, edited by Inka Mülder-Bach. Frankfurt am Main: Suhrkamp, 2004.
———. *Werke*. Vol. 6.2, edited by Inka Mülder-Bach. Frankfurt am Main: Suhrkamp, 2004.
———. *Werke*. Vol. 6.3, edited by Inka Mülder-Bach. Frankfurt am Main: Suhrkamp, 2004.
———. *Werke*. Vol. 8, edited by Ingrid Belke. Frankfurt am Main: Suhrkamp, 2005.
———. *Werke*. Vol. 9.2, edited by Ingrid Belke. Frankfurt am Main: Suhrkamp, 2004.
Kracauer, Siegfried, and Erwin Panofsky. *Siegfried Kracauer / Erwin Panofsky: Briefwechsel 1941–1966*. Edited by Volker Breidecker. Berlin: Akademie, 1996.
Kubler, George. *The Shape of Time: Remarks on the History of Things*. New Haven, CT: Yale University Press, 2008.
Kuhn, Annette, and Jackie Stacey. "Screen Histories: An Introduction." In *Screen Histories: A Screen Reader*, edited by Annette Kuhn and Jackie Stacey, 1–10. Oxford: Clarendon Press, 1998.
Kumar, Shiv K. *Bergson and the Stream of Consciousness Novel*. New York: New York University Press, 1963.
Kurtz, Rudolf. *Expressionism and Film*. Edited by Christian Kiening and Ulrich Johannes Beil. Translated by Brenda Benthien. New Barnet, UK: John Libbey Publishing, 2016.
———. "Posing the Problem." In Mertins and Jennings, G, 230.
Kuukkanen, Jouni-Matti, ed. *Philosophy of History: Twenty-First-Century Perspectives*. London and New York: Bloomsbury Academic, 2020.
LaCapra, Dominick. *Writing History, Writing Trauma*. Baltimore: Johns Hopkins University Press, 2001.
Landsberg, Alison. *Engaging the Past: Mass Culture and the Production of Historical Knowledge*. New York: Columbia University Press, 2015.
———. *Prosthetic Memory: The Transformation of American Remembrance in the Age of Mass Culture*. New York: Columbia University Press, 2004.
Lang, Fritz. "The Future of the Feature Film in Germany." Translated by Don Reneau. In Kaes, Jay, and Dimendberg, *Weimar Republic Sourcebook*, 622–23.

Latour, Bruno. *Facing Gaia: Eight Lectures on the New Climatic Regime.* Translated by Catherine Porter. Cambridge: Polity, 2017.

———. "Why Has Critique Run out of Steam? From Matters of Fact to Matters of Concern." *Critical Inquiry* 30, no. 2 (Winter 2004): 225–48.

Leibniz, Gottfried Wilhelm. *Theodicy.* Translated by E.M. Huggard. New Haven, CT: Yale University Press, 1952.

Lessing, Theodor. *Jewish Self-Hate.* Edited by Benton Arnovitz. Translated by Peter C. Appelbaum. New York: Berghahn, 2021.

Lethen, Helmut. *Cool Conduct: The Culture of Distance in Weimar Germany.* Translated by Don Reneau. Berkeley: University of California Press, 2002.

Leyda, Jay. "Toward a New Film History." *Cinema Journal* 14, no. 2 (1974): 40–41.

Lichtblau, Klaus. "Eros and Culture: Gender Theory in Simmel, Tönnies and Weber." Translated by Guenther Roth. *Telos,* no. 82 (Winter 1989–90): 89–110.

Livingston, Paisley. *Cinema, Philosophy, Bergman: On Film as Philosophy.* Oxford: Oxford University Press, 2009.

Loacker, Armin, and Ines Steiner, eds. *Imaginierte Antike: Österreichische Monumental-Stummfilme.* Vienna: Filmarchiv Austria, 2002.

Loew, Katharina. "Expressive Visual Effects from Silent to Sound Film." In *Aesthetics of Early Sound Film: Media Change around 1930,* edited by Daniel Wiegand, 49–66. Amsterdam: Amsterdam University Press, 2023.

———. *Special Effects and German Silent Film: Techno-Romantic Cinema.* Amsterdam: Amsterdam University Press, 2021.

Loewy, Hanno. *Béla Balázs – Märchen, Ritual und Film.* Berlin: Verlag Vorwerk 8, 2003.

Löwenthal, Leo. *Literature and the Image of Man.* New Brunswick, NJ: Transaction Books, 1986.

Löwenthal, Leo, and Siegfried Kracauer. *In steter Freundschaft: Briefwechsel 1921–1966.* Edited by Peter-Erwin Jansen and Christian Schmidt. Springe: Zu Klampen, 2003.

Löwith, Karl. "Nature, History, and Existentialism." *Social Research* 19, no. 1 (March 1952): 79–94.

Lukács, Georg. *The Destruction of Reason.* Translated by Peter Palmer. London and Brooklyn: Verso, 2021.

———. *Essays on Realism.* Edited by Rodney Livingstone. Translated by David Fernbach. Cambridge, MA: MIT Press, 1981.

———. *The Historical Novel.* Translated by Hannah Mitchell and Stanley Mitchell. Lincoln: University of Nebraska Press, 1983.

———. *The Theory of the Novel: A Historico-Philosophical Essay on the Forms of Great Epic Literature.* Translated by Anna Bostock. Cambridge, MA: MIT Press, 1971.

———. "Thoughts toward an Aesthetic of the Cinema." Translated by Janelle Blankenship. In Kaes, Baer, and Cowan, *The Promise of Cinema,* 377–81.

Lungstrum, Janet. "*Metropolis* and the Technosexual Woman of German Modernity." In *Women in the Metropolis: Gender and Modernity in*

Weimar Culture, edited by Katharina von Ankum, 128–44. Berkeley: University of California Press, 1997.
Lütticken, Sven. *History in Motion: Time in the Age of the Moving Image*. Berlin: Sternberg, 2013.
M., J.P. "Ein Film von Eigenart." *Vorwärts* 134 (March 13, 1920): 2.
Mahler, Gustav. *Das Lied von der Erde in Full Score*. Mineola, NY: Dover, 1988.
Malm, Andreas. *The Progress of This Storm: Nature and Society in a Warming World*. London: Verso, 2018.
Maltby, Richard. "New Cinema Histories." In *Explorations in New Cinema History: Approaches and Case Studies*, edited by Richard Maltby, Daniel Biltereyst, and Philippe Meers, 3–40. Malden, MA, and Oxford: Blackwell, 2011.
Mann, Thomas. *The Magic Mountain*. Translated by John E. Woods. New York: Alfred A. Knopf, 2005.
———. *Thomas Mann's Addresses Delivered at the Library of Congress, 1942–1949*. Washington: Library of Congress, 1963.
Mannheim, Karl. *Essays on the Sociology of Knowledge*. Edited by Paul Kecskemeti. London: Routledge & Kegan Paul, 1952.
Marcus, Steven. *Engels, Manchester, and the Working Class*. New York: Random House, 1974.
Marcuse, Herbert. "The Struggle against Liberalism in the Totalitarian View of the State." In *Negations: Essays in Critical Theory*, translated by Jeremy J. Shapiro, 3–42. Boston: Beacon Press, 1968.
Marinetti, F.T. "The Founding and Manifesto of Futurism." Translated by Lawrence Rainey. In *Futurism: An Anthology*, edited by Lawrence Rainey, Christine Poggi, and Laura Wittman, 49–53. New Haven, CT: Yale University Press, 2009.
Marinetti, F.T., Bruno Corra, Emilio Settimelli, Arnaldo Ginna, Giacomo Balla, and Remo Chiti. "The Futurist Cinema." Translated by Lawrence Rainey. In *Futurism: An Anthology*, edited by Lawrence Rainey, Christine Poggi, and Laura Wittman, 229–33. New Haven, CT: Yale University Press, 2009.
Marx, Karl. *Capital: A Critique of Political Economy*. Vol. 1, edited by Frederick Engels, translated by Samuel Moore and Edward Aveling. Chicago: Charles H. Kerr & Company, 1912.
———. *Critique of Hegel's "Philosophy of Right."* Edited by Joseph O'Malley. Translated by Annette Jolin and Joseph O'Malley. Cambridge: Cambridge University Press, 1970.
Marx, Karl, and Friedrich Engels. *The Collected Works of Karl Marx and Friedrich Engels*. Vol. 5, *1845–47*, translated by Clemens Dutt, W. Lough, and C.P. Magill. New York: International Publishers, 1976.
———. *The Communist Manifesto*. Translated by Samuel Moore. London: Penguin, 2002.
———. *The German Ideology*. Edited by C.J. Arthur. New York: International Publishers, 1970.

Marzynski, Georg. *Die Methode des Expressionismus: Studien zu seiner Psychologie.* Leipzig: Klinkhardt & Biermann, 1920.
Matuszewski, Boleslas. "A New Source of History." Translated by Laura U. Marks and Diane Koszarski. *Film History* 7, no. 3 (Autumn 1995): 322–24.
Mayer, Carl, and Hans Janowitz. *Das Cabinet des Dr. Caligari: Drehbuch von Carl Mayer und Hans Janowitz zu Robert Wienes Film von 1919/20.* Munich: edition text + kritik, 1995.
Mead, George Herbert. *The Philosophy of the Act.* Edited by Charles W. Morris. Chicago: University of Chicago Press, 1938.
Megill, Allan. "Why Was There a Crisis of Historicism?" *History and Theory* 36, no. 3 (1997): 416–29.
Meinecke, Friedrich. *Aphorismen und Skizzen zur Geschichte.* Leipzig: Koehler & Amelang, 1942.
———. *The German Catastrophe: Reflections and Recollections.* Translated by Sidney B. Fay. Cambridge, MA: Harvard University Press, 1950.
———. *Historism: The Rise of a New Historical Outlook.* Translated by J.E. Anderson. London: Routledge and Kegan Paul, 1972.
———. "Die Krisis des Historismus." *Historische Zeitschrift* 149, no. 2 (1934): 303–5.
———. *Staat und Persönlichkeit.* Berlin: E.S. Mittler & Sohn, 1933.
Mertins, Detlef, and Michael W. Jennings, eds. *G: An Avant-Garde Journal of Art, Architecture, Design, and Film, 1923–1926.* Translated by Steven Lindberg with Margareta Ingrid Christian. Los Angeles: Getty Research Institute, 2010.
Metz, Christian. *Film Language: A Semiotics of the Cinema.* Translated by Michael Taylor. Chicago: University of Chicago Press, 1991.
Michelson, Annette. "Reading Eisenstein Reading 'Capital.'" *October* 2 (Summer 1976): 27–38.
———. "The Wings of Hypothesis: On Montage and the Theory of the Interval." In *Montage and Modern Life, 1919–1942,* edited by Matthew Teitelbaum, 61–81. Cambridge, MA: MIT Press, 1992.
Mierendorff, Carlo. "If I Only Had the Cinema!" In Kaes, Baer, and Cowan, *The Promise of Cinema,* 426–33.
Moholy-Nagy, László. *Painting, Photography, Film.* Translated by Janet Seligman. London: Lund Humphries, 1967.
Moore, Jason W., ed. *Anthropocene or Capitalocene? Nature, History, and the Crisis of Capitalism.* Oakland, CA: PM Press, 2016.
———. *Capitalism in the Web of Life: Ecology and the Accumulation of Capital.* London: Verso, 2015.
Moretti, Franco. *Distant Reading.* London and New York: Verso, 2013.
Morin, Edgar. *The Cinema, or The Imaginary Man.* Translated by Lorraine Mortimer. Minneapolis: University of Minnesota Press, 2005.
Morris, Christopher. *Modernism and the Cult of Mountains: Music, Opera, Cinema.* Farnham, Surrey: Ashgate, 2012.

Moyn, Samuel. "The Trouble with Comparisons." *New York Review of Books*, May 19, 2020. www.nybooks.com/daily/2020/05/19/the-trouble-with-comparisons/.
Mülder-Bach, Inka. "History as Autobiography: The Last Things Before the Last." Translated by Gail Finney. *New German Critique* no. 54 (Autumn 1991): 139–57.
Mulhall, Stephen. "Film as Philosophy: The Very Idea." *Proceedings of the Aristotelian Society* 107 (2007): 279–94.
Mullarkey, John. *Refractions of Reality: Philosophy and the Moving Image*. New York: Palgrave Macmillan, 2009.
Mulvey, Laura. *Death 24x a Second: Stillness and the Moving Image*. London: Reaktion Books, 2006.
Münsterberg, Hugo. *The Film: A Psychological Study*. Mineola, NY: Dover, 1970.
Myers, David N. *Resisting History: Historicism and Its Discontents in German-Jewish Thought*. Princeton, NJ, and Oxford: Princeton University Press, 2003.
Nancy, Jean-Luc. *The Inoperative Community*. Edited and translated by Peter Connor. Minneapolis: University of Minnesota Press, 1991.
Nenno, Nancy P. "'Postcards from the Edge': Education to Tourism in the German Mountain Film." In *Light Motives: German Popular Film in Perspective*, edited by Randall Halle and Margaret McCarthy, 61–84. Detroit: Wayne State University Press, 2003.
Neumann, Dietrich, ed. *Film Architecture: From Metropolis to Blade Runner*. Munich: Prestel, 1996.
———. "The Urbanistic Vision in Fritz Lang's *Metropolis*." In *Dancing on the Volcano: Essays on the Culture of the Weimar Republic*, edited by Thomas W. Kniesche and Stephen Brockmann, 143–62. Columbia, SC: Camden House, 1994.
Neurath, Otto. "Anti-Spengler." In *Empiricism and Sociology*, edited by Marie Neurath and Robert S. Cohen, translated by Paul Foulkes and Marie Neurath, 158–213. Dordrecht and Boston: D. Reidel, 1973.
Nicholas of Cusa. *On Learned Ignorance*. Translated by Jasper Hopkins. Minneapolis: Arthur J. Banning Press, 1981.
Nicolson, Marjorie Hope. *Mountain Gloom and Mountain Glory: The Development of the Aesthetics of the Infinite*. Seattle: University of Washington Press, 1997.
Nietzsche, Friedrich. *The Gay Science*. Translated by Walter Kaufmann. New York: Vintage, 1974.
———. *On the Genealogy of Morals & Ecce Homo*. Edited by Walter Kaufmann. Translated by Walter Kaufmann and R. J. Hollingdale. New York: Random House, 1967.
———. *Philosophy and Truth: Selections from Nietzsche's Notebooks of the Early 1870's*. Edited and translated by Daniel Breazeale. Atlantic Highlands, NJ: Humanities Press, 1979.

———. *Untimely Meditations*. Edited by Daniel Breazeale. Translated by R. J. Hollingdale. Cambridge: Cambridge University Press, 1997.

Oexle, Otto Gerhard. "'Historismus': Überlegungen zur Geschichte des Phänomens und des Begriffs." In *Jahrbuch 1986 der Braunschweigischen Wissenschaftlichen Gesellschaft*, 119–155. Göttingen: Erich Goltze, 1986.

Die Offenbarung Sankt Johannis. Hellerau: Avalun-Verlag, 1923. Includes ten woodcuts by Bruno Goldschmitt.

Ortega y Gasset, José. *The Dehumanization of Art and Other Writings on Art and Culture*. Garden City, NY: Doubleday & Co., 1956.

Osborne, Peter. *Anywhere or Not at All: Philosophies of Contemporary Art*. London and Brooklyn: Verso, 2013.

———. *The Politics of Time: Modernity and Avant-Garde*. London and New York: Verso, 1995.

Oxford English Dictionary Online. "Historicism." Accessed September 19, 2023. www.oed.com/view/Entry/87304?redirectedFrom=historicism&.

P., E. S. "Metropolis." *Lichtbildbühne* 20, no. 9 (January 11, 1927): n.p.

Panofsky, Erwin. *Perspective as Symbolic Form*. Translated by Christopher S. Wood. New York: Zone Books, 1991.

———. "Reflections on Historical Time." Translated by Johanna Bauman. *Critical Inquiry* 30, no. 4 (Summer 2004): 691–701.

———. "Style and Medium in the Motion Pictures." In *Film Theory and Criticism: Introductory Readings*, ed. Gerald Mast and Marshall Cohen, 151–69. London: Oxford University Press, 1974.

Panofsky, Erwin, and Fritz Saxl. *Dürers "Melencolia I": Eine quellen- und typengeschichtliche Untersuchung*. Leipzig and Berlin: Teubner, 1923.

Parikka, Jussi. *What Is Media Archaeology?* Cambridge: Polity, 2012.

Peabody, Seth. *Film History for the Anthropocene: The Ecological Archive of German Cinema*. Rochester, NY: Camden House, 2023.

Pearson, Roberta. "Historical Films." In *Encyclopedia of Early Cinema*, edited by Richard Abel, 299–301. London: Routledge, 2005.

Pensky, Max. "Natural History: The Life and Afterlife of a Concept in Adorno." *Critical Horizons* 5, no. 1 (2004): 227–58.

Perlmann, Anne. "Das Kabinett des Dr. Caligari—Declafilm: Pressevorführung in den Schadow-Lichtspielen." *Der Kinematograph* 14, no. 696 (May 16, 1920): n.p.

Pestalozzi, Johann Heinrich. *Sämtliche Werke*. Vol. 16, edited by Walter Feilchenfeld and Herbert Schönebaum. Berlin and Leipzig: Walter de Gruyter & Co., 1935.

Peterson, Jennifer Lynn. *Education in the School of Dreams: Travelogues and Early Nonfiction Film*. Durham, NC: Duke University Press, 2013.

Petrarch, Francesco. *Letters on Familiar Matters*. Vol. 1, *Books I–VIII*. Translated by Aldo S. Bernardo. New York: Italica Press, 2005.

Petro, Patrice. *Aftershocks of the New: Feminism and Film History*. New Brunswick, NJ: Rutgers University Press, 2002.

———. "Classical Feminist Film Theory: Then and (Mostly) Now." In *The Routledge Companion to Cinema and Gender*, edited by Kristin Lené Hole, Dijana Jelača, E. Ann Kaplan, and Patrice Petro, 15–24. London: Routledge, 2017.

———. *Joyless Streets: Women and Melodramatic Representation in Weimar Germany*. Princeton, NJ: Princeton University Press, 1989.

Peukert, Detlev J.K. *The Weimar Republic: The Crisis of Classical Modernity*. Translated by Richard Deveson. New York: Hill and Wang, 1992.

Pinder, Wilhelm. *Das Problem der Generation in der Kunstgeschichte Europas*. Berlin: Frankfurter Verlags-Anstalt, 1926.

Pinthus, Kurt. "Lemberg und Metropolis." *Das Tagebuch* 8, no. 3 (January 15, 1927): 97–102.

———. "Sehenswerte Filme." *Das Tagebuch* 2, no. 42 (October 22, 1921): 1288–89.

Pisters, Patricia. *The Neuroimage: A Deleuzian Film-Philosophy of Digital Screen Culture*. Stanford, CA: Stanford University Press, 2012.

Pollmann, Inga. *Cinematic Vitalism: Film Theory and the Question of Life*. Amsterdam: Amsterdam University Press, 2018.

Pope, Marvin H. *The Anchor Bible: Song of Songs*. Garden City, NY: Doubleday & Company, 1977.

Popper, Karl. *The Poverty of Historicism*. London and New York: Routledge, 2002.

Postone, Moishe. "The Current Crisis and the Anachronism of Value: A Marxian Reading." *Continental Thought & Theory* 1, no. 4 (2017): 38–54.

Pound, Ezra. *Ezra Pound and the Visual Arts*. Edited by Harriet Zinnes. New York: New Directions, 1980.

Proskauer, Martin. "'Das Kabinett des Dr. Caligari'—Ein Nachwort und eine Prophezeiung." *Film-Kurier* 2, no. 51 (February 29, 1920): 2.

Pruitt, Bill. "A Former *Apprentice* Producer Responds to Donald Trump Being Elected President." *Vanity Fair*, December 21, 2016. www.vanityfair.com /hollywood/2016/12/apprentice-producer-donald-trump-president.

Rabinbach, Anson. "Nationalsozialismus und Moderne: Zur Technik-Interpretation im Dritten Reich." In *Der Technikdiskurs in der Hitler-Stalin-Ära*, edited by Wolfgang Emmerich and Carl Wege, 94–113. Stuttgart and Weimar: Metzler, 1995.

Ramsay, Stephen. *Reading Machines: Toward an Algorithmic Criticism*. Urbana: University of Illinois Press, 2011.

Rancière, Jacques. "Die Geschichtlichkeit des Films." Translated by Stefan Barmann. In *Die Gegenwart der Vergangenheit: Dokumentarfilm, Fernsehen und Geschichte*, edited by Eva Hohenberger and Judith Keilbach, 230–46. Berlin: Verlag Vorwerk 8, 2003.

———. *The Politics of Aesthetics: The Distribution of the Sensible*. Translated by Gabriel Rockhill. London: Continuum, 2004.

———. "Der Wirklichkeitseffekt und die Politik der Fiktion." Translated by Mario Horta. In *Realismus in den Künsten der Gegenwart*, edited by Dirck

Linck, Michael Lüthy, Brigitte Obermayr, and Martin Vöhler, 141–57. Zurich: Diaphanes, 2010.
Ranke, Leopold von. *The Theory and Practice of History*. Edited by Georg G. Iggers. Translated by Wilma A. Iggers. London and New York: Routledge, 2011.
———. *Zur Kritik neuerer Geschichtsschreiber*. Leipzig and Berlin: Reimer, 1824.
Rapp, Christian. *Höhenrausch: Der deutsche Bergfilm*. Vienna: Sonderzahl, 1997.
Rebentisch, Juliane. "The Contemporaneity of Contemporary Art." *New German Critique* 42, no. 1 (February 2015): 223–37.
Reitter, Paul. *On the Origins of Jewish Self-Hatred*. Princeton, NJ: Princeton University Press, 2012.
Rentschler, Eric. "Mountains and Modernity: Relocating the *Bergfilm*." *New German Critique*, no. 51 (Autumn 1990): 137–61.
Richter, Hans. "Avant-Garde Film in Germany." In *Experiment in the Film*, edited by Roger Manvell, 219–33. New York: Arno, 1970.
———. "The Avant-Garde Film Seen from Within." *Hollywood Quarterly* 4, no. 1 (Autumn 1949): 34–41.
———. "The Badly Trained Soul." In Mertins and Jennings, *G*, 146–48.
———. *Dada: Art and Anti-Art*. Translated by David Britt. London: Thames & Hudson, 1997.
———. "Dada und Film." In *Dada: Monographie einer Bewegung*, edited by Willy Verkauf, 57–66. Teufen: Niggli, 1957.
———. "Dada XYZ . . ." In *The Dada Painters and Poets: An Anthology*, edited by Robert Motherwell, 285–89. New York: Wittenborn & Schultz, 1951.
———. "Easel–Scroll–Film." *Magazine of Art*, February 1952, 78–86.
———. *Encounters from Dada till Today*. Translated by Christopher Middleton. Los Angeles: Los Angeles County Museum of Art; Munich: Prestel, 2013.
———. "*Expressionismus und Film* by Rudolf Kurtz." In Mertins and Jennings, *G*, 198.
———. "The Film as an Original Art Form." *College Art Journal* 10, no. 2 (Winter 1951): 157–61.
———. *Filmgegner von heute—Filmfreunde von morgen*. Berlin: Hermann Reckendorf, 1929.
———. "Hans Richter on the Function of Film History Writing." *Film Culture* 3, no. 18 (April 1958): 25–26.
———. "History Is What Is Happening Today." In Mertins and Jennings, *G*, 228–29.
———. "A History of the Avant-Garde." In *Art in Cinema*, edited by Frank Stauffacher, 8–21. New York: Arno Press, 1971.
———. *The Struggle for the Film: Towards a Socially Responsible Cinema*. Edited by Jürgen Römhild. Translated by Ben Brewster. New York: St. Martin's Press, 1986.
Ricoeur, Paul. "Narrative Time." *Critical Inquiry* 7, no. 1 (Autumn 1980): 169–90.

Riegl, Alois. *Gesammelte Aufsätze.* Edited by Karl Maria Swoboda. Augsburg: Filser, 1929.

———. "The Main Characteristics of the Late Roman *Kunstwollen.*" Translated by Christopher S. Wood. In *The Vienna School Reader: Politics and Art Historical Method in the 1930s,* edited by Christopher S. Wood, 87–103. New York: Zone Books, 2003.

Ringer, Fritz K. *The Decline of the German Mandarins: The German Academic Community, 1890–1933.* Hanover, NH: University Press of New England, 1990.

Rintelen, Fritz-Joachim von. "Der Versuch einer Überwindung des Historismus bei Ernst Troeltsch." *Deutsche Vierteljahrsschrift für Literaturwissenschaft und Geistesgeschichte* 8 (1930): 324–72.

Robinson, Cedric J. *Black Marxism: The Making of the Black Radical Tradition.* Chapel Hill: University of North Carolina Press, 2000.

———. *Forgeries of Memory and Meaning: Blacks and the Regimes of Race in American Theater and Film before World War II.* Chapel Hill: University of North Carolina Press, 2007.

Robinson, James Harvey. *The New History: Essays Illustrating the Modern Historical Outlook.* New York: Macmillan Company, 1912.

Rodowick, D. N. "An Elegy for Theory." *October* 122 (Fall 2007): 91–109.

———. "Historical Knowing in Film." *Iris* 2, no. 2 (1984): 2–4.

———. *Philosophy's Artful Conversation.* Cambridge, MA: Harvard University Press, 2015.

Rogowski, Christian. "Introduction: Images and Imaginaries." In *The Many Faces of Weimar Cinema: Rediscovering Germany's Filmic Legacy,* edited by Christian Rogowski, 1–12. Rochester, NY: Camden House, 2010.

Rosen, Philip. *Change Mummified: Cinema, Historicity, Theory.* Minneapolis: University of Minnesota Press, 2001.

Rosenstone, Robert A. *History on Film/Film on History.* Harlow, UK: Pearson, 2006.

———. *Visions of the Past: The Challenge of Film to Our Idea of History.* Cambridge, MA: Harvard University Press, 1995.

Ross, Ivan. "Mediating the Historical Imagination: Visual Media and the U.S. Civil War, 1861–2011." PhD diss., University of Chicago, 2012.

Rotha, Paul. *The Film till Now: A Survey of World Cinema.* New York: Twayne Publishers, 1960.

Runia, Eelco. "Presence." *History and Theory* 45, no. 1 (2006): 1–29.

Rutsky, R. L. "The Mediation of Technology and Gender: *Metropolis,* Nazism, Modernism." In *Fritz Lang's "Metropolis": Cinematic Visions of Technology and Fear,* edited by Michael Minden and Holger Bachmann, 217–45. Rochester, NY: Camden House, 2000.

Ruttmann, Walter. "The 'Absolute' Fashion: Film as an End in Itself; Beware of the *Art pour l'art* Position." Translated by Nicholas Baer. In Kaes, Baer, and Cowan, *The Promise of Cinema,* 464–65.

———. "Painting with Time." Translated by Michael Cowan. In Kaes, Baer, and Cowan, *The Promise of Cinema,* 450–52.

Sadoul, Georges. *L'invention du cinéma 1832–1897*. Paris: Denoël, 1973.
Said, Edward. *Orientalism*. New York: Vintage, 1979.
Salt, Barry. "From Caligari to Who?" *Sight and Sound* 48, no. 2 (1979): 119–23.
Scheffauer, Herman George. *The New Vision in the German Arts*. New York: B.W. Huebsch, 1924.
Scheunemann, Dietrich. "Activating the Differences: Expressionist Film and Early Weimar Cinema." In *Expressionist Film: New Perspectives*, edited by Dietrich Scheunemann, 1–31. Rochester, NY: Camden House, 2003.
Schmitt, Carl. *Land and Sea: A World-Historical Meditation*. Edited by Russell A. Berman and Samuel Garrett Zeitlin. Translated by Samuel Garrett Zeitlin. Candor, NY: Telos, 2015.
Schobert, Walter. "'Painting in Time' and 'Visual Music': On German Avant-Garde Films of the 1920s." In *Expressionist Film: New Perspectives*, edited by Dietrich Scheunemann, 237–49. Rochester, NY: Camden House, 2003.
Schoenberg, Arnold. *Style and Idea*. Edited and translated by Dika Newlin. New York: Philosophical Library, 1950.
Scholem, Gershom. *Das Davidschild: Geschichte eines Symbols*. Translated by Gerold Necker. Frankfurt am Main: Suhrkamp, 1963.
Schopenhauer, Arthur. *The World as Will and Idea*. 3 vols. Translated by R.B. Haldane and J. Kemp. London: Kegan Paul, Trench, Trübner & Co., 1909.
Schorske, Carl E. *Fin-de-Siècle Vienna: Politics and Culture*. New York: Vintage Books, 1981.
Schwartz, Frederic J. *Blind Spots: Critical Theory and the History of Art in Twentieth-Century Germany*. New Haven, CT: Yale University Press, 2005.
Segeberg, Harro. "'Is Everything Relative?': Cinema and the Revolution of Knowledge around 1900." In *Film 1900: Technology, Perception, Culture*, edited by Annemone Ligensa and Klaus Kreimeier, 67–76. New Barnet, UK: John Libbey Publishing, 2009.
Sheppard, Samantha N. "Changing the Subject: Lynn Nottage's *By the Way, Meet Vera Stark* and the Making of Black Women's Film History." *Feminist Media Histories* 8, no. 2 (Spring 2022): 14–42.
Simmel, Georg. "Alpine Journeys." Translated by Jens Klenner. In *Mountains and the German Mind: Translations from Gessner to Messner, 1541–2009*, edited by Sean Ireton and Caroline Schaumann, 184–87. Rochester, NY: Camden House, 2020.
———. "The Metaphysics of Death." Translated by Ulrich Teucher and Thomas M. Kemple. *Theory, Culture & Society* 24, nos. 7–8 (2007): 72–77.
———. *On Individuality and Social Forms: Selected Writings*. Edited by Donald N. Levine. Chicago: University of Chicago Press, 1971.
———. "On the Aesthetics of the Alps." Translated by Jens Klenner. In *Mountains and the German Mind: Translations from Gessner to Messner, 1541–2009*, edited by Sean Ireton and Caroline Schaumann, 187–92. Rochester, NY: Camden House, 2020.
———. *On Women, Sexuality, and Love*. Translated by Guy Oakes. New Haven, CT: Yale University Press, 1984.

———. "The Picture Frame: An Aesthetic Study." Translated by Mark Ritter. *Theory, Culture & Society* 11 (1994): 11–17.
Sims, Amy R. "Intellectuals in Crisis: Historians under Hitler." *Virginia Quarterly Review* 54, no. 2 (Spring 1978): 246–62.
Sinnerbrink, Robert. *New Philosophies of Film: Thinking Images*. London: Continuum, 2011.
Sloterdijk, Peter. *Critique of Cynical Reason*. Translated by Michael Eldred. Minneapolis: University of Minnesota Press, 1987.
Smith, Bonnie G. *The Gender of History: Men, Women, and Historical Practice*. Cambridge, MA: Harvard University Press, 1998.
Smith, Helmut Walser. *The Continuities of German History: Nation, Religion, and Race across the Long Nineteenth Century*. Cambridge: Cambridge University Press, 2008.
Smith, Terry. "Contemporary Art and Contemporaneity." *Critical Inquiry* 32, no. 4 (Summer 2006): 681–707.
Sobchack, Vivian. "The Insistent Fringe: Moving Images and Historical Consciousness." *History and Theory* 36, no. 4 (December 1997): 4–20.
———. "'Surge and Splendor': A Phenomenology of the Hollywood Historical Epic." *Representations*, no. 29 (Winter 1990): 24–49.
Sockness, Brent W. "Geschichte durch Ethik überwinden? Ernst Troeltsch, Moral Consciousness, and the Crisis of Historicism." In *Praktische Theologie und protestantische Kultur*, edited by Wilhelm Gräb and Birgit Weyel, 200–217. Gütersloh: Christian Kaiser, 2002.
———. "Historicism and Its Unresolved Problems: Ernst Troeltsch's Last Word." In *Historisierung: Begriff—Geschichte—Praxisfelder*, edited by Moritz Baumstark and Robert Forkel, 210–30. Stuttgart: J. B. Metzler, 2016.
Sokel, Walter H. *The Writer in Extremis: Expressionism in Twentieth-Century German Literature*. Stanford, CA: Stanford University Press, 1959.
Sombart, Werner. *The Jews and Modern Capitalism*. Translated by M. Epstein. Kitchener, ON: Batoche Books, 2001.
Sontag, Susan. "The Imagination of Disaster." *Commentary*, October 1965, 42–48.
Sorlin, Pierre. *The Film in History: Restaging the Past*. Totowa, NJ: Barnes & Noble Books, 1980.
Spengler, Oswald. *The Decline of the West*. Translated by Charles Francis Atkinson. New York: Alfred A. Knopf, 1926.
Steinskog, Erik. "Metropolis 2.0: Janelle Monáe's Recycling of Fritz Lang." In *The Black Speculative Arts Movement: Black Futurity, Art+Design*, edited by Reynaldo Anderson and Clinton R. Fluker, 173–88. Lanham, MD: Lexington Books, 2019.
Strauven, Wanda. "Media Archaeology: Where Film History, Media Art, and New Media (Can) Meet." In *Preserving and Exhibiting Media Art: Challenges and Perspectives*, edited by Julia Noordegraaf, Cosetta Saba, Barbara Le Maitre, and Vinzenz Hediger, 59–79. Amsterdam: Amsterdam University Press, 2013.

Taine, Hippolyte. *History of English Literature*. Vol. 1. Translated by Henry van Laun. Edinburgh: Edmonston and Douglas, 1871.
Tannenbaum, Eugen. "Expressionismus im Film." *Berliner Abendpost*, February 29, 1920.
Taylor, Frederick Winslow. *The Principles of Scientific Management*. New York and London: Harper & Brothers, 1915.
Thanouli, Eleftheria. *History and Film: A Tale of Two Disciplines*. New York: Bloomsbury, 2018.
Theweleit, Klaus. *Male Fantasies*. Vol. 1, *Women, Floods, Bodies, History*, translated by Stephen Conway, Erica Carter, and Chris Turner. Minneapolis: University of Minnesota Press, 1987.
Tillich, Paul. "E. Troeltsch: Historismus und seine Probleme" [1924]. *Journal for the Scientific Study of Religion* 1, no. 1 (1961): 109–14.
Traverso, Enzo. *Left-Wing Melancholia: Marxism, History, and Memory*. New York: Columbia University Press, 2016.
Troeltsch, Ernst. "Die geistige Revolution: Berliner Brief." *Kunstwart und Kulturwart* 34, no. 4 (January 1921): 227–33.
———. *Der Historismus und seine Probleme*. Tübingen: J.C.B. Mohr, 1922.
———. "Die Krisis des Historismus." *Die neue Rundschau* 33 (1922): 572–90.
———. *Die Revolution in der Wissenschaft*. Munich and Leipzig: Duncker & Humblot, 1921.
"Les Trois Lumières." *Le Matin* 39, no. 13967 (June 16, 1922): 5.
Turvey, Malcolm. *The Filming of Modern Life: European Avant-Garde Film of the 1920s*. Cambridge, MA: MIT Press, 2011.
Unruh, Fritz von. *Reden*. Frankfurt am Main: Frankfurter Societäts-Druckerei, 1924.
Usai, Paolo Cherchi. "The Philosophy of Film History." *Film History* 6, no. 1 (1994): 3–5.
Vaihinger, Hans. *The Philosophy of 'As If': A System of the Theoretical, Practical and Religious Fictions of Mankind*. Translated by C.K. Ogden. London: Routledge & Kegan Paul, 1935.
Vertov, Dziga. *Kino-Eye: The Writings of Dziga Vertov*. Edited by Annette Michelson. Translated by Kevin O'Brien. Berkeley: University of California Press, 1984.
von Moltke, Johannes. *The Curious Humanist: Siegfried Kracauer in America*. Oakland: University of California Press, 2016.
———. *No Place Like Home: Locations of Heimat in German Cinema*. Berkeley: University of California Press, 2005.
———. "Out of the Past: Classical Film Theory." *Screen* 55, no. 3 (Autumn 2014): 398–403.
Wartenberg, Thomas E. *Thinking on Screen: Film as Philosophy*. London: Routledge, 2007.
Wassermann, Jakob. *The Goose Man*. Translated by Allen W. Porterfield. New York: Harcourt, Brace and Company, 1922.

Weber, Max. "Science as a Vocation." In *Essays in Sociology*, edited and translated by H.H. Gerth and C. Wright Mills, 129–56. New York: Oxford University Press, 1946.

Wedel, Michael. *Filmgeschichte als Krisengeschichte: Schnitte und Spuren durch den deutschen Film.* Bielefeld: transcript, 2011.

Wellek, René. "The Parallelism between Literature and the Arts." In *Literary Criticism—Idea and Act: The English Institute, 1939–1972; Selected Essays*, edited by W.K. Wimsatt, 44–65. Berkeley: University of California Press, 1974.

Wells, H.G. "Mr. Wells Reviews a Current Film." *New York Times Magazine*, April 17, 1927, 4.

Westerdale, Joel. "The Musical Promise of Abstract Film." In *The Many Faces of Weimar Cinema: Rediscovering Germany's Filmic Legacy*, edited by Christian Rogowski, 153–66. Rochester, NY: Camden House, 2010.

Whissel, Kristen. *Spectacular Digital Effects: CGI and Contemporary Cinema.* Durham, NC: Duke University Press, 2014.

White, Hayden V. "The Burden of History." *History and Theory* 5, no. 2 (1966): 111–34.

———. "Historiography and Historiophoty." *American Historical Review* 93, no. 5 (December 1988): 1193–99.

———. *Metahistory: The Historical Imagination in Nineteenth-Century Europe.* Baltimore and London: Johns Hopkins University Press, 1973.

Wiene, Robert. "Expressionism in Film." Translated by Eric Ames. In Kaes, Baer, and Cowan, *The Promise of Cinema*, 436–38.

Wilmesmeier, Holger. "Entstehungsgeschichte: Le Film 100 Titres." In Bareither, Beals, Cowan, Dobryden, Fest, Müller-Richter, and Nemec, *Hans Richters "Rhythmus 21,"* 33–44.

Windelband, Wilhelm. "History and Natural Science." Translated by Guy Oakes. *History and Theory* 19, no. 2 (February 1980): 169–85.

Wolf, August. "Film as Historian." Translated by Nicholas Baer. In Kaes, Baer, and Cowan, *The Promise of Cinema*, 94–95.

Wölfflin, Heinrich. *Kunstgeschichtliche Grundbegriffe: Das Problem der Stilentwicklung in der neueren Kunst.* Munich: Hugo Bruckmann, 1917.

———. *Principles of Art History: The Problem of the Development of Style in Later Art.* Translated by M.D. Hottinger. Mineola, NY: Dover, 1950.

Wood, Christopher S. Introduction to *The Vienna School Reader: Politics and Art Historical Method in the 1930s*, edited by Christopher S. Wood, 7–24. New York: Zone Books, 2003.

Woolf, Virginia. "The Movies and Reality." *New Republic*, August 4, 1926, 308–10. Reprinted in *Authors on Film*, edited by Harry M. Geduld, 86–91. Bloomington: Indiana University Press, 1972.

Worringer, Wilhelm. *Abstraction and Empathy: A Contribution to the Psychology of Style.* Translated by Michael Bullock. Chicago: Ivan R. Dee, 1997.

Würtenberg, Gustav. "Geschichtsunterricht und Kino." *Vergangenheit und Gegenwart* 18, no. 6 (1928): 361–66.

Zamyatin, Yevgeny. "On Literature, Revolution, Entropy, and Other Matters." In *A Soviet Heretic: Essays by Yevgeny Zamyatin*, edited and translated by Mirra Ginsberg. Chicago: University of Chicago Press, 1970.

Zechner, Ingo. "Elementares Kino: Fünf Notizen zu Hans Richters *Rhythmus 21*." In Bareither, Beals, Cowan, Dobryden, Fest, Müller-Richter, and Nemec, *Hans Richters "Rhythmus 21,"* 91–102.

Ziege, Felix. "Metropolis und wir." *Kulturwille* 4, no. 6 (1927): 125.

Zimmermann, Yvonne. "Advertising and Avant-Gardes: A History of Concepts, 1930–1940." In *Advertising and the Transformation of Screen Cultures*, edited by Bo Florin, Patrick Vonderau, and Yvonne Zimmermann, 77–111. Amsterdam: Amsterdam University Press, 2021.

———. "Hans Richter and the *Filmessay*: A Media Archaeological Case Study of Documentary Film History and Historiography." In *A Companion to Documentary Film History*, edited by Joshua Malitsky, 367–89. Hoboken, NJ: Wiley-Blackwell, 2021.

———. "Hans Richter and the 'Struggle for the Film History.'" In *How Film Histories Were Made: Materials, Methods, Discourses*, edited by Malte Hagener and Yvonne Zimmermann, 209–34. Amsterdam: Amsterdam University Press, 2024.

Zweig, Arnold. *Dialektik der Alpen: Fortschritt und Hemmnis*. Berlin: Aufbau, 1997.

Index

absolute/abstract films, 109, 111*fig.*, 114–15, 117, 126, 133, 147, 165; elements of time and movement in, 112. See also *Rhythm 21* (*Rhythmus 21*, 1923–25)
absolute music, 112, 115, 117
absurdism, 160–61, 165
accumulation, 15–16, 17, 18, 41
adaptations, film: of biographies, 43; of literature, 34, 39, 41, 207n34; of poetry, 34, 182n61; of theater, 32, 33, 37, 39
Adorno, Theodor W., 3, 17, 40, 51, 88, 102, 117, 183n79; Herf's account of fascism and, 130, 131; on Mahler, 99; on metaphysics, 87, 101; natural history (*Naturgeschichte*) dialectic, 7, 128, 129, 140–41, 143, 144, 209n60; obituary for Kracauer, 101, 197n79; time spent in the Swiss Alps, 145
aesthetic modernism, 57, 59, 62, 73, 99, 107–8, 110; definition of, 105–6
aesthetics, 14, 19, 22, 26, 27, 31, 73, 165; of absolute films, 7, 112–14, 115, 117; of the Alps, 137; avant-garde, 108; of *Battleship Potemkin* (1925), 36–38; *The Cabinet of Dr. Caligari* (1920) and Expressionist, 4, 6, 62, 64, 65, 66–67, 77–78, 86; of *Destiny* (1921), 85, 88–90, 101; of *The Holy Mountain* (1926), 131–33, 138–40; introduction of sound films and, 41,

183n67; Kracauer on, 5, 31–35, 39, 43, 45, 47–48, 50, 51, 53–54, 55, 66, 101, 126; of *Metropolis* (1927), 7, 147–48, 150, 157–58, 158*fig.*, 159*fig.*; pure, 117; Rancière's "regime" of, 54–55, 104–5, 106, 108, 119; realist, 51, 65–67; theory, 118, 120
Alexander Nevsky (*Aleksandr Nevskiy*, 1938), 50
allegory, 4, 17, 50, 138, 165, 194n15, 208n55; baroque *Trauerspiel*, 94–95, 141; biblical, 153; capitalism and class, 158, 161, 162; death, 91, 95; racial capitalism, 8, 149
Allen, Robert C., 11
All for a Woman (*Danton*, 1921), 32, 48
All Quiet on the Western Front (1930), 41
Allred, Mason, 23
Alps, 131, 138–40, 145, 147; aesthetic value of, 137; Kracauer's view of, 136; perceptions and popularity of, 133–35
alterity, 99, 155, 157
analogy, 62, 67, 96, 100, 149; crises of the Weimar Republic, 8, 146, 157, 163–64; musical, 112; photographic media and historiography, 4, 16, 88, 126; poetics of parallelism, 6, 24, 89*fig.*
Ankersmit, Frank, 4, 8, 10, 18

247

Anthropocene, 18, 145–46, 148
antihistoricism, 7, 8, 67, 106, 109, 110
antiquarianism, 24, 30, 63, 106, 118, 119, 121
anti-Semitism, 98–99, 150
Apprentice, The (2004–17), 56
Arendt, Hannah, 103
Aristotle, 6, 29, 32, 50, 52, 55, 72; poetics, 51, 54, 105
Arnheim, Rudolf, 66
art, 27, 59, 72, 76, 97; absolute film and, 112–13, 113*fig.*; abstract, 64, 110–12, 114; avant-garde or modernist, 53, 105, 106, 107, 110; contemporary, 119, 121, 124, 127; Death and the Maiden motif in, 95; film history and, 21, 30–31; Hegel's lectures on, 120–21; historical paintings, 89; history/historians, 106, 109, 118, 119–20, 122–23, 125, 126; Impressionists, 57, 58, 66, 73, 74; of the masses, 152; modern technology and, 131; Romantic painters, 132, 133, 134. *See also* Expressionism; photography
authenticity, cinematic jargon of, 7, 101, 131, 141, 144
avant-garde, 1, 7, 23, 103, 105, 126–27; European, 104, 109; filmmakers, 112, 126; nonsimultaneity (*Ungleichzeitigkeit*) and, 107–8; relationship to the past, 106; Richter's journal writings and, 6–7, 108–10, 116*fig.*; term usage, 107

Baecque, Antoine de, 21
Balázs, Béla, 96–97, 132, 136–37, 196n54, 198n83; *The Spirit of Film*, 39–40, 117; *Visible Man*, 39, 73, 97, 122, 137, 139
Bambach, Charles R., 10, 28
Bann, Stephen, 20
Baptism of Fire (*Feuertaufe*, 1940), 46
Barthes, Roland, 18, 20, 29, 52, 105, 122, 134

Battleship Potemkin (*Bronenosets Potyomkin*, 1925), 36–38, 40, 46, 50, 139, 185n103
Baudelaire, Charles, 19, 106, 107, 121
Bazin, André, 51, 66–67, 91, 122, 184n81
Beard, Charles A., 11
Beck, Philip, 169n5
Beggar, The (*Der Bettler*, Sorge), 150
Beiser, Frederick C., 13
Ben-Hur (1925), 37, 46, 52, 147
Benjamin, Walter, 4, 43, 45, 86, 117, 135; critique of historicism, 15–18; study of *Trauerspiel*, 94–95, 141
Benn, Gottfried, 64
Bergson, Henri, 20, 60, 61, 109, 175n54, 187n20
biblical motifs, 90, 96, 97, 153, 154; Jesus, 52, 100, 185n112
biographies, 42–43, 45, 118, 120, 183n76
Black Square (Malevich), 112, 113*fig.*
Bloch, Ernst, 19, 84–85, 86, 107, 108, 135; *Ungleichzeitigkeit* concept, 123–24
Blumenberg, Hans, 104, 134, 145
Bong Joon-ho, 8, 149, 161–63, 163*fig.*, 164
Bordwell, David, 2–3
bourgeoisie, 16, 37, 42, 58, 61, 134, 154, 162, 197n60; ideology in *Metropolis* (1927), 151, 152, 158*fig.*; rejection of, 8, 130, 149, 150, 165
Brinckmann, Christine N., 114
Brothers Grimm, 90, 92
Buber, Martin, 99
Buchowetzki, Dimitri, 32, 33, 48
Bürger, Peter, 107
Burgoyne, Robert, 22

Cabinet of Dr. Caligari, The (*Das Cabinet des Dr. Caligari*, 1920), 2, 23, 56, 62, 85, 86, 99, 147; Dilthey's hermeneutics and, 81–82; Expressionism and narrative structure, 4, 65, 66–67, 77–78, 79*fig.*, 83, 165; framing scenes, 68–69, 70*fig.*, 71*fig.*,

Index / 249

71–72; Nietzsche's perspectivism and, 6, 78, 80*fig.*, 82; space and perspectival representation, 59, 74, 75*fig.*
Cabiria (1914), 30, 46, 48, 51, 147, 154
Cahnman, Werner, 99
camera movements, 41, 43, 44*fig.*, 74
capitalism, 19, 40, 134, 146, 148, 163–64; cinematic allegories of, 158, 161, 163; and labor, 153, 156; racial, 8, 149, 157, 161, 213n47
capitalist society, 38, 39, 149, 151, 161; bourgeoisie and, 152, 158*fig.*
Capitalocene, 146, 148
Carroll, Noël, 2–3
Cassirer, Ernst, 72, 94, 123
Castellani, Renato, 53
Cavalcade (1933), 46
Cavell, Stanley, 3, 5, 24, 25, 29, 166
Chakrabarty, Dipesh, 18
Chladenius, Johann Martin, 13, 77
Choe, Steve, 194n17
Christian theology, 102*fig.*, 144, 152–53
Cinema and Media Studies, 2, 3, 148; historical turn in, 1, 5, 10, 12, 166
Clair, René, 85
Clark, Alfred, 30
class divisions, 8, 160–63; working masses and bourgeoisie, 150–51, 156–58, 159*fig.*
close-ups, 40, 46, 53, 73, 139
Comolli, Jean-Louis, 29
Comte, Auguste, 57
Conant, James, 76
concentration camps, term usage, 164
Congress Dances, The (*Der Kongreß tanzt*, 1931), 41
consciousness: historical, 10, 18, 30, 61, 104, 149; human, 51, 72, 141; subjective, 77, 78, 81
conservative revolution, 130
contemporaneity, 104, 105, 120–21, 122, 127
contingency, 51, 65, 73, 86, 91, 101, 165
crisis of historicism, 1, 3, 4–5, 8, 12–15, 29, 30, 55–56, 166; across the human sciences, 123; avant-garde and, 105, 108, 127; *Destiny* (1921) and, 86; ecological crisis and, 146; fascism and, 128; historical study and, 22; Kracauer's and Benjamin's critiques of historicism and, 15–18, 32; nature and history and, 128–29, 141; Nietzsche and, 77; religious renewal and, 152; *Rhythm 21* (1923–25) and, 7, 109; Troeltsch on, 63, 149, 186n127; World War I and, 28
cultural synthesis (*Kultursynthese*), 14, 130, 149, 165
cyclicality, 67, 88, 91, 100; eternal, 144

Dada movement, 7, 68, 108, 115
Dagover, Lil, 85, 86, 88, 93*fig.*
Daguerre, Louis, 20–21
dance, 132, 133, 138–39, 155
Danto, Arthur, 4, 105
Danton (1921; 1931), 32, 33, 47–48, 182n64
Dasein, 7, 90, 101, 140
Das Lied von der Erde (*The Song of the Earth*, Mahler), 99, 100
Davis, Natalie Zemon, 22
Day of Wrath (*Vredens dag*, 1943), 53
death: Christian vision of, 144; gate motif and, 84, 85*fig.*; God and, 14, 57, 78; Heidegger's concept of, 90, 92; humanized depictions of, 95, 100, 101–2; inevitability and equalizing force of, 91–92, 101; life and, 71, 102, 103, 194n17; and the maiden motif, 95–96; metaphysics and, 6, 84, 86–87, 88–90, 101, 135; mourning, 94; philosophical questions on, 86–87; photography/photographic media and, 16, 46; settling patterns of Jews and, 99; time and narrative and, 90–91, 97–98
Deleuze, Gilles, 3, 5, 25, 139, 166; *Cinéma 1*, 23–24, 114; *Cinéma 2*, 152
de Man, Paul, 106, 121
Der Kinematograph, 22, 62
Der Rebell (1932), 181n49

Descartes, René, 68, 73, 78, 110, 128, 145
Destiny (*Der müde Tod*, 1921), 2, 4, 6, 23, 194n17; alterity and nonbelonging themes, 99–100; baby scene, 92, 93*fig.*, 103; death and the maiden motif, 95–96; depiction of Death figure, 95, 101–2; Expressionist characteristics, 194n15; gate and passageway motifs, 84, 85*fig.*, 89; German folk tradition and Orientalist motifs, 100, 147; metaphysics and death, 86–87, 101, 102*fig.*; poetics of parallelism and analogy, 88–89, 89*fig.*; religious and spatiotemporal themes, 91, 97–98, 102; reviews, 84–86
determinism, 12, 88, 101, 123, 124, 128
dialectics, 39–40, 42, 56, 123–24, 126, 134, 161, 165; of modernity, 104, 106, 148; nature and history, 7, 129, 140–41, 137, 143, 144; nature and technology, 133, 135
Diebold, Bernhard, 65
Dilthey, Wilhelm, 10, 11, 28, 61, 63, 96, 118, 129; Heidegger's critique of, 60; hermeneutic theory, 80–82; Kracauer's writings and, 16, 145, 172n31
Divine Lady, The (1929), 182n61
Doane, Mary Ann, 3, 122
documentaries, 1, 7, 22, 30, 108, 117; Kracauer's writings on, 42, 46, 52, 53
Don Quixote (*Don Quichotte*, 1933), 39
Dreyer, Carl Theodor, 24, 32, 40, 53, 89
Droysen, Johann Gustav, 29, 54
Dulac, Germaine, 132–33

Edison, Thomas, 5, 30, 120, 154
Edschmid, Kasimir, 64
Efron, John, 99
Eggeling, Viking, 112, 114, 115, 117
ego and id, 94
Einstein, Albert, 58, 188n27; theory of relativity, 6, 57, 59, 60–62, 63, 82–83, 187n20
Einstein, Carl, 73

Eisenstein, Sergei, 24, 47, 59; *Alexander Nevsky* (1938), 50; *Battleship Potemkin* (1925), 36–38, 46, 50, 139, 185n103
Eisner, Lotte H., 23, 26–27
Elsaesser, Thomas, 2, 12, 26–27, 59, 109, 148
empathy, theory of (*Einfühlungstheorie*), 117–18
Engels, Friedrich, 149–50, 151
Enlightenment, 10, 106, 130, 134
environmental crisis, 8, 146, 147, 149
environmental injustice, 8, 149, 157, 162–63
Enzensberger, Hans Magnus, 107, 134
episode films, 6, 50, 88, 89, 91, 97. See also *Destiny* (*Der müde Tod*, 1921)
epistemology, 10, 57, 59, 63, 64, 67, 78
Epstein, Jean, 59, 74
Ernst, Wolfgang, 20–21
Eros and Thanatos, 95–96
eroticism, 95, 140, 155–56
existence, human, 60, 129, 137; Heidegger's *Dasein*, 7, 90, 101, 140
exoticism, 95, 97, 99, 100, 147
Expressionism, 2, 62, 73, 95, 115; architecture, 133; of *The Cabinet of Dr. Caligari* (1920), 4, 6, 56, 66–67, 69, 78, 83, 165; *Destiny* (1921) and, 86, 194n15; film and, 26, 59, 66, 74, 114, 117–18; of *Metropolis* (1927), 147, 156, 157; positivism and, 63–64; theater and, 58, 150; theorists, 65
Eyers, Tom, 19

Facebook, 20
Fairbanks, Douglas, 38
fairy tales, 34, 91–92, 97, 133, 197n60; Balázs's, 96, 196n54
Fanck, Arnold, 2, 4, 7, 129, 131, 133, 138, 143–45, 147; Balázs's defense of, 136–37; book on skiing, 207n30; camera techniques, 132; Kracauer's critiques of, 127, 136, 142; *The Marvel of the Snowshoe* (1920 and 1922), 135, 136; *Mountain of Destiny* (1924), 136. See also *Holy*

Mountain, The (*Der heilige Berg*, 1926)
fantasy, 23, 26, 65, 71, 97, 138, 154; Kracauer on, 34, 40, 51–52, 101
fascism, 108, 123, 128, 130–31, 144, 164; the Alps and, 145; avant-garde and, 107; Benjamin's critique of, 135
fate, 45, 77, 88, 141, 165; *Destiny* (1921) and, 86, 100–101, 103; historicism and, 10; Jewish belief in, 98
Faure, Élie, 52, 185n112
Faust (Goethe), 140, 154
Favourite of Schonbrunn, The (*Der Günstling von Schönbrunn*, 1929), 41
Felski, Rita, 19
femininity and masculinity, 137–40, 155–56
Fickers, Andreas, 18
film history, 1, 2, 11, 20–23, 30–31, 45, 55; movements, 67, 109. *See also* New Film History
film philosophy, 2–4, 5, 23–26, 145, 166
Flaubert, Gustave, 55, 61, 105
Flute Concert of Sanssouci, The (*Das Flötenkonzert von Sanssouci*, 1930), 35, 184n101
Focillon, Henri, 108, 124–25, 126
Foucault, Michel, 2, 12, 18, 57, 97
Franju, Georges, 85
French Revolution, 10, 13, 18, 32, 48
Freud, Sigmund, 17, 86, 95, 140, 152, 154–55, 173n40; on mourning and melancholia, 94
Fridericus Rex films, 23, 35–37, 36*fig.*, 47, 49, 56; list of titles, 184n101
From Caligari to Hitler (Kracauer), 4, 26, 27, 46, 48, 68–69, 128; on fate, 100–101
Futurists: cinema, 121–22; Manifesto (1909), 106

Gadamer, Hans-Georg, 80–81
Gaines, Jane, 2, 11, 169n6
Gas I (Kaiser), 150
Gay, Peter, 7, 157, 165
Gebühr, Otto, 35, 36*fig.*, 47
Geimer, Peter, 180n27

Gemünden, Gerd, 183n76
gendered expressions, 137–40, 143–44, 155–56
geometrical forms, 4, 28, 88, 112–13, 113*fig.*, 114, 147
German Idealism, 37, 72, 87, 90, 110, 131, 135, 148; nature and history and, 128–29, 140–41
German Revolution (1918–19), 47, 151, 152
Gesellschaft Neuer Film, 115, 117
God, 101, 193n109; immediacy to, 6, 8, 14, 60, 87, 89; Nietzsche on the death of, 14, 57, 78
Goetzke, Bernhard, 88, 93*fig.*
Goldman, Jane, 61–62
Gomery, Douglas, 11
Goose Man, The (*Das Gänsemännchen*, 1915), 194n15
Gordon, Peter Eli, 90, 164
Graf, Rüdiger, 165, 166
Great War. *See* World War I
Greek mythology, 94, 95, 138, 154
Griffith, D. W.: *The Birth of a Nation* (1915), 30; *Intolerance* (1916), 24, 52, 89–90, 91, 147
Gumbrecht, Hans Ulrich, 19–20
Gunning, Tom, 85

Häfker, Hermann, 132
Hansen, Miriam, 24, 32, 33, 101, 136
Hanslick, Eduard, 110, 112, 115
Harbou, Thea von, 85, 148, 154, 155
Hartman, Saidiya, 2, 54
Hartog, François, 19
head, heart, and hands trinity, 150–51, 153, 155, 156
Hegel, G. W. F., 13, 46, 52, 65, 110, 119, 126, 128; on art and the spirit of the people, 120–21; Marxist tradition, 39, 45, 124, 141, 147; philosophy of history, 77, 141, 145
Heidegger, Martin, 3, 6, 84, 86, 87, 88, 102, 118; concept of time, 60; on existence (*Dasein*) and death, 90, 92, 101, 140; nature and history and, 7, 129, 140–41, 144

Heimat, 130, 134
Heisenberg, Werner, 83
Helena (1924), 34
Herf, Jeffrey, 130–31, 133
hermeneutics, 4, 78, 80–81
Hesse, Herman, 96, 97
Heussi, Karl, 14–15
Hewitt, Andrew, 107, 130
high-rise buildings. *See* skyscrapers
historical-film genre, 5, 21, 22, 23, 29, 30–32, 147; Kracauer's critique of, 32–35, 45, 51, 55
"historical turn," 1, 2, 5, 10–11, 12, 26, 166
historicism, definitions of, 12–15, 128. *See also* crisis of historicism
historiography, 1, 2, 5, 10–11, 14, 17, 18, 56; digital technologies and, 12; genre of modern, 4, 53; ironic mode of, 67; photographic media and, 16, 21, 126; Ranke's mode of, 63; Richter's mode of, 7, 108, 119, 126; traditional, 8, 87; of Weimar cinema, 26–28, 165; Wölfflin's mode of, 120
history, philosophy of, 1, 3, 5, 11, 14, 18, 30, 126; *The Cabinet of Dr. Caligari* (1920) and, 59, 68, 77, 82, 86; *Destiny* (1921) and, 87; episode films and, 89; Hegel's, 77, 141, 145; historical avant-garde and, 7, 109, 110; Koselleck on, 54; relationship to film, 2, 4, 23–26, 28, 32; Spengler's, 87–88
History: The Last Things before the Last (Kracauer), 4, 16, 88, 125–26, 164; on Ahasverus, 100; on general history, 53–54; on human affairs and nature, 145–46
Hitler, Adolf, 47, 56
Hobsbawm, Eric, 106
Hofmannsthal, Hugo von, 130
Hölderlin, Friedrich, 133, 143
Hollywood, 23, 27, 50, 183n76
Holy Mountain, The (Der heilige Berg, 1926), 2, 4, 7, 23, 129, 147, 153, 205n13; confrontations with nature, 141–44, 143*fig.*; gendered expressions and sea/stone metaphors, 138–40, 144, 208n55; Kracauer's critique of, 136; opening title card and camera shots, 131–33, 142*fig.*; relationship to historicism, 144–45
Horkheimer, Max, 40, 130, 131, 141, 151, 161
human sciences (*Geisteswissenschaften*), 10, 62, 81, 123
Hung, Jochen, 165
Husserl, Edmund, 53, 60–61, 76, 88, 188n27
Hymn of Leuthen, The (Der Choral von Leuthen, 1933), 47, 184n101

ideology critique, 3, 35, 51, 136
Iggers, Georg G., 13, 168n12
Impressionists, 57, 58, 66, 73, 74
individuality, principle of, 13, 29, 164
industrialism, 150, 152, 157
Institute for Social Research, 152
Intolerance (1916), 24, 52, 89–90, 91, 147
Iron Horse (1924), 36

Jameson, Fredric, 149
Janowitz, Hans, 65, 68
Jay, Martin, 76, 78, 124
Jews, 98–99, 127, 155
Joyce, James, 53, 61, 106, 147, 149, 166
Jünger, Ernst, 130, 135, 153

Kael, Pauline, 1
Kaes, Anton, 4, 27, 68
Kaiser, Georg, 64, 150
Kalbus, Oskar, 22
Kandinsky, Wassily, 65, 110–11, 114, 118, 121
Kant, Immanuel, 10, 60, 71, 134, 139, 142, 145; neo-Kantian theories, 64, 72, 123
Kaplan, E. Ann, 149
Kelley, Robin D. G., 161
Kinetoscope, 5, 30
kitsch, 33, 34, 115, 135
Kittler, Friedrich, 74, 76
Koch, Gertrud, 105

Kornblum, Hanns Walter, 59
Kortner, Fritz, 47
Koselleck, Reinhart, 18, 19, 20, 28, 54, 89, 104, 165, 186n122
Kracauer, Siegfried, 5–6, 8, 128, 175n54, 183n80, 197n60; on abstract film, 117; aging and death, 101, 197n79; on analogies, 164; on *Battleship Potemkin* (1925), 36–38, 50, 185n103; on camera movements, 43, 52–53; conception of nature, 136; correspondence with Löwenthal, 3–4; on the crisis of the novel, 61; criticism of Ufa productions, 40, 41; critique of Spengler, 88; discussion of Ahasverus, 100; discussion of historical-film genre, 31–32, 40, 180n27, 182n61; on Expressionism, 63–64, 66, 74; on Fanck's mountain films, 127, 136, 142; on fantasy, 51–52; on fate and *Destiny* (1921), 100–101, 103; on Faure, 52, 185n112; on Fridericus Rex films, 35–37, 47, 49, 56; on general history, 53–54; on historical film aesthetics, 32–35, 38–39, 45–46, 181n44, 181n49; on historicism and photographic media, 1, 15–18, 20, 172n31; on Hollywood, 50; interest in Balázs's writings, 39–40; MoMA propaganda project, 46–48; on mountain films, 129, 133, 136; on nature and human affairs, 145–46; nonsimultaneity concept, 104, 125–26; Offenbach biography and film, 42–43, 45, 183n76, 183n79; on *Paisan* (1946), 50–51, 185n103; on *The Passion of Joan of Arc* (1928), 40, 46; on realist aesthetics, 65–66; on war films, 41, 46
Kubler, George, 125
Kuh, Anton, 98
Kunstwollen (artistic will), 72, 119–20, 126
Kurtz, Rudolf, 66, 114, 117–18, 120, 122

Lang, Fritz, 27, 84–87, 147; *Die Nibelungen* (1924), 34, 112, 155; obsession with fate, 100–101. See also *Destiny (Der müde Tod*, 1921); *Metropolis* (1927)
Last Laugh, The (Der letzte Mann, 1924), 34
Latour, Bruno, 109
Legend of William Tell, The (Wilhelm Tell, 1934), 47
Leibniz, Gottfried Wilhelm, 29, 76, 109
Leidensgeschichte (history of suffering), 98
Lessing, Theodor, 98
Lethen, Helmut, 67
Leyda, Jay, 11
Lichtblau, Klaus, 140
Little Match Girl, The (Armes kleines Mädchen, 1924), 34
Livingston, Paisley, 24
Loew, Katharina, 131, 183n67
Love of a Queen, The (Die Liebe einer Königin, 1923), 32–33
Love One Another (Die Gezeichneten, 1922), 32
Löwenthal, Leo, 3–4, 144
Lubitsch, Ernst, 23, 48–49, 49fig.
Lukács, Georg, 34, 61, 64, 88, 141, 151, 188n29

Madame DuBarry (1919), 23, 48, 49fig.
magic, 154
Mahler, Gustav, 99, 100
Malevich, Kazimir, 112, 113fig.
Malm, Andreas, 149
Mann, Thomas, 90, 130, 134
Mannheim, Karl, 14, 108, 123
Marinetti, F. T., 106, 121
Marx, Karl, 124, 128, 150–51, 161, 211n12; *Das Kapital*, 209n60
Marxism, 1, 3, 15, 148, 150, 151, 152, 164; Black, 161; Hegelian, 39, 45, 124, 141, 147; Kracauer and, 35, 39, 136
Marzynski, Georg, 58
materialism, 119; historical, 17, 123; idealist shift, 26–27, 28, 35, 39, 66; new, 146

Mayer, Carl, 65
Mead, George Herbert, 76, 82
media archaeology, 12, 20
Meinecke, Friedrich, 13, 14, 15, 128, 165
melancholia, 94
Melencolia I (Dürer), 95
Merchant of Venice, The (*Der Kaufmann von Venedig*, 1923), 33
metaphysics, 3, 10, 35, 57, 76, 101; and death in *Destiny* (1921), 4, 6, 84, 86–87, 90, 98, 101–2, 165; *The Holy Mountain* (1926) and, 141, 142, 144; of presence, 107
Metropolis (1927), 2, 4, 7–8, 23, 35, 146, 147–49, 165; Christian iconography and occult symbology, 152–54; class and bourgeois ideology, 149–52, 158*fig.*, 159*fig.*, 160*fig.*; compared to *Parasite* (2019), 161–63, 164; ending, 156–57, 160; mechanization and female sexuality, 155–56; vertical cityscapes, 157–58
Metz, Christian, 122
Michelson, Annette, 59
Mierendorff, Carlo, 86
Mill at Sanssouci, The (*Die Mühle von Sanssouci*, 1926), 35
modernism: abstraction and, 114; aesthetic, 57, 59, 62, 73, 99, 105–6, 107–8, 110; *The Holy Mountain* (1926) and, 132; in interwar Germany, 90, 153; *Metropolis* (1927) and, 148; reactionary, 130; relationship to the past, 106–7
modernity, concept of, 104, 130, 148, 165
Moholy-Nagy, László, 118, 121
Moltke, Johannes von, 32, 55
Monáe, Janelle, 161
montage, 16, 17, 24, 41, 51, 55, 74, 155; in *Battleship Potemkin* (1925), 37, 40, 50; in *The Holy Mountain* (1926), 132, 141, 142*fig.*; techniques, 18, 59
mountain film (*Bergfilm*) genre, 7, 23, 129, 130, 132, 136, 147, 165. See also *Holy Mountain, The* (*Der heilige Berg*, 1926)
mourning, 94
Moyn, Samuel, 164
Mülder-Bach, Inka, 51
Mulvey, Laura, 3, 91
Münsterberg, Hugo, 25, 73
Museum of Modern Art (MoMA) Film Library, 46, 47
music, 58, 134, 142; abstract art and, 110–12, 115; Mahler's, 99, 100; musicals and operettas, 41, 43; Romantic, 133, 154; soundtracks, 149

Nancy, Jean-Luc, 84, 87
Napoléon (1927), 43, 44*fig.*, 45
narrative form, 18, 24, 27, 55, 61; of *The Cabinet of Dr. Caligari* (1920), 67, 68–69, 70*fig.*, 71*fig.*, 71–72, 77–78; of *Destiny* (1921), 88–89, 194n15; in Fanck's mountain films, 132, 133, 136; time and death and, 90–91
natality, 93*fig.*, 103
National-Zeitung Basel, 42, 45, 183n80
natural history (*Naturgeschichte*), 4, 18, 128, 132; Adorno's concept of, 7, 129, 140–41, 209n60
Nazism/National Socialism, 15, 26, 50, 123, 128, 130–31, 145; fascism and, 164; propaganda films, 46–47; rise of, 127, 166
Neumann, Dietrich, 158
New Film History, 1–2, 5, 10–12, 21, 23, 28; materialist approach, 26–27
newsreels, 42, 46
Nicholas of Cusa, 78
Nicolson, Marjorie Hope, 133
Nietzsche, Friedrich, 28, 34, 64, 69, 110, 135, 142; affirmation (*Bejahung*) concept, 118; on the antiquarianism of nineteenth-century scholarship, 30, 63, 106; death of God, 14, 57, 78; influence on Richter, 119; on perspectivism, 6, 59, 76–78, 82; three

aspects of history, 23–24; Zarathustra, 133, 139, 145
Night of Love, The (1927), 182n61
nonsimultaneity (*Ungleichzeitigkeit*), 7, 104, 110, 122, 124–26, 127, 155; avant-garde and, 107–8; Bloch's concept, 123–24
novels/novelists, 20, 33, 57, 61–62, 69, 71, 105; filmic adaptations, 34, 39, 41, 207n34; mountain-themed, 134–35; romantic literature, 74, 76; science fiction, 148, 158

observation, mode of, 10, 57, 81, 132; disinterested, 6, 68; individualizing, 13, 67, 83
Offenbach, Jacques, 42–43, 45
ontology, 103, 144; existential, 3, 102*fig.*, 129, 141; historical, 59, 90
Orientalism, 99, 100
Osborne, Peter, 104, 107, 120, 130, 148

pageants, 33, 48, 49*fig.*
Paisan (*Paisà*, 1946), 50–51, 185n103
Panofsky, Erwin, 65–66, 72, 73, 95, 108, 123, 125, 126
Parasite (2019), 8, 149, 161–63, 163*fig.*, 164
Parufamet, 147
Passion of Joan of Arc, The (*La passion de Jeanne d'Arc*, 1928), 40, 46, 53
Peabody, Seth, 158
Perlmann, Anne, 62
perspectivism: Nietzsche's usage, 6, 76–78, 80*fig.*, 82, 119; relativist, 57, 59, 68
Pestalozzi, Johann Heinrich, 151
Peter the Great (*Peter der Große*, 1922), 33–34
Petrarch, 134
Petro, Patrice, 101, 156
Peukert, Detlev, 165
philosophy of film. *See* film philosophy
philosophy of history. *See* history, philosophy of
photography/photographic media, 31, 46, 51, 74, 86, 105, 135, 184n81;

Daguerre, 20–21; historicism and, 1, 4, 15–18, 20, 88, 126, 129; movement, 115; realist aesthetics and, 65–66; still, 122; time-lapse, 18, 132
Pinder, Wilhelm, 108, 122–23, 126, 203n75
poetry/poetics, 52, 100, 106, 115, 133, 186n120; Aristotelian, 51, 54, 105; film adaptations of, 34; history and, 6, 22, 29, 32, 53–56, 185n118
Pommer, Erich, 35, 85, 86, 147, 211n19
Popper, Karl, 12, 88, 128
positivism, 15, 62–64, 65, 81, 118, 145; disinterested, 119; referentiality, 106, 110; scientistic, 19, 57
postmodernism, 148–49
Postone, Moishe, 148
power structures, 78, 79*fig.*, 156, 157
presentism, 19–20, 52, 121; antihistoricist, 7, 109, 110; perpetual present, 149; Richter's concept of, 110, 126, 127
proletariat, 150–52, 156
propaganda films, 46–49
Proust, Marcel, 20, 53, 61, 175n54
Prussian films. *See* Fridericus Rex films
Pudovkin, Vsevolod, 37, 38, 47

Rabinbach, Anson, 130–31
racism, 99, 161, 182n63
Rancière, Jacques, 21, 108, 148; on the aesthetic regime of art, 54–55, 104–5, 106, 119
Ranke, Leopold von, 10, 13, 18, 55, 77, 119, 185n118, 186n120; on an omniscient God, 193n109; on "every epoch is immediate to God," 6, 14, 60, 87; on showing the past "how it essentially was," 5, 6, 12, 17, 20–21, 54, 63, 82, 168n12
realism, 37, 48, 51, 55, 131; aesthetics, 65–67; camera, 1, 4, 16, 67; critical, 11; literary, 58, 104–5; magical, 160; photographic, 86
Reinhardt, Max, 26

relativism, 6, 14, 15, 42, 64, 87; threat of, 80, 96, 129, 144
relativity: Einstein's theory of, 6, 57–59, 60–62, 63, 82–83, 187n20; masculine and feminine, 137–38
Rentschler, Eric, 129
repetition (*Wiederholen*), act of, 90–91
Rhythm 21 (*Rhythmus 21*, 1923–25), 2, 7, 23, 108, 109, 117; opening sequence, 112–13, 113*fig.*; time and history concepts, 114, 122
Richter, Hans, 8, 105, 108–10, 111*fig.*, 124, 127; avant-garde journal writings, 6–7, 108, 116*fig.*; intellectual influences, 119–20; *Rhythm 21* (1923–25), 2, 4, 7, 23, 112–14, 113*fig.*, 122; "The Badly Trained Soul," 114–15; vision of art history, 117, 118, 120, 126
Ricoeur, Paul, 90–91
Riefenstahl, Leni, 133, 136, 142
Riegl, Alois, 72, 119–20
Riley, Boots, 8, 149, 160–61, 162*fig.*, 164
Robinson, James Harvey, 11
Rodowick, D. N., 3, 25
Rogowski, Christian, 23
Romeo and Juliet (1954), 53
Rosen, Philip, 3, 22, 30
Rosenstone, Robert, 21–22
Rossellini, Roberto, 50, 185n103
Rotha, Paul, 86
Run Lola Run (*Lola rennt*, 1998), 91
Ruttmann, Walter, 111*fig.*, 112, 114, 115, 117

Said, Edward, 99
Scheffauer, Herman, 59, 114
Schiller, Friedrich, 21, 76, 108, 119, 133
Schmitt, Carl, 130, 209n58
Schoenberg, Arnold, 110–12
Schönerer, Georg von, 150
Schopenhauer, Arthur, 65, 110–11, 114
Schorske, Carl E., 106, 150
Schwartz, Frederic J., 123

science, crisis of, 15, 63–64
science fiction, 23, 27, 52, 148–49, 154, 157, 160
sea and stone metaphors, 137–40, 142–45
second nature, 131, 141, 143, 147
"shell shock cinema," 4, 27, 166
Simmel, Georg, 33, 86, 99, 137–38, 140, 198n83; "The Metaphysics of Death," 102; "The Problem of Historical Time," 123; on the work of art, 72; writings on the Alps, 135, 137, 144
Sinnerbrink, Robert, 24
skiing, 134, 207n30
skyscrapers, 147, 148, 153, 158, 161
slapstick comedies, 33, 36–37
Sloterdijk, Peter, 67, 156
Smith, Bonnie G., 18
Social Democratic Party (SPD), 152
Sokel, Walter, 58, 69
Sorry to Bother You (2018), 8, 149, 160–61, 162*fig.*, 164
sound films, transition to, 41, 183n67
space/spatial relations: artwork and, 72–73, 112, 113; in *The Cabinet of Dr. Caligari* (1920), 66–67, 74, 75*fig.*; in *Destiny* (1921), 97–98; Expressionism and, 58, 59; of mountains, 133; photography and, 16; *Rhythm 21* (1923–25) and, 114; time and, 16, 82, 89, 100
Spengler, Oswald, 14, 67, 87–88, 125, 130, 153
spiritualism, 96–97, 154
Street, The (*Die Straße*, 1923), 34
subjectivity, 17, 20, 21, 51, 58, 63; objectivity and, 61, 77, 80, 144
Symphonie diagonale (1924), 111*fig.*, 112, 114, 117

Taine, Hippolyte, 124
Tannenbaum, Eugen, 74
Taylor, Frederick Winslow, 148, 156, 160

technology: digital culture and, 12, 18–20; in *Metropolis* (1927), 146, 147, 148, 154, 155–56; modern, 130, 131; nature and, 133, 135; photographic, 16, 21, 65, 105, 135; of sound film, 41

Teichmüller, Gustav, 76

temporality. *See* time, concepts of

theater: Expressionist dramas, 58, 150; Kracauer's critiques of, 33, 36–37, 39, 45, 181n42; realist, 73; *Trauerspiel*, 94–95, 141

Theory of Film (Kracauer), 4, 16–17, 31, 51, 53, 55, 65, 126, 133; *The Cabinet of Dr. Caligari* (1920) and, 67, 74; chapter on "History and Fantasy," 51–52; on Lang's *Destiny* (1921), 101

Thérèse Raquin (1928), 39

Theweleit, Klaus, 138

time, concepts of, 19–20, 35; art and, 106, 112, 123, 124; *The Cabinet of Dr. Caligari* (1920) and, 59, 62; chronological, 123, 124, 125; cinematic images and, 17–18, 91, 95; *Destiny* (1921) and, 6, 88–90, 91–92, 95, 102; in Hegel's philosophy, 126; historical, 108, 123, 124, 126, 127, 154; *The Holy Mountain* (1926) and, 132, 144; hourglass motif, 91, 95; modernism or avant-garde and, 104, 107–8, 127; modernist writers and, 61–62; mourning and, 94; narrative and, 90–91; perspective and, 74; photography and, 16; relativity and, 60–61; space and, 16, 82, 89, 100. *See also* presentism

Train of Death, The (*Der Zug des Todes*, Spangenberg), 92

transience (*Vergänglichkeit*), 86, 95, 141

Trauerspiel (play of mourning), 94–95, 141

Traverso, Enzo, 19

tricks, 59, 131–32, 187n14

Troeltsch, Ernst, 7–8, 15, 63, 96, 149, 165; on the crisis of historicism, 13–14, 166, 186n127

Trump, Donald, 56, 164

Turvey, Malcolm, 119

Tykwer, Tom, 91

Ufa, 35, 40, 41, 48, 147; Kulturabteilung, 111*fig.*, 112

Uncle Tom's Cabin (1927), 182n63

Ungleichzeitigkeit. *See* nonsimultaneity (*Ungleichzeitigkeit*)

Unruh, Fritz von, 150

Vaihinger, Hans, 64

Veritas vincit (1919), 24, 48, 89

verticality, 8, 157–61

Vertov, Dziga, 59

Victory in the West (*Sieg im Westen*, 1941), 46–47

war films, 22, 41, 46–47

water imagery, 137–40, 142, 144, 209n58

Weavers, The (*Die Weber*, 1927), 37–38

Weber, Max, 15, 96, 118; "Science as a Vocation," 13, 63, 86, 171n18

Weimar Republic, 7–8, 22–23, 68, 127; architecture, 133, 158; cinematic style and techniques of, 26–28, 128; culture, 67, 133, 149, 157, 165; intellectuals, 8, 87–88, 129, 166; narrative of crisis and, 1, 163–66; sociopolitical conditions, 40, 150–52

Weininger, Otto, 138

Wellek, René, 125

Wells, H. G., 148, 158

Westfront 1918 (1930), 41

Whissel, Kristen, 157

White, Hayden, 4, 18, 21, 53, 67

Wiene, Robert, 27, 42, 66–67, 68, 86, 117. *See also* Cabinet of Dr. Caligari, The (*Das Cabinet des Dr. Caligari*, 1920)

Wolf, August, 31, 42

Wölfflin, Heinrich, 120, 122, 125, 203n75
Woolf, Virginia, 53, 61–62
Working Hours Act (1927), 152
world image (*Weltbild*), 115, 117, 118–19, 120
worldview (*Weltanschauung*), 27, 45, 72, 78, 96–97, 154, 165; art and, 58, 119, 120
World War I, 15, 27–28, 41, 42, 47, 77, 100; Benjamin on, 135; "shell shock" cinema of, 4, 27, 166

Worringer, Wilhelm, 64–65, 114, 137

Yorck von Wartenburg, Paul, 186n120

Zamyatin, Yevgeny, 58
Zechner, Ingo, 113–14
Ziege, Felix, 152
Zimmermann, Yvonne, 109
Zweig, Arnold, 145

www.ingramcontent.com/pod-product-compliance
Lightning Source LLC
Chambersburg PA
CBHW021342230426
43666CB00006B/379